NOËL COWARD

NOËL COWARD

A Bio-Bibliography

Stephen Cole

Bio-Bibliographies in the Performing Arts, Number 44
James Robert Parish, Series Adviser

GREENWOOD PRESS
Westport, Connecticut • London

Library of Congress Cataloging-in-Publication Data

Cole, Stephen.
    Noël Coward : a bio-bibliography / Stephen Cole.
       p. cm.—(Bio-bibliographies in the performing arts, ISSN
  0892-5550 ; no. 44)
    Includes bibliographical references and index.
    ISBN 0-313-28599-3 (alk. paper)
    1. Coward, Noël, 1899-1973—Bibliography. I. Title. II. Series.
  Z8196.6.C65 1994
  [PR6005.O85]
  016.822'912—dc20   93-28704

British Library Cataloguing in Publication Data is available.

Library of Congress Catalog Card Number: 93-28704
ISBN: 0-313-28599-3
ISSN: 0892-5550

First published in 1993

Greenwood Press, 88 Post Road West, Westport, CT 06881
An imprint of Greenwood Publishing Group, Inc.

Printed in the United States of America

The paper used in this book complies with the
Permanent Paper Standard issued by the National
Information Standards Organization (Z39.48-1984).

10 9 8 7 6 5 4 3 2 1

For Roger Hayes, who else?

Contents

Preface   ix

Acknowledgments   xi

Chronology   xiii

Biography   1

Plays and Appearances   29

Filmography   165

Radio Broadcasts   185

Television Productions and Appearances   199

Discography   229

Awards and Honors   257

Miscellaneous Projects   259

Annotated Bibliography   261

Index   293

Preface

When I was seventeen years old I entered a talent competition at The Gil Hodge's Grand Slam Lounge in Brooklyn, New York. The year was 1973. The Lounge was part of Gil Hodge's Bowling Alley and the clientele were not part of what Noël Coward called "Nescafé Society." Nevertheless I sang a Cole Porter medley and Noël Coward's "Nina." Just right for the local bowlers, I sarcastically thought. As it happened, I was right. The medley went over well, but it was the story of Senorita Nina from Argentina, who resolutely refused to dance that knocked the socks off from under the bowling shoes of the Brooklynites.

Why did an obscure song written for a 1940's London revue win these unsophisticated bowlers? The universality of the number staggered me. They laughed in the right places and I came in second place that night. This was the just the beginning of my infatuation with Coward's words and music.

This led to a curiosity about Coward's plays and the man himself. I read everything in sight. It was soon after this fateful night at the bowling alley that Coward died. Luckily my theatrical awareness surfaced as Noël Coward's reputation was being re-evaluated. The 50's and early 60's had cruelly dismissed The Master as old hat, but the 1964 National Theatre production of *Hay Fever* (He was the first author so honored during his lifetime!) began a reassessment that crossed the Atlantic and continued with such well received major revivals of *Hay Fever, Private Lives, Design For Living, Present Laughter, Blithe Spirit and The Vortex* and the musical retrospectives *Cowardy Custard* (UK) and *Oh Coward!* (US). How well I recall the ad for *Oh Coward!* picturing a young Coward in tux (what else?) and the blurb "I came out humming the tunes."

This book is not meant to be an in-depth biography of Sir Noël Coward. There are several of those already in existence and more on the way. In 1956 an amazing book, entitled *The Theatrical Companion to Noël Coward* was published with Coward's blessing. Although this book concentrates on Coward's British theatrical career, it was for me, an incredible sourcebook. But what of the next thirty six years of a career that didn't end with Coward's death? This is where this book comes in. If one looks carefully, one can see the arcs of a career. The ups and the downs are detailed in the critical responses that have ranged from the delirious to the despicable. If one takes special note, one can see a public and it's journalistic stand-ins changing it's taste from one end of the century to the other.

This volume is divided into ten sections, as follows:

1.   a chronology of Coward's life and career.

2.   a brief biography.

3.   a listing of Coward's plays and appearances. These include the plays he appeared in and/or the plays and musicals he wrote, directed and produced, including all major West End and New York revivals. Each listing is preceded by the letter "P." Tryout dates, theatres, opening dates, number of performances, cast and credits, a short synopsis, reviews (when available) and notes are included.

4.   a filmography of the movies in which Coward appeared and/or wrote and directed and produced. Also included are the film versions of plays and musicals that Coward wrote. Studio, year of release, production and cast credits, a short synopsis, and reviews are included for each film. Each feature is preceded by the letter "F" and cross referenced with the plays on which they are based.

5.   a selected listing of Coward's radio appearances (both American and British) and radio adaptations of his stage plays. Each entry is preceded by the letter "R" and includes episode title, airdate, cast, a brief synopsis and selected reviews. The adapted plays are cross referenced with the stage versions on which they are based.

6.   a listing of Coward's television appearances (American and British) and television adaptations of his stage plays. Entries are preceded by the letter "T" and include episode title, airdate, cast and credits, brief synopsis and reviews when available.

7.   a discography of recordings made by Noël Coward and of his music and lyrics. This chapter is divided into four sections: 78's, LP's, Cassettes and CD's and subdivided into recordings Coward made and those made by others of his music. Each listing is preceded by the letter "D" and includes recording date, label, number and songs performed by or written by Coward.

8.   a listing of awards and honors bestowed upon Coward. Each entry is preceded by the letter "A."

9.   a listing of miscellaneous unrealized projects, including unproduced plays, unreleased recordings, etc. Each entry is preceded by the letter "M."

10.   a selected annotated bibliography of writings by and about Coward. This chapter includes articles, books, newspapers, magazines, trade papers and all of Coward's published works. Each entry is preceded by the letter "B."

Acknowledgments

When I made the choice to do this book about the career of Noël Coward, instead of Betty Hutton, little did I realize the scope of the work that was before me. Unlike other subjects, who are merely stars of stage, screen etc., Sir Noël was a playwright, actor, director, producer, composer, lyricist, novelist, poet, short story writer, recording artist and anything else his theatrical heart desired. He even designed the poster to one of his shows. One would not be surprised to see him tearing the tickets and sweeping out the theatre. All this is to say that I have several people to thank.

Most of my research was done at the Billy Rose Theatre Collection at the Lincoln Center Branch of the New York Public Library. The clipping files were monumental and to do a complete bibliography of Noël Coward would take many more pages and use many more trees. The library's collection is a phenomenon. The staff was helpful and I thank them.

Thanks are due to Geoffrey Johnson, Coward's friend (one of the last to see him alive) and last New York literary agent, who is now the one of the partners in Johnson-Liff Casting Associates. Although we never met, he was very helpful on the telephone and supplied much information on Coward's 70th birthday celebrations. Michael Imison, the gentleman who now represents Coward's interest in London, also deserves a large thank you as does Graham Payn, Coward's heir and co-executor for giving the project his blessing.

Mr. Jonathan Rosenthal of Research Services at the Museum of Radio and Television was most helpful and I am grateful. I'd also like to thank Miss S.M. Fewell at Independent Televison Commission in London for her efforts.

Mr. John Behrens at CBS was incredibly nice and gave me much valuable information on Coward's CBS career. Many thanks to him and to Ray Stanich who got me in touch with him and provided me with many radio logs that proved useful.

I'm very grateful to Howard Mandelbaum at Photofest for the pictures and for his wit.

Of course, I'd like to thank Jim Parish, the series adviser, for his encouragement, clippings and expertise and not to forget Jane Klain, who introduced me to Jim in the first place.

Lastly and certainly not least, I need to thank Roger Hayes, who has gone through it all with me. Without him there would certainly be no index and the entire design of the book would be very different indeed. Thanks, Roger.

Oh, and thanks to Sir Noël Coward, whom I wish I met, but I know someday I will. I think he would have enjoyed this book.

Chronology

This chronology attempts to fill in the high points in the career and life of Sir Noël Coward. Bearing in mind that there has not been one year since 1911 to his death in 1973 that Coward did not appear, write, direct, produce or compose for the stage, film, radio or television or publish non-theatrical and theatrical books, this time line will serve to point up the firsts and milestones in a major theatrical career of the twentieth century. The productions are cross referenced.

1899   Noël Pierce Coward born, December 16, at Teddington, Middlesex to Arthur Sabin and Violet Veitch Coward.

1905   Eric Coward, Noël's only brother was born.

1907   July 23; first public appearance, at end-of-term concert at St. Margaret's, Sutton (P-1).

1911   Jan. 27; professional debut in The *Goldfish* (P-2). First worked with Charles Hawtrey.

1912   Feb. 2; Directorial debut, *The Daisy Chain* (P-5).

1913   Met Gertrude Lawrence.

1915   Played first adult role, *Charley's Aunt*. Wrote both music and lyrics for first song, "Forbidden Fruit."

1916   Cabaret debut (P-16).

1917   First play produced, *Ida Collaborates*, written with Esmé Wynne. (P-19)

1918   Second play produced, *Woman and Whiskey*, written with Esmé Wynne. (P-21). Served in army. Wrote *The Rat Trap*. Film debut, *Hearts of the World*, as extra. (F-1)

1919   First song published, "The Baseball Song," Music by Doris Joel.

1920   July 21; first West End play produced, *I'll Leave It To You*. Coward played one of the leading roles. (P-25)

1921   First trip to America.

1922   First book published, *A Withered Nosegay*. (B-33).

1923   First revue produced in West End, *London Calling!*, also appeared in it with Gertrude Lawrence.

1924   *The Vortex* produced in West End with Coward in lead role. (P-35). *Fallen Angels* produced in West End (P-36). First radio sketch.

1925   Meets John C. Wilson. *Hay Fever* produced in West End. *The Vortex* produced on Broadway with Coward in lead role. Radio debut (R-2). First recording (D-1).

1927   First film version of one of his plays produced, *The Queen Was In The Parlour* (F-2).

1928   *This Year of Grace* produced in West End and on Broadway (with Coward) (P-56, P-57).

1929   *Bitter-Sweet* produced in West End and Broadway (P-58, P-59). Wrote *Private Lives* and *Post-Mortem*.

1930   *Private Lives* produced in West End starring Coward and Gertrude Lawrence (P-61).

1931   *Private Lives* produced on Broadway starring Coward and Gertrude. Lawrence (P-63). *Cavalcade* produced in West End (P-67). Met Graham Payn.

1932   *The Noël Coward Company* formed to perform his plays in repertory (P-69). *Cavalcade* wins Academy Award for Best Picture.

1933   *Design For Living* produced on Broadway with Coward and The Lunts (P-71).

1934   Played first major film role, *The Scoundrel* (F-11). Cut ties with C.B. Cochran and formed Transatlantic Productions with John C. Wilson and the Lunts to produce his plays and plays of others.

1936   *Tonight At 8:30* produced in West End (P-83).

1937   Publication of *Present Indicative*, first volume of autobiography (B-42).

1939   Sept. to April 1940; held post in Enemy Propaganda Office, Paris. First television version of his plays produced, *Hay Fever* (T-1). Published *To Step Aside*, first collection of short stories.

1940   Began singing tours for the war effort (P-92).

1941   *Blithe Spirit* starts long run in West End and Broadway (P-96, P-97). Began writing *In Which We Serve*.

1942   *In Which We Serve* (F-15) premieres. Coward wins special Academy Award for Best Production.

1943   *Present Laughter* and *This Happy Breed* produced in West End with Coward in leading roles (P-98, P-99).

1944   Continues entertaining troops. *Middle East Diary* causes an uproar in US because of line about mournful boys from Brooklyn.

1945   *Brief Encounter* premieres(F-18).

1946   Begins relationship with Graham Payn.

1947   Does 13 episodes of radio series (R-42).

1948   Last appearance with Gertrude Lawrence as a replacement for the ailing Graham Payn in *Tonight At 8:30* (P-111). Played *Present Laughter* in French in Paris.

1951   Launches a new career in Cabaret at Café de Paris (P-121). C.B. Cochran and Ivor Novello die.

1953   Played in Shaw's *The Apple Cart.*

1954   Last production of Transatlantic Productions, *Quadille*. Published second volume of autobiography, *Future Indefinate* B-53. Violet Coward (mother) dies.

1955   Television debut in *Together With Music* (T-10) with Mary Martin. Las Vegas debut (P-138).

1956   Tax exile, gave up residence in England. Carnegie Hall debut.(P-140).

1958   Last Broadway appearance in *Nude With Violin* and *Present Laughter* (P-143).

1959   Wrote first score for ballet, *London Morning* (P-150).

1960   Publication of first novel, *Pomp and Circumstance* (B-55).

1961   *Sail Away* produced on Broadway (P-154).

1963   *Private Lives* revived changing negative critical trend (P-159). *The Girl Who Came To Supper* produced on Broadway (P-160).

1964   Directs *High Spirits* (based on *Blithe Spirit*) Tony nominations for directing and book writing. Directs revival of *Hay Fever* at the National Theatre in England to great acclaim.

1965   *Pretty Polly Barlow and other stories* published (B-57). *The Lyrics of Noël Coward* published (B-61).

1966   Appears in West End for the last time in his last three plays, *Suite In Three Keys* (P-165).

1967   *Bon Voyage* and *Not Yet The Dodo* published (B-59, B-60).
Appears as Caeser in Richard Rodgers' TV musical *Androcles and The Lion*. Worked on third volume of autobiography (later abandoned) *Past Conditional*.

1968   Portrayed in film biography of Gertrude Lawrence, *Star!* (F-29) by Daniel Massey.

1969   70th Birthday celebrated with many tributes on stage, screen, television and radio.

1970   Knighted by Her Majesty the Queen of England.

1972   *Oh Coward!* and *Cowardy Custard* (P-180, P-181) produced in New York and London respectively.

1973   Makes last public appearance at a gala performance of *Oh Coward!*. (P-182). Dies March 26 in Jamaica.

NOËL COWARD

Biography

1899-1920

"I was born into a world that took light music seriously," wrote Noël Pierce Coward in the 1930's. And so he was. England in 1899 was country in which most homes, if they could afford it, had pianos in the parlor and light music was played, sung and listened to. Even the lower and middle classes had a yen for a tune and the means to play one.

Violet Coward, Noël's mother had been a fervent theatre-goer and played the piano and her husband Arthur was the possessor of a light tenor voice of great sweetness. And on December 16, 1899, when Mrs. Coward delivered her son, Noël Pierce (named for the holiday season) it is likely that her spinster sister Vida, who lived with the family, or the maid Emma had a tune on their lips.

Noël Coward was not born into the white tie and cocktail aristocracy that he so lovingly celebrated in his best remembered works, but in the working class suburb of Teddington, Middlesex in a cozy house called Helmsdale. The Cowards had lived there since their marriage in 1891. Like the family he lovingly celebrated in *This Happy Breed* (1939), his was an ordinary one. A father who sold pianos, a maiden aunt, and, eventually in 1904, a little brother named Eric. But Noël was not to have an ordinary life and at a very early age his mother Violet knew it.

From the time he was four, the talented child was in constant demand to sing and dance at parties, in Kiddie Competitions, and at church fetes. In later years Coward told of his dislike of singing at church: "there was never any applause." There is a story of Violet Coward attending a performance of a music hall mystic named Anna Eva Fay at a time when she was wondering if the stage should really be Noël's metier. She brought a piece of her son Noël's clothing for the soothsayer to touch and when the woman felt the cloth, Mrs. Coward was told "Mrs. Coward, Mrs. Coward, you ask me about your son. Keep him where he is. He has great talent and will have a wonderful career." Perhaps fittingly, years later Coward was dubbed by Alexander Woolcott as "Destiny's Tot."

Young Noël gave his first public appearance in the end of term concert as one of the students of St. Margaret's School in Sutton on July 23, 1907. He performed one of his favorite songs from the popular musical of the day, *A Country Girl*. The song was called "Coo." He was so well received that he did an encore of a song entitled "Time Flies." Unlike the other little children, he accompanied himself at the piano. His precociousness was apparent to all, but to Violet Coward he represented the key to her dreams.

Violet Coward's love of theatre had not dimmed after her marriage and throughout Noël's childhood he became an ideal theatre-going companion. This undoubtedly nurtured the boy's love for the stage. These were the days of great stars and Noël and his mother idolized Lily Elsie in *The Merry Widow* and Gertie Millar in *The Quaker Girl*. His love of stars would never dim and he would go far during his successful career to employ members of the older generation down on their luck.

If one believes in fate, and Mrs. Coward did, it was indeed a fateful day on September 7, 1910 that Noël saw an interview with Miss Lila Field in the Daily Mirror complaining that she was still badly in need of five or six boys to take part in a children's musical written by herself and Ayre O'Naut. Noël urged his mother to write to Miss Field, which she did and a positive reply came four days later.

Noël recited and sang for Miss Field and her sister and the part was his. He was to receive the staggering sum of a guinea and a half a week. Mrs. Coward and Noël thought that their fortunes had been made. *The Goldfish*, as Master Noël Coward's professional debut was called, opened at the Little Theatre on January 27, 1911 and was revived at the Crystal Palace Theatre and the Royal Court Theatre in April of the same year. At eleven years of age Master Noël received his first review. Unfortunately the performer who was given "a congratulatory pat on the back" was *Miss* Noël Coward.

Despite his first inauspicious notice, Noël evidently had caught the attention of the great Charles Hawtrey. Hawtrey, considered the best light comedian of his day, summoned the boy actor to appear in his autumn production of *The Great Name*, giving him the role of a page boy.

Young Noël, knowing that he could learn much from the great actor, followed his idol around hoping to catch some of the falling stardust. This action proved only to irritate Hawtrey to the point of his almost firing the boy. Luckily this never occurred and Noël continued to serve an on-again off-again apprenticeship with the master for the next seven years.

In 1911 Noël was asked to appear in the very first production of *Where The Rainbow Ends*. This fairy tale was so beloved that the public demanded it be played almost every Christmas for the next 40 years. During the run, which began on December 21, 1911, Hawtrey encouraged the children in the show to stage special matinees of their own device. And it was on February 12, 1912 that 12 year old Noël Coward directed 11 year old Dot Temple's first play. Noël, a natural leader, relished nothing more than pushing people around and creating life on the stage and yet another of his talents was revealed.

After appearing as a Mushroom in a ballet entitled *An Autumn Idyll* at the Savoy Theatre (the production also featuring Noël's little brother Eric), Hawtrey asked Noël to appear in a sketch at the Coliseum. Unfortunately, Noël, still underage as far as licensing was concerned, was not allowed to play any but the matinee performances. Still he stood in the wings and watched the other variety acts such as George Robey, Beattie and Babs and a Wild West Show. As he watched the pros, he learned.

Another Christmas engagement in *Where The Rainbow Ends* at the Garrick Theatre led Noël to the Liverpool Repertory and a "dream play" called *Hannele*. Cast with such other child actors as Ivy and Dorothy Moody and Harold French, Noël Coward met one of his soul mates for the first time:

> "She confided to me that her name was Gertrude Lawrence, but that I was to call her Gert because everybody did, that she was fourteen, just over licensing age, that she had been in *The Miracle* at Olympia and *Fininella* at the Gaiety, Manchester. She then gave me an orange and told me a few mildly dirty stories, and I loved her from then onwards."

After appearing at the Palladium in a dramatic spectacle entitled *War In The Air,* in which the 13 year old Noël flew a small model plane across the stage, he was engaged as an understudy in *Never Say Die*, yet another Hawtrey production. This strange turn of casting occurred when Hawtrey was unable to locate young Coward (he was away on holiday), his first choice for the role, and had to engage Reggie Sheffield instead. When Coward was finally located only the understudy role was available.

Noël was able to live down the hurt and shame of understudying with his next engagement. Having long cherished a desire to appear in the classic *Peter Pan*, Noël was thrilled to be hired to play Slightly, one of the lost boys. This production, which starred Pauline Chase as Peter, played the usual Christmas season in London's West End and toured from November to March of 1914. His mother managed to be with him and to have her travelling expenses taken care of by looking after the child actor who played Michael, one of the Darling children.

After the run of *Peter Pan* , Noël was out of work for, what seemed to a young man, a very long time. It was during this period, when he was 14 going on 15 that Noël developed two very important friendships. The first, and perhaps the most important from a personal point of view, was with artist Philip Streatfield, then 30 years old. The young Coward spent many hours in his studio and when Streatfield went to the country in search of landscapes to paint, Coward accompanied him. This may have been the first flowering of Coward's sexual orientation. There is a picture of the two which shows the younger man consciously imitating the stance of his older friend. In any case, when war broke out, Streatfield was sent to fight and was killed, but his parting gift to Noël was an introduction to a Mrs. Astley Cooper. Mrs. Cooper, a socialite with a country home, introduced the young Coward to a life of luxury to which he took like a duck to water. Since many of his early plays take place in grand country houses, it must be acknowledged that this introduction into society greatly influenced Coward's future writing.

The second important friendship developed with a girl fairly well known to Noël: Esmé Wynne. The two had appeared in *Where The Rainbow Ends* twice before, but it was during the Spring of 1914 that the acquaintance flowered into something deeper. Before then Coward always thought of Wynne as "pompous, podgy and slightly superior," but now the two began spending evenings playing games and listening to records. Before long they became inseparable. Noël and Esmé soon found nicknames for each other. He was Poj and she was Stoj. Poj and Stoj dressed in each others clothes and paraded about town and generally enjoyed their youth to the fullest. But the real tie in this relationship was their mutual desire to write. It was Wynne who first had the determination and Coward's natural competitiveness brought out his own fervent desire to create.

If Esmé wrote poems, Coward would set them to music. Soon Coward was composing short stories and Wynne was encouraging, praising and even criticizing his work.

As World War I (then known as the Great War) raged on, Coward, being too young for the army, continued in his acting career. He and Wynne appeared in the Christmas 1915 version of *Where The Rainbow Ends*. Coward, now too old for his original role and too young for the lead, played the Slacker, a cross between a man and a dragon.

Finally having finally grown into adult roles, Coward and Wynne were thrilled to be cast as Charley and Amy in a 1916 provincial tour of *Charley's Aunt*. The old warhorse had been around for over 16 seasons and showed no signs of losing steam. The tour played from February to June. Although Coward grew to dislike the unfunny title role, the experience of playing a lead in a solid farce must have proven invaluable.

After the tour ended Coward was hired to play a small role in a new musical comedy coming in to the Shaftsbury Theatre for the fall 1916 season, *The Light Blues*. Coward's role wasn't much, but he was called upon to understudy Jack Hulbert, partner to the great Cicely Courtniege, then at the beginning of a long and spectacular career. (She would later play Madame Arcati in the 1964 musical version of Coward's *Blithe Spirit*) *The Light Blues* ran only two weeks and Coward was never called upon to play Hulbert's part, but amazingly enough he was able many year later to recall lyrics and music to most of the show. This show was followed by what was to be Noël Coward's first leading role in the West End. The play was *The Saving Grace*. For the first time Coward was recognized by the public. He liked it a lot.

It was during the teens that Coward made debuts in two mediums in which he would have continued success. The first was as a cabaret performer (albeit as part of dance team) and the other on film. His cabaret debut occurred in October of 1916 and his film debut in 1918. In between these two events Coward appeared in a Christmas play entitled *The Happy Family* and got to sing and dance on the stage for the first time in years. This was followed by a strong social drama, *Wild Heather*, in which he played Helen Haye's (not the American one) son.

Although not widely noted Coward made a third debut in August of 1917. His first play, aptly titled *Ida Collaborates*, written in collaboration with his great friend Esmé Wynne was produced on tour with Wynne in the title role. Auspicious as it was, it is odd that Coward does not even mention this event in his first volume of autobiography, *Present Indicative*.

Coward's creative and interpretive talents continued to blossom and grow in all directions. At the age of 16, he wrote the music and lyrics to his first complete song, "Forbidden Fruit." It remained unpublished for thirty seven years and was finally performed fifty two years later by Coward's Godson Daniel Massay playing Coward in the film *Star*. In 1919 Noël Coward's name appeared for the first time on the cover of a published song. It was entitled "The Baseball Song" and had music by Doris Joel (known professionally as Doris Doris!). He made valiant stabs at writing a three act play and two novels. He was not to attempt fiction again for eleven years and then would not complete what was titled *Julian Kane*, a story of a young man who committed suicide because he was bored. The public would have to wait until 1960 for the first and only example of a Noël Coward novel, *Pomp and Circumstance*.

The war had made little impression on young Noël until 1918 when he was of age and was called for military service. Suffice it to say that the effete actor's nine month service was "one long exercise in futility" ending with an honorable discharge. Not a single photo of Coward in uniform remains in extant.

Within a month after his discharge Noël appeared at the Strand Theatre in *Scandal* and in 1919 Coward played Ralph in *The Knight of The Burning Pestle* in Birmingham and in 1920 moved to the West End of London. This was to be Coward's first and last stab at restoration comedy.

The 1920's

The roaring twenties were for many people the time for flaming youth to spark and flourish. The war to end all wars was over and the boys were home. Fun was the order of the day. Flappers, hooch and jazz. And to England and later the world, Noël Coward became the physical embodiment of that era of speed. It must have been fate that predestined Coward, its most representative personality, to make his West End playwriting debut in May in the first year of this most promising new decade. The city was Manchester and the play was *I'll Leave It To You*. Noël not only wrote the acclaimed play, but gave himself the juicy leading role. When the play arrived in the West End in July of 1920, he was hailed as a "Young Playwright of Great Promise," but the play only ran thirty seven performances. This phenomenon was repeated the next year with *The Young Idea*: great reviews and sixty seven performances. This lack of commercial success did nothing to dim Coward's ambitions or enthusiasms and he was perhaps soothed by such critical bouquets as "an infant prodigy," "an amazing youth" and "astonishing gifts." In print at least his future looked bright. Noël vowed to write stronger plays and began what was to be his watershed event, *The Vortex*.

While continuing to write plays, Coward took a role in the British premiere of an American farce, *Polly With A Past*. The play opened in May of 1921. Coward only stayed with the show for three months (establishing his future preference for short runs as an actor), but for whatever the reason, he got the irresistible urge to go to America. To see the lights of Broadway and try to make it in New York. Taking along a suitase full of manuscripts, he sailed to the new world with his heart full of hope and the undeniable belief in himself that would take him to the top.

Unfortunately Coward arrived in the summer, finding New York in a sweltering heat and all of the theatres (this was before air conditioning) closed and the producers hauling their bags to cooler climes. This setback allowed Coward to see the city and to make friends with people who would remain in his life till the end of it. Top of the list were Alfred Lunt and Lynn Fontanne. Not yet the stars they were all destined to become, the three laid out their "design for living": Alfred would marry Lynn, they would team up and become great theatre stars, Noël would continue to write and when they were all at the top of their form, Noël would write a play with three sparkling roles in it. The dream did come true and twelve years later the trio took Broadway by storm in *Design For Living*. He also met the great actress Laurette Taylor (chiefly remembered as Amanda in Tennessee Williams' *The Glass Menagerie*) and it was at a weekend with the actress and her author-husband that the seeds of the plot of *Hay Fever* were planted. Although Coward came away from his New York adventure neither richer or more successful, he had fallen hopelessly in love forever with the city that never sleeps.

Once back on English soil, Noël was called upon to be the entertainment at a very special Christmas party in Switzerland given by the young and very rich Lord Lathom. Known to his friends as Ned, Lord Latham numbered among his guests that great actress Gladys Cooper, the dress designer Molyneux, dancer-actor Clifton Webb and party giver and goer Elsa Maxwell. When Noël finished a dazzling selection of his own smart material at the piano it seemed inevitable that the young Lord would use his influence with his friend, the renowned impresario André Charlot to hear Coward's songs. Charlot came, Charlot heard and Coward was on his way to writing his first West End revue, *London Calling!*.

Coward not only wrote material for the revue but appeared in it opposite his once and future partner, Gertrude Lawrence. The pairing of these two elegant and dynamic performers was to reach its apex in *Private Lives* and *Tonight At 8:30*, but it was here in *London Calling!* that Gertie introduced Noël's haunting song "Parisian Pierrot." Alone in a spot in a Pierrot costume, Lawrence magically transformed an empty stage with her own brand of sorcery and Coward's sweet tune. Coward himself had material of a lesser vintage. One song entitled "Sentiment" failed to go over despite the choreography by a relatively unknown Fred Astaire. It was with great embarrassment that Coward watched the nonchalant Jack Buchanan do the very same number in New York to wild applause and cheers. Coward admitted that perhaps the material was better than he was and that he had been trying a bit too hard. The revue also contained a sketch entitled *The Swiss Family Wittlebot*, parodying the modern poetry of the Sitwell family. Edith and her family took quite a bit of offense at this sketch, which was also performed on the radio, and it was many years before they would speak to Coward. Coward further capitalized on these poetic parodies in two books *Chelsea Buns* and *Spangled Unicorn*. A third book of a satirical nature was published in London under the title of *A Withered Nosegay* and in the United States as *Terribly Intimate Portraits*.

By 1924, Noël Coward was well on his was to becoming well known, but his star was to be forever shot into the firmament on his twenty fifth birthday, December 16, 1924 when *The Vortex* opened at the Everyman Theatre in Hampstead.

The play, in which Coward portrayed a drug addict whose mother is having an affair with one of his friends shocked Hampstead and London after it. It caused the kind of stir that seems unfathomable from the vantage point of today, with our television sets filled with Amy Fishers and Yuppie Killers, but in 1924 the stark theatricality of the situations portrayed had rarely been spoken of in private, let alone seen on a public stage. Audiences were bowled over and flocked in droves to see the scandalous event. What they saw was a well constructed play with two smashing performances, one by Coward and one by Lilian Braithwaite, until then known only for her light comedy performances. For most, *The Vortex* seemed to epitomize the disillusionment of the flaming youth that filled the stalls each night and it played for a year to full houses, with Coward's role eventually being taken over by his understudy, a certain young John Gielgud.

Noël Coward had finally made it at 25 years of age. Fame and fortune came quickly and he became busier than ever. He moved from the little attic room in which he had been dwelling to an entire first floor suite decorated by set designer Gladys Calthrop. The two became great friends and Calthrop would design most of Coward's shows for years to come. Coward began work on the book, music and lyrics for *On With The Dance*, a revue to be produced by the great West End Impresario Charles B. Cochran. At first Cochran did not think that Coward's music and lyrics were strong enough and only wanted him to write the sketches, but each succeeding sketch contained an idea for a song and in the end Coward contributed all but three of the numbers for the revue. This was the show that introduced one of Coward's biggest song hits, "Poor Little Rich Girl." It was sung by the star of the show Alice Delysia to a very young "poor little rich girl" named Hermione Baddeley. This song was the first of his twenties songs that chided the mad flappers and tried to make sense of the speed at which the young were living. The next in this series of songs was "Dance Little Lady" and was introduced in 1928. During this same period Coward had the good fortune to have another of his early plays produced and acclaimed.

Fallen Angels opened at the Globe Theatre only nine days before On With The Dance at the Pavilion. Fallen Angels starred two great ladies of the theatre: Edna Best and the indefatigable Tallulah Bankhead. Bankhead was a last minute replacement for the ailing Margaret Bannerman and she learned a very large role in no time flat and gave what was by all accounts a solid and funny performance as a drunk married woman awaiting a visit from her former lover. Although it seems like an incredibly tame trifle today (and is toured in the dinner theatre circuit by the likes of Dorothy Lamour), many of the critics of the day were once again shocked and appalled at the sight of two woman drinking and discussing their mutual affair on the stage. Times certainly do change.

Now Coward had three hits running simultaneously on the West End with a fourth on its way. Success breeds success, and suddenly plays that had been rejected both in London and New York were being bid for by the very managements that had slammed their doors in Coward's face just a few years before. Not a week could go by in 1924-25 that Coward was not photographed and written about. He made his radio debut on August 5, 1925 singing his own songs. He had become the leading exponent of what he himself would term the "bright young people."

It was in 1925 that one of Coward's most enduring comedies finally opened. Having been written for and rejected by Marie Tempest, a then reigning London star, Hay Fever was finally produced with Tempest in the lead. This was the play inspired by that mad weekend in New York with the very theatrical family of Laurette Taylor. The play shows us two days in the weekend life of the Bliss clan and it continues to delight to this day (at press time the West End is enjoying a smash revival). This was to be the play to begin the Noël Coward renaissance in the 1960's, after a long period of critical exile.

Noël returned to his beloved New York in triumph in that same year of 1925. The city of closed doors now opened its welcoming arms to him. He repeated his triumphant performance in The Vortex and the results were even more gratifying than in London. The reviews were love letters to the play and the cast and Coward became as talked about on the island of Manhattan as he had been at home. The play enjoyed a long run and a not quite as successful American tour of such cities as Newark, Brooklyn, Cincinnatti and Chicago. Hay Fever also made the voyage to Broadway, but with less success. "Hay Fever nothing to sneeze at" was the general consensus and the comedy closed shortly thereafter. Without much of a breath, Coward moved on to the opening night of his next show, *Easy Virtue* starring Jane Cowl. This pleased the audiences and critics more and the play ran for many months. Nine days after the opening Noël Coward turned twenty six.

During the New York run of *The Vortex*, Noël once again met a young American stock broker whose acquainted he had made during the London run. John C. Wilson, known to his friends as Jack was handsome, was witty and interested in the theatre. Jack and Noël quickly became enamored of each other and soon became lovers. From then on until the 1950's Jack was an integral part of Noël's life and career, managing his financial and theatrical affairs. Eventually they formed their own production company (Transatlantic Production, in partnership with the Lunts) and produced all of Coward's plays. Not including the Coward plays, Wilson went on to produce and direct many Broadway hits, including *Gentlemen Prefer Blondes* and *Kiss Me Kate*. It was perhaps a shock to Coward when the homosexual Wilson wooed and married Natasha Paley, a Russian Princess, in the late 1930's, but although the sexual side of this relationship with Wilson was apparently over, Coward took to Natasha and lovingly accepted her into his theatrical family, dedicating several of his books to the Wilsons. Wilson developed a severe drinking problem (perhaps due to his sexual denial) and eventually became a burden to himself and all of his friends. He died in 1961.

Back in London for 1926 Coward witnessed the productions of four of his plays: *Easy Virtue* in June, *The Queen Was In The Parlour* in August, *The Rat Trap* in October and *This Was A Man* in November. In the midst of all this activity he rehearsed and opened in the mammoth role of Lewis Dodd in *The Constant Nymph* by Margaret Kennedy and Basil Dean, one of his few appearances in a play not his own. He received fine reviews for his portrayal, but the extremely hectic pace of the past two years finally took its toll and Coward suffered a complete nervous breakdown three weeks into the run and had to be replaced by John Gielgud. Coward was not to appear on the stage for another two years. Meanwhile *The Rat Trap* eked out only 12 showings and *This Was A Man* ran a meager 31 performances. The Midas touch seemed to be tarnishing.

The breakdown and its resultant cure put many things into perspective for Coward. He realized that he was travelling at too high a speed and giving as much attention to his private life as his professional one. He vowed to put his work above all else, for that was his lifeblood, and to frequently "get away." Travel became an important part of his life for then on giving him time to recharge his batteries and to be alone with his writing.

1927 brought unsuccessful productions of *Home Chat* in the West End and *The Marquise* on Broadway, but it was not until November 24th, 1927 that Noël Coward hit his nadir.

The play was called *Sirocco*. It was written in 1921 before fame arrived and like most of his past plays it was produced and directed by Basil Dean. Dean and Coward were lucky enough to secure the services of the enormously popular star Ivor Novello in the lead role. But success was not in the cards. Opening night of

Sirocco has passed into theatrical lore. In those days and for many years after, balcony ticket buyers, who frequently waited in line for their tickets all night, could be the most brutal of audiences. They would either take a show to its heart or could ruin a performance. This time they chose the latter. After a dullish act one, they showed their displeasure during a love scene by making sucking sounds and generally disrupting the proceedings. The last act disintergrated into complete chaos and the curtain finally fell to bedlam. Coward stoically sat in the box and watched the fiasco. When Frances Doble, one of the leads but a neophyte in the theatre, stopped the catcalls to make a speech during the curtain calls, she proudly proclaimed that this was "the happiest night of my life." The curtain was quickly rung down. When Coward left the theatre several of the audience members spat at him. *Sirocco* managed to play 27 more times before mercifully expiring. A few days later *Fallen Angels*, which had racked up a nice run in London, opened dismally in New York and closed after 36 performances.

Coward was so distressed by his sudden fall from grace that he offered to withdraw his material from the impending Cochran revue he was writing and leave town. Cockie, as he was known to friends, wouldn't hear of it. He was sure that Coward would weather the storm and his luck would change. In that assumption, he was right.

Coward accepted a role in the West End production of S.N. Behrman's play *The Second Man*. Co-starring with Raymond Massey, Ursula Jeans and Zena Dare, Coward received good reviews and began to feel a little better about himself. And then on March 22, 1928 his fortunes completely reversed with the opening of *This Year of Grace!* at the London Pavilion. Starring Jessie Matthews, Sonnie Hale, Maisie Gay, Douglas Byng and Tilly Losch, this revue, originally titled Charles B. Cochran's 1928 Revue, was hailed by the critic from the London observer with superlatives running the alphabetical gamut from "the most amusing, the most brilliant, the cleverest, the daintiest to the most uberous, the most versatile, the wittiest...." Although the other critics could never touch the exhalation of the above, the other notices were still raves. The show introduced two standards: "Dance Little Lady" (a close relation to "Poor Little Rich Girl") and "A Room With A View." *This Year of Grace!* was a major success and eventually racked up 316 performances. This was to be the first of a series of Coward-Cochran hits that would last well into the thirties. Coward was so delighted with his success that he jumped at the chance to appear in the American version of the show co-starring with Beatrice Lillie. The Noël Coward drought was over.

This Year of Grace! opened on Broadway to as much, if not more acclaim than its West End sister. "Almost too good to be true. A perfect way to spend an evening." Noël added two new numbers for the incomparable Miss Lillie, one of which would become a Coward standard, "World Weary," and several duets for the two to share. It was during this period that an idea formulated in Noël's head. After listening to some new recordings of *Die Fledermaus*, an image of gas-lit cafes of the 1870's and 80's entered his head and refused to leave. Waltzes began to spin and girls in bustles and duels and romance whirled around him. Just at the time when audiences needed it, Noël Coward came up with the antidote for the jazz and speed of the twenties and a perfect capper for his decade of wild success: *Bitter-Sweet*.

In 1927 the first film version (albeit silent) of one of Coward's plays was released by Gainsborough Pictures in England. It was *The Queen Was In The Parlour*. It was successful enough to encourage the filming of *The Vortex*, preserving not Coward's brilliant performance, but Ivor Novello's. At about the same time Alfred Hitchcock was directing another Coward's adaptation, *Easy Virtue*. Michael Balcon, the producer of the Hitchcock film, realized how difficult it was adapting these plays for the silent screen and asked Coward to write an original scenario expressly for the camera. Coward complied and the result was called *Concerto*. Although it was never filmed, Coward was able to used the plot about a young girl who runs away with her singing teacher to a bohemian life for his projected romantic operette for the stage, *Bitter-Sweet*.

Lavishly produced by Cochran with sets and costumes by Gladys Calthrop and Ernst Stern this operette was the first production with music, book, lyrics and direction by Noël Coward. Having first envisioned his darling Gertrude Lawrence in the lead role of Sari, as the composing of the score went on he realized that the range of singing was well beyond her capabilities and had Cochran approach the great musical star Evelyn Laye. Laye, harboring a grudge against Cochran for casting her husband Sonny Hale opposite Jessie Matthews in *This Year of Grace!* (the two became lovers), refused the role point blank, a mistake she regrets to this day.

Finally, American star Peggy Wood was hired and it was she who created the role and introduced "I'll See You Again" and "Zigeuner" among other exquisite items. One much overlooked number, the first of Coward's male operetta quartets, was entitled "Green Carnations" and was an incredibly "out" number for 1929 England. The fey men who sing the song tell us that they are the reason for the nineties being gay and you can tell who they are because they all wear a green carnation. This number must have raised a few eyebrows in a country that punished its homosexuals with prison sentences and was famous for ruining Oscar Wilde's career and life. It must have been very couragous for Coward, who was never really "out" to the public (it was illegal after all) to write and stage this number. When the show was revived on tour by the Shubert's in the early thirties, the song was cut for a while, but reinstated when the tour arrived on Broadway. The homosexual Noël Coward surely had a hand in that.

But it was Ivy St. Helier, in the supporting role of Manon, the poor tragic singer of songs, who got to sing what was perhaps Coward's professional credo, "If Love Were All." With its lines about having "just a talent to amuse," the song grew through the years, sung by everyone from Helier (who repeats her role in the first film version) to Judy Garland. Coward himself would use it at the end of his medleys in cabaret in the fifties. Whether he believed its sentiment or not, it was a beautiful and heartfelt song in a score of amazing versatility and charm. *Bitter-Sweet* would go on to a run of 697 performances in London and an additional 159 performances on Broadway, where, having finally realizing her folly, Evelyn Laye starred. Coward bid farewell to the 1920's with his most beloved and best received musical play.

The 1930's

After mounting the Broadway production of *Bitter-Sweet*, which was co-produced by Florenz Ziegfeld, Coward went off on a six month trip to the Orient with his close friend Jeffrey Amherst. Their itinerary included Japan, Korea and Shanghai. With nothing on his mind but a dim promise to Gertie Lawrence to write a suitable play in which the two could star, Coward and Amherst embarked. When Amherst contracted ameobic dysentery in Singapore, Coward was forced to await his friend's recovery. Coward got the flu and while in bed wrote what would be one of his most famous songs, "Mad Dogs And Englishmen" and, as per his promise to Lawrence, a three act comedy designed especially for the talents of Noël and Gertie. He called it *Private Lives* and he wrote it in four days. Noël was so pleased with the play that he cabled Gertie at once with the news and a copy of the script followed. Gertie cabled back: NOTHING WRONG THAT CAN'T BE FIXED, to which Coward replied: NOTHING TO BE FIXED EXCEPT YOUR PERFORMANCE.

With nothing to do in Singapore Noël wandered and came across an English theatrical touring company that was appearing in repertory. After discovering that they were performing *Journey's End*, a favorite play of his, he expressed his wish to play the part of Stanhope. This he did and enjoyed very much. He might have gone on with the company, but Amherst recovered and they completed their own journey.

Returning to home, Coward and Cochran (for he was to produce the play) got ready to do *Private Lives*. With Noël and Gertie in the lead roles of Elyot and Amanda, Coward cast their respective mates with Adrianne Allen and Laurence Olivier. Coward felt that the roles of the mates were so dull that they required actors of great skill and good looks. In Olivier's book, *On Acting*, he tells how Coward helped him at his craft:

> "I had been fired from several productions for giggling. Noël Coward broke me of it when we were doing *Private Lives* by deliberately saying, 'Look, you're a giggler and I'm going to cure you. I'll tell you how I'm going to do it. I warn you. I'm going to make you giggle all I can, and between Gertie and me we can do it anytime we feel like. We can kill you. And you know it. And at the end of each performance, every time you do it, I'm

going to tick you off in front of the entire cast and staff, and you are going to learn not to.' It took seven months."

Private Lives opened the newly built Phoenix Theatre in London and ran as long as Coward and Lawrence stayed with it. By now, Noël had a hard and steadfast rule about appearing on the stage for no more than a three month run. So despite full houses and good reviews, the star took a holiday in preparation for the New York run, which opened at the Times Square Theatre on January 27, 1931 and received even better notices from the New York dailies. As per his pact, Coward, along with Lawrence, left the show after the allotted three months, but the roles of Elyot and Amanda were played by Otto Kruger and Madge Kennedy and the show ran more than twice as long on Broadway as the West End. Luckily for posterity, Noël and Gertie recorded two scenes from *Private Lives* and one can hear at least a bit of their inimitably incandescent performances on disc today.

Difficult as it was to follow such a triumph as *Private Lives*, Coward surpassed himself with his next production. Wanting to test his directorial powers on a large scale, Coward searched for a subject. When he came across some old magazines with pictures of men going off to fight the Boar War, an idea came Noël for what would become *Cavalcade*. Rather like the later-to-be-famous BBC series, *Upstairs Downstairs* (the similarity was to annoy Coward), the show followed two classes of families, the upstairs Marryots and the downstairs Bridges, from December 31, 1899 to the present (1930). Making ingenious use of the enormous theatrical resources at Theatre Royal Drury Lane in London (which included hydraulic lifts aplenty), Coward filled his stage with troops leaving for war, musical shows, hordes of celebrating people in Trafalger Square, the funeral of Queen Victoria and the sinking of the Titanic. The play was more like a film come to life; one last stab by the theatre to counterattack the movies. It was wildly successful. Once again Coward seemed to tap into the British public's tastes and needs and came up with a patriotic pageant just when the country was entering into new political waters by electing its first labour government. *Cavalcade* ran for 405 spectacular performances and was filmed as a guide for the Oscar winning Fox movie version, released in 1932.

With *Cavalcade*, Noël Coward had become something of a national treasure. A repertory company was formed to perform only his plays. It was called *The Noël Coward Company* and toured with *Private Lives, Hay Fever, Home Chat, Weatherwise* (a sketch),*The Vortex, Rain Before Seven* (a sketch), *Fallen Angels, The Queen Was In The Parlour* and *I'll Leave it To You*. The whole affair was supervised by Coward and lasted over a year.

Despite all this theatrical activity Noël Coward still found time for travel. Having done the Far East, he took off for South America and it was on this trip that he received a cable from the Lunts: OUR CONTRACT WITH THEATRE GUILD UP IN JUNE WHAT ABOUT IT?

It had been years since the trio vowed to become famous and work together and now the time had come for Coward to make good on his end of the bargain, but first came another revue for Cochran called *Words and Music*. Although not as successful as their last revue, *This Year of Grace!*, *Words and Music* could boast of introducing "Mad Dogs and Englishmen" (to the British public that is. It had already been interpolated into *The Third Little Show* in New York in 1931 and was sung by Bea Lillie.), "Something To Do With Spring" and one of the few numbers that Coward himself didn't attempt to perform (except perhaps at private parties), "Mad About The Boy." The score on the whole was top of the barrel, but the lack of stars (a primary ingredient for good revues) perhaps doomed it to the second echelon of Coward revues. Despite this it ran a respectable 134 performances.

Words and Music also introduced Coward to a very young man (13 at the time) who become a very important part of his life in future years. When Graham Payn was brought in by his mother to audition for Mr. Coward, the young man wanted so to please that he sang and tap danced. At the same time. Coward did not heed his own warning to Mrs. Worthington and put the boy on the stage. Several years later the two would share more than good reviews.

With the revue out of the way, Coward could concentrate of the promise of the play for the himself and the Lunts. This promise finally bore fruit on January 24, 1933 when the Ethel Barrymore Theatre in New York played host to the trio of stars in *Design For Living*. This was one of the few Coward plays to have its premiere on this side of the Atlantic and it was wildly successful, only coming off when the stars decided to close.

Coward enjoyed working on Broadway and even appeared in two benefits on his nights off from *Design For Living*. When the usual three months were over he went back to England to direct a revival of *Hay Fever* with Constance Collier taking the lead. It only lasted 26 performances. He also bought a house in the country which he called Goldenhurst. There he put his mother, father and Aunt Vida and himself. It became a retreat for the busy writer and his friends. And perhaps it was on one those weekend retreats that Coward thought of writing an operette specifically for the talents of french actress-singer Yvonne Printemps. Noël had gone to see the enchanting Miss Printemps in as many performances in Paris as he was able and fashioned his story and score for her delectable charms. This homage became *Conversation Piece* and it was the first and only show in which Printemps sang in English.

At first Noël was content to only write the play, the music, the lyrics and direct the large cast, which included Romney Brent in the role of the Duc, guardian to Melanie (played by Miss Printemps), but when it became apparent in rehearsal that Mr. Brent (also a writer) was miscast, it was Coward himself who took over the role and played from the opening, February 16 until April 23, 1934, when he was replaced by Printemp's husband Pierre Fresney, who was apparently so good in the part that when the show went to Broadway in October of the same year, he re-created his role of the Duc.

Critically and musically the show played stepchild to *Bitter-Sweet*, but still contained such goodies as "I'll Follow My Secret Heart," "Nevermore," and the witty "Regency Rakes." The last named was one of Coward's famous male quartets which include "Green Carnations" and "The Stately Homes of England." *Conversation Piece* was to be the last in a very successful line of collaborations between Noël Coward and Charles B. Cochran. Coward, perhaps prodded by his lover John C. Wilson or greed or just the power to do what he wanted, broke with Cochran and decided to produced his plays and musicals himself. With Wilson and the Lunts as partners, he formed Transatlantic Productions, Inc. although all productions produced by the company had posters and playbills that read "John C. Wilson presents." The arrangement called for profits made by any one of the participants to be shared with the others. So presumably plays starring the Lunts and not produced by Wilson would be part of the deal and of course Coward's work without the Lunts would also be part of the pot. Having been an actor, author, composer and director, now Noël Coward was a manager.

The first production under the new banner was the 1934 West End premiere of S.N. Behrman's hit Broadway comedy, *Biography*. To ensure success, Coward himself directed a cast that included Laurence Olivier, Ina Claire and Frank Cellier. Despite all these merits the show only ran for 45 performances. Transatlantic Productions, Inc. was not off to a good start.

Theatre Royal, the firm's next production, was more successful. A retitled (Coward's title) West End version of the very popular comedy, *The Royal Family*, by George S. Kaufman and Edna Ferber, this tale of a theatrical clan not unlike the Barrymores was directed by Coward and played by the likes of Marie Tempest, Laurence Olivier and Madge Titheradge. It ran for a respectable 174 performances.

Producing is not only a matter of nuts and bolts and budgets. Charles B. Cochran's taste was impeccable and it is likely if Coward delivered a play that Cochran felt unworthy, he might not produce it. With Cochran out of the way, Coward would make several mistakes and he would never have another musical hit. The first of these errors was another play for the Lunts called *Point Valaine*.

Both Lynn and Alfred had many misgivings when sent the script of this rather dour piece about an innkeeper and her black Russian lover. The play contained a scene where Lunt had to spit in Fontanne's face and ended with his suicide. Not the usual Coward-Lunt fare. But despite their misgivings the Lunts, remembering the great hit that *Design For Living* had been, signed on for the Broadway run. After tryouts in Boston and Philadelphia, everyone involved knew where the chips would fall. When the show reached New York it turned out to be the only flop that the Lunts had ever or would ever appear in. Eventually, after being away from the play and seeing the London production years later (without the Lunts) Coward realized that the play was neither big enough for tragedy nor light enough for comedy. So far none of the Transatlantic productions were smash hits.

When movies learned to talk in the late twenties (although it took the British Cinema a few more years than the Americans) it was inevitable that Coward's plays with their verbal wit, which had proven elusive in the silent days, would be better bets for the silver screen. With the stage triumph of *Private Lives* both in England and America in 1930 the Hollywood studios bid for the film rights and MGM won. At first it was thought that Coward and Lawrence might repeat their stage roles and they were even screen tested (quite unsuccessfully). Then it was speculated that the Lunts would follow up their first screen appearances in *The Guardsman* by playing Elyot and Amanda, but instead chose to return to stage and never again darken Hollywood's door. Finally the choice roles went to the queen of the lot, Norma Shearer (wife to studio head, Thalberg) and Robert Montgomery.

Although neither actor was very British the film managed to capture the sharp wit of the play, despite the usual Hollywood changes. The reviews were good and Coward was not displeased with the results. Amazingly, there would be another film version of *Private Lives* in 1936, albeit in French, under the title of *Les Amants Terrible*.

Paramount next filmed *The Queen Was In The Parlour* under the new title of *Tonight Is Ours*. It was mildly successful. But it was in 1931, when Coward's lawyer the redoubtable Fanny Holtzman (she also represented Gertrude Lawrence) shopped around and sold the film rights to *Cavalcade* (which never played in New York) to the Fox Film Company, that a truly satisfying film version of one of Noël Coward's plays was produced.

Fox sent a film crew to the Theatre Royal Drury Lane to film Coward's production as a model for the movie and the care that they, director Frank Lloyd and screen writer Reginald Berkeley took still is in evidence today. The reviews were raves and *Cavalcade* won the Academy Award for Best Picture and for Lloyd's direction. Coward was very pleased with the transformation of his play to the new medium.

In 1933 both *Bitter-Sweet* and *Design For Living* were put before the cameras with varying results. Although announced as a vehicle for Jeanette MacDonald in Hollywood (she was destined to re-make the film in 1940 with Nelson Eddy), *Bitter-Sweet* turned out to be a British production spearheaded by Herbert Wilcox for his wife, Anna Neagle. The very popular, but marginally talented Miss Neagle valiantly played the demanding role of Sari, while Ferdinand Graavey portrayed her doomed lover, Carl. The casting coup of the film was Ivy St. Helier who recreated her poignant performance as the sparrow-like Manon. It is indeed lucky to have her renditions of "Kiss Me" and most especially "If Love Were All" preserved on film. Although the screenplay deleted Act III of the stage version altogether, it remains the most faithful of the two film versions of the operette.

The film version of *Design For Living* can boast many virtues, but not of being faithful to its source. Directed by the stylish Ernst Lubitsch at Paramount, the screen adaptation was done by Ben Hecht. Due to the rather lascivious nature of the plot, almost all of the Coward's lines were tossed to the wind and Hecht was heard to boast that there was only one line of Coward's left in the film. Coward himself was unable to find it. Despite all of the above the film was successful and the performances of Miriam Hopkins, Frederic March and Gary Cooper were praised.

After the closing notice for *Point Valaine* went up Coward was in the embarrassing position of being short of cash. So it was with great prudence and a little reluctance that he accepted the starring role in a film to be written and directed by Ben Hecht and Charlie MacArthur then called *Miracle in 49th Street*.

Hecht and MacArthur, authors of such Broadway smashes as *The Front Page* and *Twentieth Century*, had set up a production company of their own to film their works. They worked out of the Astoria Studios in New York and had already released *Crime Without Passion* starring Claude Rains and now focused on the story of Anthony Mallare (to be played by Coward), a successful and heartless book publisher who dies and must redeem his soul.

Coward became excited by the project when, at first, Helen Hayes (MacArthur's wife) was announced to play the lead role opposite him, but began to be disillusioned when Hayes withdrew and was replaced by Julie Haydon (today chiefly remembered as the original Laura in *The Glass Menagerie*). The shooting went smoothly and advance publicity predicted that Noël would give Gary Cooper a run for his money. When the picture opened at Radio City Music Hall on May 2, 1935, under the title of *The Scoundrel*, the reviews were very good, but the sophisticated nature of the film put it in the cult class rather than that of a hit. It won the Academy Award for Best Original Story and faded from public memory, although it shows up on Public Television and in astute revival houses. Film was never to prove to be Coward's medium as an actor and it would be several years before he would go in front of the cameras again.

It was then that Noël Coward, producer thought it was time for Noël Coward, actor to team up again with Gertrude Lawrence and so he summoned Noël Coward, author to come up with a play in which the two would not bore themselves too terribly if they had to play it eight times a week. One of the Noëls came up with the smashing idea of writing not one, but ten plays (although only nine were used) that the two stars could perform in various combinations over a three night span. The one act plays (a neglected form which Coward was determined to revive) ran the gamut from light comedy, to psychological drama, to music hall, to farce, to musical fantasy and operetta, to melodrama.

And so in 1936, following a nine weeks tour of the provinces, Gertrude Lawrence and Noël Coward triumphantly opened *Tonight At 8:30* (as the whole cycle was called) with the first cycle of plays consisting of *Family Album*, a Victorian musical, *The Astonished Heart*, a drama, and *Red Peppers*, a music hall interlude. Several nights later they premiered *Fumed Oak*, "a brisk and bitter" comedy, *Hands Across The Sea*, a farce showcasing Miss Lawrence and *Shadow Play*, a musical fantasy. These were joined by perhaps the most famous of the plays,

Still Life (later to be filmed as *Brief Encounter*), *Ways and Means* and *We Were Dancing*.

Not all the critics agreed on the merits of all of the plays, but the sheer theatrical hat trick was enough to draw full houses for the limited run and the plays all proved durable properties which Coward and other would adapt for the screen, television, radio and recordings again and again. They became his nest eggs. During the run at the end of a normal matinee, Sir Seymour Hicks presented Noël with Edmund Kean's sword. The sword, which had Kean's signature inscribed on the scabbard, was handed down via Irving, who was given it by a character actor from Kean's company. Hicks felt that Coward as an actor was worthy of the honor. It now sits in the National Theatre Museum in England. Coward and Lawrence took the plays to Broadway in November of the same year and the results were just as gratifying.

It was about this time that Coward took stock of his life and wrote his first volume of memoirs. It was published to good reviews and better sales in 1937 under the title of *Present Indicative* and spanned the years from birth to 1930.

Production-wise, Coward devoted the rest of the thirties to two musical productions, both only moderately successful. *Operette* (1938) was yet another attempt to mine the *Bitter-Sweet* vein. It was a period piece and one again starred Peggy Wood. The critics were unimpressed and only one song (although several are beautiful) went on to fame, "The Stately Homes of England." The second musical was more or less the American edition of his 1930 revue *Words and Music*. This time called *Set To Music* (1939), it starred the great Beatrice Lillie and had her introduce one of her most famous pieces of Coward material: "I've Been To A Marvelous Party." She also sang "Mad About The Boy" and "Three White Feathers" and audiences cheered her with gales of laughter for 129 performances.

In April and May of 1939 Coward wrote two plays in which he would star in repertory. The first play, *Present Laughter* was semi-autobiographical, being a comedy about a famous actor and his theatrical "family." But where Noël Coward was homosexual, his alter ego, Garry Essendine was straight. Despite the necessary switch in sexual orientation, Garry was Noël and Noël was Garry. The other play, *This Happy Breed* went back to Coward's roots. It was about a middle class family not unlike the Coward's of Teddington. Like *Cavalcade* before it, the play spanned many years and used historical references as signposts for the characters.

With the storm clouds gathering all over Europe, war seemed imminent. But Coward proceeded to cast and rehearse both *Present Laughter* and *This Happy Breed* getting as far as dress rehearsals on August 30 and 31st. When war was declared on September 3, 1939, the plays were scrapped not to be taken up again until three years later. Coward felt that he could be of better use to his country in this time of drama and Sir Campbell Stuart agreed. He asked Coward to set up a British propaganda machine in Paris and four days after the outbreak of war, Coward was on a plane to France.

The 1940's

The office that Noël Coward and David Strathallan organized became a model of efficiency and boredom. The tasks were few and far between during what came to be known as the Phoney War. After several months Noël was given a leave of absence and went to America, just missing the German invasion of France.

With the disbanding of the French office, Coward's first mission was to stay in America and try to gage the American reaction to the war, but he was soon inducted by Sir William Stephenson, known as "Little Bill" for intelligence work. Whether Coward was a spy (as several sources insist) or not, he did his best to serve his nation in need, but ultimately found that his contributions should be within his field of expertise: entertainment. And so in the 1941, during some of the darkest days of the war, Noël Coward wrote a patriotic song ("London Pride") and one of his funniest and most enduring comedies, *Blithe Spirit*.

Blithe Spirit was an improbable farce about death. Once again Noël Coward tapped right into the needs of the British public. With the Blitz all around them, what was required was to exorcise the demons. The tale of Charles Condomine and the return of his dead wife Elvira, did just the trick. *Blithe Spirit* also contained a strong theme that ran through some of the best of Coward's plays. In *Private Lives*, in *Design For Living* and in *Present Laughter* there are characters who cannot live together and cannot live apart. In *Blithe Spirit* this theme is made hilariously obvious, when Elvira tries to kill her husband so that he can be with her after having said that she died to get away from him.

Although he would play the role many times though the years, Coward did not originate the role of Charles (but he did direct it), that honor went to Cecil Parker. The play ran for 1,997 performances and set a record for a straight play in London. That record was only broken in 1957 by the West End phenomenon, *The Mousetrap* (still running). It opened that same year on Broadway, produced and directed by John C. Wilson and starring Clifton Webb, Peggy Wood, Mildred Natwick and Leonora Corbett. It ran for 657 performances and was chosen as one of Burn Mantle's 10 Best Plays of 1941-42 and won the coveted New York Drama Critics Circle Award.

Never having been entirely satisfied with the film versions of his plays (eg. *Bitter-Sweet, Design For Living, Private Lives*), Coward formed a film company called Two Cities to produce his own movies. The first of these films took shape in Coward's mind after hearing his good friend Lord Mountbatten tell the sad tale of the sinking of his ship. Coward felt that the story of this ship and its brave men would make a moving testament to the Royal Navy and its struggles. The fictionalized story became *In Which We Serve*. Coward asked film editor David Lean to co-direct and got the young director's career off to a rousing start. The 1942 film proved as popular with war time audiences as with the critics and won a special Academy Award for Coward's outstanding production achievement. Coward's production company went on to produce the film versions of *This Happy Breed, Blithe Spirit* and one of the one act plays in *Tonight At 8:30* called *Still Life*. This last was retitled *Brief Encounter* and became one of the most beloved English romances of the screen.

Still concerned about doing his bit for the war, in 1942 Coward put together a package of *Blithe Spirit* and the as-yet unproduced *Present Laughter* and *This Happy Breed* and with the help of H.M.Tennent as producer began a 25 week tour of England. The plays brought live theatre to war-weary Britishers, who didn't even have a movie theatre in their towns. The tour culminated with *Present Laughter* and *This Happy Breed* finally making their bows in the West End at the Haymarket Theatre in April of 1943.

Unlike other of his theatrical brethren, Coward did not want to be part of ENSA (the British equivalent of the USO) and along with his accompanist took off on his own singing tours of Australia, Trinidad, South Africa, Ceylon, Chittagong, Dozahri, Denchapalong, Tambru Gat and Cox's Bazaar. These tours included many radio broadcasts, including the famous Australia Visited series in 1940 and the 14th Army Broadcast in 1944. It was during this time that Coward wrote one of his most sardonic and explosive songs, "Don't Let's Be Beastly To The Germans." When he broadcast the satirical number the British public evidently were not listening to the words and took the title at face value. Coward and the BBC received hundreds of letters of protest.

In December of 1944 he gave in and did join ENSA on a tour of Versailles, Paris and Brussels.

When the war finally seemed to be drawing to a close, Coward wanted the British Theatre-going public to have a gift and he wrote a revue entitled *Sigh No More*. It opened at the Piccadilly Theatre starring Cyril Ritchard, Madge Elliot, Joyce Grenfell and a young man whom Noël had met several years earlier, Graham Payn. This was the same Graham Payn who tapped and sang for Noël in 1931, except that he had grown up to be a handsome actor-singer-dancer. Before long Noël and Graham were living together.

Perhaps it was love or just good theatrical sense, but Coward's next opus was a musical romance set in 1860 on a fictional island and it was to star his new romance, Graham and the up and coming Broadway star, Mary Martin. The musical, entitled *Pacific 1860* was to re-open the Theatre Royal, Drury Lane, which was heavily damaged in the Blitz, in the fall of 1946, but reconstruction took so long that the show opened in the dead of what was one of the coldest winters in London memory. Although graced with lovely melodies and witty and romantic lyrics, the stale operetta plot pleased neither the critics nor the public. (although Ivor Novello continued to do the same type of thing for years, and to great acclaim). Beset by backstage spats, the show managed to run 129 freezing performances before closing to make way for a musical fresh from America. This musical signaled the wave of the future and sounded the deathknell for British musicals until the

Andrew Lloyd Webber resurgence in the seventies. The show was *Oklahoma!*. This event also marked the beginning of Coward's commercial and critical decline. A decline that would continue until his own renaissance in the 1960's.

Although *Present Laughter* had played at the Haymarket in 1943, it had only lasted for 38 performances, so Coward decided to revive it with himself in the starring role. It was a huge success and ran for 528 performances (most of those with Hugh Sinclair in the lead).

Wondering what it would have been like if England had been conquered as France was, Coward sat down and wrote *Peace In Our Time*. It was a moderate success, but the British public did not seem to want to be reminded of the war. *Point Valaine* finally made the trip abroad and ran a dismal 37 times. Hoping to repair the family fortunes, Coward agreed to let a young American producing team send out a tour of six of his ten plays in *Tonight At 8:30*. The commercial lure was to be Gertrude Lawrence in her original roles and Noël Coward as director. In Coward's roles, he cast his lover Graham Payn. This tour began in Baltimore in November of 1947 and ended on Broadway in February of 1948, lasting a mere 26 performances in New York. Most of the critics felt that Coward's presence was badly needed and that the plays themselves were not enough. Coward did perform the plays for one last time in January of 1948 in San Francisco, when Payn took ill. This and the two other times he played for the ailing Payn proved to be the last time that Gertrude Lawrence and Noël Coward shared a stage. She died in 1952 during the run of her greatest Broadway hit *The King And I*.

Theatrically speaking, the rest of the 1940's were taken up with Coward's Parisian theatrical debut in the French production of *Present Laughter*, entitled *Joyeux Chagrin* and the film version of *The Astonished Heart* (one of the plays in *Tonight At 8:30*). The former, which Coward played in flawless French, was the more successful of the two ventures.

The 1950's

The fifties began with a Noël Coward musical unlike others. More musical comedy and influenced by the Americans, *Ace of Clubs* took place in the seedy nightclub of the title in Soho and concerned gangsters and their molls. Rather like *Guys and Dolls*, which was running on Broadway, the music and lyrics reflected the new tough Coward mood and the score was first rate, but obviously not good enough to counterattack the onslought of American product, such as *South Pacific, Brigadoon* and *Oklahoma!* It ran 211 performances in the days when the American shows ran thousands.

Perhaps becoming dispirited, Coward turned back to the form of writing he knew best, the light comedy and produced *Relative Values*. Starring Gladys Cooper and Angela Baddeley, the witty play seemed to harken back to the glamorous thirties and London theatre-goers kept it going for 477 performances.

Despite this relative success, Coward began to realize that his career and his bank account needed a shot in the arm. Due to the heavy British tax laws, money was rolling out to the state as quickly as his royalty checks came in. Since the war, when he was forced to entertain without the benefit of footlights, character or orchestra, Coward knew that he could do it and in June of 1951, at one of the Charity Garden Parties he annually gave to aid the Actor's Orphanage (of which he was President), Coward tried out his cabaret act. It proved so successful that he was engaged by the stylish Café de Paris in London for a season beginning on October 29, 1951. Using his own witty material, Noël Coward, became, what he had never before been, a cabaret star. He now had a new product to peddle and returned to the Café de Paris on June 10, 1952 to great acclaim. If he was not as successful as a writer, he was hailed as a performer.

Success breeds the same and his next play, *Quadrille* at the Phoenix Theatre, had a nice run of 329 performances, no doubt helped by the box office allure of the Lunts in the leading roles. Coward himself helped to light a marquee with a well received Coronation revival of George Bernard Shaw's *The Apple Cart* in 1953, doubling in his cabaret act at the Café de Paris and appearing in benefits at the Palladium and the Savoy Hotel.

Perhaps noticing the successful American trend at musical adaptations, Coward tried his hand at adapting Oscar Wilde's *Lady Windermere's Fan* for the musical stage. The combination of Wilde and Coward, now called *After The Ball*, should have jelled but did not, leaving behind a lovely score and the inevitable cries of "weak book." But his next book was acclaimed. It was the second volume of autobiography entitled, *Future Indefinite* and the critics agreed that this was Coward's most mature work to date.

The Coward cabaret bonanza came to a climax when he was approached by Wilbur Clark to appear at his Desert Inn in Las Vegas. Vegas, used to stars like Sinatra, Durante and Liberace was not prepared for the dapper Englishman in tux singing his witty and risqué songs. No showgirls, no frills, just "hilarity itself," as Variety put it. Noël Coward, at the age of 54 wowed them in the desert. His engagement brought out Hollywood's elite and the audience was packed nightly with the likes of Bogart, Bacall, Zsa Zsa, Jack Benny, Cole Porter etc., eating up what "the Master" chose to serve to them. The engagement was recorded by Columbia records and released as a best selling album entitled *Noël Coward At Las Vegas* and led to a three part television contract with Columbia's parent company CBS and the Ford Motor Company.

For his television debut (his plays had been adapted for the small screen as early as 1939), Coward chose to appear with the more experienced Mary Martin (she had already appeared with Ethel Merman and in her fabulous recreation of *Peter Pan*) in a ninety minute entertainment to be written and directed by himself. He and Mary got together at his home in Jamaica to rehearse what would be shown live and in color on the *Ford Star Jubilee* as *Together With Music*. It consisted of parts of Coward's act, highlights from Mary's career and the two of them bickering as if in a real life version of *Red Peppers*. The result was delightful and the critics bent over backwards to welcome Noël Coward to American television.

1956 was another busy year for the fledgling television star. He found himself adapting, directing and starring in TV versions of *Blithe Spirit* and *This Happy Breed*, appearing on Edward R. Murrow's *Person To Person* and *The Ed Sullivan Show* and making his Carnegie Hall debut reciting *Carnival of the Animals* with André Kostelanetz's orchestra. With all this television work and the resulting publicity surrounding it, Noël Coward became famous all over again, but this time to a couch-potato public that may have never entered a legit theatre.

He also had two new plays *(South Sea Bubble*, starring Vivien Leigh and *Nude With Violin* starring John Gielgud) debut in the West End. This was also the year in which Coward (along with his lover Payn and secretary Cole Leslie) took up residence in Bermuda in order to avoid the heavy British taxes. Despite a storm of protest from the British press, Coward felt it was time to begin thinking about his old age "which begins next Tuesday," to quote the Master. This tax exile, which would last till he died, finally had him taking up residency in Jamaica and Switzerland, never being able to be in England for more than a certain period of time, lest he be liable for taxation. This decision pained Coward, but the thought of destitution after years of hard work and success pained him more. Living and working in his own fashion had also necessitated turning down the two coveted musical theatre roles: The King in *The King and I*, opposite his beloved Gertrude Lawrence and Henry Higgins in *My Fair Lady*.

1957 brought Noël Coward back to Broadway in *Nude With Violin*, which had been such a success in London. Coward hadn't appeared on the New York stage since 1932, but although welcomed back as an actor, the play itself suffered from the powerful axes of the critics. Coward made a quick decision to rehearse his old stalwart, *Present Laughter*, and take the two plays to the west coast in repertory. Both plays were well received in San Francisco and Hollywood and did good business. Noël Coward never appeared on Broadway again.

The fifties had Coward composing his only ballet score *(London Morning)*, unsuccessfully adapting a Feydau farce *(Look After Lulu)* and appearing in a cameo role in *Around The World In 80 Days* and a much larger role in Carol Reed's film of Graham Greene's *Our Man In Havana*. Although busy and more famous than ever, his pre-war successes and post-war failures continued to haunt him and made him wonder if he was, as many of his critics implied, over the hill.

The 1960's

With the new decade, Noël Coward entered his 61st year. He celebrated his declining years with a role in Stanley Donen's *Surprise Package* (the only film in which he was seen singing and dancing) and by writing a new play for the West End about a home for old actresses, entitled *Waiting In The Wings*. The play was originally to be produced by Coward's old friend Binkie Beaumont, head of H.M. Tennent, but the two men had a falling out about changes in the script and Coward gave the play to Michael Redgrave to produce. As with most of his work since the war, the critics savaged the play and it ran 191 performances on the strength of Dame Sybil Thorndike and a cast of "gallant old troupers" whose combined age was too much to count.

Amazingly, Coward still had some tricks up his sleeve. For years he had been planning to write a musical based on his very successful cabaret number "A Bar On The Piccolo Marina." The song concerned a certain middle-aged widow, Mrs. Wentworth-Brewster and her sordid adventures on a holiday in Capri. As Coward originally planned the show, he wrote it as a vehicle for either Rosalind Russell, Kay Thompson, or Judy Holliday. When none of them signed on, he changed the premise, set the show on a cruise ship and hired Elaine Stritch to play Mimi Paragon. Gone was Mrs. Wentworth-Brewster and her holiday. Now the main plot concerned Verity, a married woman in love with an older man. Coward wrote the book, music and lyrics and directed. He even did the poster art.

When the show, now called *Sail Away* (after one of the songs from *Ace of Clubs*), played its tryout on the road, drastic surgery was needed and Coward cut the main plot, enlarged Elaine Stritch's role (giving her the love interest) and made the show work. Of course after all that, the critics were not impressed. The score, which was dismissed, showed little signs of an aging songwriter. The music and lyrics were fresh, up-to-date, funny and romantic. Listening to the cast album today, one wonders what was wrong? The book perhaps was revue-like and not too serious, but with Stritch and the songs, it should have run longer than 167 times. Coward obviously felt the show deserved another chance and directed it again in London (once again with Stritch). The reviews were worse than ever.

As the sixties moved forward it seemed that Noël Coward was a forgotten old has-been from the 1920's, until a small British theatre in Hampstead decided to revive one of his relics from a bygone age, *Private Lives*. Over the years the show had several successful revivals including a major American tour starring Tallulah Bankhead. But the play had been dismissed as no more than a vehicle for camp queens to ride on. Suddenly, out of the blue, this little production directed by James Roose-Evans took the town by storm. For the first time in a long while, the critics recognized that here was a comedy of worth that still had life after thirty.

Noël Coward didn't know it but April 24, 1963 marked the beginning of what he came to call "Dad's Renaissance."

Meanwhile, "Dad" prepared two musicals for the 1963-64 Broadway season. The first to open merely had music and lyrics by Coward. The book, based on Terrence Rattigan's *The Sleeping Prince*, was by Harry Kurnitz and the entire production was directed by Joe Layton. It was called, against Coward's wishes, *The Girl Who Came To Supper* (He preferred the title *Passing Fancy*). The show was splendidly produced by Herman Levin, the producer of *My Fair Lady*, but unfortunately the musical seemed to be trying to be too much like that landmark hit. Some of the reviews were positive, but the show could only manage to last a few months and did not have a West End production.

Coward's other entry for that season did a bit better. Several years before, he had been approached by the team of Hugh Martin and Timothy Gray for the musical rights to his play *Blithe Spirit*. Impressed with the book and score that the team came up with Coward agreed to direct *High Spirits*, as it was dubbed, starring Beatrice Lillie, Tammy Grimes and Edward Woodward. It was a fun evening with a superior score and it ran most of the season against such gargantuan competition as *Hello, Dolly* and *Funny Girl* and was produced in London in the fall.

Before *High Spirits* reached London, Coward had another milestone that absolutely solidified his "renaissance." When Laurence Olivier, then head of the National Theatre, approach Coward about directing a revival of his 1920's comedy *Hay Fever*, Coward thought the actor barmy. But faced with a cast that included Edith Evans, Lynn Redgrave, Maggie Smith, Robert Stephens and Derek Jacobi (Coward: "they could play the Albanian telephone book") he directed the old play as if it were freshly minted. It was the first play done by the National by a living playwright and the reviews were raves. The critics and the public had decided that it was alright to like Noël Coward's writing again. From here on the 65 year old genius had smooth sailing.

Realizing that he was getting on, Coward decided to stage his own swan song. He wrote three plays under the banner title, *Suite In Three Keys* and planned an orgy of acting. Illness postponed the opening of the plays until April of 1966, but his return to the West End stage (his first since the late forties) was greeted with huzzahs. The plays themselves were not hailed (although at least one of them, *Song At Twilight*, in which Coward played a closeted homosexual writer, is a minor masterpiece) but Coward's swan song was. He played his usual three months and intended to take the plays to Broadway, but the dysentery that struck him before the London run, returned. Sadly, Coward would never be fully well again.

Still happily living with Graham Payn, whose career had not quite gone as well as he and Coward had planned, Noël seemed content to live out his years in Jamaica and Switzerland, travelling to New York and London and revisiting the parts of the world that had pleased him most. For age and illness hadn't changed the man who wrote "I Travel Alone" and "Why Do The Wrong People Travel?."

Now that the critics okayed Coward's plays again, revivals abounded of *Fallen Angels, Tonight At 8:30, Hay Fever, Private Lives, Blithe Spirit* and *Present Laughter*. Although Coward's musicals seemed unrevivable, due to antiquated books, the songs were sturdier than ever and sought new homes in revues such as *Noël Coward's Sweet Potato, Oh Coward! and Cowardy Custard*.

As Noël Coward approached his seventieth birthday, plans were in the works to honor him. The National Film Theatre put together a program of his films at which he appeared, the BBC produced his plays on radio and television and even televised his birthday party from the Lancaster Room at the Savoy Hotel. There was so much Cowardian activity that it caused the Master to dub it "holy week." To top it off several dozen theatrical luminaries got together and put on a midnight matinee at the Phoenix Theatre (which Noël Coward and Gertrude Lawrence christened with *Private Lives*). It was a show beyond anything London or Broadway had running, with stars that no management could afford. And they all appeared to honor "the Master" on his birthday. There were songs and sketches and poems and tributes, all written by Noël Coward. The evening lasted until the wee hours of the morning and when it was over and Coward took the stage to thank one and all, there wasn't a dry eye in the house.

Although it seemed that nothing could top this tribute, Coward's name finally appeared on the Honor's List of Her Majesty the Queen of England. He was to be knighted for his service to the Crown. This honor had eluded him for many years and he accepted it with great humility and joy. Now he joined Sir John Gielgud, Sir Laurence Olivier and the other theatrical knights as Sir Noël Coward. A happier entry in the 1970's was hard to come by.

The Last Years

As he entered his eighth decade, Coward's health continued to decline. Always a heavy smoker, he refused doctor's orders to quit and was also disinclined to exercise bringing on a worsening arteriosclerosis. Mere movement became a painful challenge.

The theatrical world, now used to "Dad's Renaissance," continued to eulogize the aging Master. In London there was *Cowardy Custard*, a revue of his songs and in New York, *Oh Coward!*, an equally laudatory tribute to Coward's music and lyrics. In fact, Coward made one of his last public appearances at a gala performance of *Oh Coward!*, accompanied by his old friend, Marlene Dietrich.

In his diaries, Coward alluded to not wanting to have a lingering old age and his wish was to come true. On March 22, 1973, his old friend and sometime producer, Binkie Beaumont died suddenly, shocking the ailing Coward. Four days later, Sir Noël Coward died of a heart attack in his sleep in Jamaica. His friends Cole Leslie, Geoffrey Johnson and especially Graham Payn were there.

Although Coward was buried in Jamaica, both London and New York held memorials. Sir Laurence Olivier, Yehudi Menuhin and Sir John Gielgud participated in a Service of Thanksgiving at St. Martin-in-the-Fields and Radie Harris, Roderick Cook, Geoffrey Johnson and Margalo Gillmore organized a celebration at the New Theatre (where *Oh Coward!* was playing), the sight of Coward's last public appearance. Helen Hayes, Cyril Ritchard, Glynis Johns and Cathleen Nesbit appeared. In 1984 a memorial stone was unveiled in Westminster Abbey in London to commemorate the life and career of Sir Noël Coward.

Noël Coward's fame and luster have not dimmed since his death at the age of 73, twenty years ago. In the 20 years since his demise, there have been five major revivals of *Private Lives*, four each of *Present Laughter* and *Blithe Spirit*, three each of *Design For Living* and *Hay Fever*, two of *The Vortex* and one each of *Fallen Angels, Bitter-Sweet, Cavalcade, Easy Virtue* and *Look After Lulu*. Perhaps more astonishing is the fact that both *Post-Mortem* and *Semi-Monde* have had posthumous world premieres. The book world has seen several biographies, the publication of his diaries and several picture books devoted to preserving the reputation of the man who had much more than just "a talent to amuse." There have been television shows, records and CD's and videos of his films. Perhaps the 1990's need a bit of his glamour, a bit of the man who epitomized the style and speed of the 1920's. A man whose "cheap music" is as potent today as it was when it was composed, but not written down by the composer. A man who grew into his title of "The Master."

Plays and Appearances

This chapter features the stage career of Noël Coward as an actor/performer, writer, director, producer, composer and lyricist. These include various children's shows, plays written by others and most especially plays, revues and musicals that Coward wrote and/or produced and directed. This section will only be concerned with London and NY premieres and major revivals. As Coward mostly appeared in works of his own writing, there will be many cross references with chapters featuring his writing, his recordings and his publications. Each entry in this section is preceded by the letter "P." To delineate Coward's contribution to each production, his name and credit are in bold print. Where he is listed as only of the cast, his name will be bold. The dates first listed refer to opening nights.

P-1   *End of Term Concert* St. Margaret's School, Sutton. July 23, 1907

   Master **Noël Coward** (8 years old) made his first public appearance performing with other pupils. He sang "Coo" from "A Country Girl" and did "Time Flies" at the piano. The latter song demanded an encore.

P-2   *The Goldfish* The Little Theatre, London. Jan. 27, 1911 Revived at Crystal Palace Theatre (2 matinees) and at the Royal Court Theatre April 17, 1911 (9 performances)

   A children's musical by Lila Field and Ayre O'Naut. Produced and Directed by Miss Field. Musical Direction by Harold Robertson Grimston.

   CAST: June Tripp (Princess Sole), Alfred Willmore (King Goldfish), Burford Hampden (King Starfish), **Noël Coward** (Prince Mussel, Jack),

Nellie Terriss (Sea Nymph, Eva), Peggie Bryant (Dolly)Irene Palotta (White Moonstone), Cuthbert Howard (Vivian), Eric Lascelles (Prince Sole, Garnet), Stella Reed (Golden Sea Nymph, Sylvia), Olga Warneford (Sea Nymph, Nell), Ruby Warneford (Pink Pearl, Molly), Kathleen Ross Lyell(Spirit of Shells), Eileen Esler (Blue Moonstone), Doris Harris (Amber, Myra), Fred Warneford (Amemone, Violet), Lorna Reed (Red Coral), Beatrice Beauchamp (Sea Foam, Kitt), Tyrell Hinton (Amethyst, Claud), Arthur Wynne (Gossamer)

REVIEWS:
London Daily Telegraph, Jan. 28, 1911: "Among other tiny artists who deserve a congratulatory pat on the back are Miss Noël Coward, Miss Nellie Terriss and Miss Peggie Bryant."

London Daily Telegraph, April 12, 1911: "[Coward]...his robust appearance gave excellent point to his woebegone song of love for the Queen of the Coral Islands."

NOTES: This was Master Coward's professional debut. As seen above, his first notice was less than auspicious, referring to him as *Miss* Noël Coward, but this was softened at the time by the Royal Court engagement. Master Alfred Willmore grew up and changed his name to the original Irish and became known as Michael Mac Liammoir. Ironically this innocent children's show played the same theatre at which Coward was to make his adult mark as a drug addict in his own play, *The Vortex.*

P-3   *The Great Name* Prince of Wales Theatre, London. Sept. 7, 1911
       (51 performances)

A play by James Clarence Harvey. Produced and directed by Charles Hawtrey. Costumes by Mme. Neville. Sets by Arthur de Lissa.

CAST: Charles Hawtrey (John Harcourt), James Hearn (Robert Brand), Arthur Playfair (Isaac Manhard), Ronald Squire (Hubert Last), Charles B. Vaughan (Webber), Sydney Sherwood (Tristan), Henri Laurent (Marks), Edgar B. Payne (Eversfield), Lionel Williams (Hilton), Franc Stoney (Wilburn), Charles E. Vernon (Andrews), **Noël Coward** (Cannard), Lydia Bilbrook (Stephanie Julius), Dorothy Thomas (Clara Brand), Enid Leslie (Senta Brand), Mona Harrison (Anna), Violet Graham (Mary), Hilda Moore (Lady Roderick), Mary Rorke (Mrs. Harcourt)

NOTES: Playing Cannard, a page boy in the last act of Charles Hawtrey's production, Coward had only one line, but it was addressed to Hawtrey himself. The line was "Stop that noise at once, please. In there they're playing The

Meistersingers. Making such a horrible noise. We're used to good music here." Coward took this opportunity to follow Hawtrey around and learn everything he could about comic acting from him. What Hawtrey thought of Coward is unknown, as his 300 page autobiography (1924) barely mentions him as one of the actors with whom he worked who eventually made good in the theatre. The play ran 2 months. Coward was paid 2 pounds a week.

P-4   *Where the Rainbow Ends*   Savoy Theatre, London. Dec. 21, 1911
       (69 performances)

A play by Clifford Mills and John Ramsey. Directed by Charles Hawtrey. Music by Roger Quilter. Ballet Mistress-Italia Conti. Designed by Tom Heslewood.

CAST: Esmé Wynne (Rosamond Carey), Philip Tonge (Crispian Carey), **Noël Coward** (William), Mavis Yorke (Will-o'-the Wisp), Sidney Sherwood (Jim Blunders), Dot Temple (Betty Blunders), Guido Chiarletti (Cuba) C.W. Somerset (Joseph Flint), Henry Morrell (Schlapps), Norman MacOwan (Genie), Reginald Owen (St. George of England), Clifton Anderson (Dragon King), Reginald P. Lamb (Dunks), Harry Duff (The Slacker), Maurice Tosh (The Slitherslime), J.K. Edro (Dragon Sentry), Jeannie Thomas (Matilda Flint), Helen Vicary (Sea Witch), Grace Seppings (Spirit of the Lake), Zoe Gordon (Hope), Iva Williams (Mother)

NOTES: Once again, Master Coward appeared under the direction and banner of the great Charles Hawtrey.

P-5   *The Daisy Chain*   Savoy Theatre, London. Feb. 2, 1912 (1 performance)
       Special matinee.

A one act play by Dot Temple (11 years old). **Directed by Noël Coward** (12 years old).

NOTES: While appearing in *Where The Rainbow Ends* (P-4), Coward, encouraged by Hawtrey to stage special matinees, made his directorial debut.

P-6   *An Autumn Idyll*   Savoy Theatre, London. June 25, 1912 (1 performance)

A ballet produced and danced by Ruby Ginner. Music by Chopin.

CAST: Ruby Ginner (Autumn Leaf) Alan Trotter (The Wind), Joan Carrol (Toadstool) **Noël Coward** (Mushroom) Eric Coward (Fungus)

REVIEWS:
The LondonTimes, June 26, 1912: "Miss Joan Carrol and Mr. Noël Coward as the Toadstool and the Mushroom headed delightfully a little troupe of various small and engaging fungi."

NOTES: Coward's brother Eric also appeared in the play.

P-7   *A Little Fowl Play* Coliseum, London. Oct., 1912

A sketch by Harold Owen starring Charles Hawtrey and featuring Master **Noël Coward**.

NOTES: At that time in London, boys under 14 years of age were required to be licensed to work in the theatre. As this sketch was to go on at 11:00 PM, Coward was denied a license to play evening performances and could only do matinees. This was a four week run on a bill including George Robey, Beattie and Babs, Mme. Alicia Adelaide Needham and her choir, The Grotesques and a Wild West show.

P-8   *Where The Rainbow Ends* Garrick Theatre, London. Dec. 11, 1912
(84 performances)

See P-4. **Noël Coward** and most of the same cast were re-engaged for this return engagement.

P-9   *Hannele* Liverpool Repertory Company. Mar., 1913: Liverpool and Manchester.

A dream poem by Gerhardt Hauptmann. Translated by William Archer. Directed by Basil Dean. Music by Arnold Clubborn.

CAST: Fanny Ovie (Tulpa), Beatrice Smith (Hedwig), Wilfred E. Shine (Pleschke), Grace Seppings (Hannele) Baliol Holloway (Gottwald, the schoolmaster). Children in the cast included Ivy and Dorothy Moody, Roy Royston, Harold French, **Noël Coward** and Gertrude Lawrence.

NOTES: This was the first professional union of the future team of Coward and Lawrence, who were to star together in only three more productions, (P-32, P-61, P-82), but would become forever identified as a team in the public's mind and indeed, Coward would deem her his favorite interpreter of his work. Coward played an angel in a dream sequence, as well as a real child. This was also Noël's first professional association with Basil Dean, who would direct many of his later plays.

P-10   *War in the Air*   Palladium Theatre, London. June 23, 1913.

A Dramatic Spectacle by Frank Dupree following a first act bill of variety artistes including Nellie Wallace, Phil Ray and Maidie Scott. **Noël Coward** played Tommy, the infant Aviator in the prologue and flew a small model aeroplane across the stage. The sketch also made brief appearance at the Willesden Hippodrome and the Shoreditch Olympia.

P-11   *Never Say Die*   Apollo Theatre, London.   Sept. 13, 1913 (216 performances)

A play by W.H. Post.   Directed by Charles Hawtrey.   Produced by Henry Lowenfeld.

CAST: Charles Hawtrey (Woodbury), Reginald Sheffield (Buster), Louis Goodrich (Hector Walters), E. Holman Clark (Virgil Galesby), John Clulow (Sir John Fraser), A. Van-Tempest (Griggs), Daniel McCarthy (Berchesi), E.W. Tarver (Mr. Gibbs), Marie George (La Cigale), J.R. Tozer (Servant), S. Grenville Darling (Auction Man), Doris Lytton (Violet Stevenson), Winifred Emery (Mrs. Stevenson)

NOTES: **Noël Coward** understudied Reggie Sheffield as Buster. He never went on.

P-12   *Peter Pan*   Duke of York's Theatre, London Dec. 23, 1913 (40 performances) and on tour Nov. 13-Mar. 1914.

Play by J.M. Barrie. Directed by Dion Boucicault. Toured to Glasgow, Edinburgh, Newcastle, Birmingham, Wimbledon, Hammersmith and Kennington and returned in Dec., 1915 at the Duke of York's Theatre.

CAST: Pauline Chase (Peter), Godfrey Tearle (Capt. Hook), Basil Foster (Mr. Darling), Nina Sevening (Mrs. Darling), Mary Glynne (Wendy), Alfred Willmore (John), Donald Buckley (Michael), Edward Sillward (Nana), Jane Wren (Tinkerbell), Gertrude Lang (Tootles), Marjorie Graham (Nibs), **Noël Coward** (Slightly), Purcence Bourchier (Curly), Doris McIntyre (First Twin), Joan Courlthurst (Second Twin), George Shelton (Smee) Pirates: Charles Trevor, Charles Medwin, James Prior, William Luff, James English, John Kelt, Dora Sevening (Mermaid), Moya Nugent (Baby Mermaid, Liza) D. Buickley and F.W. Cecil (Crocodile), Gordon Carr (Ostrich)

SYNOPSIS: After finding his shadow, the unaging Peter Pan wisks the

Darling children off to Neverland to join the Lost Boys in numerous adventures with Pirates and Indians.

REVIEWS:
The LondonObserver: "[Coward was]...an excellent Slightly."

P-13   *Where the Rainbow Ends* Garrick Theatre, London. Dec. 27, 1915 (87 performances)

CAST: Mostly same as P-4, except for Christopher Frere (William), Goodwin Nock (Genie), H.R. Hignett (St. George of England), Frank Petley (Dragon King), E.G. Browne (Dunks), **Noël Coward** (The Slacker), A. Dixon (The Slitherslime), Charles Cleather (Dragon Sentry), Nellie Bouviere (Matilda Flint), Mona Harrison (Sea Witch), Harold French (Crispian), Violet Marley (Betty)

NOTES: Having outgrown his original role, Coward now played the part of The Slacker, a cross between a man and a dragon.

P-14   *Charley's Aunt* Tour Feb-June 1916

Tour of play by Brandon Thomas. Produced by Cecil Barth. Directed by J.R. Crawford. This played split weeks in such towns as Rugby, Peterborough, Chester, Manchester, Hanley, Bristol, Torquay, Wolverhampton.

CAST: **Noël Coward** (Charley) Esmé Wynne (Amy) Arnold Raynor (Jack), James Page (Spettigue) Sidney Compton (Brasset), J.R. Crawford (Colonel) Norah Howard.

NOTES: This was the umpteenth revival of the wildly popular farce, that was eventually filmed with Jack Benny in the lead. Frank Loesser and George Abbott musicalized it into *Where's Charley?* in 1948 combining the roles of Charley and the Lord who impersonates the aunt into one and and Ray Bolger played this role on stage and in the Warner Brothers film version in 1954.

P-15   *The Light Blues* Shaftesbury Theatre, London. Sept. 14, 1916 (20 performances)

A new musical comedy by Mark Ambient and Jack Hulbert with music by Talbot and Fink. Tried out for three weeks in Cardiff, Newcastle and Glasgow. Produced and Directed by Robert Courtneidge.

CAST: Cicely Debenham (Topsy), Albert Chevalier (Father), Cicely Courtneidge (Cynthia), Jack Hulbert (Arthur), Shaun Glenville (Gundy), Fred Lewis (Sir Oliver), Nancie Lovat (Mildred), Phyllis Hughes (Peggy), Joan Beryl (Rose), Stephanie Stephens (Doris), Ivy Louis (Gertrude), Mona Finucane (Kate), Madget Compton (Phyllis), Leslie Graham (Phoebe), Noel Dainton (Sydney Pontine), Alice Mansfield (Mrs. Budd), **Noël Coward** (Basil Pyecroft)

SYNOPSIS: The excruciating adventures of a jolly actress called Topsy Devigne, who dresses up as an undergraduate at Cambridge during May week and gets herself into a series of scrapes.

REVIEWS:
London Era, Sept. 20, 1916: "Mr. Noël Coward puts the requisite touch of ec-centricity into the character of Sydney Pontine [sic]."

NOTES: The role of Sydney Pontine mentioned in the above review was actually played by Noel Dainton. Coward played what was known as the "dude" part. He sported morning clothes, silk hat and false moustache. He appeared for five minutes in the first act and four in the second. He also understudied Jack Hulbert as the dancing lead. Many years later Cicely Courtneidge would star as Madame Arcati in the rather unsuccessful West End premiere of the musical version of Coward's play *Blithe Spirit* (see P-161). Although Coward directed the Broadway version he only supervised Courtneidge's performance.

P-16   *Cabaret Debut* Elyseé Restaurant (later the Café de Paris) Oct., 1916.

NOTES: **Noël Coward** was partnered with Eileen Dennis. The couple danced during dinner and supper at the sight of Coward's 1950's cabaret triumphs. They did a slow waltz, a tango and a one-step.

P-17   *The Happy Family* Prince of Wales Theatre, London. Dec. 18, 1916
        (41 performances)

A Christmas play by Cecil Aldin and Adrian Ross with music by Cuthbert Clarke. Directed by Arthur Aldin and Donald Calthrop. Musical Direc-tion by Cuthbert Clarke. Designed by Cecil Aldin.

CAST: George Tawde (McLachlan), Molly Burton (Mary), Cecil War-wick (Giles), C.V. France (Theophilus Pennithorne), Mimi Crawford (Barbara), Bertram Siem (Robert), Fabia Drake (Elsie) Olga Ward (Aimee), Jim (Himself), Helene Stirling (Miss Desmond) **Noël Coward** (Jack Morrison, a Sandhurst cadet).

NOTES: For the first time since *The Goldfish* (P-2), Coward sang and danced on stage. He sang a military number entitled "Sentry Go."

P-18   *Wild Heather* Gaiety Theatre, Manchester. Aug. 17, 1917, Three week run.

A play by Dorothy Brandon.

CAST: Edith Goodall, Helen Haye, Lyn Harding & **Noël Coward** (Leicester Boyd)

P-19   *Ida Collaborates* Theatre Royal, Aldershot and tour. Aug. 20, 1917

A light comedy by Noël Coward and Esmé Wynne.

CAST: Esmé Wynne (Ida)

SYNOPSIS: Ida, a charwoman's daughter is unrequitedly in love with a distinquished author.

NOTES: Written in collaboration with his good friend Esmé Wynne, this is the first play with Coward's name as author to reach the stage.

P-20   *The Saving Grace* Garrick Theatre, London. Oct. 10, 1917 (167 performances)

A comedy by Haddon Chambers. Produced by Gilbert Miller. Directed by Charles Hawtrey. Tried out at Gaiety Theatre. Manchester.

CAST: Charles Hawtrey (Blinn Corbett), Emily Brook (Susan Blaine), Ellis Jeffries (Mrs. Guildford), May Blayney (Ada Parsons), A.E.George (William Hogg), Mary Jerrold (Mrs. Corbett), **Noël Coward** (Ripley Guildford)

NOTES: Coward played one of his first leading roles and was recognized by the public for the first time. The play was a success despite WWI, which seemed to the Londoners to be interminable. There were a series of air raids during the show.

P-21   *Woman and Whisky* Tour, 1918.

A play by Noël Coward and Esmé Wynne.

P-22   *Tails Up!* Comedy Theatre, London June 1, 1918

A musical entertainment presented by Andre Charlot with music by Philip Braham. **"Peter Pan" written by Noël Coward** and Doris Joel.

NOTES: This marked the firt time that **Noël Coward** got credit as a lyricist in a London program. The song was "Peter Pan" and the music was by Doris Joel. It was performed by J. M. Campbell and Phyllis Titmuss as Peter himself. The first night program credited the lyric to Noel Farque, but this was corrected in later issues. The song was published under the title of "The Story of Peter Pan" by Herman Darewski Music and also wrongly credited the lyric to both Coward and Joel. The song was recorded by Louise Leigh.

P-23   *Scandal* Strand Theatre, London Dec. 7, 1918 (237 performances)

A play by Cosmo Hamilton.

CAST: Arthur Bourchier (Pelham Franklin), Kyrle Bellew (Beatrix Hunchcliff), Gladys Ffolliot (Honoria Hinchcliff), Norah Swinburne (Regina Waterhouse), Mary Robson (Mrs. Larpent), Millie Hylton (Lady Wickham), Clare Greet (Mrs. Keene), **Noël Coward** (Courtney Borner), Gilbert Laye (Pewsey), Alex Scott-Gatty (Malcolm Fraser), William Stack (Sutherland York), Fred Lewis (Alec Thatcher), George Dellaway (Carter), Stanley Lathbury (Lord Wickham), Arthur Dixon (Mr. Jones) Esmé Beringer (Mrs. Lee-Rivers), Hazel Hamilton (Helene)

NOTES: Coward's small and nebulous role called for him to appear in Act two in a grey suit and in Act three dressed as Sir Walter Raleigh.

P-24   *The Knight of the Burning Pestle* Birmingham Repertory Theatre. Aug., 1919. Three week run.

A play by Beaumont and Fletcher. Directed by Nigel Playfair. Produced by Bronson Albery. Costumes by Norman Wilkingson. Sets by Victor Hembrow.

CAST: E.M. Robson (Tapster), **Noël Coward** (Ralph), Ivan Berlyn (Humphrey), Eric Morgan (Jasper), Roger Livesey (George), Sydney Leon (Luce), Thomas Weguelin (Citizen), Halliwell Hobbes (Venturewell), Stanley Newman (Merrythought), Deric Zoya (Tim), Philip Cuningham Jr. (Barber), J.B.S. Davies, Neil Gow, Barry Jones, Donald Macardle, Cyril Woodward (Gallants), Betty Chester (Citizen's Wife), Dorothy Cheston (Pompiona), Hermione Baddeley (Michale), Mary

Barton (Mistress Merrythough), Cherry Carver, Guinevere Day, Doris Deane, Sylvia Forde, Dorthy Oliver, Daphne Sedgewick, Dorothy Wakefield, Esmé Welman, Ann Desmond (Dancers)

NOTES: This Elizabethan comedy was Coward's first and only foray into the genre.

P-25   *I'll Leave It To You* New Theatre, London. July 21, 1920 (37 performances)

First play written by **Noël Coward** to be produced in the West End. (Written in 1919) Tried out at the Gaiety Theatre, Manchester, May 3, 1920. (24 performances). Presented by Gilbert Miller in Manchester and by Mary Moore in London.

CAST: Kate Cutler (Mrs. Dermott), Douglas Jefferies (Oliver), Muriel Pope (Evangeline), Stella Jesse (Sylvia), **Noël Coward** (Bobbie), Moya Nugent (Joyce), E. Holman Clark (Daniel Davis), Lois Stuart (Mrs. Crombie), Esmé Wynne (Faith Crombie), David Clarkson (Griggs)

SYNOPSIS: Finding a family of ne're-do-wells, Uncle Daniel, who has been supporting them with checks, stirs them into activity by announcing that he will leave his fortune to whichever of them the most successfully turns over a new leaf and makes good. In the end, even though the Uncle hasn't any money, all realize the message of his game.

REVIEWS:
Manchester Guardian, May 4, 1920: "...the neatest thing of its sort we have lately had in Manchester. The play was most warmly received."

The London Daily Mail, July 22, 1920: "Freshly written and brightly acted. Mr. Noël Coward, the author, who is not yet twenty-one, is almost too successful in making the younger nephew a most objectionable boy."

NOTES: This is a milestone in Coward's career. It was the first time he appeared in a play written by himself. It would not be the last. Renowned producer Gilbert Miller suggested the idea of the play to Coward meaning him to write it for Charles Hawtrey. The play opened successfully in Manchester, but was not thought strong enough for Hawtrey to perform in London. When Miller closed the play, Coward gained the interest of Lady Wyndham (Mary Moore) and it was she who presented it in London two and a half months later. Although it was not a success, Coward sold the amateur rights to Samuel French and set to work on another play. The role of Daniel Davis was played by Farren Soutar in Manchester. *I'll Leave It To*

You was the first Coward play to be seen in America. It was produced in Boston in 1923.   Coward also turned the play into a short story for *The Metropolitan Magazine,* for which he was paid $500.00. When asked if he could accomplish the task of reducing his play to short story form, he replied that for five hundred dollars he would gladly consider turning *War and Peace* into a music hall sketch. When the play was revived in July of 1926 at the "Q" Theatre (a small fringe theatre) *The American* reported that it was "suprisingly juvenile – a sort of amateur entertainment, as it were, and quite devoid of the subtle Coward sex topics in general." For publications see B-76, B-90.

P-26   *Knight of the Burning Pestle* Kingsway Theatre, London. Nov. 24, 1920
(96 performances).

See P-24 for cast and credits.

NOTES: Coward contracted mumps and a fever of 102 just before Christmas and Nigel Playfair was forced to play his role. Bad business and the rest of the company contracting the mumps finally forced the play to close.

P-27   *Polly With A Past* St. James Theatre, London. Mar. 2, 1921 (110 performances)

An American farce by George Middleton and Guy Bolton. Produced and directed by Gilbert Miller.

CAST: Edna Best (Polly), Donald Calthrop (Rex Van Zile), C. Aubrey Smith (Prentice Van Zile), Helen Haye (Mrs. Davis), Alice Moffat (Myrtle Davis), Claude Rains (Stranger), Arthur Hatherton (Stiles), Edith Evans (Mrs. Van Zile), Henry Kendall (Harry Richardson), **Noël Coward** (Clay Collins), Nancye Kenyon (Parker)

SYNOPSIS: Polly, an honest chorus girl, agrees to pose as a naughty French actress. During a weekend in Long Island, Polly falls in love.

NOTE: In *Bring On The Girls* by Guy Bolton and P.G. Wodehouse, Coward was remembered as being part of a brilliant cast. In 1929 the play was musicalized and retitled *Polly*. The music and lyrics were by Herbert Stothart, Philip Charig and Irving Caesar. Coward's role was taken by William Seabury.

P-28   *The Co-Optimists* Palace Theatre, London. May, 1922

NOTES: This "Pierrotic Entertainment" opened at the Royalty Theatre on June 24, 1921 and moved to the Palace Theatre in October of 1921. **Noël Coward** contributed two items to the third edition of the revue: "The Co-Communists" performed by Laddie Cliff, Davy Burnaby, Gilbert Childs and Stanley Holloway and "Down with the Damn Lot!." The music for the songs was by Melville Gideon. On October 11, 1923 (now at the Prince of Wales Theatre) Coward contributed another item entitled "There May Be Days" (also with music by Gideon). The latter two songs were published by Francis, Day, and Hunter.

P-29   *The Better Half* Little Theatre, London. May 31, 1922 (29 performances)

A one act comedy by Noël Coward. Produced by Jose G. Levy in the 8th Series of London's Grand Guignol. Directed by Lewis Casson. Sets & Costumes by Francis H. Bull. Written in 1921.

CAST: Auriol Lee (Alice), Ivy Williams (Marion), Ian Fleming (The Husband)

SYNOPSIS: Alice is sick of her husband's nobility and tries to provoke him to a little human brutality. When she succeeds, she calls him a bully. In the end she leaves him in search of a less noble mate.

REVIEWS:
London Clarion, June 22, 1922: "There is a sense of character, though lax, And this is irony, though smartish. Withal there is the assurance that Mr. Coward is one of our most promising young playwrights.

P-30   *The Young Idea* Savoy Theatre, London. Feb 1, 1923 (60 performances). Tried out at the Prince's Theatre, Bristol. Sept. 25, 1922 (6 wks. tour).

A Comedy of Youth by Noël Coward. (written in 1921) Produced & Directed by Robert Courtneidge.

CAST: Herbert Marshall (George Brent), Ann Trevor (Gerda), **Noël Coward** (Sholto), Kate Cutler (Jennifer), Muriel Pope (Cicely), Leslie Banks (Rodney Masters), Phyllis Black (Priscilla Hartleberry), Ronald Ward (Claud Eccles), Naomi Jacob (Julia Cragworthy), Clive Currie (Eustace Dabbit), Mollie Maitland (Sybil Blaith), Ambrose Manie (Hiram J. Walkin), Walter Thompson (Huddle), Irene Rathbone (Maria)

SYNOPSIS: Brother and Sister (Sholto & Gerda), determine to reunite their divorced parents. After easily ridding themselves of father's second wife, they return to mother in Italy to complete the reconciliation.

REVIEWS:

Saturday Review, Feb. 17, 1923: "Superficially it is exhilarating and great fun....an original talent, a feeling for the theatre, and a quite extraordinary belief in the existance of an audience capable of intellectual delight. As Sholto, Mr. Coward gives an admirable performance of — Mr. Coward."

Boston Transcript, March 5, 1923: "If you examine it closely, it reaches after more than it can grasp — a good fault in a young writer. Superficially it is exhilarating and great fun."

NOTES: Although Coward blatently cribbed the idea of the play from George Bernard Shaw, when he sent the play to Shaw, he received a letter back telling him that he would some day be a good playwright, if he never read another of Shaw's plays! Like *I'll Leave It To You, The Young Idea* was turned into a short story for *Metroplitan Magazine*. For publications see B-76, B-125.

P-31   *Yoicks!* Kingsway Theatre, London. June 11, 1924 (271 performances)

A revue presented by Donald Calthrop and John Hastings Turner. Costumes by Doris Zinkeisen.

NOTES: This revue contained two items by **Noël Coward**: "I'd Like To See You Try" sung by Mary Leigh and Richard Dolman (choreographed by Fred Astaire) and "It's The Peach" (later entitled "Forbidden Fruit," and performed years later in the film *Star* by Daniel Massey, see F-29) sung by Leigh. This last was the first song with music and lyrics by Noël Coward.

P-32   *London Calling!* The Duke of York's Theatre, London. Sept. 4, 1923 (316 performances)

A Revue presented by André Charlot. **Book by Noël Coward.** and Ronald Jeans. **Music and Lyrics by Noël Coward.** Staged by Herbert Mason. Additional numbers by Philip Braham and Sissle and Blake.

CAST: Gertrude Lawrence, Maisie Gay, Tubby Edlin, Arthur Lowrrie, Eileen Molyneux, Winifred Satchell, Billy Fry, Jill Williams, Tony Williams, April Harmon, Dolores Sisters, Betty Nicholas, Wyn Clare & **Noël Coward**.

MUSICAL NUMBERS (By Noël Coward): Breaking it Gently (with Ronald Jeans)-Coward, Lawrence, Gay, Edlin, Lowrie, Molyneux; Tamarisk Town-Lawrence & Chorus; Devon-Edlin; Other Girls-Coward; When My Ship Comes Home-Satchell; Carrie-Lawrence; There's Life in the Old Girl Yet-Gay & Chorus; Russian Blues-Coward, Molyneux, Brothers, Sisters, Nicholas & Chorus; Sentiment (music by Braham)-Coward; Parisian Pierrot-Lawrence, Molyneux, Williams & Chorus; What Love Means-Gay; Follow A Star-Lawrence & Company

REVIEWS:
The London Times, Sept. 5, 1923: "With some condensation, *London Calling!* would emerge the best review that even Mr. Charlot has given us. Mr. Noël Coward is the Pooh-Bah of the production. He takes a leading part in it, and acts, dances and sings with credit; he helped Mr. Ronald Jeans to write book and also wrote the lyrics and music. To him therefore the greatest praise is due, for it was his handiwork that gave the others many of their opportunities of shining."

NOTES: This was Noël Coward's first adult professional association with Gertrude Lawrence. She sang one of his first hit songs, "Parisian Pierrot" and together they sang and danced Sissle and Blake's "You Were Meant For Me." The latter song and one other Coward solo ("Sentiment"-Lyric by Coward, Music by Philip Braham) were choreographed by Fred Astaire. Coward deemed his performance of "Sentiment" a complete and glorious failure. Maisie Gay also made a big hit singing Coward's "What Love Means to Girls Like Me" and "There's Life In the Old Girl Yet." A second edition of the revue was produced on Dec. 1, 1923 with Dorothy Clarke and Joyce Barbour replacing Gertrude Lawrence and Eileen Molyneux. Coward sang a new song of his own entitled "Temperemental Honeymoon" and wrote "I Prefer to Be on the Safe Side" for Joyce Barbour. A third edition opened on Feb. 20, 1924 with only Maisie Gay remaining of the original stars. Coward wrote two new songs: "When We Were Girls" and "A Spanish Grandee." Coward remained in the revue for 6 months. See D-44, 45, 46 for recordings from the score, See B-40 and B-61 for publications of sketches and songs.

P-33   *Charlot's Revue (Andre Charlot's London Revue of 1924)* Times Square Theatre, NY. Jan. 9, 1924 (285 performances)

NOTES: This New York edition of several of Charlot's revues included **Noël Coward** material from *London Calling!* (P-32). The show made international stars of Gertrude Lawrence, Beatrice Lillie and Jack Buchanan. Coward had to wait until his next play to acheive what this trio had with this show. His songs were: "There's Life in the Old Girl Yet" sung by Lillie, "Parisian Pierrot" sung by Lawrence and "Sentiment" sung by Buchanan (evidently with more success than Coward himself in *London Calling!*)

P-34   *Charlot's Revue* Prince of Wales Theatre, London. Sept. 23, 1924 (518 performances)

NOTES: This London version of P-33 was staged by Dion Titheradge and Laddie

Cliff with costumes by G.K. Benda and sets by Mark Henry. **Noël Coward** contributed the following items: "That'll Be Very Useful Later On" sung by Phyllis Monkman, "A Scotch Interlude" and "Jessie Hooper" sung by Morris Harvey, "After Dinner Music" (a sketch with songs) performed by Maisie Gay, "Specially for You" sung by Monkman and Henry Kendall, "Love, Life, and Laughter"(a sketch with a song) performed by Gay, Harvey, Hugh Sinclair, Nellie Bowman, and Leonard Henry. When the American edition opened on March 23, 1925, the same material as P-33 was used. In July of 1932 Coward added a sketch from *London Calling!* entitled "Early Mourning." It was performed by Gertrude Lawrence and Sybil Chester. In September Lawrence sang Coward's song "Carrie" (also from *London Calling!*)

P-35   *The Vortex*   Royalty Theatre, London. Dec. 16, 1924 (224 performances)Tried out at The Everyman Theatre, Hampstead, London Nov. 25, 1924 (12 performances). Moved to the Comedy Theatre, London Mar. 9, 1925 and to the Little Theatre, London. May 4, 1925.

A play written and directed by Noël Coward. Presented by Norman Macdermott. Designed by G. E. Calthrop.

CAST: Claire Keep (Preston), Mary Robson (Helen Saville), F. Kinsey Peile (Pauncefort Quentin), Millie Sim (Clara Hibbert), Lilian Braithwaite (Florence Lancaster), Alan Hollis (Tom Veryan), **Noël Coward** (Nicky Lancaster), Bromley Davenport (David Lancaster), Molly Kerr (Bunty Mainwaring), Ivor Barnard (Bruce Fairlight)

SYNOPSIS: Middle aged and married, Florence Lancaster is having an affair with Tom Veryan, who is the same age as her son, Nicky. When Nicky brings his fiance, Bunty home to meet his parents, Bunty and Tom fall in love, leaving Nicky and Florence to face the facts. Florence reveals her affairs and Nicky admits to taking drugs. The curtain falls on Mother and son vowing to give up vice for each other.

REVIEWS:
Sunday London Times, Nov. 30, 1924: "Mr. Coward has brains to spare. The scene of the discovery is as good a bit of theatre as I have seen for a long time. It might be just disagreeable, but Mr. Coward, by a stroke of pure genius, lifts it into the region of philosophic comment. The piece was magnificently acted by Mr. Coward, who lived the part with his nerves, and was so lifelike that you seemed to be in the same room with him."

NOTES: The play was an immediate success, despite the last minute replacement of leading lady Kate Cutler by Lilian Braithwaite and the near refusal of license by the Lord Chamberlain, whose duty it was to judge and license all productions presented in London. The play's rather adult themes of drugs and sex almost was its undoing. Luckily Coward was able to convince the L.C. that the play was little more than a moral tract and the license was finally granted. Nonetheless the play established Coward as both a playwright and actor. Coward's understudy was John Gielgud and he played the role on three occasions: Mar. 16 & 17, 1925 when Coward was required to go to Manchester for the dress rehearsal and opening of his revue, *On With The Dance* (see P-37) and on April 21, 1925 when Coward attended the first night of *Fallen Angels* (see P-36). He also finished the run in London after Coward left to appear in the Broadway Production (See P-39) For the film version see F-3. For publications of play see B-67, B-72, B-74, B-112. Also see P-69 for *The Noel Coward Company*. See Also P-124, P-219, T-24, T-36, T-57.

P-36   *Fallen Angels* Globe Theatre, London. April 21, 1925 (158 performances)

A Comedy by Noël Coward. Producted by Anthony Prinsep. Directed by Stanley Bell. Sets and Costumes by Joseph and Phil Harker. Written in 1923.

CAST: Tallulah Bankhead (Julia Sterroll), Arthur Wellesley (Frederick Sterroll), Mona Harrison (Saunders), Gerald Ames (William Banbury), Edna Best (Jane Banbury), Austin Trevor (Maurice Duclos)

SYNOPSIS: With their husbands away on a golfing trip, Julia and Jane get a postcard from their mutual ex-lover, Maurice, announcing his arrival in London. Begowned and bejewelled, the friends await his arrival and drink, getting wildly drunk and quarrelling bitterly. Their husbands return home the next morning in time for Maurice's belated arrival. When he moves into the flat upstairs, the husbands wonder if it is wise to leave their wives alone.

REVIEWS:
Punch (London) April 29, 1925: "Mr. Coward has written it so gaily and wittily and they play it so lightly and briskly that it is relieved of all offensiveness. I don't remember a better piece of stage-craft in this type of play since Mr. Maugham's *Home and Beauty*. A tour de force indeed."

The London Sketch, May 6, 1925: "Brilliant in execution, brilliant in dialogue, and brilliantly acted, it is still nothing more than a clever play."

NOTES: The above reviews were in the minority. The play was described as vulgar, disgusting, shocking, nauseating, vile, obscene and degenerate. All of this did the box office no harm at all. The play was originally bought as a vehicle for Margaret Bannerman. During reheasals she had a nervous breakdown and was replaced with four days of rehearsal by Tallulah Bankhead. According to *Tallulah* by Tallulah Bankhead (Harper & Bros. 1952.), Coward called her one morning to ask "'Tallulah, can you learn one hundred sides in four days?' 'Four days. I can get up in it in four hours. Why?' 'Come up and see me at once.' Although I didn't know a thing about *Fallen Angels*, I agreed to play the part. 'What's your salary?' asked Noël. 'One hundred pounds a week.' 'But you were only getting forty pounds in *Rain*.' 'That's true, but I wanted to play Sadie Thompson. I don't give a good goddam if I play this or not.' 'Agreed,' said Noel, 'if you can open Tuesday.'" And she did. For publications of play see B-62, B-72, B-75, B-86. See also P-54, P-69, P-114, P-139, P-193, T-30.

P-37   *On With The Dance* London Pavilion, London. April 20, 1925 (229 performances). Tried out at the Palace, Manchester. March 17, 1925

Book & lyrics by Noël Coward. Music by Philip Braham and **Noël Coward.** Staged by Frank Collins. Produced by Charles B. Cochran. Dances by Leonide Massine & Max Rivers. Conducted by J.B. Hastings. Costumes and Sets by William Nicholson, Doris Zinkeisen and G.E. Calthrop. Masks by Betty Muntz

CAST: Alice Delysia, Florence Desmond, Hermoine Baddeley, Max Rivers, Greta Fayne, Richard Dolman, Terri Storri, Pat & Terry Kendall, Douglas Byng, Nigel Bruce, Lance Lister, Ernest Thesiger

MUSICAL NUMBERS: Cosmopolitan Lady-Delysia; So In Love-Kendalls; Georgie-Delysia; On With The Dance-Chorus; Poor Little Rich Girl-Baddeley, Delysia & Chorus; First Love-Baddeley, Lister & Delysia; Couldn't We Keep On Dancing?-Chorus; Soldier Boys-Max Rivers and the Trocadero Four; Come A Little Closer-Fayne & Dolman

REVIEWS:
London Morning Post, May 1, 1925: "As befits Mr. Coward's genius, many of the incidents are as Nature seen through a glass crookedly, and when we see some normal little typical revue duet-dance face to face, it seems positively dull. Those arid, futile people that Mr. Coward puts into his plays dash about the stage, worked into a frenzy by the syncopated music."

NOTES: Along with *Fallen Angels*, and *The Vortex* this completed the trio of Coward hits running in the West End. A second edition of the revue, called "Still Dancing" was produced on Nov. 19, 1925, but no Coward material was retained. One sketch, "Oranges and Lemons" was revived in *Non Stop Revels* in 1936. This was the subject of court case, which Coward won, preventing the sketch from being performed with unauthorized changes in the text. For recordings see D-47, D-48.

P-38   *Hay Fever*   Ambassadors Theatre, London. June 8, 1925. Moved to the Criterion Theatre Sept. 7, 1925 (337 performances)

A comedy written and directed by Noël Coward. Produced by Alban B. Limpus. Sets and Costumes by G.E. Calthrop.

CAST: Marie Tempest (Judith Bliss), W. Graham Browne (David Bliss), Helen Spencer (Sorel Bliss), Robert Andrews (Simon Bliss), Hilda Moore (Myra Arundel), Athole Stewart (Richard Greatham), Ann Trevor (Jackie Coryton), Patrick Susands (Sandy Tyrell), Minnie Rayner (Clara)

SYNOPSIS: A weekend in the country with the Bliss family (retired actress Judith, her author-husband and their eccentric children) is complicated when each invites a guest. The incredibly egocentric family ignore and humiliate their non-theatrical guests until the weekend finishes with the guests escaping, leaving the unbelievably theatrical Blisses on their own.

REVIEWS:
The London Times, June 9, 1925: "It will be seen that it is all, as usual, Mr. Coward's fun. All the better fun, be it added, for being punctuated, as usual, with Mr. Coward's wit. The audience were delighted, and insisted on a speech from Mr. Coward."

NOTES: This is considered by many to be his best comedy. Coward was inspired to write it after a weekend with Laurette Taylor and her family. It was this play that was chosen by the National Theatre to be revived in 1964, making Coward the first living playwright thus honored. That revival, coming on the heels of a very successful fringe production of *Private Lives*, solidified what Coward termed as "Dad's Renaissance." For publications see B-67, B-74, B-81, B-88. See also P-40, P-68, P-69, P-74, P-94, P-160, P-166, P-174, P-204, P-208, R-17, R-41, R-76, T-1, T-2, T-25.

P-39   *The Vortex*   The Henry Miller Theatre, NY. Sept. 16, 1925 (157 performances) Tried out at the National Theatre, Washington D.C. Sept. 7, 1925.

Broadway debut of **Noël Coward's play.** Produced by J.P. Brickerton Jr. & Basil Dean. Directed by Basil Dean with the help of **Noël Coward.** After Broadway, toured to Broad St. Theatre, Newark, NJ Feb. 1, 1926, Werbers Brooklyn Theatre, B'klyn, NY Feb. 6, 1926, Grand Theatre, Cincinnati, OH Feb. 15, 1926, Selwyn Theatre Chicago, Il. Mar. 1, 1926 and Ohio Theatre Cleveland, OH. Mar. 7, 1926.

CAST: George Harcourt (Preston), Auriol Lee (Helen Saville), Leo G.

Carroll (Pauncefort Quentin), Jeanette Sherwin (Clara Hibbert), Lilian Braithwaite (Florence Lancaster), Alan Hollis (Tom Veryan), **Noël Coward** (Nicky Lancaster), David Glassford (David Lancaster), Molly Kerr (Bunty Mainwaring), Thomas Braidon (Bruce Fairlight)

SYNOPSIS: see P-35

REVIEWS:
New York World, Sept. 17, 1925: "The walls of Henry Miller's pretty theatre shook last evening with the first cheers of the new season – the honest, hearty, well earned cheers. I suspect the young Noël Coward will have to live on and on for an almost intolerably long time before he will be able to forget a night that was a true triumph for himself – a triumph for his work both as a playwright and an actor. A completely engrossing and sometimes glittery play, brilliantly acted. Mr. Coward's performance is unforgettable."

New York Tribune, Sept. 17, 1925: "A good, thrilling, glib and seriously amusing play. Mr. Coward was quite overwhelmed last night when, at the end of *The Vortex* those present refused to go away until he had thanked them for their approval. This praise was loud and from the heart. The season's best new play."

New York Post, Sept. 17, 1925: "*The Vortex* is only within two or three feet of being the sort of play to burn the town down about. But Mr. Coward, who can do many things, is no preacher, and his last act is preaching. *The Vortex* is laughable, deft and sophisticated entertainment."

New York Telegram, Sept. 17, 1925: "Mr. Coward showed some of the qualities that have made him the toast of the younger English intellectuals. The strain of being both author and actor seemed to check his histrionic activity in the early stages, but the quality of his performance grew with the enthusiasm of the audience."

NOTES: Braithwaite, Hollis, Kerr, and Coward repeated their London roles (see P-35). The play, which was an unparalleled success, was originally to be produced by Dillingham and Erlanger, but, according to Coward's autobiography, *Present Indicative* (B-42), Erlanger got cold feet about the last act, in which the mother and son admit to nymphomania and drug addiction respectively. The playbills and ads read as above, but Coward states in *Present Indicative* that Sam Harris and Irving Berlin took over the play and the original handbills prove this to be true.

P-40   *Hay Fever* Maxine Elliot Theatre, NY Oct. 5, 1925 (49 performances)

Broadway premiere of **Noël Coward's comedy. Directed by Noël Coward** and Laura Hope Crews. Produced by Messrs. Shubert.

CAST: Laura Hope Crews (Judith Bliss), Harry Davenport (David Bliss), Frieda Prescourt (Sorel Bliss), Gavin Muir (Simon Bliss), Phyllis Joyce (Myra Arundel), George Thorpe (Richard Greatham), Margot Lester (Jackie Coryton), Reginald Sheffield (Sandy Tyrell), Alice Belmore Ceiffe (Clara)

SYNOPSIS: See P-38.

REVIEWS:
New York Times, Oct. 6, 1925: "Stage business, stage direction and an uncommonly well organized performance combine to make a generally frothy, enjoyable evening. If Mr. Coward had packed his play with half the humor the actors bring to their parts, *Hay Fever* might be steadily amusing; at present, it has many colorless moments."

P-41   *Modern Drama From the English View Point* Biltmore Hotel, NY. Nov. 4, 1925

NOTES: **Noël Coward,** along with Basil Dean, Lillian Braithwaite, Auriol Lee, Ashley Dukes and Marc Connolly discussed the subject of modern drama at a ladies club luncheon.

P-42   *Charlot's Revue of 1926* Selwyn Theatre, NY. Nov. 10, 1925

NOTES: *Charlot's Revue* was so successful that many new editions were mounted. **Noël Coward** numbers in this version included: "Russian Blues" sung by Gertrude Lawrence, "After Dinner Music" performed by Beatrice Lillie, "Poor Little Rich Girl" sung by Lawrence, "Early Mourning" performed by Lawrence and Eve Wynne and "Carrie" sung by Lawrence.

P-43   *Easy Virtue* Empire Theatre, NY. Dec. 7, 1925 (147 performances). Tried out at the Broad Theatre, Newark, NJ Nov. 23, 1925

A play by Noël Coward. Produced by Charles Frohman Inc. Directed by Basil Dean. Sets & Costumes by George W. Harris.

CAST: Mabel Terry-Lewis (Mrs. Whittaker), Marda Vanne (Marion), Halliwell Hobbes (Colonel Whittaker), Joan Clement Scott (Hilda), Lionel Hogarth (Furber), Robert Harris (John), Jane Cowl (Larita), Joyce Carey (Sarah Hurst), Vernon Kelso (Charles Burleigh), Peter Carpenter (Philip Bordon), William Podmore (Mr. Harris), Gipsy O'Brien (Nina

Vansittart), Peter Macfarlane (Hugh Petworth), C. Bailey Hick (Bobby Coleman), Constance Best (Lucy Coleman), Wallace Wood (Henry Furley), Grace Hampton (Mrs. Hurst), Nancy B. Marsland (Mrs. Phillips), Marlon Evensen (Mary Banfield)

SYNOPSIS: When John Whittaker brings his new wife home to meet the family, they are aghast to find Larita is older than her husband and infinitely more sophisticated. Only John's father, the Colonel is kind to her and realizes that she is bored. When Larita is cordially uninvited to a dance the Whittaker women are giving, she decides to be the woman of easy virtue they think her to be. She makes a large scene and exits from the fold.

REVIEWS:
New York Times, Mar. 8, 1926: "Mr. Coward knows the people of whom he is writing, and with unerring precision goes to the source of their various weaknesses. It seems to be a flash rather than a play. In spite of the fact that Mr. Coward's piece frequently makes conventionality, prejudice and complacence look as ridiculous as they do in the more penetrating plays of George Bernard Shaw."

NOTES: This was the first Coward play to receive its world premiere in America. For West End production see P-44. For revival see P-213. For publications see B-67, B-75, B-81, B-87.

P-44   *Easy Virtue* Duke of York's Theatre, London. June 9,1926
(124 performances) Tried out as *A New Play in Three Acts* at the Opera House, Manchester. May 31, 1926.

A play by Noël Coward. Produced and directed by Basil Dean. Sets and Costumes by George W. Harris. (for American production see P-43)

CAST: The same as P-43, except: Marcus Barron (Colonel Whittaker), Claud Graham (Furber), James Raglan (John), Deering Wells (Philip Bordon), Philip Wade (Mr. Harris), Humphrey Morton (Bobby Coleman), Diana Beaumont (Lucy Coleman), Gertrude Sterroll (Mrs. Hurst), Edith Barker-Bennet (Mrs. Phillips), Anne Hyton (Mary Banfield)

SYNOPSIS: See P-43

REVIEWS:
Sunday London Times, June 13, 1926: "Mr. Coward gets younger with every play, and in *Easy Virtue* has attained to that pure idealism which prompts the schoolboy

who has been taken to see *La Dame aux Camelias* to believe for the next ten years that a cocotte is the noblest work of man if not of God."

NOTES: The Manchester Watch Committe, for some reason, refused to allow the producer to use the the title *Easy Virtue,* and thus was announced as *A New Play in Three Acts.* Ironically the movie house next door openly advertised a film entitled *Flames of Passion.* For film version see F-4.

P-45   *The Queen Was In The Parlour* St. Martin's Theatre, London. August 8, 1926. Transferred to the Duke of York's Theatre October 4, 1926. (136 performances)

A play by Noël Coward. Produced and Directed by Basil Dean. Sets by George W. Harris. Decor by Gladys Calthrop. Written in 1922.

CAST: Madge Titheradge (Nadya), Francis Lister (Sabien Pastal), Fred Godfrey (Zana), C.M. Hallard (General Krish), Ada King (Miss Phipps), C. Disney-Roebuck (Court Usher), Herbert Marshall (Prince Keri), Lady Tree (The Grand Duchess)

SYNOPSIS: Taking place in Paris and the mythical Krayia, the play concerns Nadya, the queen of the latter country, a revolution and of course true love.

REVIEWS:
London Daily Mail, Aug. 25, 1926: "Mr. Coward shows that he can construct what is called a well-made play with the best of the Victorians. It is impossible not to feel that Mr. Coward wrote the play with his tongue in his cheek. When those who had expected something typical of Mr. Coward had recovered from the shock of being given something different, they set themselves to enjoy scenes of violence and romance. And at the end the applause was a loud and as long as anything ever given to the same author's alleged 'nasty' plays."

NOTES: This "Ruratanian" play was more in the style of Ivor Novello's operettas than Coward's comedies, showing yet another side to the youthful talent. For film versions see F-2, F-7. For publications see B-76, B-102.

P-46   *The Constant Nymph* New Theatre, London. Sept. 14, 1926 (387 peformances)

A play by Margaret Kennedy and Basil Dean. Directed by Basil Dean. Produced by Mary Moore. Sets by Alick Johnston. Costumes by Paris Trades Ltd.

CAST: **Noël Coward** (Lewis Dodd), Edna Best (Teresa Sanger), Cathleen Nesbitt (Florence Churchill), Aubrey Mather (Sir Barthlemy Pugh), Kenneth Kent (Jacob Birnbaum), Ton de Lungo (Robert), Cecil Parker (Charles Churchill), Harold Scott (Peveril Leyburn), Craighall Sherry (Dr. Dawson), David Hawthorne (Mjr. Robert Mainwaring), Guy Pelham Boulton (Usher), Charles Garry (Fireman), Elissa Landi (Antonia), Mariey Ney (Kate), Muriel Lambert (Katrina), Mary Clare (Linda Cowland), Elsie Clark (Susan), Margot Sieveking (Erda Leyburn), Marjorie Gabain (Lydia), Margaret Yarde (Mme. Marxse)

REVIEWS:
London Observer, Sept. 19, 1926 "The play was beautifully acted. Mr. Noël Coward gave Dodd the charm that he must have had to be able to rouse love for him in such dissimilar women as Florence and Tessa. Mr. Coward is beginning to control his attractive cheekiness. His performance is a fine one and I hope that he will not, in his popularity as a dramatist, forget that he has abilities as an actor."

NOTES: Coward played the role of Dodd for just over three weeks before suffering a breakdown. He was successfully replaced for the rest of the run by John Gielgud. This was one of the few times after 1925 that Coward was to play in a theatrical work other than his own. Just as in the film of *The Vortex*, Ivor Novello played Coward's role on the screen.

P-47   *The Rat Trap* Everyman Theatre, Hampstead, London. Oct. 18, 1926
         (12 performances)

         A play by Noël Coward. Produced by George Carr, Raymond Massey & Allan Wade. Directed by George Carr. Sets & Costumes by Peggy Fremantle. Written in 1918.

         CAST: Mary Robson (Olive Lloyd-Kennedy), Joyce Kenney (Sheila Brandreth), Robert Harris (Keld Maxwell), Elizabeth Pollock (Naomi Frith-Bassington), Raymond Massey (Edmund Crowe), Clare Greet (Burrage), Adrianne Allen (Ruby Raymond)

         SYNOPSIS: The consequences when a brilliant and successful playwright and an equally brilliant, but first time novelist marry.

REVIEWS:
Sunday Times, Oct. 24, 1926: "What a pity it is that Mr. Noël Coward ever published *The Rat Trap*, thereby making impossible any juggling with dates! What should we have said, I wonder, if this play had followed the Ruritanian excursion with the usual West End fanfare and implication that this was Noel's very latest

thing in nolly dialogues! To produce the piece on the fringe of Town, half apologetically and as a work of youth and curiosity, was to damage it in advance."

NOTES: Coward never saw this, the first production of one of his first plays, as he was in America. Of this play he wrote in the Introduction to *Play Parade, Volume III*, "It is not without merit. There is some excruciatingly sophisticated dialogue in the first act of which, at the time, I was inordinately proud." For publications see B-72, B-76, B-103.

P-48   *This Was A Man* Klaw Theatre, NY. Nov. 23, 1926 (31 performances)

    A comedy in three acts by Noël Coward. Produced and Directed by Basil Dean. Sets and Costumes by George W. Harris and G.E. Calthrop.

    CAST: Francine Larrimore (Carol Churt), Terence Neill (Harry Challoner), A.E. Matthews (Edward Churt), Violet Campbell (Lary Margot Butler), Leonard Loan (Berry), Mackenzie Ward (Lord Romford), Auriolee (Zoe St. Mervin), Nigel Bruce (Major Evelyn Bathurst), Horace Pollack (Blackwell)

SYNOPSIS: Carol Churt carries on boldly with almost anyone except her husband, Edward, a famous portrait painter. He is too bored to even care. His friend, Major Bathurst, conspires to teach Carol a lesson by seducing her and berating her for her loose morals. In the end Edward sends Carol abroad and divorces her. "There is still time for you to shoot yourself," she says sweetly as the curtain falls.

REVIEWS:
New York Times, Nov. 24, 1926: "By the time the first act is half over, one begins to suspect that Mr. Coward has contributed very meagerly to the occasion."

NOTES: Due to rejection of license by the Lord Chamberlain, this play was never produced in the West End. Coward was reported to have said "I shall in future concentrate on New York, where I am taken seriously as a serious writer, whereas in England people think I am out for salacious sensations. I shall from time to time write a pleasant little trifle for London."

P-49   *The Marquise* Criterion Theatre, London. Feb. 16, 1927 (129 performances)

    A comedy by Noël Coward. Produced by Alan B. Limpus. Directed by W. Graham Browne. Sets and Costumes by William Nicholson.

CAST: W. Graham Brown (Comte Raoul de Vriaac), Eileen Sharp (Adrienne), Robert Harris (Jaques Rijar), Frank Cellier (Esteban), Godfrey Winn (Miquel), Colin Johnston (Father Clement), Rupert Lister(Hubert), Marie Tempest (The Marquise Eloise de Kestournel), Lilian Cavanagh (Alice)

SYNOPSIS: The Comte Raoul de Vriaac is about to marry his daughter, Adrienne to Miquell, the son of his former boon companian. Adrienne loves Jacques, her father's secretary, while Miquel has lost his heart to a dancer in Paris. When the Marquise Eloise de Kestournel, the Comte's former lover and mother to Adrienne, arrives it is discovered that she is also Miquel's mother! All is settled after a duel when Adrienne gets Jacques, and Comte Raoul gets the Marquise.

REVIEWS:
London Morning Post, Feb. 17, 1927: "A very amusing and well constructed piece it proved to be. This is the first of Mr. Coward's plays to have a good first act. The quality of the craftmanship was kept up in the second and third acts, with a bad lapse, not in craft, but in feeling, when the young lovers, Rijar and Adrienne, told their love for each other. Mr. Coward still cannot write an effective love scene. But the rest of the play is delicious and done with dexterity and delicacy. If some of the wit was too facile, more of it was brilliant, and the surprise at the beginning of the second act was as good a surprise as any dramatist has ever invented. The audience seemed to be delighted with the play."

London Telegraph,Feb. 17, 1927: "Whatever you may think of Mr. Noël Coward's plays, you must not deny his possession of a superb sense of theatre, and a feeling for situation. The first audience gave the play a good send off and the public will doubtlessly flock to the Criterion."

NOTES: See P-52 for New York production and T-59 for TV version. For publications see B-76, B-92.

P-50   *Whitebirds* His Majesty's Theatre, London. May 31, 1927 (80 performances)

NOTES: Noël Coward contributed one song to this Lew Leslie revue, "What's Going To Become of the Children?" sung by Maisie Gay. It was only done for part of the run. This song was re-written and used in *Together With Music* (T-8) as "What's Going To Happen To The Tots?"

P-51   *Home Chat* Duke of York's Theatre, London. Oct. 25, 1927 (38 performances)

A play by Noël Coward. Produced and Directed by Basil Dean. Sets and Costumes by G.E. Calthrop.

CAST: Pauline Newton (Pallett), Marda Vanne (Mavis Wittersham), George Relph (Paul Ebony), Nina Boucicault (Mrs. Chilham), Henrietta Watson (Mrs. Ebony), Helen Spencer (Lavinia Hardy), Madge Titheradge (Janet Ebony), Arthur Margetson (Peter Chelsworth), Tom Woods (Turner), George Curzon (Alec Stone)

SYNOPSIS: Janet Ebony is wrongly suspected of having an affair with Peter Chelsworth. She does very little to deny this to her friends and family. When the truth is finally revealed, she has great difficulty in making her husband believe that she is really having an affair with Major Stone.

REVIEWS:
Westminster Gazette, Oct. 26, 1927: "'We expected better.' 'So did I.' This conversation piece between a voice in the gallery and Noël Coward when he came forward to take a call at the end of his new play, *Home Chat*, last night is a succinct criticism of the piece. As it is endorsed by the author, it can confidently be put on record. A play which is slender in plot and not particularly scintillating in dialogue. The gallery was right. We expected better."

NOTES: This justly forgotten play was another in a series of flops that nearly ruined Coward's playwriting career. For publications see B-73, B-76, B-87.

P-52   *The Marquise* Biltmore Theatre, NY. Nov. 14, 1927 (80 performances)

Broadway debut of **Noël Coward's play.** Directed by David Burton. Produced by Kenneth MacGowan & Sidney Ross. Sets by Jo Mielziner.

CAST: Arthur Byron (Comte Raoul de Vriaac), Madge Evans (Adrienne), Theodore St. John (Jacques Rijar), Reginald Owen (Esteban), Rex O'-Malley (Miquel), Harry Lillford (Father Clement), William Kershaw (Hubert), Billie Burke (The Marquise Eloise de Kestournel), Dorothy Tree (Alice)

SYNOPSIS: See P-49.

REVIEWS:
New York Times, Nov. 15, 1927: "It is a play written with all of Mr. Coward's impudence and about half of his accustomed skill at dialogue, the result being a pleasant and forgetable evening in the theatre."

P-53   *Sirocco* Daly's Theatre, London. Nov. 24, 1927 (28 performances)

A play by Noël Coward. Produced and Directed by Basil Dean. Sets and Costumes by G.E. Calthrop. Written in Spring of 1921.

CAST: Ada King (Miss Johnson), Margaret Watson (Mrs. Breeze), Helen Ferrers (Mrs. Griffin), Blyth Daly (Francine Trott), Frances Doble (Lucy Griffin), Ivor Novello (Sirio Marson), Aubrey Mather (Rev. Crutch), David Hawthorne (Stephen Griffin), Tony de Lungo (Pietro), Margery Gabain (Giulia), Doris Garrick (Gianetta), Arturo Gomez (Antonio Piocchi), George Coulouris (Giuseppe), Mario Mariani (Waiter), Elizabeth Vaughan (Maria)

SYNOPSIS: Young Mrs. Griffin, married to an oaf, is obliged to spend too much time in Italy in the society of elderly, frosty and mentally bankrupt persons. She finds relief from her boring life in the passionate arms of Sirio Marson. After living with him, she becomes disgusted and they part.

REVIEWS:
The London Times, Nov. 27, 1927: "How dreadfully silly and solemn it became, the solemner the sillier! There was a time when it seemed that a derisive gallery would put an end to our discomfort, but the curtain to the second act was happily quicker than their impatience...A more uncomfortable conclusion to the evening may we never experience. The worst of it was that Mr. Coward had brought it on himself."

London Observer, Nov. 27, 1927: "There is more theme, more idea in *Sirocco* than there has been in any play by Mr. Coward since he wrote *The Vortex.* The evening seemed to be a sad one, but it will probably prove to be the turning-point in Mr. Coward's career. I regard *Sirocco* as the most significant and hopeful play he has yet produced."

NOTES: The first night of this play has passed into theatrical lore as one of the most gruelling in the history of the English theatre. The first act was received dully, but the storm broke during a love scene, at which time the balcony shrieked with mirth and made sucking sounds. The last act was complete chaos. The curtain finally fell to bedlam. After reading the notices (none as good as the above), and literally having audience members spitting at him, Coward's first instinct was to leave England immediately. He was so distressed that he offered to withdraw his material from his next Cochran revue. *Sirocco* was the only time that Novello and Coward's theatrical careers crossed, although Novello made the film version of *The Vortex* playing Coward's original role. For publications see B-73, B-76, B-105.

P-54   *Fallen Angels* 49th Street Theatre, NY. Dec. 1, 1927 (36 performances)

Broadway debut of **Noël Coward's comedy**. Produced by The Actor's Theatre Inc. Directed by Guthrie McClintic. Sets by Jo Mielziner.

CAST: Fay Bainter (Julia Sterroll), Gordon Ash (Frederick Sterroll), Eileen Beldon (Saunders), Gerald Haner (William Banbury), Estelle Winwood (Jane Banbury), Luis Alberni (Maurice Duclos)

SYNOPSIS: See P-36.

REVIEWS:
New York Times, Dec. 2, 1927: "As his previous plays have revealed him, Mr. Coward has a pretty talent, but a slight one. *Fallen Angels* is not exception to the rule that if the prettiness does not win the slightness will."

P-55   *The Second Man* Playhouse Theatre, London. Jan. 24, 1928 (109 performances)

A play by S.N. Behrman. Directed by Basil Dean. Sets by G.E. Calthrop.

CAST: **Noël Coward** (Clark Storey), Raymond Massey (Austin Lowe), Ursula Jeans (Monica Grey), Zena Dare (Mrs. Kendall Frayne)

REVIEWS:
*New York Times,*Feb. 12, 1928 (London Jan. 26, 1928): "Mr. Coward's performance as Clark Storey was received with enthusiasm."

P-56   *This Year of Grace!* London Pavilion, London. March 22, 1928 (316 performances). Tried out as *Charles B. Cochran's 1928 Revue* at the Palace Manchester. Feb. 28, 1928. A revue with **book, lyrics and music by Noël Coward**. Dances by Tilly Losch and Max Rivers. Staged by Frank Collins. Produced by Charles B. Cochran. Conducted by Ernest Irving. Pianist, Leslie Hutchinson.

CAST: Jessie Matthews, Sonnie Hale, Douglas Byng, Tilly Losch, Adrienne Brune, Maisie Gay, Sheilah Graham, Madge Aubrey, Lauri Devine, Moya Nugent, Jean Barry, Jack Holland, Lance Lister, Tommy Hayes, Robert Algar, Betty Shale, Betty Davis, Ann Codrington, Dinka Starace, Arthur Warren, Cecil Stafford, William Cavanagh, Joan Clarkson, Billy Shaw, Fred Groves, Nora Oliver, Syd Shields, Charles Farey, Eddie Grant, Edward Conventry

MUSICAL NUMBERS: Waiting in a Queue-Hale; Mary Make Believe-Matthews and Girls; Mad About You-Graham, Cavahagh & Girls; Lorelei-Brune, Hale, Devin, & Cavanagh; A Room With a View-Matthews, Hale & Brune; It Doesn't Matter How Old You Are-Gay; Teach Me To Dance Like Grandma-Matthews & Girls; Little Woman-Matthews, Graham, Aubrey & Nugent; Lido Beach-All; Mother's Complaint-Codrington, Clarkson, Aubrey & Shale; Britannia Rules the Waves-Gay & Company; Dance Little Lady-Hale, Devin & Dancers; Chauve Souris-Lister, Gay, Groves, Hale, Byng & Algar; Try To Learn To Love-Matthews, Hale & Girls; Caballero-Barry & Holland; Finale-Company

REVIEWS:
London Observer, Mar. 25, 1928: "I must be careful with my superlatives, so I will say only this, that *This Year of Grace!* is the most amusing, the most brilliant, the cleverest, the daintiest, the most exquisite, the most fanciful, the most graceful, the happiest, the most ironical, the jolliest, the most kaeidoscopic, the loveliest, the most magnificent, the neatest and nicest, the most opulent, the pithiest, the quickest, the richest, the most superb and tasteful, the most uberous, the most versatile, the wittiest ...After that marvelous exhibition of self restraint, I will now let myself go, and say that if any person comes to me and says that there has ever, anywhere in the world, been a better revue that this, I shall publicly tweak his nose. Mr. Coward has many and various gifts; nearly all of them are displayed in this entertainment."

NOTES: After the fiasco of *Sirocco* (P-53), Coward felt it would be unfair to write this revue for Cochran and tried to withdraw, but Cochran wouldn't hear of it, and forced Coward to write one of their greatest successes, re-establishing his good name in the theatrical community. Coward and Cochran were to have a string of successes ending only when Coward decided to produced his own works himself. For recordings see D-1, D-2, D-3, D-4. For publications see B-40, B-61, B-110.

P-57   *This Year of Grace* Selwyn Theatre, NY. Nov. 7, 1928 (158 performances) Tried out at Maryland Theatre, Baltimore, MD Oct. 29, 1928. Bea Lillie toured with the show to Toronto, May, 1929.

A revue produced by C.B. Cochran and Archie Selwyn with **book, music and lyrics by Noël Coward**. Directed by Frank Collins, Choreographed by Max Rivers & Tilly Losch. Settings by Marc Henri & Laverdet, Oliver Messel, G.E. Calthrop, Costumes by Idear, Norman Hartnell, Christabel Russell, Messel, Calthop. Musical Direction by Frank Tours. (For London Production see P-56)

CAST: Beatrice Lillie, **Noël Coward**, Florence Desmond, Dick Francis, Madeleine Gibson, Queenie Leonard, Marjorie Moss & George Fontana,

Billy Milton, G.P. Huntley Jr., Tommy Hayes, Phyllis Harding.

REVIEWS:
NewYork Tribune, Nov. 8, 1928: "Coward's song and satires were upper class, ranging from competent to superlative. And the fleet manner in which they came along made the revue one of the merriest of its closet type. Mr. Coward was not, however so brilliant as a musical comedian. His efforts were slightly laborious and he sang in a tweedy voice and danced with small facility. But when he grew dramatic (Dance Little Lady) he stirred his audience to transports similar to those he used to arouse in *The Vortex.*"

The New York World, Nov. 9, 1928: "That astonishingly brilliant young man, Mr. Noël Coward, not content with writing, composing and inventing dances for the best revue that I have ever seen, now takes the principal man's part in it and almost convinces the amazed onlooker that if he put his mind to it he could perform the entire revue by himself. Coward doth make conquest of us all."

New York Evening World, Nov. 8, 1928: "It was all grand and glorious. The audience took Mr.Coward's revue with a whole heart, as to a message of grace from our British cousins."

The New York Post, Nov. 8, 1928: "Almost too good to be true. A perfect way to spend an evening. Seldom have more good things been packed into one show."

NOTES: The show was unchanged from the London production except for the interpolation of two single numbers for Beatrice Lillie: "World Weary" and "I Can't Think" (an imitation of Gertrude Lawrence), two duets between Coward and Lillie: "Lilac Time," an opera bouffe burlesque and "Love, Life, and Laughter," a sketch and song of Paris night life in the 80's which had originally been created by Maisie Gay in another Cochran revue. See B-40, B-61 for publications of sketches and songs.

P-58   *Bitter-Sweet* His Majesty's Theatre, London. July 12, 1929 (697 performanes) Moved to the Palace Theatre, Mar. 2, 1931. Tried out at the Palace Theatre, Manchester. July 2, 1929.

An Operette with **book, music, lyrics and direction by Noël Coward.** Produced by Charles B. Cochran. Sets and Costumes by G.E. Calthrop and Ernst Stern. Conducted by Reginald Burston. Orchestrations by Orellana.

CAST: Peggy Wood (Sarah Millick), George Metaxa (Carl Linden), Elaine Inescort (Mrs. Millick), Robert Newton (Hugh Devon), Robert

Algar (The Marquis of Steere), Millie Sim (Lotte), Betty Huntley-Wright (Freda), Marjorie Rogers (Hansi), Norah Howard (Gussi), Ivy St. Helier (Manon), Austin Trevor (Captain August Lutte), Clifford Heatherley (Herr Schlick), Gerald Nodin (Capt. Schenzi), Arthur Alexander (Lt. Transich), Anthony Brian (Burley), Alan Napier (The Marquis of Shayne), Mary Pounds (Effie), Jose Fearon (Victoria), Maie Drage (Harriet), Rose Hignell (Gloria), Eileen Carey (Jane), Isla Bevan (Honor), Dorothy Boyd (Dolly), Penryn Bannerman (Lord Henry), Billy Milton (Vincent Howard)

SYNOPSIS: In the year 1929 the Marchioness of Shayne, confornted with a young couple's romance, remembers her youth, flashing us back to 1875 when she, Sari, ran away from an arranged marriage with her music teacher, Carl Linden. Once married to Sari, Carl finds work in Vienna in a café. When Capt. Lutte sets his sights for Sari it ends with a duel and Carl dies in Sari's arms. Fifteen years later Sari has become a famous singer of her late husband's songs and she accepts the proposal of Lord Shayne, a longtime suiter. In the last scene, the present day of 1929, the Marchioness of Shayne scoffs at youth and remembers real love and real romance as she sings her dead lover's song.

MUSICAL NUMBERS: That Wonderful Melody-Singer;The Call of Life-Wood & Chorus; If You Could Only Come With Me-Metaxa; I'll See You Again-Wood & Metaxa; What Is Love?-Wood & Chorus; The Last Dance-Algar, Robson, Nodin, Russell, Gatrell, Cornish, Drage, Fearon, Hignell, Bevan, Carey & Pounds; Life In the Morning-Chorus; Ladies of the Town-Sim, Huntley-Wright, Rogers & Howard; If Love Were All-St. Helier; Evermore and a Day-Wood & Metaxa; Little Café-Wood & Metaxa; Officers' Chorus-Chorus; Tokay-Nodin & Chorus; Bonne Nuit, Merci-St. Helier; Kiss Me-St. Helier & Chorus; Ta Ra Ra Boom De Ay-Chorus; Alas, the Time is Past-Fearon, Drage, Hignell, Bevan, Carey & Pounds; Green Carnations-Male Quartet; Zigeuner-Wood; Finale-Wood and Chorus

REVIEWS:
London Morning Post, July 18, 1929: "A simple little story, but told (after a quiet opening act) with a wealth of light and colour and movement in which scenery, costumes, and music are charmingly blended, the entrancing lilt of Viennese waltzes, grave and gay, ever in the background."

Sunday London Times, July 21, 1929: "Mr. Coward shows himself to be possessed of the triple gift of your true man of the theatre — the faculty for entertaining both the eye, the ear and the mind."

NOTES: Although published in the score and script, the duet "Evermore and a Day" was cut from the English production and used in the NY production. Coward had intended the role of Sari for Gertrude Lawrence, but found that in the composing he was writing it for a far larger voice than Lawrence's. He promised her his next play would be one in which the two of them would star. (see P- 61) For Film versions see F-9, F-13. For Recordings of the score see D-10, D-25, D-43, D-49, D-50, D-51. For Publication of the script see B-61, B-68, B-74, B-80, B-81. The company toured to Streatham Hill and Golders Green for 3 weeks and then returned to the Lyceum Theatre, April 13, 1931 for 32 additional performances.

P-59   *Bitter-Sweet*   Ziegfeld Theatre, NY. Nov. 5, 1929 (159 performances)
Tried out at the Tremont theatre, Boston, MA October 22, 1929

Broadway premiere of **Noël Coward's Operette** (P-58). Produced by Florenz Ziegfeld & Arch Selwyn. Personal same as P-58, except for Conducted by Arthur Jones.

CAST: Evelyn Laye (Sari), Gerald Nodin (Carl), Mireille (Manon), Max Kirby (Vincent Howard), Tracy Holmes (Hugh Devon), Sylvia Leslie (Gussi), John Evelyn (Marquis of Shayne), Isabel Ohmead (Mrs. Millick), Donald Gordon (The Marquis of Steere), Zoe Gordon (Lotte), Nancy Barnett (Freda), Dorothy Debenham (Hansi), Sylvia Barnett (Gussi), Desmond Jeans (Captain August Lutte), Charles Mortimer (Herr Schlick & Sir Arthur), Louis Miller (Lt. Transich), Vesta Sylva (Effie), Marjorie Raymond (Victoria), Audrey Pointing (Harriet), Nancy Brown (Gloria), Winifred Talbot (Jane), Isla Bevan (Honor), Audrey Pointing (Dolly), Trevor Glyn (Parker), Patrick Ludlow (Lord Henry), Kathleen Lambelet (Lady Devon), Richard Thorpe (Lord Edgar James), Hopper Russell (Lord Sorrell), Leslie Bannister (Mr. Vale), Anthony Neville (Mr. Bethel), Douglas Graeme-Brooke (Mr. Proutie)

SYNOPSIS & MUSICAL NUMBERS: See P-58

REVIEWS:
New York Times, Nov. 6, 1929: "Mr. Coward is the master of little things, and the virtuosity of his talents amounts to genius. Although considerable showmanship has gone into the staging and the organization of the story, it is not a musical show in the rapid, flamboyant style to which we have become accustomed. But it is sheerly delightful by reason of the delicate perfection of the workmanship and the radiant splendor of Evelyn Laye, who has the principal role. It is charming; it is subtle and witty. By his mastery of little things Mr. Coward has mastered the artisty of musical entertainment in a refreshingly civilized style."

NOTES: Evelyn Laye finally took the role that was originally offered her in London. She had turned it down due to what she considered an indescretion on the part of Charles Cochran. It seems that he introduced her husband, Sonnie Hale to Jessie Matthews. Hale left Laye for Matthews and Laye blamed Cochran. After seeing what a mistake she made in turning down the role, she fought to get the Broadway company. She also replaced Peggy Wood for two weeks in London.

P-60   *Journey's End* Victoria Theatre, Singapore. April, 1930. (3 performances) A play by R.C. Sherriff

CAST: The Quaints including John Mills (Raleigh), **Noël Coward** (Stanhope)

SYNOPSIS: A depiction of the effect of warfare on a small group of English officers during WWI. When Lt. Raleigh joins the group, he is dismayed to see the changes which have taken place in his former school idol, Captain Stanhope. Tension mounts as a German attack is imminent. Raleigh is fatally wounded and the entire dugout is destroyed by shellfire at the final curtain.

NOTES: Coward was on a 6 month trip to Japan, Korea, and Shanghai (a trip which cost $7,500.00) with close friend Jeffrey Amherst, when Amherst was stricken with ameobic dysentery. Awaiting his friend's recovery, Coward contracted flu and wrote "Mad Dogs and Englishmen" (see P-65, P-70) and the whole of *Private Lives* (see P-61, P-63) in four days, in bed in Singapore. While Amherst recovered, Coward discovered an English theatrical touring company that was appearing in repertory. When he discovered that they were playing *Journey's End* he expressed his longing to play Stanhope. The company was thrilled and he learned the role and performed it for 3 performances. According to an interview with *The Sun* on Feb. 2, 1931 Coward commented on his performance: "at two of them I was lousy, but on the last night I was fair." Performing in this play inspired Coward to write an anti-war play of his own, *Post-Mortem*.

P-61   *Private Lives* Phoenix Theatre, London. Sept. 24, 1930 (101 performances). Tried out at the Kings Theatre, Edinburgh. Aug. 18, 1930 (5 weeks tour, Liverpool, Birmingham, Manchester and Southsea).

An intimate Comedy written and directed by Noël Coward. Produced by Charles B. Cochran. Production Designed by G.E. Calthrop.

CAST: Adrianne Allen (Sybil Chase), **Noël Coward** (Elyot Chase), Laurence Olivier (Victor Prynne), Gertrude Lawrence (Amanda Prynne), Everley Gregg (Louise, a maid)

SYNOPSIS: When Elyot and Amanda (formerly married to each other) meet unexpectedly on their respective honeymoons, they find that they are still very much in love and run off together to Paris. There they fight and quarrel, remembering what tore them apart in the first place. When their spouses find them, they too get into a violent quarrel, leaving Amanda and Elyot to slip away together once more.

REVIEWS:

London Era (re: Edinburgh opening), Aug. 20, 1930: " The play, apart from its entertainment qualities, was a triumph for the actors. Mr. Coward gave a performance in which consummate ease and a fine sense of humor revealed a thorough mastery of his art. The play was beautifully staged."

London Times, Sept. 25, 1930: "Amanda and Elyot are the fine, flippant flower of Mr. Coward's talent...and the dialogue, which might seem in print a trickle of inanities, becomes in the theatre a perfectly timed and directed interplay of nonsense. Mr. Coward can pad as no one else can pad; he has made of dramatic upholstery an art."

London Weekend Review, Oct. 4, 1930: *"Private Lives,* as put before you at the Phoenix, is a piece of immensely skilled labor, but the writing is the least part of it. The brilliance of the business lies in Mr. Coward's capacity, as a director and actor, to persuade us that his lines are witty and that his thin little projections of humanity are the real and triumphant clowns of eternal comedy. He does persuade us. He enormously entertains. Within a few years the student of drama will be sitting complete bewilderment before the text of *Private Lives,* wondering what on earth those fellows in 1930 saw in so flimsy a trifle."

London Era, Oct. 1, 1930: "Mr. Noel Coward has an uncanny sense of theatre and as he has directed *Private Lives* himself he has brought out every syllable. Badly acted it would have been unendurable, but in the hands of Mr. Coward and Miss Lawrence the play is almost high comedy."

NOTES: Having denied the leading role in *Bitter-Sweet* to Gertrude Lawrence because she was not up to the operatic demands of the score, Coward promised her that he would write a play in which they both could appear. On a trip to the Orient (see P-60), a picture of Lawrence in a Molyneux gown appeared before him and *Private Lives* took its place in his head. Coward wrote it in four days. He also wrote a song to be performed in the play, "Someday I'll Find You." Both he and Lawrence sang it. For recordings see D-5, D-52, D-53 and for publications of play see B-68, B-74, B-100. For film version see F-6, F-12. For subsequent productions see P-63, P-69, P-103, P-112, P-157, P-167, P-170, P-177, P-187, P-195, P-201, P-218, P-222. For TV version see T-71.

P-62   *Some Other Private Lives* Hippodrome, London. Dec. 1930. Charity Matinee.

A parody sketch of *Private Lives* **written and directed by Noël Coward.**

CAST: **Noël Coward** (Fred), Gertrude Lawrence (Flossie), Laurence Olivier (Alf), Adriannie Allen (Elsie)

NOTES: This parody sketch takes the upper class characters of *Private Lives* and transposes them into Fred and Flossie, two cockneys. The production of *Private Lives* at the Phoenix was nearing the end of its run when the parody was produced. See P-69 for *The Noel Coward Company*. For publication see B-40.

P-63   *Private Lives* Times Square Theatre, New York. Jan. 27, 1931 (256 perfor mances)

Broadway debut of **Noël Coward's comedy**. Production credits same as P-61.

CAST: Jill Esmond (Sybil Chase), **Noël Coward** (Elyot Chase), Laurence Olivier (Victor Prynne), Gertrude Lawrence (Amanda Prynne), Therese Quadri (Louise, a maid)

SYNOPSIS: See P-61

REVIEWS:
The New York Sun, Jan. 28, 1931: "Noël Coward, irrepressible in his universal facility, bubbled up last evening with a play in one hand and a comic performance in the other and writing jokes with his eyebrows. *Private Lives* is as irresistable a comedy as ever turned old situations into new fun. It is a Coward evening."

The New York Evening World, Jan. 28, 1931: "A rare blessing of the theatre, a merry, witty, smart light comedy with the airy grace of a feather brushing an idea true as sentiment. Mr. Coward gave an adroit, engaging performance as Elyot in his most intimate and irresistably funny comedy."

The New York World, Jan. 28, 1931: "An admirable piece of fluff acted as brilliantly uproariously and happily, with as much resourceful neatness and variety as I have ever seen. Mr. Coward's skill brings the freshness of surprise to things we have all seen before."

NOTE: Coward and Lawrence were replaced after three months by Otto Kruger and Madge Kennedy.

P-64   *Charles B. Cochran's 1931 Revue* London Pavilion, London. March 19, 1931 (27 performances). Tried out at Palace Theatre, Manchester. Feb. 18, 1931.

NOTES: Although the program read "**Music by Noël Coward** and others," Coward only contribued the following: "Opening Chorus," "City" sung by Bernardi, "Any Little Fish" sung by Ada-May, "Bright Young People" sung by Queenie Leonard, Edward Cooper and Effie Atherton and "Half Caste Woman" done by the company. "Foolish Virgins" was performed by Atherton, Leonard and Jane Welsh only in Manchester.

P-65   *The Third Little Show* Music Box Theatre, NY. June 1, 1931 (136 performances)

NOTES: **Noël Coward** contributed "Mad Dogs and Englishman" performed by Beatrice Lillie and chorus and a sketch entitled, "Cat's Cradle" peformed by Lillie and Ernest Truex. Truex also sang "Any Little Fish" during the tryout at the Shubert Theatre, New Haven, CT (May 4, 1931)

P-66   *The Ziegfeld Follies of 1931* Ziegfeld Theatre, NY. July 1, 1931 (165 perfmormances)

NOTES: "Half Caste Woman" by **Noël Coward** was performed by Helen Morgan.

P-67   *Cavalcade* Theatre Royal, Drury Lane, London. Oct. 13, 1931 (405 performances)

A play written and directed by Noël Coward. Produced by Charles B. Cochran. Sets and Costumes by G.E. Calthrop. Conducted by Reginald Burston.

CAST: Mary Clare (Jane Marryot), Edward Sinclair (Robert Marryot), Una O'Conner (Ellen Bridges), Fred Groves (Alfred Bridges), Irene Browne (Margaret Harris), Alison Leggatt (Edith Harris), Arthur Macrae (Edward Marryot), John Mills (Joe Marryot), Binnie Barnes (Fanny Bridges), Veronica Vanderlyn (Edith as a child), Peter Vokes (Edward as a child), Leslie Flack (Joe as a child), Dorothy Keefe (Fanny as a child), Stella Wilson (Mirabelle), Eric Purveur (Lt. Edgar), Maidie Andrews (Ada), Billy Fry (Tom Jolly), Laura Smithson (Cook), Merle Tottenham (Annie), Edie Martin (Mrs. Snapper), Dorothy Monkman (Flo Grainger), Bobby Blythe (George Grainger), Moya Nugent (Daisy Devon), Betty Hare (Marion Christie), Betty Shale (Connie Crawshay), Philip Clarke (Tim Bateman), John Beerbohm (Douglas Finn), Anthony Pelissier

(Chubby), Aly Ford (Uncle Harry), Charles Wingrove (Uncle George), Walter Rayland (Uncle Dick), Tod Squires (Uncle Jack), Tom Carlisle (Uncle Bob), William McGuigan (Uncle Jim), Lena Brand (Freda Weddell), Marcelle Turner (Olive Frost), Dorothy Drover (Gladys). Anthony Blair (A Communist), Enid Clinto-Baddely (Religious Fanatic), W.A.H. Harrison (Wireless Announcer), Jack London (Pianist), Leslie Thompson (Trumpet)

SYNOPSIS: As the title suggests, a cavalcade of British history from Sunday December 31, 1899 to the present (1930), as seen through the eyes of an upper class family, the Marryots and their servants, the Bridges. Along the way, the Boar War, the death of Queen Victoria, the sinking of the Titanic and other significant moments are illustrated.

REVIEWS:
London Daily Mail, Nov. 1, 1931: "When the curtain fell there was an ovation such as I have not heard in very many years playgoing. *Cavalcade* is a magnificent play in which the note of national pride pervading every scene and every sentence must make each of us face the future with courage and high hopes. I have so often paised Coward the playwright that I want to devote myself tonight to Coward the director. These huge, unruly crowd scenes were superbly handled. Hundreds and hundreds of people thronged the stage, and yet the story lives throughout. Drury Lane has come into its own again — our national theatre has a theme worthy of itself."

NOTES: "I felt an urge to test my directing powers on a large scale," wrote Coward, about *Cavalcade* and this was one of the most spectacular productions ever staged. The action spanned Coward's lifetime to date and hit upon his anti-war philosophies and his intense patriotism. The original production was filmed in its entirety as a guide for the film makers. The film version won the Academy Award for Best Picture. For film version see F-8. For TV version see T-7. For publications see B-69, B-74, B-83.

P-68   *Hay Fever* (revival) Avon Theatre, NY. Dec. 29, 1931 (95 performances)

Revival of **Noël Coward's comedy**. Produced by Patterson McNutt. Directed by Constance Collier.

CAST: Constance Collier (Judith Bliss), Eric Cowley (David Bliss), Betty Linley (Sorel Bliss), Anthony Kemble-Cooper (Simon Bliss), Julia Hoyt (Myra Arundel), Edward Cooper (Richard Greatham), Valerie Cossart (Jackie Coryton), Terence Neill (Sandy Tyrell), Alice Belmore Cliffe (Clara)

SYNOPSIS: See P-38.

REVIEWS:
New York Times, Dec. 30, 1931: "As usual, Mr. Coward is a pastmaster at the game of entertaining satire. While he pinions his victims he tosses out impish comedy to the audience. It is theatrical satire, and infernally delicate and accomplished. It is dry subtle, mettlesone comedy, and it is enormously entertaining."

P-69   *The Noël Coward Company: Private Lives, Some Other Private Lives, Hay Fever, Home Chat, Weatherwise, The Vortex, Rain Before Seven, Fallen Angels, The Queen Was In The Parlour, I'll Leave It To You.* Opened at Festival Theatre, Malvern Sept. 1, 1932. A Repertory Company devoted to the plays of Coward opened in Malvern and toured to the Prince of Wale's, Birmingham, The Royal Court, Liverpool, Theatre Royal, Exeter, Devonshire Park, Eastbourne, Theatre Royal, Brighton, New Theatre, Oxford, The Pavilion, Bournemouth, returning to and closing in Eastborn Nov. 28, 1932. General Manager: Gatenby Bell. **Supervised by Noël Coward.**

CAST: Kate Cutler, Agatha Carrol, Janet Burnell, Marjorie Harwood, Joyce Wodeman, Marjorie, Taylor, Wilson Barrett, James Mason, Keith Shephard, and Farries Moss.

P-70   *Words and Music* Adelphi Theatre, London. Sept. 16, 1932.
(134 performances) Tried out at the Opera House, Manchester. Aug. 25, 1932

A revue with **book, lyrics, music and direction by Noël Coward.** Produced by Charles B. Cochran. Costumes and Decor by G.E. Calthrop. Dances by Buddy Bradley. Conducted by Hyam Greenbaum. Orchestrations by Spike Hughes.

CAST: Ivy St. Helier, Romney Brent, Phyllis Harding, Betty Hare, Moya Nugent, John Mills, Steffi Duna, Gerald Nodin, Bill Harn, Doris Hare, Tommy Hayes, Norah Howard, Effie Atherton, Kenneth Ware, Elizabeth Corcoran, Naomi Waters, Ann Codrighton, Joyce Barbour, Edward Unerdown, Kenneth Carten, Rita Lyle, Millie Sim, Joy Spring, Jack Spurgeon, Graham Payn (added after opening night)

MUSICAL NUMBERS: Opening Chorus-St. Helier & All; Debutantes-Harding, Betty Hare & Nugent; Let's Live Dangerously-Mills, Hare, Duna, Waters & Codrington; Children of the Ritz-Barbour & Girls; Mad Dogs & Englishman-

Romney Brent & Chorus; Let's Say Goodbye-Lyle & Underdown; The Hall of Fame-Barbour & Celebrities; Mad About the Boy-Barbour, Sim, Duna, Howard, Spring, Doris Hare, Payne, Lincoln & All; Journey's End-St. Helier, Lyle, Brent, Ware, Duna, Barbour, Mills, Nodin, Harn & All; Housemaid's Knees-Atherton & Girls; Three White Feathers-Hare; Something to Do With Spring-Barbour, Mills & Chorus; The Wife of An Acrobat-St.Helier; The Younger Generation-Lyle, Harding, Betty Hare, Nugent, Spring; Midnight Matinee-All; The Party's Over Now-Company

REVIEWS:
London Times, Sept. 17, 1932: "Mr. Coward has, above all else, the gift of satire, and this review, being primarily satirical, is his best work in the musical kind."

The Sketch (London), Sept. 28, 1932: " Thanks to Mr. Noël Coward, the revue as a form of dramatic art is rehabilitated. It is a kind of model and a masterpiece, and one that is so vastly amusing that we are only too willing to overlook the arid patches in a field so rich. The whole merry affair was a feast of wit, wisdom and mockers, charmingly assembled in a picturesque frame. It will enjoy a long life and add to the laurels of Mr. Noël Coward's genius."

NOTES: "Mad Dogs and Englishmen," one of Coward's most famous songs was first performing in *The Third Little Show* in New York 1931 (P-65) . It was introduced by Beatrice Lillie and became one of the cornerstones her act and also of Coward's successful cabaret and TV career in the 1950's. The bulk of *Words and Music* became *Set To Music* on Broadway in 1939 (see P-89). For recordings of the score see D-11, D-12, D-41, D-54. For publication see B-61.

P-71   *Design For Living* Ethel Barrymore Theatre, NY.   Jan. 24, 1933 (135 performances)Tried out at Hanna Theatre, Cleveland, OH Jan. 2, 1933.

> **A comedy written and directed by Noël Coward** (written in 1932). Presented by Max Gordon. Designed by G.E. Calthrop.

> CAST: Lynn Fontanne (Gilda), Campbell Gullan (Ernest Friedman), Alfred Lunt (Otto), **Noël Coward** (Leo), Gladys Henson (Miss Hodge), Ward Bishop (Photographer), Philip Tonge (Mr. Birbeck), Ethel Borden (Grace Torrence), Phyllis Connard (Helen Carver), Alan Campbell (Henry Carver), Macleary Stennett (Matthew)

SYNOPSIS: Gilda, Leo and Otto, all artistically inclined, are dear friends. When Gilda and Otto fight, Gilda leaves them both to marry the staid Ernest. Leo and Otto appear, disrupt her life and marriage and when Ernest leaves, the three decide to live their own design for living.

REVIEWS:
New York Times, Jan. 25, 1933: "When *Design for Living* sounds serious, you wish impatiently that Mr. Coward would cut the cackle and come to the main business, which is his brand of satire comedy. When he is in an impish mood, which is most of the time, he is enormously funny. But the acting supplies the final brilliance. *Design for Living* is written for actors — in fact for three actors who are now most conspicuous in it. They are extraordinarily well balanced. Miss Fontanne, with her slow languorous deliberation, Mr. Lunt with his boyish enthusiasm, Mr. Coward with his nervous, biting charity create more variety in the acting than Mr. Coward has got into the parts."

NOTES: The play was a culmination of a promise by Coward to his good friends the Lunts that he would write a play in which the three of them could star. This was one of the few times a Coward play premiered in the US. For publications of play see B-69, B-74, B-85. For film version see F-10. For subsequent productions and revivals see P-90, P-184, P-203, P-206. See also R-8, T-72.

P-72   *Actor's Fund Benefit* Imperial Theatre, NY. Jan. 29, 1933

NOTES: On his night off from *Design For Living,* **Noël Coward** appeared along with such stars as Ethel Barrymore.

P-73   *Stage Relief Fund* Hotel Biltmore Supper Room, NY. March 23, 1933

NOTES: **Noël Coward** appeared along with such stars as Ethel Merman, the Lunts, Beatrice Lillie and MC, Julius Tannen.

P-74   *Hay Fever* (revival) Shaftesbury Theatre, London. Nov. 17, 1933 (26 performances)

> Revival of **Noël Coward's comedy. Directed by Noël Coward.** Produced by Charles B. Cochran. Designed by G.E. Calthrop.

> CAST: Constance Collier (Judith Bliss), Eric Cowley (David Bliss), Helen Spencer (Sorel Bliss), Louis Hayward (Simon Bliss), Joyce Barbour (Myra Arundel), Alan Napier (Richard Greatham), Ann Trevor (Jackie Coryton), Hargrave Pawson (Sandy Tyrell), Gladys Henson (Clara)

SYNOPSIS: See P-38.

REVIEWS:
London Times, Nov. 13, 1933: "It is in the highest mood of fantastic comedy, deliciously heartless and, therefore, deliciously alive and fresh."

P-75   *Conversation Piece* His Majesty's Theatre, London. Feb. 16, 1934 (177 performances)

A Romantic Comedy with music written and directed by Noël Coward (written in 1933). Presented by Charles B. Cochran. Designed by G.E. Calthrop. Conducted by Reginald Burston. Orchestrated by Charles Prentice.

CAST: Heather Thatcher (Sophie), Moya Nugent (Martha), Betty Shale (Mrs. Dragon), **Noël Coward** (Paul, Duc de Chaucigny-Varennes), Yvonne Printemps (Melanie), Maidie Andrews (Rose), Louis Hayward (The Marquis of Sheere), George Sanders (Earl of Harringford), Pat Worsley (Lord Braceworth), Antony Brian (Lord Doyning), Sydney Grammer (Mr. Hailsham), Winifred Davis (Duchess of Beneden), Athole Stewart (Duke of Beneden), Irene Browne (Lady Julia Charteris) Elizabeth Corcoran (Her maid), Tommy Hayes (A Tiger), Everley Gregg (Miss Goslett), Molly Lumley (Miss Mention), Penryn Bannerman (Lord Kenyon), Kim Peacock (Lord St. Marys), Sheila Pattrick (Countess of Harringford), Betty Elburn (Lady Braceworth), Winifred Campbell (Mrs. Hailsham), St. John Laurie (Julian Kane), Alex Robertson (Mr. Amos), Claude Farrow (Butler), Leonard Michel (Mr. Jones), Jean Barnes (Courtesan)

SYNOPSIS: In the Regency Brighton of 1811, Paul, the Duc de Chaucigny-Varennes concocts a plan to pass off Melanie as his ward, a young girl orphaned by the French revolution. With this deception they hope to ensnare a rich husband, the Marquis of Sheere, ensuring both of their financial futures. Despite their own mechanations, true love triumphs in the end for Paul and Melanie.

MUSICAL NUMBERS: The Parade; I'll Follow My Secret Heart-Printemps; Regency Rakes-Sanders, Worsley, Brian & Grammer; Charming, Charming-Printemps, Andrews, Thatcher & Nugent; Dear Little Soldiers-Printemps, Andrews, Thatcher & Nugent; There's Always Something Fishy About The French-Thatcher & Nugent; English Lesson-Printemps; There Was a Little Village by The Sea-Thurgood, McGuigan, Jones & Hall; Finale Act II-Printemps; Nevermore-Printemps

REVIEWS:
The London Daily Telegraph, Feb. 17, 1934: "Last night at His Majesty's was a great occasion. Since Coward is the author, composer, director and chief male actor in this brilliant show, he enjoys a separate triumph all to himself. If you cannot afford a ticket for this show any other way, sell your wife's jewellery or your children's school books. You will never regret the sacrifice. It is a continued

delight to the eye."

The London Observer, Feb. 19, 1934: "Mr. Coward has been more concerned to provide a medium for Mlle. Printemps than to prepare a balanced play."

NOTES: Coward wrote this "operette" for french star Yvonne Printemps, despite her apparent unaquaintence with English. She learned the part by rote and by all accounts was enchanting. During rehearsals it became apparent to Coward that Romney Brent, whom he engaged to play Paul, was not working out. Brent gladly passed the role on to Coward asking only to be at rehearsals to watch Coward discover "what a bloody awful part it is". On April 23, 1934 Pierre Fresnay (Printemps' husband. He would also introduce the role on Broadway.) replaced Coward in the role. On July 2, 1934 Coward returned to the play only to hand over the role to Fresnay again on July 12, 1934 when he was taken ill with appendicitis. The run ended on July 21, 1934. For American production see P-78. For recordings of the score see D-16, D-17, D-55, D-56, D-57, D-97, D-111. For publication see B-69, B-75, B-84. For radio version see R-14.

P-76   *Biography* Globe Theatre, London. April 25, 1934 (45 performances)

A comedy by S.N. Behrman. **Directed by Noël Coward**. Produced by John C. Wilson as the first production of Transatlantic Productions, Inc. Sets by Alick Johnston. Costumes by Molyneux.

CAST: Laurence Olivier (Richard Kurt), Ina Claire (Marion Froude), Frank Cellier (Leander Bunny Nolan) Sam Livesay (Orrin Kinnicott), Alexander Sarner (Melchoir Feydak), Reginald Tate (Warwick Wilson), Annie Esmond (Minnie), Joan Wyndham (Slade Kinnicott)

SYNOPSIS: When Marion Froude, a portrait artist, decides to publish a serialized account of her colorful life, she has Bunny Nolan, her politically ambitious former lover in an uproar. When he has Richard Kurt, the editor in charge of the project, fired, he fires Kurt up to use the biography as a weapon againt the established social order he hates. When Marion destroys what she has written, she also ends the love that Kurt has come to feel for her.

REVIEWS:
New York Times, May 20, 1934 (from London May 3, 1934): "Since the first night's performance I have heard it said by more than one of those who profess to be able to estimate the public's mood that *Biography* will not run, partly because it has an unhappy ending, partly because it has few dramatic high-lights. I am inclined to think that these prophets are unnecessarily gloomy. It has a freshness, an honesty and an intelligence which English audiences, tired of empty theatrical tricks, can

scarcely fail to recognize."

NOTES: Originally produced in NY at the Guild Theatre Dec. 12, 1932.

P-77   *Bitter-Sweet* (revival) 44th Street Theatre, NY. May 7, 1934

Revival of **Noël Coward's operette.** Produced by Messeurs Shubert. Staged by Edward J. Scanlon. Sets by Watson Barratt. Costumes by Ernest Schraps. Orchestra directed by Pierre Dereeder.

CAST: Evelyn Herbert (Sari), Alan Jones (Carl), Hannah Toback (Manon), Cameron York (Vincent Howard), Henry Rabke (Hugh Devon), Kay Simmons (Gussi), Clyde Kelly (Marquis of Shayne), Elizabeth Crandall (Mrs. Millick), Jay Conley (The Marquis of Steere), Carol Boyer (Lotte), Beatrice Berenson (Freda), Marion Carlisle (Hansi), Kay Simmons (Gussi), Leonard Ceeley (Captain August Lutte), Victor Casmore (Herr Schlick & Sir Arthur), Beulah Blake (Effie), Martha Boyer (Victoria), Marion Carlisle (Harriet), Beatrice Berernson (Gloria), Anna Werth (Jane), Ruth Adams (Honor), Mary Wrick (Dolly), Jack Richards (Lord Henry), Frances Marion Comstock (Lady Devon), Samuel Thomas (Lord Edgar James), Brian Davis (Lord Sorrell), Jack Richards (Mr. Vale), Harold Abbey (Mr. Bethel), Truman Gaige (Mr. Proutie)

SYNOPSIS & MUSICAL NUMBERS : See P-58

NOTES: This marked the Broadway debut of Allan Jones. When this production was on its pre-broadway tour in Dec. 1933 at the National Theatre in Washington D.C., a song entitled "It's Always The Man That's Pursued" was performed by Schlick, Fritz and Lizzi in Act II. Whether this song was by Coward or not is unknown, but it was gone by the time the revival opened in May.

P-78   *Conversation Piece* 44th St. Theatre, NY. Oct. 10, 1934 (55 performances)

Broadway premiere of **Noël Coward's Operette.** Produced by Arch Selwyn & Harold Franklin with Charles B. Cochran. Personel the same as P-75 except conducted by Victor Baravalle.

CAST: Sylvia Leslie (Sophie), Moya Nugent (Martha), Betty Shale (Mrs. Dragon), Pierre Fresnay (Paul, Duc de Chaucigny-Varennes), Yvonne Printemps (Melanie), Maidie Andrews (Rose), Carl Harbord (The Marquis of Sheere), George Sanders (Earl of Harringford), Pat Worsley (Lord Braceworth), Anthony Brian (Lord Doyning), Sydney Grammer (Mr. Hailsham), Winifred Davis (Duchess of Beneden), Athole Stewart

(Duke of Beneden), Irene Browne (Lady Julia Charteris) Elizabeth Corcoran (Her maid), Leonard Goodman (A Tiger), Phyllis Harding (Miss Goslett), Dorothy Drover (Miss Mention), Penryn Bannerman (Lord Kenyon), George Sanders (Lord St. Marys), Sheila Pattrick (Countess of Harringford), Eileen Clifton (Lady Braceworth), Winifred Campbell (Mrs. Hailsham), St. John Laurie (Julian Kane), Alex Robertson (Mr. Amos), Claude Farrow (Butler), Leonard Michel (Mr. Jones), Brenda Clether (Courtesan)

SYNOPSIS: Same as P-75

REVIEWS:
New York Times, Oct. 24, 1934: "Neither the conversation nor the piece has the vivid distinction of most of Mr. Coward's work. Even when he is not in top form he has a genius for theatrical presentation. Although the plot is not ingenious, Mr. Coward is the sort of theatrical magician to give it a real patina on the stage."

New York Sun, Oct. 24, 1934: "There are songs to help it, also written by Mr. Coward and set to tunes by Mr. Coward, which are not very distinctive.

NOTES: Of the cast brought over from London, only George Sanders remained and became a Hollywood star.

P-79   *Theatre Royal* Lyric Theatre, London. Oct. 23, 1934 (174 performances) Tried out at the Lyrceum Theatre, Edinburgh.

West End premiere of a comedy by George S. Kaufman & Edna Ferber (originally titled *The Royal Family*). **Directed by Noël Coward.** Produced by John C. Wilson. Designed by G.E. Calthrop.

CAST: Marie Tempest (Fanny Cavendish), Laurence Oliver (Tony Cavendish), Madge Titheradge (Julie Cavendish), Anthony Pelissier (Jo), Patrick Susands (McDermott), George Zucco (Herbert Dean), Wallace Douglas (Perry Stewart), W. Graham Brown (Oscar Wolfe), Tristan Rawson (Gilbert Marshall), Tommy Hayes (Hallboy), Charles Schofield (Second Hallboy), George Chamberlain (Chauffeur), Arthur Carino (Gunga), Mona Harrison (Della), Mary Merrall (Kitty Le Moyne), Margaret Vines (Gwen), Lumena Edwards (Miss Peake)

SYNOPSIS: The inner goings on of a Broadway theatrical clan not unlike the Barrymores. When Julie decides to marry again and leave the stage, the clan tries to stand behind her. Her daughter takes her place and her mother plans a touring season. Her brother Tony (read John Barrymore), a silent film star, hides out from the press. In the end Julie abandons love for the stage and Fanny dies before returning to the boards.

REVIEWS:
New York Times, Nov. 11, 1934 (from London Oct. 25, 1934): "I think Mr. Coward ought to have made up his mind whether he intended the audience to grovel at the feet of the Cavendish family or to mock at them. As it is, he seems to have directed the play, not with an eye to the general significance and effect, but scene by scene."

NOTES: Coward retitled the Broadway hit, as the *The Royal Family* would be misconstrued in England as being about the Royal Family rather than an acting clan. He appeared at one performance at the Lyceum Theatre, Edinburgh as an Indian Servant, surprising Olivier et al.

P-80   *Point Valaine*   Ethel Barrymore Theatre, NY. Jan. 16, 1935 (55 performances).Tried out at the Colonial Theatre, Boston, MA Dec. 25, 1934 and Chestnut St. Opera House, Philadelphia, PA

A play written and directed by Noël Coward. Produced by John C. Wilson. Sets and Costumes by G.E. Calthrop.

CAST: Grayce Hampton (Mrs. Tillett), Fred Leslie (Major Tillett), Lilian Tonge (Mrs. Birling), Osgood Perkins (Mortimer Quinn), Alfred Lunt (Stefan), Ruth Boyd (Lola), Alberta Perkins (May), Broderick Crawford (George Fox), Philip Tonge (Ted Burchell), Lynn Fontanne (Linda Valaine), Gladys Henson (Mrs. Hall-Fenton), Phyllis Harding (Gladys),Margaret Curtis (Phyllis), Valerie Cosart (Sylvia), Everly Gregg (Hilda James), Louis Hayward (Martin Welford)

SYNOPSIS: The Point Valaine Hotel on a secluded island near Trinidad is run by Linda Valaine. Stefan, her Russian head waiter is also her lover. Among her guests are a famous novelist and a gallant young aviator resting up from an accident. The aviator falls in love with the middle aged hotel proprietor and she surrenders to him in spite of herself. When her lover discovers her disloyalty, he slashes his wrist and hurls himself into the sea. The play ends with Linda Valaine seeking a new head waiter.

REVIEWS:
New York Times, Jan. 17, 1935: "If there is an Coward manner discernible among all his talents, he has departed from it in *Point Valaine*. It is unmistakably the work of a master of the stage. The story has a sense of impending horror. Mr. Coward is ingenious enough to capture the fullness of the evil in his staging of the play."

New York American, Jan. 17, 1935: "This is not the Noël Coward of *Design For Living* say, or even of that paper valentine, *Conversation Piece*. I might continue to deny that it is another *Cavalcade*, another *Vortex*, another anything previous by Squire Coward and then I should admit that it doesn't try to be."

NOTES: Sometime in March 1934, Coward, John C. Wilson and the Lunts formed a production company called Transatlantic Productions, Inc. The arrangement called for profits made by any one of the participants to be shared with the others. After the first production, S.N. Behrman's *Biography* (P-76) opened in London, the first joint venture was *Point Valaine*. The Lunts were reluctant about the play from the start, but went on with it remembering the great success of *Design For Living*. *Point Valaine* proved to be the only flop of the Lunt's duel career. In retrospect Coward saw the flaws in the play, which he felt was neither big enough for tragedy nor light enough for comedy. After more than two decades Transatlantic Productions, Inc. was dissolved at the end of the run of *Quadrille* (P-137). For publication see B-79, B-97.

P-81   *Post Depression Gaieties* New Amsterdam Theatre, NY. Feb. 24, 1935

NOTES: Alexander Woollcott, Ben Hecht, Charles MacArthur, Helen Hayes and **Noël Coward** appeared in one sketch.

P-82   *Personal Appearance* at the Cinema in Ashford, Kent Aug. 18,. 1935

NOTES: **Noël Coward** appeared with Jeanne de Casalis in a benefit for the Actor's Orphanage and the Ashford Hospital. Also appearing were Vivien Leigh, Douglas Fairbanks and Joyce Barbour.

P-83   *Tonight At 8:30* Phoenix Theatre, London. Jan. 9, 1936 (157 performances) Tried out at the Opera House, Manchester. Oct. 15, 1935. A nine week tour followed including Leeds, Glasgow, Edinburgh, Liverpool, Newcastle and Birmingham.

Three Evenings of One-Act Plays written and directed by **Noël Coward**. Presented by John C. Wilson. Sets and Costumes by G.E. Calthrop. Conducted by Clifford Greenwood. Dances by Ralph Reader. A group of ten one-act plays and musicals combined in various orders to make three evenings, each consisting of three plays.

THE PLAYS AND THEIR CASTS: *We Were Dancing*: Kenneth Carten (Ippaga), Edward Underdown (George Davies), Moya Nugent (Eva Blake), Gertrude Lawrence (Louise Charteris), **Noël Coward** (Karl Sandys), Alison Leggatt (Clara Bethel), Alan Webb (Hubert Charteris),

Anthony Pelissier (Major Blake); *The Astonished Heart*: Alison Leggatt (Barbara Faber), Everly Gregg (Susan Birch), Anthony Pelissier (Tim Verney),Edward Underdown (Ernest), Alan Webb (Sir Rebinald), Gertrude Lawrence (Leonora Vail), **Noël Coward** (Christian Faber); *Red Peppers*: Gertrude Lawrence (Lily Pepper) **Noël Coward** (George Pepper), Kenneth Carten (Alf), Anthony Pelissier (Bert Bentley), Alan Webb (Mr. Edwards) Alison Leggatt (Mabel Grace); *Hands Across The Sea*: Moya Nugent (Walters) Gertrude Lawrence (Piggie), **Noël Coward** (Her husband), Edward Underdown (Alastair Corbett), Alison Leggatt (Mrs. Wadhurst), Kenneth Carten (Mr. Burnham), Everly Gregg (Clare Wedderburn), Anthony Pelissier (Bogey); *Fumed Oak*: **Noël Coward** (Henry Gow), Gertrude Lawrence (Doris Gow), Moya Nugent (Elsie), Alison Leggatt (Mrs. Rocket); *Shadow Play*: Moya Nugent (Lena) Gertrude Lawrence (Victoria Gayforth), Everly Gregg (Martha Cunningham), **Noël Coward** (Simon Gayforth), Kenneth Carten (Hodge), Edward Underdown (Michael Doyle), Alison Leggatt (Sybil Heston), Anthony Pelissier (A Young Man), Alan Webb (George Cunningham); *Family Album*: **Noël Coward** (Jasper Featherways), Gertrude Lawrence (Jane, his wife), Everly Gregg (Harriet Winter), Anthony Pelissier (Charles Winter), Moya Nugent (Emily Valance), Kenneth Carten (Edward Valance), Edward Underdown (Richard Featherways), Alison Leggatt (Lavinia Featherways), Alan Webb (Burrows); *Star Chamber*: **Noël Coward** (Johnny Bolton), Gertrude Lawrence (Xenia James), Everly Gregg (Dame Rose Maitland), Anthony Pelissier (J.M. Farmer), Moya Nugent (Hester More), Kenneth Carten (Jimmie Horlick), Edward Underdown (Maurice Searle), Betty Hare (Violet Vibart) Alan Webb (Julian Breed), Lumena Edwards (Elise Brodie), Charles Peters (Photographer); *Ways and Means*: **Noel Coward** (Toby Cartwright), Gertrude Lawrence (Stella Cartwright), Everly Gregg (Nannie), Anthony Pelissier (Murdock), Moya Nugent (Elena), Kenneth Carten (Gaston), Edward Underdown (Stevens), Joyce Carey (Olive) Alan Webb (Lord Chapworth); *Still Life*: **Noël Coward** (Alec Harvey), Gertrude Lawrence (Laura Jesson), Everly Gregg (Dolly Messiter), Anthony Pelissier (Johnny), Moya Nugent (Beryl Waters), Kenneth Carten (Stanley), Edward Underdown (Bill), Betty Hare (Mildred) Alan Webb (Albert Godby), Joyce Carey (Myrtle Bagot), Charles Peters (Young Man);

SYNOPSIS:

We Were Dancing: On the island of Samolo, Louise Charteris and Karl Sandys dance until the dance becomes a kiss, seen by Louise's husband. Karl makes Louise's husband admit that he no longer loves his wife and the two plan to sail together to Australia. When the cold light of dawn comes, the two see that the magic has vanished and they part.

The Astonished Heart: As Barbara Faber, Susan Birch and Tim Verney await the arrival of Leonora Vail to the dying psychiatrist, Christian Faber's bedside, they remember how it all came about. It was one year ago when Leonora came into their lives and lured Chris away from his loving wife, only for him to become obsessed in his love. Knowing about the affair, his wife Barbara tells him to go away with Leonora and see the thing through. When the affair goes sour, Faber hurls himself from a window, bringing us to the present. When Leonora arrives at his bedside, Chris doesn't recognize her, but calls her by his wife's nickname, Baba.

Red Peppers: George and Lily Pepper, small time music hall performers do their act and bicker backstage. They fight with the conductor about tempos and are rewarded by the racing speed of their next number.

Hands Across The Sea: Lady Maureen Gilpin (Piggie) and her husband Commander Peter Gilpin have a cocktail party for two people they met in the Far East and now can hardly recall. When two other people show up, they take them for their guests and treat them with great manners. When a phone call comes which says their original guests cannot make it, they beautifully go on with the charade, no one the wiser.

Fumed Oak: Middle class suburbanite, Henry Gow finally has had it with his nagging wife, his mean old mother in law and his nasty daughter. The worm turns and he leaves them forever to stew in their own juices.

Shadow Play: Victoria and Simon Gayforth are having a rocky time in their marriage and divorce seems imminent. When Victoria takes some sleeping tablets, she recalls happier times in their lives: when they met, when they honeymooned and how it all went wrong. When she awakes, Simon and she make it up.

Family Album: The Victorian Featherway clan gathers after the funeral of their tyranical father. They drink wine and bring out the box of their old toys, reviving memories. The old maid of the clan who took care of Daddy to the death, reveals that she has destroyed the will that would have cut them all off and they all drink and dance to her decision.

Ways and Means: Toby and Stella Cartwright are stranded in the south of France without any funds at the home of a rich friend. They can't leave and they can't let anyone know they are broke. When they are almost robbed, they concoct a plan to make it seem like they were. The crook, whom they know, ties them up and they await the morning when they will be discovered.

Still Life: In a teashop in a London railway station Dr. Alec Harvey and suburban housewife, Laura Jesson meet innocently. After running into each other again, the two married people begin a romance that lasts a brief while, until Alec takes a position in Africa, parting them forever.

Star Chamber: On the stage of a West End theatre, a meeting of a theatrical charity is kept waiting by Xenia James, its president. When she finally arrives the meeting comes to order and much is discussed.

MUSICAL NUMBERS: *We Were Dancing*: We Were Dancing-Coward; *Red Peppers*: Has Anyone Seen Our Ship & Men About Town-Coward & Lawrence; *Shadow Play*: Then, Play Orchestra Play, You Were There-Coward & Lawrence; *Family Album*: Here's A Toast, Princes and Princesses, Let's Play a Tune on the Music Box, Hearts and Flowers-Coward, Lawrence and All

REVIEWS:
The London Observer, Jan 12, 1936: "The first piece, *Family Album*, is sometimes nearly vulgar, sometimes nearly mawkish, and sometimes modernly smart; but thanks to Mr. Coward's uncannily tactful direction, the gearchanges are not harsh. Next *The Astonished Heart*. Mr. Coward and Miss Lawrence play the desperated lovers in the tight-lipped, back-to-the-audience, self-suppressive, word-swallowing style of emotional acting which is fashionable today. Of this style they offer a first rate example, but it is not a good style of acting for a play the paramount interest of which lies in violence of erotic passion and in the virtuosity with which this demonic possession is portrayed. *Red Peppers*: This, the least ambitious feature of the triple bill, is certainly the most successful. But the variety of the programme is a tribute to Mr. Coward's interest in experiment. The presentation of it is a real piece of work.

The London Observer, Jan. 19, 1936: "The second programme maintains a better level than his first. *Fumed Oak* is a brisk and bitter entertainment. Coward somehow contrives to make this sad and sour story immensely diverting. *Hands Across The Sea*: The pith of this piece is the production, and Mr. Coward has created a wonderful rattle of smart idiocy. In *Shadow Play*, Mr. Coward once more demonstrates, with music, that nobody can put a brisker, fresher look than he does on the surface of a simple and threadbare theme."

The Sunday London Times, May 24, 1936: "In *Still Life* Coward is almost at his best. The play is a tiny masterpiece of economical writing and is beautifully acted by Mr. Coward and Miss Lawrence. The author is less happy in the characteristic trifle, *Ways and Means*. Mr. Coward and Miss Lawrence chatter in the hard, glittering manner of the author's earlier plays, and the piece ends in an entirely arbitrary way."

NOTES: Coward achieved a rare achievement in the theatre. Not only as author, but as actor, Coward proved his incredible versatility in one fell swoop. In three evenings he & Lawrence ran the gamut from comedy to tragedy, melodrama, music hall & musical comedy. Besides single handedly reviving the once dead one act play programme, almost all these plays proved durable on their own and Coward got much mileage out of film, radio, record and TV versions of these works throughout the years. *Star Chamber* was performed only once on Mar. 29, 1936. For American Production see P-85. For recordings see D-19, D-20, D-21, D-22.

P-84   *Mademoiselle* Wyndham's Theatre, London. Sept. 15, 1936 (136 performances)

A play by Jacques Deval. Adapted by Audrey and Waveney Carten. **Directed by Noël Coward**. Produced by John C. Wilson. Designed by G.E. Calthrop. Costumes by Molyneux.

CAST: Cecil Parker (Lucien Galvoisier), Victor Boggetti (Jean), Nigel Patrick (Maurice), Laidman Browne (Georges Boutin), Edward Mac-Cormack (Edouard), Isobel Jeans (Alice), Ann Farrer (Helene), Greer Garson (Christianne), Madge Titheradge (Mademoiselle), Dorothy Lane (Therese), Willeen Wilson (Juliet)

P-85   *Tonight at 8:30* National Theatre, NY. Nov. 24, 1936 (118 performances). Tried out at Colonial Theatre, Boston Oct. 26, 1936. Production credits same as P-83, except Conducted by John McManus.

CAST: Plays and cast essentially the same as P-83. *Star Chamber* was not played.

REVIEWS:
New York Times, Nov. 25, 1936: "The point of *Tonight at 8:30* is that Mr. Coward and Miss Lawrence are in fine fettle. Give them the wisp of an idea, and they can trip-clip-clop it into good theatre festivity, making the most of the gaudy world of make-believe."

New York Times, Nov. 28, 1936: "*Fumed Oak* is a little masterpiece of sour-puss dramaturgy, and *Shadow Play* is an extraodinarily precise stage expression of a dance of rueful phantoms and if *We Were Dancing* is no piece of wizardry, it suffices for opening Mr. Coward's fashionable vaudeville show. No student of the drama will ever grind out his doctor's thesis on Mr. Coward's contribution to thought on the basis of the current one act panels. Nor will anyone, save Mr. Coward and Miss Lawrence give them much vibrancy on the stage. For they are personal vehicles."

New York American, Nov. 25, 1936: "They are cause for everyone to crow of Mr. Coward's versatility all over again."

NOTES: In a survey in the *New York Times* on Nov. 30, 1936 as to which of the one-acts was most popular with the audiences, *The Astonished Heart* and *Fumed Oak* tied for top honor followed by *Hands Across The Sea, Shadow Play, Family Album, Still Life, Ways and Means, Were Were Dancing* and *Red Peppers* trailing last. Just as Gertrude Lawrence had suffered from nervous exhaustion during the London run, Coward succumbed to the strain of playing nine difficult roles and had his second breakdown, necessitating closing the plays one month ahead of schedule. He was advised by doctors to stay off the stage for two years. In fact, he did not appear again until 1942. For Publications see B-61, B-69, B-70, B-77, B-111. For major revivals, film, TV & radio versions see P-111, P-165, P-175, P-199, F-14, F-18, F-19, F-20,T-5, T-6, T-8, T-21, T-26, T-58, T-67, R-15, R-19, R-20, R-22, R-35, R-37, R-39, R-40, R-43, R-44, R-46, R-47, R-50, R-54, R-62.

P-86   *Benefit for Flood Victims*   Radio City Music Hall. Feb. 11, 1937.

NOTES: **Noël Coward** appeared along with Ethel Merman, Gertrude Lawrence, Maurice Evans, Evelyn Laye, Helen Hayes, Ruth Gordon, Richard Rodgers, Arthur Schwartz, Bert Lahr, Beatrice Lillie. Coward hosted and performed "Dance Little Lady." The grand climax of the evening was Coward, Lawrence and Reginald Gardiner joining the Cab Calloway orchestra in a few dozen choruses of "Minnie the Moocher."

P-87   *George and Margaret*   Morosco Theatre, NY   Sept. 22, 1937 (86 performances) Tried out in Toronto.

A comedy by Gerald Savory. **Directed by Noël Coward** (uncredited in the Playbill). Produced by John C. Wilson. Sets by Geoffrey Nare.

CAST: Moya Nugent (Gladys), Morland Graham (Malcolm Garth-Bander), Irene Browne (Alice Garth-Bander), Arthur Macrae (Dudley), Rosalyn Boulter (Frankie), Richard Warner (Claude), Alan Webb (Roger), Gladys Henson (Beer)

SYNOPSIS: Malcolm and Alice Garth-Bander and their three children live in a London suburb. They are expecting George and Margaret to arrive as weekend guests and hating the thought of it. George and Margaret are bloody bores. While they wait Frankie falls in love with Roger and Claude decides that he wants to marry Gladys, the maid. Their parents make the comic best of things and then George and Margaret arrive.

REVIEWS:
New York Times, Sept. 23, 1937: "If it is in bad taste to say that *George and Margaret* is thin entertainment, this column is going to be indecorous this morning. *George and Magaret* is the sort of scribbled skit this column does not like very much until it becomes a classic."

NOTES: Coward wanted and received no credit for directing the play. He apparently replaced the previous director as a favor to Jack Wilson. Despite its Broadway reception, the play was a summer stock favorite for many years hence.

P-88   *Operette*   His Majesty's Theatre, London. Mar 16, 1938 (133 performan ces). Tried out at The Opera House, Manchester. Feb. 17, 1938

An Operette written, composed and directed by Noël Coward. Produced by John C. Wilson. Sets and costumes by G.E. Calthrop.

CAST: Phyllis Monkman (Maisie Welbey), John Laurie (Phillip Johns), Edward Cooper (Eddie Gosling), Pamela Randell (Grace Mentheith), Linda Gray (Violet Travers), Peggy Wood (Rozanne Gray)Lisa d'Esterre (Lala Montague), Hedli Anderson (Eleanor West), Jean Barnes (Doreen Manners), Fritzi Massary (Liesle Haren), Tommy Hayes (Duggie), Winifred Davis, Decina Drury), Gerald Nodin (Edgar Fawcett), Max Oldaker (Paul Trevor), Duncan Rider (Albert), Muriel Barron (Elsie Jewell), Gladys Henson (Dora), Violet Oldak (Trudi), Molly Lumley (Lily), Griffith Jones (Nigel Vaynham), Peter Vokes (David Messiter), Hugh French (Lord Elderley), Kenneth Carten (Lord Camp), John Gatrell (Lord Sickert), Ross Landon (Lord Borrowmere), Denis Carew (Humphrey Gordon), J. Grant Anderson (Jenner), Marcelle Turner (Mabel), Rosemary Lomax (Doris), Leonard Morris (George), Richard Haydn (Johnny Knowles), George Butler (Charles Hobson), Irene Vanbrugh (Countess of Messiter)

SYNOPSIS: In 1906, the musical comedy "The Model Maid" plays in the ficticious Jubilee Theatre. When Rozanne, one of the sextette who is love with Lord Vaynham, achieves overnight stardom, she is forced to choose between love and the stage. When he rejoins his regiment in India for the next five years, her choice becomes plain. She clearheadedly chooses her career.

MUSICAL NUMBERS: Prologue-Chorus; Opening Chorus-Chorus; Countess Mitzi-Massary & Chorus; Dearest Love-Barron & Oldaker; Foolish Virgins-Sextette; The Stately Homes of England-French, Landon, Gatrell, & Carten; Where are the Songs We Sung?-Wood; The Island of Bollamazoo-Copper & Chorus; Sing for Joy-Wood & Chorus; Operette-Massary & Sextet

REVIEWS:

Manchester Guardian, Feb. 18, 1938: "Cutting loose among composers and producers of that period, Mr. Coward has some fine larks. Mr. Coward has added to kindly parody many tuneful waltzes in his own manner. At least two of them, "Dearest Love" and "Where Are the Songs We Sung?" are as attractive as any in *Bitter-Sweet*."

The Sketch, March 30, 1938: "A modishly nostalgic, gently romantic and show a definite dislike, except in one song, for smartness and brilliance. The music is sweet and soothing, and wholly suitable."

NOTES: Coward felt that this was the least successful musical play that he ever wrote. This, he attributed to the overabundace of story and underabundance of song. Only "The Stately Homes of England" went on to become a Coward standard and was also used in *Set to Music* (P-90). "Countess Mitzi" was used again in *The Girl Who Came To Supper* (P-158), under the guise of "My Family Tree." Coward himself conducted several performances. For Recordings see D-23, D-24, D-25, D-58, D-59, D-60. For publications see B-61, B-75, B-94.

P-89   *Benefit for the Negro Actor's Guild* 46th Street Theatre Dec. 11, 1938.

NOTES: **Noël Coward** and Beatrice Lillie were among those appearing.

P-90   *Set To Music* Music Box Theatre, NY. Jan. 18, 1939 (129 performances). Tried out at the Shubert Theatre, Boston, MA Dec. 26, 1938.

A revue with **book, lyrics, music and direction by Noël Coward**. Decor and Costumes by G.E. Calthrop. Conducted by John McManus. Orchestrations by Hans Spialek.

CAST: Beatrice Lillie, Richard Haydn, Hugh French, Bronson Dudley, Anna Jackson, Laura Duncan, Ruby Green, Leonard Gibson, Mary Ann Carr, Ray Dennis, Gladys Henson, Robert Shackleton, Anthony Pelissier, Eva Ortega, Florence Britton, Sarah Burton, Maidie Andrews, Moya Nugent, Rosemary Lomax, Penople Dudley Ward, Tilda Getze, Angus Menzies, Kenneth Carten.

MUSICAL NUMBERS: A Fragonard Impression; Three Little Debutantes-Jackson, Duncan, Green; Mad About The Boy-Ward, Lomax, Henson, Duncan, Lillie, Nugent; The Stately Homes of England-French, Menzies, Pelisier; Weary of It All-Lillie; Children of The Ritz-Ortega; Never Again-Ortega & French; Midnight Matinee-Lillie, Haydn & All; Three White Feathers-Lillie; Marvellous Party-Lillie; The Party's Over Now-Ward & French

REVIEWS:
New York Times, Jan. 19, 1939: "Whether Noël Coward is Beatrice Lillie's best friend of whether the honors are the other way round is an academic question at best. For the simple fact is that *Set to Music* represents both of them at their best. It seems like the best show he has written."

New York Herald Tribune, Jan. 19,1939: "With the exception of one or two scenes, Mr. Coward's own work in the new revue reveals a surprising laziness. His work is tired, brittle, and strangely lacking in vitality."

New York Post, Jan. 19, 1939: "When Mr. Coward turns author for Lady Peel the results are bound to be convulsing. Mr. Coward has written some of his most biting lyrics."

NOTES: This was more or less the American edition of *Words and Music* (P-70) with new material for Beatrice Lillie. "The Stately Homes of England" was introduced in *Operette* (P-88), which was never produced in NY. "Weary of It All" & "Marvellous Party" were later heard in *All Clear*, (P-92) and "Never Again" was introduced to London in *Sigh No More* (P-106). Coward appeared in one sketch in Boston. For recordings of songs see D-61, D-62, D-63, D-64. For publications see B-61.

P-91   *Design For Living* The Haymarket Theatre, London. Jan. 25, 1939 (203 performances) Tried out at Theatre Royal, Brighton Jan. 16, 1939. Moved to the Savoy Theatre June 13, 1939. Run interrupted by outbreak of WWII. After tour run was resumed at the Savoy on Dec. 23, 1939 (33 performances)

West End premiere of **a comedy by Noël Coward**. Direced by Harold French. Sets and costumes by Roger K. Furse.

CAST: Diana Wynyard (Gilda), Alan Webb (Ernest Friedman), Anton Walbrook (Otto), Rex Harrison (Leo), Dorothy Hamilton (Miss Hodge), Cyril Wheeler (Mr. Birbeck), Everley Gregg (Grace Torrence), Cathleen Cordell (Helen Carver), Ross Landon (Henry Carver), James McIntyre (Matthew)

SYNOPSIS: see P-71.

REVIEWS:
The London Times, Jan. 26, 1939: "Mr. Coward's dialogue dips and swings and glitters as though he were writing a dazzling farce. The theme is not faced; the subject is not worked out. For these reasons, the play is disappointing."

NOTES: According the Rex Harrison's second autobiography, *A Damned Serious Business* (Bantam Books, 1991): "Some actors actually wrote the parts which fitted their own personalities, and the style they wanted to play, like Noël Coward, whose characters were him, and generally he played them on the stage himself the first time round. This made it pretty difficult to follow him, which I had to do in 1939 in *Design for Living*. This was a situation you couldn't win, and may well have been when Noel first uttered his much quoted remark about me, 'Rex Harrison is the best light comedian in the business — after me!'"

P-92   *All Clear* Queen's Theatre, London. Dec. 20, 1939 (162 performances) Tried out at the Theatre Royal, Brighton Dec. 4, 1939.

A revue presented by H.M. Tennent Ltd. Directed by Harold French. Decor by G. E. Calthrop. Orchestra under the direction of Dennis Van Thal.

NOTES: **Noël Coward** contributed the following items: "Cat's Cradle" (sketch) performed by Beatrice Lillie and Bobby Howes (originally from *The Third Little Show*), "Secret Service" (sketch) performed by Lillie, Gladys Henson, Moya Nugent, John Stevens, Robert Eddison, Hugh French, Tony Hully, Hilde Palmer, Mary Lynn, "Marvelous Party" sung by Beatrice Lillie, "Weary of it All" sung by Lillie with Nugent, French, Hulley, and Eddison. The last three items were written for *Set To Music* (P-90).

P-93   *Singing Tours* 1940-43

Noël Coward went on tour entertaining the troops and the public in such Australian locales as Sydney, Melbourne, Adelaide, Perth, Fremantle, Canberra, Brisbain, Launceston, Hobart, and New Zealand ending in Wellington. Middle East tours included Algiers, Syria, Iraq, Iran, Cairo, Alexandria, Beruit, Bagdad, Tripoli.

NOTES: In these and the 1944 tours Coward chose not to join ENSA, but to go off on his own tours. They are detailed in *Future Indefinite* (B-53) and *Middle East Diary* (B-48).

P-94   *London Wings Club and Nuttfield Centre* Oct., 1941

P-95   *Hay Fever* (revival) The Vaudeville Theatre, London April 1, 1941 (8 performances)

Revival of **Noël Coward's comedy**. Produced by Wilson Barnett. Directed by Charles Hickman.

CAST: Enid Sass (Judith Bliss), George Larchet (David Bliss), Joan Benham (Sorel Bliss), John Marquand (Simon Bliss), Phyllis Barker (Myra Arundel), Owen Reynolds (Richard Greatham), Joan Lang (Jackie Coryton), Neil Crawford (Sandy Tyrell), Kitty de Legh (Clara)

SYNOPSIS: See P-33.

P-96   *Up and Doing* Saville Theatre, London. April 17, 1940 (171 performances) Run interrupted by the Blitz. Returned May 20, 1941 (332 performances)

NOTES: During the second run **Noël Coward** contributed one song, "London Pride" sung by Binnie Hale.

P-97   *Blithe Spirit* Piccadilly Theatre, London July 2, 1941. Moved to St. James Theatre Mar. 23, 1942 and to the Duchess Theatre Oct. 6, 1942. (1,997) performances. Tried out at Opera House, Manchester on June 16, 1941 and then played Leeds.

An Improbable Farce written and directed by Noël Coward. Presented by H.M. Tennent Ltd. and John C. Wilson. Sets and Costumes by G.E. Calthrop.

CAST: Ruth Reeves (Edith), Fay Compton (Ruth Condomine), Cecil Parker (Charles Condomine), Martin Lewis (Dr. Bradman), Moya Nugent (Mrs. Bradman), Margaret Rutherford (Madame Arcati) Kay Hammond (Elvira)

SYNOPSIS: When novelist Charles Condomine and his wife Ruth invite Madame Arcati to perform a seance, they are wildly surprised when she succeeds in materializing Elvira, the ghost of Charles' first wife. Elvira wants Charles back, but the only way to his heart is to kill him. In this she fails, but succeeds in killing Ruth, whose ghost Madame Arcati also materializes. Charles' two wives drive him crazy until Madame Arcati finally exorcises them and Charles leaves the country hopefully leaving his "blithe" spirits to wreck havoc on his house.

REVIEWS:
The London Daily Mail, July 3, 1941: "This is riotously witty stuff. I laughed and laughed and laughed. If there are suggestions of bad taste, they are swamped by the delicious fun of it all, by the immaculate productions and by the fine performances."

London Times, July 3, 1941: "Without a single lapse into improbability it achieves the impossible. The author's light, easy, amusing way with ectoplasm, poltergeists, hypnotic trances and the like is so adriotly sustained, so much a matter of cause and effect on the comic plane.

NOTES: Beginning Aug. 20, 1942, while the production was at St. James Theatre, London, Coward played the role of Charles for two weeks. Cecil Parker then returned to the cast. The run of 1,997 performances was a record for a straight play in London, beaten only by the still running "Mousetrap" on Sept. 13, 1957. A touring company went out in Feb., 1942 starring Ronald Squire, Irene Brown, Ursula Jeans, and Agnes Lauchlan. The play also toured with *Present Laughter* (P-100) and *This Happy Breed* (P-101) under the banner of *Play Parade*. In Feb., 1942 there was a tour featuring Ronald Squire (Charles), Irene Browne (Ruth), Ursula Jeans (Elvira), Agnes Lauchlan (Madame Arcati). In Feb., 1944 E.N.S.A. sent out a company to the Middle East and the Continent with Emlyn Williams as Charles, Jessie Evans as Arcati, Adrianne Allen as Ruth and Leueen MacGrath as Elvira. From Oct. , 1945-Feb., 1946 another E.N.S.A. company featured John Gielgud playing Charles, Irene Browne this time as Arcati, Marian Spenser as Ruth and Hazel Terry as Elvira. *Sigh No More* (P-107) contains a ballet based on the play. For the film version see F-17. For the TV versions see T-3 , T-4, T-33, T-42. For the musical version entitled *High Spirits* see P-161. For subsequent productions see P-99, P-175, P-191, P-211, P-214, P-218. For radio versions see R-33, R-38, R-52. For publications see B-70, B-78, B-82.

P-98   *Blithe Spirit* Morosco Theatre, NY. Nov. 4, 1941 (657 performances)

Broadway premiere of the **light comedy by Noël Coward**. Produced & Directed by John C. Wilson. Sets by Stewart Chaney.

CAST: Clifton Webb (Charles Condomine), Peggy Wood (Ruth Condomine), Mildred Natwick (Madame Arcati), Leonora Corbett (Elvira), Philip Tonge (Dr. Bradman), Valerie Cossart (Mrs. Bradman), Doreen Lang (Edith)

SYNOPSIS: See P-97.

REVIEWS:
New York Daily News, Nov. 5, 1941: "Deliberately impudent. One of his most ingenious plots."

New York Journal-American, Nov. 5, 1941: "Hilariously funny, brilliantly clever and about as cockeyed as a play can be and still stay on the stage."

NOTES: The play was chosen as one of the ten best plays of 1941-42 and won the Drama Critics Circle Award as best play. After ending its run in July, 1942 the cast took a summer hiatus and reopened Sept. 1943 and ran 32 performances, preliminary to a road tour that included Chicago and San Francisco. For radio broadcast with this cast see R-38.

P-99   *Blithe Spirit* 25 wk. tour of **Noël Coward**'s light comedy beginning Sept. , 1942 beginning in Grand Theatre, Blackpool and going to Leeds, Bristol, Nottingham, Manchester, Liverpool, Sheffield, Hul, Newcastle, Edin- burgh, Glasgow, Aberdeen, Inveress, Carlisle, Cardiff, Northampton, Ox- ford, Leicester, Southsea, Coventry, Exeter and Bournemouth. Alternating with *This Happy Breed* (see P-101) and *Present Laughter* (see P-100) under the title *Play Parade*.

CAST: **Noël Coward** (Charles Condomine), Joyce Carey (Ruth Con- domine), Judy Campbell (Elvira) and Beryl Measor (Madame Arcati).

P-100   *Present Laughter* Haymarket Theatre, London. April 29, 1943 (38 perfor- mances). This was preceeded by a 25 week tour beginning on Sept. 20, 1942 in Grand Theatre, Blackpool and going to Leeds, Bristol, Nottingham, Manchester, Liverpool, Sheffield, Hul, Newcastle, Edinburgh, Glasgow, Aberdeen, Inverness, Carlisle, Cardiff, Northampton, Oxford, Leicester, Southsea, Coventry, Exeter and Bournemouth. Alternating with *This Happy Breed* (see P-101) and *Blithe Spirit* (see P-99) under the title *Play Parade*.

A Comedy written and directed by Noël Coward. Presented by H.M. Tennent Ltd. and John C. Wilson. Sets and costumes by G.E. Calthrop.

CAST: Jennifer Gray (Daphne), Molly Johnson (Miss Erikson), Billy Thatcher (Fred), Beryl Measor (Monica), **Noël Coward** (Garry Essen- dine), Joyce Carey (Liz Essendine), James Donald (Roland Maule), Gerald Case (Henry Lyppiatt), Dennis Price (Morris Dixon), Judy Campbell (Joanna Lyppiatt), Gwen Floyd (Lady Saltburn)

SYNOPSIS: Garry Essendine is, like Noël Coward, a famous and very theatrical actor about to begin a theatrical tour of Africa. He is surrounded by an entourage of loving friends including a Swedish maid, a efficient secretary, a valet, an estranged wife, a business manager and a producer. Their tight little crew is thrown by Henry's (the producer's) new wife, Joanna, who seduces Garry. The consquen- ces lead Garry back to the arms of his wife.

REVIEWS:
The Daily Telegraph, April 20, 1943: "Mr. Coward has laughed at the absurdities of his own world of the theatre before. This time his view is more detached than

of old. His chief characters are all members of a highly successful theatrical firm, with Mr. Coward himself playing Garry Essendine, the romantic actor who is the firm's chief asset. A production gleaming with polish like a lacquer cabinet."

NOTES: Although originally entitled *Sweet Sorrow*, the current title is taken from the Clown's Song in "Twelfth Night": "Present mirth hath present laughter." Coward wrote both *Present Laughter* and *This Happy Breed* for himself during April and May of 1939. Due to the war, they were not to be produced in 1939, despite getting as far as dress rehearsals on Aug. 30 & 31, 1939. War was declared on Sept. 3, 1939. Interrupted by Coward's war work, it was not until 1942 that the plays were produced. Two other plays (*Time Remembered* and *Blithe Spirit*) had been written in the interim and *In Which We Serve* (F-15) was written and filmed. Coward played in *Present Laughter* three more times. See P-110, P-115, P-147, P-148. For Broadway version see P-108. For TV versions see T-32, T-43, T-70. For publications see B-70, B-77, B-99. Also see P-108, P-164, P-190, P-194, P-198, P-202.

P-101   *This Happy Breed* Haymarket Theatre, London April 20, 1943 (38 performances)

A play by Noel Coward.   For production credits and tour see P-100. Produced alternately with *Present Laughter*.

CAST: Gwen Floyd (Mrs. Flint), Judy Campbell (Ethel), Joyce Carey (Sylvia), **Noel Coward** (Frank Gibbons), Gerald Case (Bob Mitchell), Billy Thatcher (Reg), Jennifer Gray (Queenie), Molly Johnson (Vi), Dennis Price (Sam), Meg Titheradge (Phillis Blake), Beryl Measor (Edie), James Donald (Billy)

SYNOPSIS: Beginning in June of 1919 when the Gibbons family first moves in to their new house at Clapham Common, we follow the family over the years until June 1939 when they move out. Along the way the family encounters Communism, the General Strike of May 1926, the depression, the abdication of King Edward and the entrance of WWII. Despite their daughter Queenie's running away and returning the family survives.

REVIEWS:
London Daily Telegraph, May 1, 1943: "*This Happy Breed* is Mr. Coward's tribute to John Citizen, the ordinary Englishman. It represents a most important development in the author's quality and power. Here for the first time in his brilliant career, we have him writing with sympathy, understanding, and admiration of the common man. As for Mr. Coward himself, he has never acted better than in this part, as the ex-soldier who is so sound of heart and so quietly proud of his English heritage."

NOTE: This was a sort of working class version of *Cavalcade* (see P-67) For film and TV version see F-16 & T-11, T-28, T-56. For publications see B-70, B-77, B-108.

P-102   *Noel Coward Singing Tours*: Jan., 1944 Trinidad, Feb. 21, 1944-May, 1944 South Africa,Indian tour included Ceylon, Chittagong, Dozahri, Denchapalong, Tambru Gat, Cox's Bazaar.

P-103   *ENSA Tour* November, 1944. Paris, Versailles Brussels. **Noël Coward** toured in the company of Bobby Howes, Nervo and Knox, Frances Day and Josephine Baker.

P-104   *Stage Door Canteen* London 1944. **Noël Coward** sang his songs.

P-105   *Private Lives* (revival) Apollo Theatre, London Nov. 8, 1944 (716 performances) Culmination of a 14 week tour beginning July 10, 1944 at Theatre Royal, Newcastle.

Revival of **Noël Coward's comedy**. Directed by John Clements. Designed by G. E. Calthrop. Produced by H.M. Tennent Ltd. and John C. Wilson.

CAST: Peggy Simpson (Sybil), John Clements (Elyot), Raymond Huntley (Victor), Kay Hammond (Amanda), Yvonne André (Louise)

SYNOPSIS: See P-61.

NOTES: Sybil was played by Leslie Brook on tour. On Dec. 10, 1945 Hugh Sinclair replaced John Clements and Googie Withers replaced Kay Hammond. The play was now set in the period "a few years ago."

P-106   *Stage Door Canteen* Concert Paris 1945
        Noël Coward appeared in the company of Marlene Dietrich and Maurice Chevalier.

P-107   *Sigh No More* Piccadilly Theatre, London. Aug. 22, 1945 (213 performances). Tried out at the Opera House, Manchester July 11, 1945. Then moved to Liverpool.

A revue written, composed and directed by Noël Coward. Decor by G.E. Calthrop. Choreography by George Carden, Sheila Nicholson and Wendy Toye. Conducted by Mantovani.

CAST: Cyril Ritchard, Madge Elliott, Graham Payn, Joyce Grenfell, Gail Kendal, Tom Linden, Gwen Bateman, Joy O'Neill, Daphne Anderson, Betty Matthews, Lance Hamilton, Ann Martin, Renee Stocker, John Hugo, Alan Clive, Josephine Wray, Howard Gilbert, Silvia Shmole, Gretta Grayson, Fedora Bernard, Cliff Gordon, Marion Gordon, Tom Linden.

MUSICAL NUMBERS: Sigh No More-Payn & All; Parting of Ways-Elliott & Ritchard; Mother and Daughter-Bateman & O'Neill; I Wonder What Happened to Him-Ritchard; Never Again-Payn & Girls; That is the End of the News-Grenfell; Loch Lomond-Kendal; Willy-Linden, Elliott & Ritchard; Wait a Bit, Joe-Payn; Nina-Ritchard, Kendal & Linden; The Merry Wives of Windsor-Elliott, Ritchard & Girls; Matelot-Payn; Blithe Spirit Ballet-Dancers; The Burchells of Battersea Rise-Ritchard, Elliott, Grenfell & Payn

REVIEWS:
London Times, Aug. 23, 1945: "A light easy, amusing entertainment, disconcertingly without the impress of a definite style—disconcertingly, because it has been 'written, composed, and directed' by Mr. Noël Coward. Mr. Coward's touch throughout is of the lightest. In one or two songs its is instantly recognizable and the stage is suddenly alive with acid wit."

NOTES: Coward appeared in the revue on the evenings of Sept. 5-6, 1945 in place of Cyril Ritchard, who had laryngitis. The understudy played the Sept. 5, 1945 matinee. The song "Nina" was written in during Coward's South African tour (P-102) and was premiered by Coward in Pretoria, South Africa. For recordings see D-31, D-32, D-33, D-65, D-66. For publications see B-61.

P-108   *Present Laughter* Plymouth Theatre, NY. Oct. 29, 1946 (158 performances)Tried out at Playhouse, Wilmington DE. Sept. 26, 1946

Broadway Premiere of **a comedy by Noël Coward**. Produced and directed by John C. Wilson. Sets by Donald Oenslager. Costumes for Miss Dalton and Miss Linden by Castillo. Other costumes supervised by Sylvia Saal.

CAST: Clifton Webb (Garry Essendine), Jan Sterling (Daphne), Grace Mills (Miss Erikson), Aidan Turner (Fred), Evelyn Varden (Monica), Doris Dalton (Liz Essendine), Chris Alexander (Rolan Maule), Gordon Mills (Hugo Lyppiatt), Marta Linden (Joanna Lyppiatt), Leonore Harris (Lady Saltburn)

SYNOPSIS: See P-100.

REVIEWS:

New York Times, Oct. 30, 1946: "Although *Present Laughter* is one of Noël Coward's unworthiest enterprises, this review will not be so dolorous as the occasion warrants. For, good or hackneyed, Mr. Coward can give casual lines hilarious inflections, and his whole point of view toward ordinary affairs is suitably crack-brained. At the moment he is writing a narrative of inferior quality—conventional, unimaginative and generally commonplace; and although Clifton Webb acts the chief part brilliantly, the pace of the performance would be slow even for a burial."

The New York Sun, Oct. 30, 1946: "Noël Coward's *Present Laughter* is far from being Noël Coward's best comedy. It is not continuously or devastatingly funny, but if offers a measure of entertainment and a precise, sharp and well-sustained performance from Clifton Webb. *Present Laughter* is second best Noël Coward, but it still has enough waggish moments to afford a generally entertaining evening."

NOTES: All of the critics commented on the poor manners of the opening night audience, who arrived late and seemed to compete with the actors for attention. When Coward finally saw this production on Feb. 7, 1947, he was appalled by the direction by Wilson, his former lover. He felt that the cast was tatty and fifth rate, except for Webb, who he thought was lacking in fire and virility, but compensated by comedy technique.

P-109   *Pacific 1860* Theatre Royal, Drury Lane, London. Dec. 19, 1946 (129 performances)

> **A musical romance written, composed and directed by Noël Coward.** Produced by Prince Littler on behalf of the Board of Theatre Royal, Drury Lane, Ltd. Sets and Costumes by G.E. Calthrop. Conducted by Mantovani. Orchestrations by Mantovani and Ronald Binge. Coward's Musical Assistant-Robb Stewart.

> CAST: Mary Martin (Elana Salvador), Sylvia Cecil (Rosa Cariatanza, her duenna), Maria Perilli (Solang, her maid), Winefride Ingham (Trudi, her cook), Maidie Andrews (Mrs. Stirling), Ann Martin (Louise), Irlin Hall (Caroline), Peggy Thompson (Henrietta), Joy O'Neill (Agnes), Daphne Peretz (Sarah), Ann Sullivan (Georgiana), Rose Hignell (Mrs. Cawthorne), Daphne Anderson (Penelope), Gwen Bateman (Mrs.Pehlham), Celia Lamb (Melia), Helen Horsey (Lady Grayshott), Moya Nugent (Miss Scobie), Betty Hare (Miss Teresa Scobie), Jacqueline Jones (Primrose Larch), Carol Graye (Kara), Elizabeth Todd (Maliane), Lucy Peters (Teleete), Jacqueline Browning (Laiela), Graham Payn (Kerry Stirling), Pat McGrath (Rollo), Tudor Evans (Mr. Stirling), Carl Jaffe (Felix Kammer), Cyril Butcher (Sir Lewis Grayshott), Denis Martin (Aden

Grayshott), John Warwick (D'Archy Grayshott), Peter Evans (Capt. Edward Harmby), Angus Menzies (Lord William Ravenscar), David Carey (James Culross), Peter Mosley (Evan St. Mawes), Grant Tyler (Canon Banks), Harry Weste (Hubert Cawthorne), Emlyn Weeks (Mr. Marryot), Gustav Sacher (Ayano), Howard Gilbert (Saul), Ronald Evans (Elisha), Anthony Kay (Paeno), Lionel Baker (Niahu)

SYNOPSIS: On the Cowardian island of Samola in 1860 a beautiful and famous diva, Elana Salvador arrives and meets the young planter's son, Kerry Stirling. They fall in love, part due to their age difference and, of course, reunite in time for the finale.

MUSICAL NUMBERS: Family Grace-T. Evans; If I Were A Man-A. Martin, Thompson, O'Neill, Peretz, Sullivan, & Hall; Dear Madame Salvador-Payn; My Horse Has Cast A Shoe-Martin & Payn; I Wish I Wasn't Quite Such A Big Girl-Anderson & Girls; Ka Tahua-Sacher & Servants; Bright Was The Day-Martin & Payn; Invitation to The Waltz-A. Martin, Thompson, O'Neill, Peretz, Sullivan, Hall, D. Martin, Warwick, P. Evans, Menzies & Carey; His Excellency Regrets-A. Martin, Thompson, O'Neill, Peretz, Sullivan, Hall, D. Martin, Warwick, P. Evans, Menzies & Carey; Dear Friends, Forgive Me, Pray-T. Evans; Make Way For Their Excellencies-Company; Fumfumbolo-Payn & Servants; One, Two, Three-Martin; This Is A Night For Lovers-Cecil, Perilli & Ingham; I Never Knew-Martin & Payn; This Is A Changing World-Cecil; Come Back to The Island-Company; Poor Lady in the Throes of Love-Cecil, Perilli & Ingham; This Is The Night-Company; Mother's Lament-Andres, Hignell & Bateman; Pretty Little Bridesmaids-A. Martin, Thompson, O'Neill, Peretz, Sullivan, & Hall; I Saw No Shadow-Martin; Wedding Chorus-Company; Finale-Bright Was The Day-Martin & Payn

REVIEWS:
The London Times, Dec. 20, 1946: "Mr. Coward no doubt judges the public mood shrewdly when he sets his daisy chain story in a beautiful, little known island of the Samolan Archipelago in 1860. ...music, which is amusing, tuneful and equable...and always there is Mr. Coward's sure handling of the stage to make it clear that this effect of the other, however simple is precisely what he intends it to be."

London Telegraph, Dec. 20, 1946: "Mr. Coward never falls below a certain degree of accomplishment and the entertainment he provides had the smooth grace and finished charm that we have learned to expect from his work."

London Evening Standard, Dec. 20, 1946: "Halfway through *Pacific 1860* I began to wonder if Noël Coward was having an excellent joke at our expense. Finally the awful thought occured that he might not be joking at all."

NOTES: Coward tailored this operette (which was earlier entitled both *Samolo* and *Scarlet Lady* and at one point intended for Yvonne Printemps) for Mary Martin (making her London debut) and for his current lover, Graham Payn (who would appear in several more Coward pieces). At first Coward was delighted with Martin, calling her "a dream girl, quick and knowledgeable; she has all the mercurial charm of Gertie at her best with a sweet voice and with more taste." This honeymoon soon ended as Martin's husband, Richard Halliday got into a great row over whether Mary would wear a hat on stage or not. This arguement, coupled with the show's failure, divided Martin and Coward for several years. Throughout the short run of the show Coward called the theatre which housed it "Dreary Lane." After the opening Coward added three new songs: "Uncle Harry"-Payn, McGrath, A. Martin, Thompson, O'Neill, Peretz, Sullivan, & Hall; "The Party's Going With A Swing"-Payn, McGrath, Anderson, & Lamb; "Gipsy Melody"-Cecil, with Perilli & Ingham; This last song replaced "Poor Lady in the Throes of Love." The original script called for a song called "Alice Is At It Again" for Mary Martin's Act II entrance, but Miss Martin found it dirty and refused to sing it. Coward later recorded it himself (See D-98). For recording of score see D-34, D-35, D-42, D-67, D-68, D-69, D-70, D-71, D-72, D-125, D-126. For publications see B-61, B-78, B-95.

P-110   *Present Laughter* (revival) Haymarket Theatre, London. April 16, 1947
(528 performances). Tried out at the Royal Court Theatre, Liverpool
April 7, 1947.

A revival of the **comedy by Noël Coward**. Same production credits as
P-100.

CAST: Same as P-100, except Avis Scott (Daphne), Daphne Newton (Miss
Erikson), Joan Swinstead (Monica), Robert Essison (Roland), Peter Gray
(Morris), Moira Lister (Joanna).

NOTES: Coward was replaced by Hugh Sinclair on July 14, 1947. Coward went to the Haymarket to say goodbye on July 24, 1947 to find Sinclair playing the first act with almost no voice. Coward played the last two acts himself.

P-111   *Peace In Our Time* Lyric Theatre, London. July 22, 1947 (167 performances).   Moved to the Aldwych Theatre on Sept. 29, 1947.Tried out at the Theatre Royal, Brighton, July 15, 1947.

A play by Noël Coward. Produced by H.M. Tennent Ltd. and John C. Wilson. Directed by Alan Webb, **under the supervision of Noël Coward.** Sets and Costumes by G.E. Calthrop.

CAST: Helen Horsey (Alma), Bernard Lee (Fred Shattock), Elspeth March (Janet Braid), Maureen Pryor (Doris Shattock), Trevor Ward (Mr. Grainger), Sybil Wise (Mrs. Grainger), Beatrice Varley (Nora Shattock), Hazel Terry (Lyia Vivian), Douglas Vine (A Man), Kenneth More (George Bourne), Stella Chapman (A Woman), Olaf Pooley (Charley Bannister), Derik Aylward (Bobby Paxton), Ralph Michael (Albrecht Richter), Dora Bryan (Phyllis Mere), Geroge Lane (Mr. Lawrence), Irene Relph (Maudie), Daphne Maddox (Gladys Mott), Brian Carey (Alfie Blake), Charles Russell (German Soldier), Richard Scott (Herr Huberman), Betty Woolfe (Frau Huberman), Anthony Peek (First SS Guard), William Murray (Second SS Guard), Philip Guard (Billy Grainger), Michael Kent (Dr. Venning), Manfred Priestley (Ben Capper), Dandy Nichols (Lily Blake), William Murray (Mr. Williams), Alan Badel (Stevie), John Molecey (Archie Jenkins), Michael Anthony (Kurt Forster), Janet Barrow (Mrs. Massiter), Peter Drury (Third SS Guard), Douglas Vine (Fourth SS Guard)

SYNOPSIS: Taking place in a pub from 1940-45, the play explores what England would have been like under Nazi occupation.

REVIEWS:
London Daily Telegraph, July 21, 1947: "The play is one long thrill. Mr. Coward's account rings true. No less than his sincerity one admires his theatrical skill, which enables him to build up to a finish at once plausible and telling. This play cannot possibly fail. It is too moving, too exciting, too deft — and too timely. We need to be reminded, just now, that we are people of spirit."

NOTES: The working title was *Might Have Been*. For publications see B-78, B-96.

P-112   *Point Valaine* Embassy Theatre, London Sept. 3, 1947 (37 performances)

London premiere of **Noël Coward's play.** Produced by Envoy Productions. Directed by Peter Glenville. Designed by Tanya Moiseiwitsch.

CAST: Marjorie Hellier (Mrs. Tillett), Charles Cameron (Major Tillett), Doris Rogers (Mrs. Birling), Aurdrey Fildes (Elise), Anthony Ireland (Mortimer Quinn), Ben-Astar (Stefan), Pauline Henriques (Lola), Louise Tammavoh (May), Basil Appleby (George Fox), Neville Mapp (Ted Burchell), Mary Ellis (Linda Valaine), Isobel Ohmead (Mrs. Hall-Fenton),

Pat Smylie (Gladys), Prudence Hyman (Phyllis), Alexis Milne (Sylvia), Ambrosine Phillpotts (Hilda James), Allan Cuthbertson (Martin Welford)

SYNOPSIS: See P-80.

REVIEWS:
London Times, Sept. 4, 1947: "For all its rather calculated violence the scene holds, and should communicate the pathos of a woman who is time's fool. If in this performance the pathos is suggested rather than communicated the fault would not seem to be in the writing. Some passes, no doubt, are emotionally overwrought, but their weakness is unduly stressed by the sluggish pace of the acting."

The London Observer, Sept. 7, 1947: "Happily, there are gleams of the other, wittier Coward—expressed in the irony of the peripatetic novelist who is for a moment a guest at the hotel, peeping and botanizing with a grim pleasure that has begun to fray into boredom."

NOTES: This production was performed by the Old Vic Company at the Playhouse in Liverpool for 37 performances beginning Oct. 18, 1944 with most of the same cast.

P-113   *Tonight At 8:30* Limited Tour of 6 American Cities opening in Baltimore Nov. 10, 1947 continuing to Boston, Dec., 1947, Philadelphia, San Francisco Jan. 1948, Los Angeles, National Theatre, NY Feb. 20-Mar. 13, 1948 (26 performances on Broadway)

Revival of 6 of the 10 **one act plays by Noël Coward** (see P-83). Produced by Homer Curran in association with Russell Lewis and Howard Young. **Directed by Noël Coward.** Sets by George Jenkins. Gowns by Hattie Carnegie. Costumes supervised by James Morgan. Conducted by Frank Tours. Dances by Richard Barstow.

CAST: Gertrude Lawrence, Graham Payn, Norah Howard, Valerie Cossart, Philip Tonge, Sarah Burton, Booth Colman, William Roerick, Rhoderick Walker.

The plays were: *Ways and Means, Family Album, Red Peppers, Hands Across The Sea, Fumed Oak & Shadow Play*

REVIEWS:
New York Times, Feb. 21, 1948: "Under Mr. Coward's adroit direction, the plays are produced with taste. The cast is a good one. Everything crackles except the entertainment. Miss Lawrence still looks as mischievous and sinful as Eve, cast

luster around her everywhere, sings in an enchantingly round and coquettish style, wears costumes magnificently and chops the wit cleanly out of the dialogue. We miss the brisk clicking of Mr. Coward's harp style, the lines rattling out like machine-gun fire. There is not much point in reviving these trifles without Mr. Coward in the battery."

New York Herald-Tribune, Feb. 21, 1948: "Noël Coward is badly missing in the revival of his *Tonight At 8:30.* The Coward touch is still there in the staging; his great leading lady, Gertrude Lawrence, is as supremely artful as ever, and the incidental songs are even more mellifluous now than they were in 1936. Where the theatre's jack-of-all-trades has made a lamentable mistake is in not appearing in the vignettes which he and Miss Lawrence made so peculiarly their own."

NOTES: The performance began with an overture which included: "Dance Little Lady," "Room With a View," "Someday I'll Find You," "You Were There" and "I'll Follow My Secret Heart." On Jan. 24, 1948 in San Francisco, Graham Payn was taken ill. Coward played the matinee which included *Shadow Play* and *Hands Across The Sea.* In all Coward subbed for Payn two other times. This was the last time Coward and Lawrence performed together on a stage.

P-114   *Private Lives* (revival) Plymouth Theatre, NY. Oct. 4, 1948 (248 performances)

A revival of **Noël Coward's comedy.** Produced by John C. Wilson. Directed by Martin Manulis. Set by Charles Elson. Miss Bankhead's clothes by Mainbocher.

CAST: Tallulah Bankhead (Amanda), Barbara Baxley (Sybil), Donald Cook (Elyot), William Langford (Victor), Therese Quadri (Louise)

SYNOPSIS: See P-61.

REVIEWS:
New York Times, Oct. 5, 1948: "After seventeen years, Noël Coward's *Private Lives* is still outrageously amusing. Since virtually the same thing is true of Tallulah Bankhead, the revival at the Plymouth is the funniest item in the season so far. Among the sardonic delights of *Private Lives* is the cheerful disdain with which the chief egotists dismiss respectability. Mr. Coward has a genius for venomous phrases."

New York Daily News, Oct. 5, 1948: "*Private Lives* is a tour de force which had sophisticates chattering when Mr. Coward and Gertrude Lawrence first played it here. It was, one said, slight and brittle, and in other than expert hands it wouldn't be much. The same can be said today—but the swivelnecked Mr. Cook and the hag-voiced Miss Bankhead struck me as experts."

New York Post, Oct. 5, 1948: "Noël Coward's *Private Lives* is a kind of theatrical tightrope, stretched high and perilously across nothingness, and playwright and actors must move back and forth on it and balance themselves with great care and brilliance, lest they tumble down into oblivion."

NOTES: This was the end of very successful tour including the Harris Theatre in Chicago (July 22, 1947) where it broke Coward records and played 26 weeks and the Curran Theatre in San Fransico (June 1, 1948). It also played Columbus, Ohio April 5-7, 1948, Indianapolis April 8-10, 1948, the American Theatre in St. Louis April 12-24, 1948, Cedar Rapids, IA April 26, 1948, Des Moines, IA April 27, 1948, Kansas City, MO April 28-May 1, 1948, Joplin, MO May 3, 1948, Tulsa, OK May 4, 1948, OK City, OK May 5, 1948, Wichita May 6, 1948, Pueblo, CO May 7, 1948, Colorado Springs May 8, 1948, Denver May 10-11, 1948, Salt Lake City, UT May 14, 1948, Seattle, WA May 17-22, 1948, Portland, OR May 24-27, 1948, Sacramento May 29, 1948. On the road Sybil was played by Buff Cobb and Victor by Phil Arthur.

P-115   *Joyeux Chagrins* (*Present Laughter*) Theatre Edouard VII, Paris. Nov. 17, 1948. Played until Dec. 26, 1948. Tried out in Bruxelles Oct. 29, 1948.

A French translation of **Noël Coward's comedy.**

NOTES: Noël Coward appeared in this french translation of his play (see P-100.) as Max Aramont, the renamed Garry Essendine.

P-116   *Fallen Angels* (revival) Ambassadors Theatre, London. Nov. 29, 1949 (299 performances) Culmination of tour that opened at the Shakespeare Memorial Theatre, Stratford-on-Avon, Nov. 14, 1949 and at Plymouth Nov. 21, 1949. *Fumed Oak* was played as a curtain riser.

Revival of **Noël Coward's comedy.** Produced by Lance Hamilton and Charles Russell and Peter Daubeny Productions. Directed by Willard Stoker. Designed by Anthony Holland.

CAST: *Fumed Oak*: Hermione Baddeley (Doris Gow), Diana Lincoln (Elsie Gow), Maurice Denham (Henry Gow), Hermione Gingold (Mrs. Rocket); *Fallen Angels*: Hermione Baddeley (Julia Sterroll), Gerald Case (Frederick Sterroll), Diana Lincoln (Saunders), Maurice Denham (William Banbury), Hermione Gingold (Jane Banbury), Paul Dupuis (Maurice Duclos)

SYNOPSIS: See P-36.

REVIEWS:
The London Tatler, Jan. 8, 1950: "I have the greatest respect for the two queens of revue, Hermione Baddeley and Hermione Gingold: but they are juvenile bubblers and their handling of the comedy has the mature vigour of experienced comediennes. On those lines much of it is wildly funny....It is the fifties laughing uproariously at what the twenties thought daring and faintly disquieting."

NOTES: The show included a curtain raiser of *Fumed Oak*. When Coward saw this production and the outrageous camping of the two Hermiones on Nov. 23, 1949 in Plymouth, he was just a tad livid. He called their performances vulgar, silly, unfunny, and disgraceful. Although he advised cutting *Fumed Oak,* the show went on and was a large success, making Coward all the more bitter. According to *Stage By Stage* by Peter Daubeny (John Murray, London 1952) "I was astonished that Noel approved the casting of the two Hermiones. He went further. He would not, he said, consent to a London production of *Fallen Angels* except with these two players." Tunes were meant to change.

P-117   *Ace of Clubs* Cambridge Theatre, London. July 7, 1950 (211 performances)

> A new musical play **written, composed and directed by Noël Coward**. Sets and Costumes by G.E. Calthrop. Conducted by Mantovani. Orchestrations by Ronald Binge and Mantovani.
>
> CAST: Bubbly Rogers (Elaine), Sylvia Cecil (Rita Barbury), Raymond Young (Benny Lucas), Robb Stewart (Sammy Blake), Myles Eason (Felix Fulton), Jean Carson (Baby Belgrave), Victor Harman, Ronald Francis, Stanley Howlett (Hercules Brothers), Elwyn Brook-Jones (Joseph Snyder), Patrick Westwood (Gus), Pat Kirkwood (Pinkie Leroy), Graham Payn (Harry Hornby), Eileen Tatler (Clarice), Renee Hill (Eva), Jean Inglis (Yvonne Hall), Gail Kendall (Mavis Dean), Jack Lambert (Detective-Inspector Warrilove), Michael Darbyshire (Policeman), Philip Rose (Mr. Price), Stella White (Mrs. Price), Peter Tuddenham, Colin Kemball, Norman Warwick (Juvenile Delinquents), Manfred Priestley (First Plain-Clothes Man), Christopher Calthrop (Second Plain-Clothes Man), Don Fitz Stanford (Drummer), George Selfe, Richard Gill, Jacques Gautier(Waiters), Sylvia Veerney, Margaret Miles, June Whitfield, Erica Yorke, Pamela Devis, Lorna Drewes, Vivien Kearns (Ace of Clubs Girls)

SYNOPSIS: At the Soho night club, The Ace of Clubs, the lead singer, Pinkie Leroy is rescued from a thug's advances by a young sailor names Harry Hornby.

When she inadvertently takes a mackintosh with a dangerous parcel in its pocket it gets into Harry's hands. Pinky and Harry fall in love, but at one of her floor shows, Harry, who still has the mob's parcel, is kidnapped. When he escapes, package still in tow (which we by now know is an emerald necklace), the package somehow gets switched with one of the showgirl's gag birthday presents (a pair of falsies!). Pinkie returns the wrong package to the mob. The show girl gets the emeralds and the mob gets the falsies. The police discover the mix up and arrest the gangsters leaving Pinkie to Harry and the finale of the Ace of Clubs to be cheered by the audience.

MUSICAL NUMBERS: Top of the Morning-Carson and Girls; My Kind of Man-Kirkwood; This Could be True-Kirkwood & Payn; Nothing Can Last Forever-Cecil; Something About a Sailor-Payn; I'd Never, Never Know-Kirkwood; Three Juvenile Delinquents-Tuddenham, Kemball & Warwick; Sail Away-Payn; Josephine-Kirkwood; Would You Like to Stick a Pin in My Balloon?-Girls; In a Boat On a Lake with My Darling-Sextet; I Like America-Payn & Girls; Why Does Love Get In the Way-Kirkwood; Evening In Summer-Cecil; Time for Baby's Bottle-Carson, Inglis & Kendall; Chase Me, Charlie-Kirkwood;

REVIEWS:
London News Chronicle, July 2, 1950: "It is not the ace of trumps. But it will serve to take a trick. Early on Miss Kirwood and Mr. Payn have a shy little duet with a shy little dance "This Could be True," which is to my way of thinking and responding, the most charming item in a score quite reasonably full of charming items. The wittiest is a trio for 'Three Juvenile Delinquents'. The show is lively and well ordered. Coward put out his witty tongue three of four times, but for the rest he keeps it in either cheek, alternately, achieving a little masterpiece of convention, banality, puiqancy, freshness, cuteness, impudence and characteristic self-expression."

Variety, July 10, 1950: "The expected Noël Coward touch of slick sophisticating and acid humor is missing from his new all-British musical. There's no lack of tuneful, scintillating numbers. Two or three, at least, may soon be popular hits. But the best numbers have nothing to do with the plot."

NOTES: One song "Three Theatrical Dames" was intended as a cabaret number, but was dropped. It was performed eventually as an item in *The Night of 100 Stars* at the London Palladium on June 28, 1956 by Peter Ustinov, Laurence Harvey, and Paul Scofield. For recording see D-102. For a recording of the score see D-36, D-37, D-39, D-73, D-74, D-75. For publications see B-61, B-79.

P-118   *Charity Matinee* Drury Lane Theatre, London

Noël Coward sang at this annual event.

P-119 *Actor's Orphanage Garden Party* June 19, 1951

Noël Coward made a personal appearance for this, his favorite charity.

P-120 *Island Fling* Country Playhouse, Westport, CT July 22, 1951
(8 performances). Played the next week at the Cape Playhouse, Dennis, MA;
Returned to Country Playhouse, Westport for another 8 performances.

CAST: Chester Stratton (John Blair Kennedy), Edith Meiser (Maud
Witterby), Gordon Mills (Capt. Christopher Mortlock*), Berry Kroeger
(Sir Georg Shotter), Claudette Colbert (Lady Alexandra Shotter),
Reginald Mason (Punalo Alani), Don Glenn (Sanyamo), Peter Boyne
(Edward Honey), Cherry Hardy (Cuckoo Honey), A. J. Herbert (Admiral
Turling), Esther Mitchell (Mrs. Turling), Roy Johnson (Robert Frome),
Leon Janney (Hali Alani)

SYNOPSIS: Taking place on the Cowardian island of Samola, the play concerns
the wife of a Governor of the colony, Lady Alexandra Shotter and an islander Hali,
who developes quite a yen for her.

REVIEWS:
New York Telegraph, Aug. 20, 1951: "When I say that I had one of the pleasantest
playgoing evenings in a long time, it is an understatement. Mr. Coward is no
profound writer, but he is a deft comedian and he has certainly written a funnier
and better play than his *Present Laughter*, which ran a season on Broadway."

NOTES: For London production see P-143.

P-121 *The Lyric Revue* Lyric Theatre, Hammersmith May 24, 1951 (141 performances) Transferred to to Globe Theatre, London Sept. 26, 1951 (313
performances) Tried out at the Pavilion, Bournemouth, May 7, 1951 and
Brighton the following week.

A revue presented by Tennent Productions Ltd. Directed by William
Chappell. Decor by Loudon Sainthill.

NOTES: Noël Coward contributed one quartet, "Don't Make Fun of The Festival"
sung by Graham Payn, Dora Bryan, Robert Huby and Ian Carmichael

P-122 *Concert of his songs* at the Theatre Royal, Brighton. Oct., 1951. Tryout for
Noël Coward's cabaret act at the Café de Paris, London.

P-123   *Café de Paris*, London. Oct. 29, 1951. **Noël Coward** debuted his cabaret act, despite his failing voice, to great acclaim and good business.

P-124   *Relative Values* Savoy Theatre, London. Nov. 28, 1951 (477 performances)

A light comedy written and directed by Noël Coward. Produced by H.M. Tennent Ltd. and John C. Wilson. Sets and costumes by Michael Relph.

CAST: Richard Leech (Crestwell), Renee Hill (Alice), Angela Baddeley (Moxie), Gladys Cooper (Felicity, Countess of Marshwood), Dorothy Batley (Lady Hayling), Simon Lack (Peter Ingleton), Charles Cullum (Sir John Hayling), Judy Campbell (Miranda Frayle), Ralph Michael (Nigel), Hugh McDermott (Don Lucas)

SYNOPSIS: When film star Miranda Frayle decides to marry Sir John, son of the Countess of Marshwood the whole estate is upset. Most especially Moxie, the Countess' maid. She decides to leave when Miranda is to pay a visit. It seems that Moxie is Miranda's sister and they haven't seen each other for many, many years. The Countess convinces Moxie to stay and she gets to hear the incredible lies about her sister's supposed past. When she finally reveals her identity, she confronts Miranda with the truth, sending the film star back to Hollywood and leaving the class system status quo.

REVIEWS:
London Daily Mail, Nov. 29, 1951: "There remains the old Coward genius for giving near wit the sparkle of pure wit."

Variety, Dec. 1, 1951: "Though this latest Coward opus is written in his inimitable style it lacks the piquant whimsicality of *Blithe Spirit,* his last straight play in London [sic]. But it is, first and last, Gladys Cooper's evening supplying, as she does, a perfect foil for the traditional Cowardesque technique."

John o' London's Weekly, Dec. 14, 1951: "Coward's sense of humour has not changed radically through the years. It is his theatricality that, I feel, will harm Coward's comedies in years ahead. They will act well as period pieces. *Relative Values* is a return journey to the best days of the younger Coward, the period that produced, within five years or so, *Hay Fever* and *Private Lives.*"

NOTES: When the show toured to the Hippodrome, Conventry on May 4, 1953, Moxie was played by Mona Washbourne, Sir John by Donal Finlay, Nigel by Peter Gray, Miranda by Glen Alyn and Don Lucas by Gordon Tanner. On May 11, 1956 the *New York Herald Tribune* mentioned that the play might be done in the 1956-57 season with Gladys Cooper recreating her role and Edna Best playing Moxie. This never happened. For subsequent productions see P-137, P-183. For publications see B-71, B-78, B-104.

P-125   *Café de Paris*, London. Jan. 13, 1952. **Noël Coward** did a double act with Mary Martin, then starring in the London production of *South Pacific*. This was a special benefit for the Actor's Orphanage, of which Coward was president. This was their first professional reunion since the debacle of *Pacific 1860* (P-109). According to Coward's diaries, "Mary tore the place up."

P-126   *The Vortex* (revival) The Lyric Theatre, Hammersmith, London Mar. 4, 1952 (75 performances). Tried out at the Theatre Royal, Brighton Feb. 18, 1952 and at Cambridge Feb. 25, 1952. Moved to the Criterion Theatre, London April 9, 1952.

Revival of **Noël Coward's play**. Produced by Tennent Productions. Directed by Michael Macowan. Sets by G.E. Calthrop. Costumes by William Chappell.

CAST: Neville Prescott (Preston), Adrianne Allen (Helen Saville), Robert Andrews (Pauncefort Quentin), Sylvia Coleridge (Clara Hibbert), Isabel Jeans (Florence Lancaster), Anthony Forwood (Tom Veryan), Dirk Bogarde (Nicky Lancaster), Nicholas Hannen (David Lancaster), Janet Butler (Bunty Mainwaring), Peter Jones (Bruce Fairlight)

SYNOPSIS: See P-35.

REVIEWS:
London Daily Mail, April 10, 1952: "It may be laboriously stagey in contrivance, and what were once arresting effects — like the frantic piano-playing at every crisis in this neurotic household — may have faded with the years into rather tiresome tricks. But the wit still sparkles and that final hysterical scene between the son and the mother with a lover of just his own age has lost little of its old dramatic sting."

NOTES: This production is set in the original period the 1920's. On April 9, 1952 Michael Gough took over the role of Nicky.

P-127   *Café de Paris,* London. June 16, 1952. A return engagement of **Noël Coward's act**. Celebrities at the opening included the Duchess of Kent, Danny Kaye, Errol Flynn, Claudette Colbert, Alfred Lunt and Lynn

Fontanne, The Oliviers (Larry & Vivien Leigh) & Douglas Fairbanks Jr. Coward played until July 12, 1952.

REVIEWS:
New York Post, July 3, 1952: "A distinguished evening of wit and hilarity"

P-128   *The Globe Revue* Globe Theatre, London, July 10, 1952 (234 performances) Tried out at the Theatre Royal, Brighton, June 30, 1952.

A revue presented by Tennent Productions Ltd. Directed by William Chappell. Decor by Loudon Sainthill.

NOTES: **Noël Coward** contributed two numbers: "Kensington By-pass" sung by Graham Payn and "There Are Bad Times Just Around the Corner" sung by Payn, Dora Bryan, Joan Heal and Ian Carmichael.

P-129   *Quadrille* Phoenix Theatre, London. Sept. 12, 1952 (329 performances)Tried out at the Opera House, Manchester July 15, 1952 (8 wks tour including Manchester, Edinburgh, Glasgow & Liverpool.)

A comedy written and directed by Noël Coward (Direction with grateful acknowledgement to Miss Fontanne and Mr. Lunt). Produced by H.M. Tennent Ltd. and John C. Wilson. **Incidental Music by Noël Coward.** Sets and Costumes by Cecil Beaton.

CAST: John Gill (Rev. Edgar Spevin), Moya Nugent (Sarah), Pamela Grant (Gwendolyn), Michael Allison (Waiter), Timothy Forbes Adam (Courier), Griffith Jones (The Marquess of Heronden), Marian Spencer (Mrs. Charlotte Diensen), Gordon Phillott (Catchpole), Lynn Fontanne (The Marchioness of Heronden), Joyce Carey (Lady Harriety Ripley), Sybil Wise (Foster), Rhoderick Walker (Footman), Alfred Lunt (Axel Diensen), Sylvia Coleridge (Octavia), Charles Rennison (Waiter), Allegra Nichole, Derek Prouse, Betty Hare, Gillian Raine, Richard Scott, Dorothy Blythe (Travellers)

SYNOPSIS: When the Marquess of Heronden runs away with the wife of a Railroad magnate, their spouses follow after, only to fall in love with each other, and beginning the whole circle again.

REVIEWS:
Morning Advertiser, Sept. 13, 1952: "Does not reach Coward's high standard. Nevertheless, it has a number of merits. A variant of *Private Lives* has been richly decked with Victorian elaborations. There is no looseness about the knitting of

the threads, and the play has a satisfying symmetry and a high polish. His incidental music is exactly attuned to the matters in hand."

NOTES: For publications see B-78, B-101.

P-130   *Café de Paris*, London. Nov. 9, 1952. Another benefit for the Actor's Orphanage with **Noël Coward** doubling with Mary Martin, on the night after her closing in *South Pacific*.

P-131   *The Apple Cart* Haymarket Theatre, London. May, 1953 played until Aug. 1, 1953. (100 performances)

A play by George Bernard Shaw. Directed by Michael Macowan. Produced by Tennent Productions. Sets and costumes by Loudon Sainthill.

CAST: **Noël Coward** (King Magnus), Margaret Leighton (Orinthia), Geoffrey Dunn (Pamphilius), John Humphry (Sempronius), George Rose (Boanerges), Sylvia Syms (Princess Alice), Hugh Manning (Balbus), John Moffatt (Nicabar), Peter Bayliss (Crassus), Archibald Batty (Pliny), Laurence Naismith (Proteus), Margaret Rawlings (Lysistrata), Alexis France (The Queen), Cecil Trouncer (Mr. Vanhattan)

NOTES: This, one of the few times Coward appeared in a play not his own, was to be the last.

P-132   *Café de Paris,* London. May ?-June 20, 1953. **Noël Coward** played his act at the same time as appearing in Shaw play.

P-133   *Stars At Midnight* London Palladium. May 28, 1953. **Noël Coward** appeared at special performance benefitting the Actor's Orphanage.

P-134   *Coronation Gala* Savoy Hotel, London June 3, 1953

Noël Coward performed his Cabaret act two more times for the Gala, after appearing in *The Apple Cart* (P-131) and at the *Café de Paris* (P-132).

P-135   *After The Ball* Globe Theatre, London. June 10, 1954 (188 performances). Tried out at the Royal Court Theatre, Liverpool. Mar. 1, 1954 (12 wks. tour included Cardiff, Bournemouth, Birmingham, Bristol, Manchester, Leeds, Newcastle, Edinburgh, Glasgow, Brighton, and Southsea)

A musical play with book, music and lyrics by Noël Coward. Directed by Robert Helpmann. Sets and Costumes by Doris Zinkeisen. Orchestrations by Philip Green. Conducted by Philip Martell. Based on *Lady Windermere's Fan* by Oscar Wilde.

CAST: Betty Felstead (Lady Jedburgh), Anna Halinka (Lady Paisley), Ailsa Gamley (Lady Cowper-Cowper), Lois Green (Lady Plymdale), Pam Marmount (Lady Stutfield), Dennis Bowen (Mr. Dumby), John Morley (Lord Paisley), Tom Gill (Cecil Graham), Vanessa Lee (Lady Windermere), Peter Graves (Lord Windermere), Graham Payn (Mr. Hopper), Shamus Locke (Lord Darlington), Irene Browne (The Duchess of Berwick), Patricia Cree (Lady Agatha Carlisle), Leslie Pearson (Parker), Donald Scott (Lord Augustus Lorton), Mary Ellis (Mrs. Erlynn), Raymond Savigear (Guy Berkeley), Bill Horsley (Mr. Rufford & Footman), Silvia Beamish (Lady Ruckinge), Maureen Quinney (Miss Graham), Marion Grimaldi (Mrs. Hurst-Green), Margaret Gibson (Mrs. Arthur Bowden)

SYNOPSIS: When the young Lady Windermere, who believes there is an absolute standard of morality, finds that her husband has been seeing Mrs. Erlynn, a woman of tarnished reputation, she decides to run off with Lord Darlington. At this point we find out that Mrs. Erylnne is actually Lady Windermere's mother. In the end, with the help of Mrs. Erlynn, Lady Windermere learns that morality and the appearance of morality are not the same.

MUSICAL NUMBERS: Oh What A Century It's Been-All; I Knew That You Would Be My Love-Lee & Graves; Mr. Hopper's Chanty-Payn, Bowen & Gill; Sweet Day-Lee; Stay on the Side of the Angels-Locke; Oh What A Century (reprise)-Green, Marmount, Bowen & Morley; Sweet Day (reprise)-Lee; Creme de la Creme-All; Light Is The Heart-Ellis; May I Have The Pleasure-Browne, Cree, & Payn; I Offer You My Heart-Lee & Locke; Sweet Day (reprise)-Lee; Why Is It The Woman Who Pays?-Marmount, Green & Grimaldi; Aria-Lee; Go. I Beg You, Go-Ellis & Lee; London at Night-Scott, Bowen, Gill, Payn, Graves & Locke; Clear Bright Morning-Lee; All My Life Ago-Ellis; London at Night (reprise)-Scott, Bowen, Payn & Gill; Oh, What a Season This Has Been-Ladies; Farewell Song-Scott; Something On A Tray-Browne, Felstead, Halinka & Gamley; Faraway Land-Payn; May I Have The Pleasure (reprise)-Cree & Payn, I Knew That You Would Be My Love (reprise)-Graves; Sweet Day (reprise)-Lee; Light Is The Heart (reprise)-Ellis

REVIEWS:
Punch (London), June 16, 1954: "One of Coward's difficulties in turning *Lady Windermere's Fan* into a musical comedy is that, not unnaturally, he finds the

Victorians period-funny, so that, although he used some of Wilde's epigrams in addition to his own, he cannot escape a pointed note of burlesque. There is still a good deal in *After The Ball* to be enjoyed simply as musical comedy. Mr. Coward has written pleasing music and a number of extremely nimble lyrics."

NOTES: This musical version of Wilde's play should have been right up Coward's alley, but somehow it did not gel, although the score is beautiful. The conductor and orchestrator were replaced in Liverpool. The Liverpool personel were Norman Hackforth (conductor) and J. Marr Mackie (orchestrator). Three songs, "Good Evening, Lady Windermere," "What Can It Mean?," and "Letter Song" were cut. "Clear Bright Morning" was added. For recording of the score see D-127. For publications see B-61.

P-136   *Night of 100 Stars* London Palladium. July 24, 1954. **Noël Coward** appeared in a Gala performance benefitting the Actor's Orphanage.

P-137   *Café de Paris,* London. Oct. 24, 1954. **Noël Coward** opened a four week run of his new act.

NOTES: Coward introduced some new songs including "A Bar On The Piccolo Marina."

P-138   *Royal Command Performance* London Palladium Nov. 1, 1954.

NOTES: According to Noël Coward's diaries, after arriving to find Bob Hope tight-liped, Jack Buchanan quivering and Norman Wisdom sweating, he knew that the audience would be vile. Nevertheless, he sang "Uncle Harry" (*Pacific 1860*), "Mad Dogs," and "There Are Bad Times Just Around The Corner" (*Globe Revue*) to a cheering reception. The press called him the hit of the evening.

P-139   *Quadrille* Coronet Theatre, NY Nov. 3, 1954 (149 performances)

> Broadway premiere of **Noël Coward's romantic comedy.** Produced by John C. Wilson and H.M. Tennent, Ltd. Directed by Alfred Lunt. Sets and costumes by Cecil Beaton. Sets supervised by Charles Elson. Costumes supervised by Stanley Simmons. Lighting by Jean Rosenthal.

> CAST: Madeleine Clive (1st Woman), Byron Mitchell (1st Man), Patricia Quinn O'Hara (Buffet Manageress), Jerome Kilty (Rev. Edgar Spevin), Phyllis Connard (Sarah), Nina Reader (Gwendolyn), Bruce Webster (Courier), Brian Aherne (Hubert), Edna Best (Mrs. Axel Diensen), Harold Crane (Catchpole), Lynn Fontanne (Serena, Marchioness of Heronden), Brenda Forbes (Lady Harriet Ripley), Mildred Clinton

(Foster), Rhoderick Walker (Footman), Alfred Lunt (Axel Diensen), Dorothy Sands (Octavia), Mildred Clinton (2nd Woman), Michael Lewis (2nd Man)

SYNOPSIS: see P-129.

REVIEWS:
New York Times, Nov. 4, 1954: "It lacks the hard, ricocheting wit of Mr. Coward's characteristic works and it looks suspiciously like the libretto for a Viennese operetta. But this theatregoer is not throwing any stones at it this morning. For there is some excellent writing in *Quadille*, especially a rhapsody about railroading in America. There is also a respect for the two chief character, who are people of mind and valor, and free of piety. *Quadille* is an acting piece for the Lunts, and the Lunts are, as always, superbly accomplished."

New York Daily Mirror, Nov. 4, 1954: "Coward wrote this romantic comedy to display the virtuosity of his friends and partners. It is a disarming work—not robusly amusing, never very moving, but freighted with some of the master's more incisive and urbane lines. There is little plot and not too much action, but the characters are quite wonderful."

New York Post, Nov. 4, 1954: "If it by no means reveals Mr. Coward in one of his wittiest or most urbane moods, it does show him writing what he correctly calls a 'romantic comedy' with considerable grace and style."

NOTES: This is the last production under the banner of Transatlantic Productions, Inc. (see P-80) Due to severe drinking problems, Jack Wilson, who was Coward's first lover, was becoming impossible to deal with and the Lunts and Coward disbanded the corporation that began with *Point Valaine*.

P-140   *Wilbur Clark's Desert Inn*, Las Vegas, NV. June 7, 1955

> **Noël Coward** made his Vegas Debut singing his own songs accompanied and arranged by Peter Matz. He was accompanied by Carlton Hayes and His Orchestra.

MUSICAL NUMBERS: Opening Medley: I'll See You Again, Dance Little Lady, Poor Little Rich Girl, A Room With A View, Someday I'll Find You, I'll Follow My Secret Heart, If Love Were All, Play Orchestra Play; Uncle Harry; Loch Lomond; A Bar On The Piccola Marina; World Weary; Nina; Mad Dogs and Englishmen; Matelot; Alice Is At It Again; A Room With A View; Let's Do It (Music by Porter); The Party's Over Now

REVIEWS:

Variety, June 15, 1955: "Las Vegas, Flipping, Shouts 'More!' As Noël Coward Woos 'Em in Cafe Turn. Mr. Coward socked across his message to a glittering first night audience of theatrical luminaries here last week. 'A Bar on the Piccolo Marina' is hilarity itself."

NOTES: Celebrities attending the opening included: Frank Sinatra, Judy Garland, The Bogarts (Bogie & Bacall), The Nivens, Joan Fontaine, Zsa Zsa Gabor, the Joe Cottens, Peter Glenville, Laurence Harvey. As the run went on Burns and Allen, the Jack Bennys, Kay Thompson, Jeanette MacDonald, Cole Porter, Tallulah Bankhead, the Van Johnsons, and the Sam Goldwyns were reported in the audience. On June 27 & 28, 1955 four performances were recorded live by Columbia Records. See D-97. The closing on July 5, 1955 attracted the likes of Ethel Merman and Bankhead once again.

P-141   *Fallen Angels* (revival) The Playhouse, NY. Jan. 17, 1956 (239 performances)

Revival of **Noël Coward's comedy**. Produced by Charles Bowden and Richard Barr in association with H. Ridgely Bullock Jr. Directed by Charle Bowden. Sets and lighting by Eldon Eldor. Costumes by Patton Campbell. Hats by Mr. John.

CAST: Nancy Walker (Julia), William Windom (Frederick), Alice Pearce (Jasmine Saunders), William LeMessena (William Danbury), Margaret Phillips (Jane), Efrem Zimbalist Jr. (Maurice)

SYNOPSIS: See P-36.

REVIEWS:
New York Post, Jan. 18, 1956: "Since *Fallen Angels* always was distinctly minor Coward, those of us who are among his veteran admirers certainly can't say he is being betrayed in this rather free revival. As a latecomer to the ranks of Miss Walker's enthusiasts, I think her humor justifies everything."

New York Journal-American, Jan. 18, 1956: "It seems utterly incredible that anybody, including Noël Coward, would attempt to write a three-act play about two women getting drunk. But that's what Mr. Coward has done in *Fallen Angels*, which was revived at the The Playhouse last night, and thanks to Nancy Walker, one of the drunks, he very nearly gets away with it. The final tote of *Fallen Angels* indicates that Nancy Walker is certainly one of our funniest ladies."

NOTES: Saunders was played by Louise Hoff from Feb. 6-22, 1956. This was the first American revival of the comedy.

P-142 *Carnival of the Animals* Carnegie Hall, NY. April 7, 1956

Noël Coward appeared as part of a one night only concert conducted by André Kostelanetz to recite the Ogden Nash verses.

REVIEWS:
New York Times, April 9, 1956: "Mr. Coward's British accent makes him perhaps not the ideal reciter of such un-British humor. His great personal charm, however, captivated Saturday night's audience."

New York Daily Mirror, April 9, 1956: "The suave and urbane Noël Coward delighted us with his reading of Ogden Nash verses set to Saint-Saen's tuneful and satiric *Carnival of Animals*. It was evident that the orchestra as well as the audience had a high old time of during this amusing interlude."

NOTES: A cut version of the piece was presented on the Ed Sullivan Show (see T-12) and Coward recorded the poems on Columbia Records (see D-86, D-101)

P-143   *South Sea Bubble* Lyric Theatre, London April 25, 1956 (276 performances). Tried out at the Opera House, Manchester Mar. 19, 1956 and toured to Liverpool, Edinburgh, Glasgow and Newcastle.

West End premiere of **a light comedy by Noël Coward** (*Island Fling* in US, originally titled *Home and Colonial*) Produced by H.M. Tennent. Directed by William Chappell. Sets and costumes by Peter Snow.

CAST: Arthur Macrae (John Blair Kennedy), Peter Barkworth (Capt. Christopher Mortlock), Ian Hunter (Sir George Shotter), Vivien Leigh (Lady Alexandra Shotter), Alan Webb (Punalo Alani), William Peacock (Sanyamo), John Moore (Edward Honey), Joyce Carey (Cuckoo Honey), Nicholas Grimshaw (Admiral Turling), Daphne Newton (Mrs. Turling), Eric Phillips (Robert Frome), Ronald Lewis (Hali Alani)

SYNOPSIS: see P-120.

REVIEWS:
The Sunday London Times, April 29, 1956: "*South Sea Bubble* is an almost perfect example of cooperation between author, company and director. It is the best play Mr. Coward has written for a long time."

NOTES: This was a revision of *Island Fling* (P-120) which in turn was subsequently entitled *Home and Colonial*. Although intended for Gertrude Lawrence, she never played it. Due to her pregnancy Vivien Leigh was replaced by Elizabeth Sellers on Aug. 13, 1956, thus causing the early demise of the show. On Sept. 21, 1956 Joyce Carey was replaced by Daphne Newton and she was repleaced by Betty Woolfe. See T-13 for details of Act II being televised. Capt. Mortlock was played by Clifford Elkin in Manchester. For publications see B-79, B-106.

P-144   *Nude With Violin* Globe Theatre, London. Nov. 7, 1956. Tried out at the Olympia, Dublin Sept. 24, 1956 followed by 4 wks tour of Liverpool, Manchester, Newcastle & Edinburgh.

A light comedy by Noël Coward. Produced by H.M. Tennent Ltd. Directed by John Gielgud and Noël Coward. Sets and Costumes by Paul Anstee.

CAST: John Gielgud (Sebastien), Gillian Webb (Marie-Celeste), John Sterland (Clinton Preminger, Jr.), Joyce Carey (Isobel Sorodin), Anne Castle (Jane), Basil Henson (Colin), Patricia Raine (Pamela), David Horne (Jacob Friedland), Patience Collier (Cherry-May Wateron), Douglas Robinson (Fabrice), Thomas Baptiste (Obadiah Llewellyn), Keith Green (George), Nicky Edmett (Lauderdale)

SYNOPSIS: When the famous modern artist, Paul Sorodin dies, it is revealed to his family that he painted none of his own pictures. They were done by anyone handy: his mistresses, a Jamaican missionary, a small boy.

REVIEWS:
New York Times, Dec. 2, 1956: "An evening that starts brilliantly and ends in anticlimax."

NOTES: The end of Act I and both scenes of Act II were televised. See T-14 . Michael Wilding replaced John Gielgud. For publications see B-79, B-93.

P-145   *Nude With Violin* Belasco Theatre, NY Nov. 14, 1957 (80 performances) Tried out in Wilminton, DE Oct. 14, 1957 and at the Forrest Theatre, Philadelphia Oct. 2, 1957.

Broadway premiere of a comedy written and directed by Noël Coward. Produced by The Playwrights Company and Lance Hamilton and Charles Russell. Sets by Oliver Smith. Costumes by Peggy Clark. Costumes by Frank Thompson

CAST: Noël Coward (Sebastien), Therese Quadri (Marie-Celeste), William Traylor (Clinton Preminger, Jr.), Joyce Carey (Isobel Sorodin), Angela Thornton (Jane), John Ainsworth (Colin), Iola Lynn (Pamela),

Morris Carnovsky (Jacob Friedland), Luba Malina (Anya Pavlikov), Mona Washurne (Cherry-May Waterton), Robert Thurston (Fabrice), Cory Devlin (Obadiah Lewellyn), Robert Wark (George), Bobby Alford (Lauderdale)

SYNOPSIS: See P-144.

REVIEWS:
New York Mirror, Nov. 16, 1957: "Coward is quite amusing as the resourceful gentleman's gentleman. *Nude With Violin* spells hilarity as slick as a seals overcoat."

New York Times, Nov. 15, 1957: "He [Coward] plays the part of the valet. But even here the clipped phrase seems a little slovenly. The cackling vocal style of twenty years ago, the meticulous design of the spoken sentence and the acid emphasis has succumbed to maturity and good nature. With the sting gone there is not much exhileration left."

New York Herald Tribune, Nov. 15, 1957: "It is delightful to have Mr. Noël Coward back in the theatre. It would be even more delightful to have him back in a play."

NOTES: The play was cancelled from Jan. 24-30, 1957 due to Coward's illness. Ironically *Present Laughter* opened on Jan. 31, 1957 and alternated with *Nude With Violin* for the next two weeks. See P-147.

P-146   *Conversation Piece* (revival) Barbizon-Plaza Theatre, NY   Nov. 18, 1957
(8 performances)

Off Broadway revival of **Noël Coward's operette**. Produced by David Shaber, Philip Wiseman and William Synder by special arrangement with Lance Hamilton and Charles Russell. Directed by Philip Wiseman. Sets and Lighting by Tony Walton. Musical Direction by John Kander. Musical Numbers staged by John Heawood. Costumes by Audre. Orchestrations by Peter Matz.

CAST: Louise Troy (Sophie), Sasha von Scherler (Martha), Mildred Cook (Mrs. Dragon), Rene Paul (Paul, Duc de Chaucigny-Varennes), Joan Copeland (Melanie), Joan Kibrig (Rose), Gerald Garrigan (The Marquis of Sheere), William Woodson (Earl of Harringford), Cherry Hardy (Duchess of Beneden), Sarah Burton (Lady Julia Charteris), Jonathan Morris (Lord St. Marys), Mabel Cochran (Countess of Harringford), Elwyn Harvey (Lady Braceworth), Corinna Manetto (Hannah), James Valentine (Butler), Leamond Dean (Sailor), Gloria Kaye (Girl)

SYNOPSIS & MUSICAL NUMBERS: See P-75.

REVIEWS:

New York Times, Nov. 19, 1957: "It is difficult, if not impossible to separate *Conversation Piece* from the daintiness and exquisite charm of the actress who played it first. As a theatrical conceit the play is probably as good as it ever was. Mr. Coward was not trying to devastate the populace with wit and brilliance, but to write a mannered entertainment with music."

New York Post, Nov. 19, 1957: "Noël Coward has a romantic as well as a cynical mood. Despite a few humorous songs and a couple of waspish Coward lines of dialogue, he is completely on the level. It seems rather heavy-handed and uninspired romanticism and only intermittenly interesting. *Conversation Piece* is mild Coward."

New York Journal-American, Nov. 19, 1957: "A highly stylized piece-I think it may do very well this time around."

NOTES: Although Arthur Miller's sister, Joan Copeland has had a nice career, and Louise Troy went on to star in the Coward production of *High Spirits*, the only real star to emerge from this production was musical director John Kander, who is one half of the very successful Kander and Ebb.

P-147   *Present Laughter* Belasco Theatre, NY Jan. 31, 1958 (6 performances) Alternating with *Nude With Violin*.

A revival of a comedy written and directed by **Noël Coward**. Personel the same as P-145, except Miss Gabor's Gown's by Scaasi.

CAST: **Noël Coward** (Garry), Eva Gabor (Joanna), Therese Quadri (Contesse de Vriac), William Traylor (Roland Maul), Joyce Carey (Liz), John Ainsworth (Morris), Mona Washbourne (Monica), Robert Thurston (Fred), Avril Gentles (Miss Erikson), Winston Ross (Henry), Angela Thornton (Daphne)

NOTES: This was a start of a West Coast tour alternating with *Nude With Violin* (see P-148 for tour). After suffering the slings and arrows of *Nude With Violin*'s reception, Coward allowed no critics to review *Present Laughter*. On Feb. 8, 1958 Coward gave his last two performances on the Broadway stage: *Nude With Violin* in the afternoon and *Present Laughter* in the evening.

P-148   *Present Laughter* alternating with *Nude With Violin*. Curran Theatre, San Francisco Feb. 11, 1958 (4 wks.), Huntington Hartford Theatre, Hollywood Mar. 10, 1958 (*Present Laughter*) Mar. 11, 1958 (*Nude*) (2 wks ending on Mar. 22, 1958)

Same personnel as P-145.

CAST: Same cast as P-147 for *Present Laughter* and same cast as P-145 for *Nude*, except for Patricia Devon playing Pamela and Avril Gentiles playing Anya Pavlikov.

SYNOPSIS: See P-100.

REVIEWS:
Nude With Violin:
San Francisco Examiner, Feb. 12, 1958: "Never has a vehicle been driven more amusingly or at such a fast comic pace. It's ripping fun. The play is naughty and clever, awfully simple, but simply delightful."

Present Laughter:
Los Angeles Examiner, Mar. 11, 1958: "The advent of Noël Coward in the Los Angeles theatre last night made us regret all the years we have spent without him. He brought with him the glitter of mock wickedness, the tingle of the choicely framed epigram, the atmosphere of delightfully impossible wit and divertingly malicious banter."

NOTES:
The reviews were much more hospitable on the west coast than on the east and the plays did well.

P-149   *Night of 100 Stars* London Palladium July, 1958

Noël Coward did his medley of hits, "What's Going To Happen To The Tots?" and "Let's Do It"

P-150   *Look After Lulu* Henry Miller's Theatre, NY. Mar. 3, 1959 (39 performances). Tried out in New Haven Jan. 19, 1959

A farce by Noël Coward. Based on "Occupe-toi d'Amelie" by Feydeau. **Directed by** Cyril Ritchard & **Noël Coward**. Sets and Costumes by Cecil Beaton. Lighting by Raymond Sovey.

CAST: Tammy Grimes (Lulu), Rory Harrity (Bomba), Craig Huebling (Valery), Bill Berger (Emile), Barbara Loden (Gaby), Sasha Von Scherler (Yvonne), Grace Gaynor (Paulette), George Baker (Philippe de Croze),

Paul Smith (Adonis), Eric Christmas (Gigot), Polly Rowles (Claire), Roddy McDowall (Marcel Blanchard), Ellis Rabb (General Koschnadieff), Jack Gilford (Herr Van Putzeboum), David Fauklner, David Thurman (Florist's Boys), Kurt Kasznar (Prince of Salestria), Reva Rose (Rose), Earl Montgomery (Oudatte), John Alderman (Cornette), Arthur Malet (Mayor), William Griffis (Photographer), Philippa Bevans (Aunt Gabrielle), Ina Cummings (Little Girl), David Hurst (Inspector of Police)

SYNOPSIS: Lulu, an attractive tart, is entrusted to Marcel while her true love, Phillipe goes off to the army. Marcel lures her into a mock wedding and the farce begins.

REVIEWS:
New York Herald Tribune, Mar. 4, 1959: "Mr. Coward has not neglected the stout old maxim that a true-blue farce should roll. *Look After Lulu* rolls. The only trouble is that it keeps rolling backward."

New York Daily News, Mar. 4, 1959: "There were excellent moments of gay and truly farcical humor, but they were followed by moments of desperation in which people seemed to be trying to keep things going while the stagehands changed the grand sets or the girls changed their wonderful robes and hats or the men took off their pants."

New York Daily Mirror, Mar. 4, 1959: "A swanky first-night audience relished Noel's charade. The white-tie-and-chinchilla set shook the Miller with howls of delight. As for your aisle-sitter, he won't have to visit a doctor this morning to have his ribs taped up. And he cannot recommend that you *Look after 'Lulu.'*"

NOTES: This was the only time that Coward adapted the work of another playwright. For publication see B-91.

P-151   *Look After Lulu* Royal Court Theatre, London July 29, 1959 (165 performances)

West End premiere of **Noël Coward's adaptation of Feydeau's farce**. Directed by Tony Richardson. Decor by Roger Furse. Produced by England Stage Company in association with H.M. Tennent and L.O.P. Ltd.

CAST: Vivien Leigh (Lulu), Robert Stephens (Philippe de Croze), Sean Kelly (Adonis), Peter Sallis (Gigot), Meriel Forbes (Claire), Anthony Quayle (Marcel Blanchard), Lawrence Davidson (General Koschnadieff), George Devine (Herr Van Putzeboum), Max Adrian (Prince of Salestria), Anne Bishop (Rose), Arnold Yarrow (Oudatte), Peter Wyatt (Cornette),

Richard Golden (Mayor), David Ryder (Photographer), Barbara Hicks (Aunt Gabrielle), Michael Bates (Inspector of Police)

SYNOPSIS: See P-150

P-152 *London Morning* London Festival Ballet Company, Festival Hall, London. July 14, 1959. Barcelona May, 1959. In repertoire for three years.

A ballet with scenario and music composed by Noël Coward. Choreographed by Jack Carter. Conducted by Geoffry Corbett. Designed by William Constable. Costumes by Norman McDowell.

CAST: John Gilpin, Jeanette Minty, Anton Dolin, Marilyn Burr

REVIEWS:
London Times, July 15, 1959: "Anyone who tries to approach *London Morning* as a ballet is doomed to disappointment...*London Morning* is much more accurately revue dance-sketches which are to be seen in variety shows or on televison. The atmosphere is frankly artificial and it is out of date too, so is the music, much of which would not have seemed avant-garde if Sullivan had penned it in the rein of our previous queen."

London Stage, July 23, 1959: "Mr. Coward has created a tableu vivant which has been set in motion by Jack Carter, far less inspired than usual, to a commonplace Coward score."

New York Morning Telegraph, July 24, 1959: "Jack Carter's choreography is impeccable. The reception was enthusiastic and Mr. Coward beamed from his box—as in old days..."

NOTES: Although the critics carped as usual, there were eight curtain calls at the opening of this thirty minute ballet. When asked by the press, "Is there anything you can't do, Mr. Coward?," he replied, "I could not dance in my own ballet." For recording see D-128.

P-153 *Waiting In The Wings* Duke of York's Theatre, London. Sept. 7, 1960 (191 performances). Tried out at Olympia Theatre, Dublin Aug. 8, 1960.

A play by Noël Coward. Directed by Margaret Webster. Produced by F.E.S. Plays Ltd in association with Michael Redgrave Productions Ltd. Sets and Costumes by Motley.

CAST: Sybil Thorndike (Lotta Bainbridge), Lewis Casson (Osgood Meeker), Marie Lohr (May Davenport), Graham Payn (Perry Lascoe), Mary Clare (Almina Clare), William Hutt (Alan Bennet), Una Venning (Cora Clarke), Maidie Andrews (Bonita Belgrave), Norah Blaney (Maude Melrose), Maureen Delaney (Deidre O'Malley), Edith Day (Estelle Craven), Margot Boyd (Miss Archie), Betty Hare (Dora), Jean Conroy (Doreen), Nora Nicholson (Sarita Myrtle), Jessica Dunning (Zelda Fenwick), Molly Lumley (Topsy Baskerville), Eric Hillyard (Dr. Jevons)

SYNOPSIS: The adventures and escapades of the dwellers of a home for aged actresses. How are they to get a new sun room and still retain the poise of stardom?

REVIEWS:
Sunday London Times, Sept. 11, 1960: "*Waiting In The Wings* will give a great deal of quiet and legitimate pleasure to many theatregoers."

The Theatre (London), Nov., 1960: "There is no one quite like Coward for sentimentalizing the magic world beyond the footlights. This time he takes us further showing a group of elderly actresses living in a theatrical charity home. They say and do very funny things but somehow it is all rather sad. Mr. Coward never sets foot in the door that might lead to an answer to their fates. If he had done so his play would have been much more plausible."

NOTES: Although the play was to be produced by Coward's old friend, Binkie Beaumont for H.M. Tennent, the two had a falling out over the play and Coward was very hurt by the whole sordid mess, thus giving the play to the inexperienced producer, Michael Redgrave. Coward felt that if Beaumont had produced it, it may have been more of a hit. For publications see B-71, B-79, B-113.

P-154 *Sail Away* Broadhurst Theatre, NY Oct. 3, 1961 (167 performances). Tried out at the Colonial Theatre, Boston, MA Aug. 9, 1961, then Forrest Theatre, Philadelphia, PA Sept. 5, 1961.

A new musical comedy **written, composed and directed by Noël Coward**. Produced by Bonard Productions in association with Charles Russell. Musical numbers and dances staged by Joe Layton. Sets by Oliver Smith.

Costumes by Helene Pons and Oliver Smith. Lighting by Peggy Clarke. Musical Direction and Dance Arrangements by Peter Matz. Orchestrations by Irwin Kostal. Vocal Arrangements by Fred Werner.

CAST: Elaine Stritch (Mimi Paragon), James Hurst (Johnny), Grover Dale (Barnaby Slade), Charles Braswell (Joe, the Purser & Ali), Keith Prentice (Shuttlworth), James Pritchett (Rawlings), C. Stafford Dickens (Sir Gerald Nutfield), Margaret Mower (Lady Nutfield), Henry Lawrence (Elmer Candijack), Betty Jane Watson (Maimie Candijack), Alan Helms (Glen Candijack), Patti Mariano (Shirley Candijack), Jon Richards (Mr. Sweeney), Paula Bauersmith (Mrs. Sweeney), Alice Pearce (Elinor Spencer-Bollard), Patricia Harty (Nancy Foyle), Paul O'Keefe (Alvin Lush), Evelyn Russell (Mrs. Lush), Margalo Gillmore (Mrs. Van Mier), David Evans (Carrington), James Frasher (Deck Steward), Richard Woods (Man from American Express) Bobby Allen, Paul Gross, Bridget Knapp, Mary Ellen O'Keefe, Dennis Scott, Christopher Votos (The Little Ones), Ann Fraser (Girl Passenger), Jere Admire, Don Atkinson, Gary Crabbe, Pat Ferrier, Dorothy Frank, Gene Gavin, Curtis Hood, Wish Mary Hunt, Cheryl Kilgren, Nancy Lynch, Alan Peterson, Alice Shanahan, Dan Siretta, Gloria Stevens (Chorus)

SYNOPSIS: The good ship Coronia is about to set sail from NY on a Mediterranean cruise. After everyone is safely shown to their cabins, we meet Mimi Paragon, the cruise director. When youthful passenger, John Van Mier meets the older Mimi he begins to fall in love with her. At the same time, Nancy Foyle and Barnaby Slade begin their "beatnik love affair." When they arrive in Tangiers Mimi and Johnny move forward in their love story, until on the last night of the cruise Mimi tries to explain to Johnny why they could never make a success of life together. By the time the passengers disembark in NY, Nancy has her Barnaby and Johnny comes back and takes Mimi away with him for the happy ending.

MUSICAL NUMBERS: Come to Me-Stritch & Stewards; Sail Away-Hurst; Come to Me (reprise)-Stritch; Sail Away (reprise)-Hurst & Company; Where Shall I Find Him?-Harty; Beatnick Love Affair-Dale, Harty & All; Later Than Spring-Hurst; The Passenger's Always Right-Braswell & Stewards; Useful Phrases-Stritch; Where Shall I Find Her (reprise)-Dale; Go Slow, Johnny-Hurst; You're A Long, Long Way From America-Stritch & Company; The Customer's Always Right-Braswell & Arabs; Something Very Strange-Stritch; Italian Interlude-The Company; The Little One's ABC-Stritch & Children; Don't Turn Away From Love-Hurst; When You Want Me-Dale & Harty; Later Than Spring (reprise)-Stritch; Why Do the Wrong People Travel?-Stritch; When You Want Me (Reprise)-The Company; Finale-All

REVIEWS:

Show Business Illustrated, Oct. 3, 1961: "In its dry dock at the Colonial Theatre in Boston, *Sail Away* looked like a first class cruise for the New York season. After 50 years in the theatre, his versatility remains undiminished. When Coward hits the mark, the wings begin to waver. In its tryout stage *Sail Away* had three rousers: a jingoistic first act final, a wicked children's number salted with sly poison, and a showstopper on the stupidity of travelers. In addition, the music is melodious, the lyrics alternately tender and clever."

New York Times, Oct. 4, 1961: "It was a delightful idea of Mr. Coward's to have Mimi Paragon air a leash of dogs on the deck. It was a poodle's own idea to forget that he was a performer. No sooner had an actor responded with the resourcefulness his role as a steward required when the young man in Mimi's life entered and murmered romantically that here was something unusual in the air tonight."

New York Herald Tribune, Oct. 4, 1961: "The librettist-composer never does get around to introducing all of his amiable people to one another. let alone welding them together into a cheerful 'party-mix.'"

New York Journal-American, October 4, 1961: "It struck me that the power was missing from the revered Coward dialogue. Not the Noël Coward I used to know. *Sail Away*, in spite of all the rooting and the shouting, doesn't really go anywhere."

New York World-Telegram & Sun, Oct. 4, 1961: "*Sail Away* easily could have qualified as the musical of the year if it had opened in 1936."

NOTES: Originally planned as a vehicle for Rosalind Russell, Kay Thompson, Judy Holliday and even announced as a possibility for Ethel Merman (Leonard Lyons, April 4, 1961: "Ethel Merman's next starring role may be in Noel Coward's new musical."), Elaine Stritch was finally engaged to play Mimi Paragon, co-starring with Jean Fenn. *Sail Away* underwent some very extreme sea changes in its out-of-town tryout. A leading lady (Verity) played by Jean Fenn was eliminated and merged with the character played by Elaine Stritch, combining both the romantic and comic leads into one. This entailed cutting the character of Fenns's husband played by William Hutt and losing several songs were cut on the road: "Bronxville Darby and Joan," "This Is A Night For Lovers," "This Is A Changing World" (both originally from *Pacific 1860*), and "I Am No Good At Love." The first two were recorded by Coward and Layton as opening night gifts. For recording of these two numbers see D-115. "Go Slow Johnny" and "Don't Turn Away From Love" were added to the score for Johnny. Besides all of his other contributions, Coward created the poster art and was the voice of Captain Wilberforce. For Original Cast see D-129. See also D-109, D-171 for Coward's own recording of the score.

P-155   *Gallery First Nighters' Dinner in Honor of Noël Coward.* Criterion Restaurant, London. May 23, 1962.

NOTES: Noël Coward was given a tribute dinner followed by a cabaret in which he participated. Coward sang some of his hits ending with "I'll See You Again." Peter Greenwell accompanied. Elaine Stritch also sang. Also appearing were Kenneth MacDonald, Tony Sumpson and Jill and Terry. The cabaret was arranged by Leslie Bloom.

P-156   *Sail Away* Savoy Theatre, London June 21, 1962. Tried out in Bristol May 31, 1962.

West End Premiere of **Noël Coward's musical**. Produced. by Harold Fielding. **Directed by Noël Coward**. Choreographed by Joe Layton. Sets and costumes by Loudon Sainthill. Lighting by Michael Northen. Musical direction by Gareth Davies.

CAST: Elaine Stritch (Mimi Paragon), David Holliday (Johnny), Grover Dale (Barnaby Slade), John Hewer (Joe, the Purser & Ali), Tony Adams (Shuttlworth), David Henderson-Tate (Rawlings), Edward Steel (Sir Gerald Nutfield), Hester Paton Brown (Lady Nutfield), Kim Grant (Elmer Candijack), Stella Moray (Maimie Candijack), Nicholas Chagrin (Glen Candijack), Gillian Martindale (Shirley Candijack), Sydney Arnold (Mr. Sweeney), Edith Day (Mrs. Sweeney), Dorothy Reynolds (Elinor Spencer-Bollard), Sheila Forbes (Nancy Foyle), Stephen Ashworth (Alvin Lush), Margaret Christensen (Mrs. Lush), Mavis Villiers (Mrs. Van Mier), Betty Hare (Eileen Leopard)

SYNOPSIS: See P-154

MUSICAL NUMBERS: Same as P-154, except for the addition of "Bronxville Darby and Joan," which was cut from the Broadway production.

REVIEWS:
London Observer, June 24, 1962: "As musicals go nowadays, Noël Coward's *Sail Away* is a lightweight affair. The score fades instantly from memory, but serves as a peg for two good numbers. But on the whole it's a smooth, well drilled, old fashioned excuse for spending three hours sweltering underground."

London Financial Times, June 22, 1962: "Basically, its a good old fashioned musical: colour scenes, and comedy scenes, backdrops of Tangier and the Pantheon, travel jokes, American jokes, and smutty jokes, and a clutch of shipboard romances. The second act of *Sail Away* offers just about the most enjoyable hour to be found in the West End at the moment."

London Daily Sketch, June 22, 1962: "By the first curtain I was hating the whole thing. Then suddenly unexpectedly the star Elaine Stritch burst into life. She gave a solo show that saved the night."

NOTES: For recording of London Cast see D-130.

P-157 *Sail Away* Her Majesty's Theatre, Sydney, Australia July 19, 1963

> Australian Premiere of **Noël Coward's musical.** Directed by John Hewer. **Supervised by Noël Coward.** Musical direction by Terry Vaughan. Produced by J.C. Williamson Theatres Ltd. by special arrangement with Harold Fielding. Sets and costumes by Loudon Saint Hill. Dances directed by Brenda Averty from Joe Layton's originals.
>
> CAST: Maggie Fitzgibbon (Mimi Paragon), Kevin Colson (Johnny), Jon Dennis, Carol Walker, Diana Bell, Alathea Siddons, Letty Craydon, Alton Harvey, Shirley Donald, Ron Shand, Charley McCallum.

SYNOPSIS AND MUSICAL NUMBERS: See P-154

REVIEWS:
Mellba Herald: "Most polished, fast moving musical for many a day."

P-158 *Charity Gala*, Washington DC Nov. 9, 1963.

> **Noël Coward performed** songs from his cabaret act.

P-159 *Private Lives*(revival) Hampstead Theatre Club, London April 24, 1963. Transferred to the Duke of York's Theatre July 3, 1963 (216 performances)

> Revival of **Noël Coward's comedy.** Produced by Michael Codron. Directed by James Roose-Evans. Designed by Christian Kurvenal.
>
> CAST: Rosemary Martin (Amanda Prynne), Edward de Souza (Elyot), Sarah Harter (Sybil), Roger Booth (Victor), Janie Booth (Louise)

SYNOPSIS: See P-61.

NOTES: This highly acclaimed revival was the beginning of what Coward termed "Dad's Renaissance."

P-160   *The Girl Who Came To Supper* Broadway Theatre, NY Dec. 8, 1963 (112 performances). Tried out in Boston Sept. 28, 1963, Toronto Oct., 1963, and Philadelphia Nov. , 1963.

A new musical with **music and lyrics by Noël Coward**. Book by Harry Kurnitz. Based on 'The Sleeping Prince' by Terrence Rattigan. Entire Production staged by Joe Layton. Produced by Herman Levin. Musical direction and vocal arrangments by Jay Blackton. Sets by Oliver Smith. Costumes by Irene Sharaff. Orchestrations by Robert Russell Bennett. Lighting by Peggy Clark. Dance Music by Genevieve Pitot.

CAST: José Ferrer (Regent), Florence Henderson (Mary Morgan), Tessie O'Shea (Ada Cockle), Irene Browne (Queen Mother), Roderick Cook (Peter Northbrook), Sean Scully (King Nicholas), Carey Nairnes (Major-Domo), Chris Gampel (Colonel Hofmann), Lucie Lancaster (Baroness Brunheim), Peter Pagan (Mr. Grimes), Marian Haraldson (Jessie Maynard), Jack Eddleman (Tony Morelli), Maggie Worth (Violetta Vines), Murray Adler (Simka), Ilona Murai (Lady Sunningdale), Donna Monroe (First Girl), Ruth Shepard (Second Girl), Nancy Lynch, Julie Drake, Sheila Forbes, Jami Landi, Sandy Leeds, Carmen Morales, Mari Shelton, Gloria Smith, Mary Zahn, Ivan Allen, Robert Fitch, José Gutier-rez, Peter Holmes, Scott Ray, Paul Reid Roman, Dan Siretta, Mike Toles (Dancers), Jeremy Brown, Kellie Brytt, Carol Glade, Elaine Labour, Donna Monroe, Ruth Shepard, Maggie Worth, Jack Eddleman, John Felton, Dell Hanley, Barney Johnston, Art Matthews, Bruce Peyton, Jack Rains, Mitchell Taylor (Singers)

SYNOPSIS: On the night before the coronation of King George V in 1911, chorus girl Mary Morgan catches the eye of the Prince Regent of Carpathia and he invites her to dine at the Embassy. When they are alone, the Regent plies her with vodka, but his attempts at seduction are constantly interrupted. After having too much to drink, Mary passes out. When morning comes Mary assumes that she has given her all for love. When the Queen Mother's lady-in-waiting is taken ill, Mary is commandeered and bejewelled and besabled, is swept off to Westminster Abbey for the Coronation. Mary and the Regent eventually fall in love, but realize in the end the impossibility of their union. They part with the frail hope that they will meet again someday.

MUSICAL NUMBERS: Swing Song; Yasni Kozkolai-Ensemble; My Family Tree-Ferrer; I've Been Invited To A Party-Henderson; When Foreign Princes Come To Visit Us-Nairnes & Chorus; Sir or Ma'am-Cook & Henderson; Soliloquies-Ferrer & Henderson; Lonely-Ferrer; London: London Is A Little Bit Of All Right, What Ho Mrs. Brisket, Don't Take Our Charlie For the Army, Saturday Night at the

Rose and Crown-O'Shea, Scully & Ensemble; Here And Now-Henderson; Coronation Chorale-Henderson, Ferrer & Ensemble; How Do You Do, Middle Age-Ferrer; Curt, Clear And Concise-Ferrer & Cook; The Coconut Girl: Welome To Pootzie Van Doyle, The Coconut Girl, Paddy MacNeil And His Automobile, Swing Song, Six Lilies Of The Valley, The Walla Walla Boola-Henderson; This Time It's True Love-Ferrer & Henderson; I'll Remember Her-Ferrer

REVIEWS:
New York World Telegraph, Dec. 10, 1963: *"The Girl Who Came To Supper* is elegant, charming and delightfully cast. Mr. Coward has evokes, brought back to us and put into graceful, gracious melody a time of elegance and good living. A shining musical offering a theatrical treat."

New York Times, Dec. 9, 1963: "In this quartet of tunes — 'London Is A Little Bit of All Right,' 'What Ho, Mrs. Brisket,' 'Don't Take Our Charley For The Army,' and 'Saturday Night at the Rose and Crown' — Mr Coward has recaptured the pawky humors of another era. The second act sets out as if it means to sustain high spirits Miss O'Shea and her friends have released. Seated in four tiers in Westminster Abbey, the ensemble sings a dryly diverting commentary called 'Coronation Chorale.' *The Girl Who Came to Supper* brings shrewd skill to its earnest attempt to record the gaiety and deviltry of a sentimental past."

NOTES: After Rex Harrison, George Sanders and Christopher Plummer turned down the starring role, Keith Michell was engaged. When Jose Ferrer became available, Keith Michell was paid off and sent packing. Ironically he played the role in the BBC radio version years later (see R-74). Among the cut numbers were: 'Put Not Your Trust In Princes,' 'If Only Mrs. Applejohn Were Here,' 'Time Will Tell' (from The Coconut Girl sequence), 'Just People,' 'What's The Matter With A Nice Beef Stew?' (from the London Sequence), and 'Long Live The King (If He Can).' The last mentioned was deleted the day after President Kennedy was assassinated, as the song dealt comically with attempts at killing a king. It was replaced by 'My Family Tree,' whose melody was a quick re-write of 'Countess Mitzi' from *Operette* (see P-88). The London sequence was performed in its entirety on the Ed Sullivan Show (see T-32). This was the first Coward musical for which Coward did not also author the book, although oddly enough he is sighted as being nominated, along with Kurnitz for the Tony Award for Best Book of a Musical. For recordings see D-110, D-131, D-170.

P-161   *High Spirits* Alvin Theatre, NY April 7, 1964 (375 performances)Tried out in New Haven Feb. 3, 1964, Boston and Philadelphia.

A musical version of **Noël Coward**'s comedy *Blithe Spirit*. Book, music and lyrics, vocal direction and arrangements by Hugh Martin & Timothy Gray.

Directed by Noël Coward. Produced by Lester Osterman, Robert Fletcher and Richard Horner. Sets and costumes by Robert Fletcher. Miss Grimes costume by Valentina. Lighting by Jules Fisher. Musical Direction by Fred Werner. Orchestrations by Harry Zimmerman. Dance Music by William Goldenberg. Dances and musical numbers by Danny Daniels.

CAST: Beatrice Lillie (Madame Arcati), Tammy Grimes (Elvira), Edward Woodward (Charles Condomine), Louise Troy (Ruth), Carol Arthur (Edith), Margaret Hall (Mrs. Bradman), Lawrence Keith (Dr. Bradman), Robert Lenn (Bob), Beth Howland (Beth), Gene Castle (Rupert), Adrienne Angel, Syndee Balaber, Gene Castle, Jerry Craig, Jackie Cronin, Altovise Gore, Judith Haskell, Jack Kauflin, Bill Kennedy, Al Lanti, Miriam Lawrence, Renee Lee, Robert Lenn, Alex MacKay, Jaqueline Maria, Stan Mazin, Joe McGrath, Don Percassi, Kathy Preston, Sybil Scotford, Tom Thornton, Ronnie Walken, Anne Wallace (Chorus)

SYNOPSIS: see P-98. A new final scene was added in which Arcati and Condomine drink hemlock which was planted earlier by Elvira. They both die and the finale is sung from heaven.

REVIEWS:
New York Daily News, April 8, 1964: "*High Spirits* has elevated by several notches the tone of Broadway's current musical theatre simply by being beguiling."

United Press International, April 8, 1964: "The best musical show of the season-the funniest, the most melodious, the most enchanting and the most literate."

NOTES: Coward was pleasantly surprised by this adaptation of his play, which was originally entitled *Faster Than Sound* , and even before he agreed to direct the production, he dreamed of a perfect one starring Gwen Verdon as Elvira, Celeste Holm as Ruth, Keith Michell as Charles, Kay Thompson as Madame Arcati, and all of them directed and choreographed by Bob Fosse. Since Thompson had already turned down *Sail Away* and vowed never to appear on Broadway (she never did), it is unlikely that she was a serious contender, but after Coward took over the directorial helm, both Verdon and Holm were very seriously considered. Ultimately none of the dream cast made it to the Alvin Theatre. Although they retained credit, Coward and Daniels were both "helped" out of town by Gower Champion with the direction and choreography. On the other hand it is acknowledged that Coward had a hand in many of the lyrics for Tammy Grimes' showstopper "Home Sweet Heaven." An interesting side note: The song "Faster Than Sound" had been previously used and cut from the film *Athena*. Although that score was written by Hugh Martin, Timothy Gray had nothing to do with the film, which had lyrics by Ralph Blane. Coward recorded four songs from the show on

EP. (see D-111). For original cast recording see P-132.

P-162   *Hay Fever* National Theatre, Old Vic, London Oct. 27, 1964

A revival of **Noël Coward's comedy**. Directed by Coward. Lighting by Brian Freeland. Sets and costumes by Motley.

CAST: Edith Evans (Judith Bliss), Lynn Redgrave (Jackie), Maggie Smith (Myra), Robert Stephens (Sandy), Derek Jacobi (Simon Bliss), Louise Purnell (Sorel Bliss), Barbara Hicks (Clara), Anthony Nicholls (David Bliss), Robert Lang (Richard)

SYNOPSIS: See P-97.

REVIEWS:
Sunday London Telegraph, Nov. 8, 1964: "The National Theatre's *Hay Fever* shows us Coward in danger of being mistaken for Pinter. There is barely one witty epigram in the entire dialogue."

London Times, Oct. 28, 1964: "The interesting thing about *Hay Fever*, after nearly forty years, is the way in which its two groups of characters have responded to time — the Bliss family in their never-never land remaining untouched by it, and their guests stiffening into period caricatures. The production dwells pointedly on this contrast, weighting down the outsiders with cricket-blazers, and waxed moustaches, and leaving their hosts in dress that spans both periods. The use of costume is one of the many delights of the production."

Plays and Players, December 1964: "Mr. Coward has the distinction of having created an entire era which possibly never existed, but it has the more fascination for that reason."

NOTES: This revival astounded most critics and proved that Coward's plays were not unbearably dated, but eminently playable and funny. This really solidified 'Dad's Renaissance.' Celia Johnson replaced Edith Evans as Judith for the last 8 performances.

P-163   *High Spirits* Savoy Theatre, London Nov. 3, 1964 (94 Performances)

West End premiere of the musical adaptation of **Noël Coward**'s *Blithe Spirit*. Same personnel as P-162, except for: Directed by Graham Payn and Timothy Gray. **Supervised by Noël Coward**. Sets and Costumes by Hutchinson Scott. Lighting by Michael Northen. Produced by Geoffrey Russell for Linnit & Dunfee Ltd.

CAST: Cicely Courtneidge (Madame Arcati), Denis Quilley (Charles Condomine), Jan Waters (Ruth), Marti Stevens (Elvira), Ann Hamilton (Mrs. Bradman), Peter Verno (Dr. Bradman), Matt Zimmerman (Bob), Maurice Lane (Rupert), Denise Coffey (Edith), Peta Palham (Beth), Rita Cameron, Kathy Kunkerly, Julia Meadows, Joan Ryan, Clare Welch, Brian Beaton, Brian Handley, James Hunt, Barry Kennington (Singers) Sarah Flemington, Jackie Gentle, Pamela Grant, Jill Holmes, Gloria Johnson, Valerie Smith, Richard Fox, Bob Hogan, Norman Leggatt, Fernand Monast, Alex Morrow, Leon Ward (Dancers)

SYNOPSIS: See P-162

REVIEWS:
Sunday Telegraph, Nov. 8, 1964: "*High Spirits* emerges as an evening of low jinks."

NOTES: This production was less successful than its Broadway predecesor. Coward merely supervised and let one of the authors and his lover Payn direct.

P-164   *Present Laughter* (revival) Queen's Theatre, London April 21, 1965. (364 performances)

Revival of **Noël Coward's comedy**. Directed by Nigel Patrick. Produced by H.M. Tennent Ltd. and John Gale. Sets by Hutchinson Scott. Lighting by Joe Davis.

CAST: Anna Palk (Daphne), Sheila Keith (Miss Erikson), Drewe Henley (Fred), Avice Landon (Monica), Nigel Patrick (Garry Essendine), Phyllis Calvert (Liz Essendine), Richard Briers (Roland Maule), John Lee (Henry Lyppiatt), Graham Payn (Morris Dixon), Maxine Audley (Joanna Lyppiatt), Jacqueline Maude (Lady Saltburn)

SYNOPSIS: See P-100.

P-165   *Suite In Three Keys* Queens Theatre, London April 14, 1966

Three plays by Noël Coward taking place in the same hotel suite in Switzerland: *Shadows Of The Evening, Come Into The Garden, Maud* and *A Song At Twilight*. The first two opened on April 14, 1966 and the third on April 25, 1966. Produced by H.M. Tennent Ltd. . Directed by Vivian Matalon. Sets by Brian Currah. Costumes by Molyneux-Paris. Lighting by Joe Davis.

PLAYS AND CASTS: *Shadows Of The Evening*: Lilli Palmer (Linda

Savignac), Sean Barret (Felix, a waiter), Irene Worth (Anne Hilgay), **Noël Coward** (George Hilgay); *Come Into The Garden Maud*: Irene Worth (Anna-Mary Conklin), Sean Barret (Felix, a waiter), **Noël Coward** (Verner Conklin), Lilli Palmer (Maud Caragnani); *A Song At Twilight*: Irene Worth (Hilde Latymer), Sean Barret (Felix, a waiter), **Noel Coward** (Hugo Latymer), Lilli Palmer (Carlotta Gray)

SYNOPSIS: *Shadows Of The Evening*: A worldly and successful publisher discovers that he has only a few months to live. The wife whom he has deserted and his mistress of seven years join forces to make his twilight more than an inexorable surrender to death. *Come Into The Garden Maud*: A last minute defection leaves an American couple, Verner and Anna-Mary Conklin, with thirteen dinner guests. To even up the table, Verner is ordered to dine in his rooms. Attractive, aristocratic Maud joins him there later with perfectly delightful results for Verner. *A Song At Twilight*: Aging and married author, Sir Hugo Latymer has a visit from Carlotta Gray, which whom he had an affair over sixty years ago. At first, she asks for permission to print his love letters to her in her autobiography. When he refuses, she gives him the letters, but tells him that he cannot have the others: the love letters he has written to the one true love of his life, Perry. In the course of the evening Carlotta tries to open Sir Hugo's eyes to his own hypocrisy and self deceipt. She finally leaves, giving him the letters and, visibly moved, he reads them as the curtain falls.

REVIEWS:
London Daily Express, April 15, 1966: "Mr. Coward doesn't merely stand on a stage. He colonises it. His is a kind of acting that has passed from the London stage perhaps forever and many last night were grateful for a reminder of an era when urbanity, subtlety and an overwelming sense of sheer style counted for something."

New York Times, June 19, 1966: "Coward's technique as a craftsman is as fine as ever and his acting is impeccable. Yet somehow the play (*A Song At Twilight*) strikes this member of the audience as curiously harmless."

NOTES: This triumphant return to the West End was to be the last stage performance of Coward and his last three plays produced. Coward intended to take the plays and his performance to NY in 1966-67 under the banner of David Merrick and co-starring Irene Worth and Margaret Leighton, but illness forced first a postponement to the 67-68 season and finally the plays had to wait till after Coward was dead to be produced on Broadway (see P-187).

P-166   *Fallen Angels* (revival) Vaudeville Theatre, London April 4, 1967.

Revival of Noël Coward's comedy. Directed by Philip Wiseman.

CAST: Joan Greenwood, Constance Cummings

P-167   *Tonight At 8:30* (revival) Anta Theatre, NY May 3, 1967 (16 performances)

Revival of three of **Noël Coward's one act plays:** *Ways and Means* Directed by Nina Foch, *Still Life* Directed by Jack Sydow & *Fumed Oak* Directed by G. Wood. Produced by Michael Dewell and Frances Ann Dougherty for The American National Theatre and Academy. Sets by Will Steven Armstrong. Costumes by Alvin Colt. Lighting by Tharon Musser.

CAST: *Ways and Means*: Joan Bassie (Stella Cartwright), John Church (Toby Cartwright), Les Barkdull (Gaston), Geddeth Smith (Lord Chapworth), Jeanne Hepple (Olive Lloyd-Randsome), Patricia Guinan (Princess Elena), John Straub (Murdock), Joan Force (Nanny), Herbert Foster (Stevens); *Still Life*: Jeanne Hepple (Myrtle Bagot), Patricia Guinan (Beryl Waters), John Church (Stanley), G. Wood (Albert Godby), Denholm Elliot (Alec Harvey), Priscilla Morrill (Laura Jesson), Joan Bassie (Mildred), Les Barkdull (Young Man), Geoff Garland (Bill), Geddeth Smith (Johnnie), Joan Force (Dolly Messiter); *Fumed Oak*: Sloan Shelton (Doris Gow), Patricia Guinan (Elsie Gow), Joan Force (Mrs. Rocket), Geoff Garland (Henry Gow)

REVIEWS:
New York Times, May 4, 1967: "Drop in on the National Repertory Theatre's revival of Noël Coward's *Tonight At 8:30* around 10:30 and you'll have a good time. It is perhaps easier to explain why the first two plays don't work than to explain why *Fumed Oak* does. The clever dialogue is routine 1920's clever and the players plow through it with a nervous speed that they or their director have confused with high style."

New York Post, May 4, 1967: "They are good plays that well represent the versatility of Mr. Coward's notable writing talent, and the visiting company, which hasn't been finding the local going exactly easy, was at it best in presenting them with spirit, freshness and understanding appreciation. Among the admirable qualities of Noël Coward, not the least is his inspirational capacity for bringing out the best in the National Repertory Theatre."

P-168   *Hay Fever* (revival) Duke of York's Theatre, London Feb. 14, 1968. (9 wks.)

Revival of **Noël Coward's comedy**. Directed by Murray MacDonald. Designed by Motley.

CAST: Roland Culver (David Bliss), Celia Johnson (Judith Bliss), Lucy Fleming (Sorel Bliss), Simon Williams (Simon Bliss), Diana Fairfax (Myra Arundel), Richard Vernon (Richard Greatham), Prunella Scales (Jackie Coryton), Michale Graham Cox (Sandy Tyrell), Betty Bascomb (Clara)

REVIEWS:
London Observer, Feb. 18, 1968: "The current production, though glittering less than its predecessor, is perfectly adequate corroboration that *Hay Fever* belongs with "Twelfth Night," "Love For Love" and "The Important of Being Earnest" in the gallery of classic English comedies. It is Coward's profoundest play."

P-169   *Private Lives* (revival) Theatre De Lys, NY May 19, 1968 (9 performances)

Off Broadway revival of **Noël Coward's comedy**. Directed by Richard Barr. Produced by Haila Stoddard, Mark Wright, Duane Wilder. Sets by Herbert Senn and Helen Pond. Lighting by David F. Segal. **Noël Coward's music** arranged and performed by Don Elliott.

CAST: Betsy Von Furstenberg (Sybil Chase), Russell Nype (Elyot Chase), Howard Erskine (Victor Prynne), Elaine Stritch (Amanda Prynne), Anita Palacine (Louise)

NOTES: This not too successful rendering is best remembered by some for Miss Stritch's stamping of her foot whenever she could not remember her lines, which was often.

P-170   *Noël Coward's Sweet Potato* Ethel Barrymore Theatre, NY Sept. 29, 1968 (17 performances). Moved to the Booth Theatre on Nov. 1, 1968 (36 performances).

A revue comprised of **Noël Coward's words and music** from a conception by Roderick Cook. Directed and Choreographed by Lee Theodore. Settings by Helen Pond and Herbert Senn. Costumes by David Toser. Lighting by Peter Hunt. Musical supervision and arrangements by Charles Schneider. Co-choreography by Robert Tucker. Production supervised by Robert Linden. Material assembled and adapted by Roderick Cook and Lee Theodore.

CAST: George Grizzard, Dorothy Loudon, Carole Shelley, Arthur Mitchell, Tom Kneebone, Bonnie Schon, Ian Tucker, Robert LuPone,

Stephen Reinhardt

MUSICAL NUMBERS: Useful Phrases, Dance Little Lady, Mad Dogs and Englishmen, World Weary, A Bar On The Piccola Marina, Why Does Love Get In the Way?, Men About Town, Matelot, Mad About The Boy, I Wonder What Happened To Him?, A Room With A View, I Like America, Let's Do It, Three White Feathers, Mrs. Worthington, Alice, If Love Were All, Teach Me To Dance Like Grandma

REVIEWS:
New York Times, Sept. 9, 1968: "The material itself is thin and bland, and this is hardly the fault of Mr. Coward. Revue writing is the stage's equivalent of journalism and not intended to last. To resurrect old sketches is almost an act of cruelty, and the old revue songs — even when revamped — more often than not seemed to have outstayed their welcome. The trouble with too much of the material is that it is now a little too late in the century for it. An except from *Red Peppers* showing a fading song and dance vaudeville act, is celebrating a forgotten world."

New York Daily News, Sept. 30, 1968: "*Noël Coward's Sweet Potato* offers a beguiling evening of song, dance and sketch performed by an attractive, versatile company. I wish the sooty players in "Hair" could see it some time and learn how the other half lives. At the Barrymore, Coward seems bright and new again."

NOTES: This oddly 60's revue had such items as "A Room With A View" sung to a looking-glass, and the lady doing the singing finds that she's locked on the balcony with nothing but a view. "Mad About The Boy" was sung by one and the balcony scene from *Private Lives* found Amanda and Elyot on roller skates. Roderick Cook found his senses and produced *Oh Coward!* two years later. When the show moved to the Booth Theatre, Mary Louise Wilson replaced Dorothy Loudon, who went into "The Fig Leaves Are Falling." The show was originally called *And Now Noël Coward.*

P-171   *Mr. & Mrs.* Palace Theatre, London Dec. 11, 1968

A musical version of two of **Noël Coward's one act plays** from *Tonight At 8:30: Fumed Oak & Still Life*. Book, music and lyrics by John Taylor. Adapted, staged and directed by Ross Taylor. Produced by George W. George and Frank Granat in association with John Roberts. Orchestrations by Johnnie Spence. Musical Direction by Derek New.

CAST: John Neville (Henry Gow & Alec Harvey), Honor Blackman (Doris Gow & Laura Jesson), Hylda Baker (Mrs. Rockett & Myrtle

Bagot), Liz Emiston (Elsie), Alan Breeze (Albert Godby), Leslie Meadows (Stanley), Ursula Smith (Paul Weston), Brian Casey (Mr. Saunders)

SYNOPSIS: See P-83

REVIEWS:
London Evening Standard, Dec. 12, 1968: "*Mr. & Mrs.* at the Palace take two fragile Noel Coward stories, expands them with irrelevant production numbers, stuffs them with banal music, inflates them with inconsequential lyrics and offers up the grossly contrived concoction as a musical."

Variety, Feb. 19, 1969: "The show appears fragile at least for a high overhead West End berth, where only a fluke is likely would save it."

Christian Science Monitor, Dec. 23, 1968: "Two of Noël Coward's best short plays have been turned into a musical under the title of *Mr. & Mrs.* They are memorable for reintroducing to the London stage John Neville. They are not, unfortunately, memorable for anything else."

NOTES: Why Coward ever gave his consent to musicalize *Fumed Oak* and *Still Life* remains a mystery. Perhaps he knew that even the worst musical, which this turned out to be, could not dim the value of these great properties. In either case the show flopped leaving only a dismal original cast record to remind buffs of its inadequacies.

P-172   *Private Lives* (revival) Billy Rose Theatre, NY Dec. 4, 1969 (204 performances)   Moved to the Broadhurst Theatre Arpil 27, 1970.

Revival of **Noël Coward's play**. Directed by Stephen Porter. Produced by David Merrick and the APA. Sets and Lighting by James Tilton. Costumes by Joe Eula. Miss Grimes costumes by Barbara Matera.

CAST: Suzanne Grossmann (Sybil Chase), Brian Bedford (Elyot Chase), David Glover (Victor Prynne), Tammy Grimes (Amanda Prynne), J.J. Lewis (Louise)

REVIEWS:
New York Times, Dec. 5, 1969: "Gorgeous – that would be one word for Stephen Porter's restaging of *Private Lives*. Delicate might be another word, dazzling if you want a third. *Private Lives* is, of course, a great test of style for both director and actors. Tammy Grimes is outrageously appealing. She plays every cheap trick in the histrionic book with supreme aplomb and adorable confidence. Everything

came together to make me at least realize that *Private Lives* is not a revival but a classic."

New York Daily News, Dec. 5, 1970: "The sharp and catty dialogue, which once seemed so brilliant and which also was enjoyable when Tallulah Bankhead and Donald Cook battled it back and forth in 1948, now strikes me as quite dated. Bedford seems to have the Coward style, but Miss Grimes doesn't."

NOTES: Tammy Grimes won a "Tony" Award for Best Actress for this performance.

P-173   *John Player Lecture-Noel Coward* National Film Theatre. Dec. 14, 1969 4:00 PM

Personal appearance by Noël Coward as part of the National Film Theatre's tribute to his films. He taked about his long career in the cinema and answered questions from the audience. Artists involved with *In Which We Serve* (F-15) (which was shown at 6:15 PM) also attended. Other films shown in the season were: *Hearts of The World* (F-1), *The Vortex* (F-3), *Private Lives* (F-6), *Cavalcade* (F-8), *The Scoundrel* (F-11), *This Happy Breed* (F-16), *Blithe Spirit* (F-17), *Brief Encounter* (F-18), *The Astonished Heart* (F-19), *Our Man In Havana* (F-22), *Surprise Package* (F-23), *Bunny Lake Is Missing* (F-26), *The Italian Job* (F-30).

P-174   *A Talent To Amuse* Phoenix Theatre, London Dec. 16, 1969 (1 performance)

A midnight matinee in celebration of **Noël Coward's seventieth birthday**. Directed by Wendy Toye, Nigel Patrick & Douglas Squires. Produced by Martin Tickner. Lighting by Michael Northen. Decor by Hutchinson Scott. Musical direction by Grant Hossack. Orchestrations by Bruce George. Productions supervised by Robert Nesbitt.

CAST: Robert Morley and Richard Attenborough (Co-hosts), Richard Briers, Susannah York, John Gielgud, Cyril Ritchard, Dame Anna Neagle, Stanley Holloway, Joyce Grenfell, John Schlesinger, Maggie Fitzgibbon, Irene Worth, Betty Hare, Danny La Rue, Gretchen Franklin, Alison Leggatt, Dandy Nichols, Elsie Randolph, Dorothy Reynolds, George Benson, Robert Coote, Jack Kruschen, John Merival, Daphne Anderson, Amanda Barrie, Sheila Bernette, Joyce Blair, Josephine Gordon, Gay Soper, Billy Boyle, Neil Fitzwilliam, John Gower, Terence Knapp, Rod McLennan, Terry Mitchell, Cheryl Kennedy, David Kernan, Faith Brook, Patricia Burke, Judy Campbell, Dulcie Gray, Marion Grimaldi, Glynis

Johns, Vaness Lee, Moira Lister, Dinah Sheridan, Eleanor Summerfield, Kim Grant, Lewis Fiander, Norman Warwick, Stephen Warwick, Patrick Allan, Ray Barrett, Michael Denison, Caryl Little, Sheila White, Jonathan Dennis, Graham James, Tony Britton, Peter Graves, John Moffatt, John Standing, Celia Johnson, Anne Rogers, Mark Wynter, Nicky Henson, Julian Holloway, Bunny May, Gary Bond, Anthony Roberts, Hubert Gregg, Gordon Jackson, David Knight, Bryan Forbes, Guy Hamilton, Joan Heal, Ian Carmichael, Graham Payn, Terry Mitchell, Tessie O'Shea, Susan Hampshire, Denis Quilley, Pat Kirkwood, Elisabeth Welch, Jessie Matthews, Avril Angers, Hy Hazell, Stella Moray, June Whitfield, Patricia Routledge, Richard Rodney Bennett, Jeremy Brett, June Bronhill, Una Stubbs, Cliff Richard, Cleo Laine, The Mike Sammes Singers

MUSICAL NUMBERS AND SKETCHES: The Boy Actor-Gielgud; This is Not a Day Like Any Other Day-Fitzgibbon; Early Mourning-Worth, Hare; Marvelous Party-La Rue; What's Going To Happen To The Tots-Franklin, Hare, Leggatt, Nichols, Randolph, Reynolds, Benson, Coote, Kruschen, Merivale; Room With A View-Kennedy & Kernan; Ladies of the Town-Brook, Burke, Campbell, Gray, Grimaldi, Johns, Lee, Lister, Sheridan, Summerfield, Grant, Fiander, Warwick & Warwick; Private Lives (scene)-York & Briers; Green Carnation-Allen, Barrett & Denison; If Love Were All-Grenfell; Any Little Fish-Little, White, Dennis, James; The Stately Homes of England-Britton, Graves, Moffatt, Standing; I've Just Come Out From England-Johnson; Sigh No More-Rogers; Matelot-Wynter; Three Juvenile Delinquents-Henson, Holloway, May, Bond, Roberts, Warwick, Gregg, Jackson, Knight, Forbes, Hamilton, Schlesinger; There Are Bad Times Just Around The Corner-Heal, Carmichael & Payn; London Pride-Holloway; London-O'Shea; You Were There-Hampshire & Quilley; Chase Me Charlie-Kirkwood; Twentieth Century Blues-Welch; Why Do The Wrong People Travel?-Fitzgibbon; Mary Make Believe-Matthews; That Is The End Of The News-Angers, Hazell, Moray, Whitfield; I'll Follow My Secret Heart-Routledge; Nina-Ritchard; Poor Little Rich Girl & Parisian Pierrot-Bennett; Time and Again-Rogers & Brett; Dance Little Lady-Neagle; Melanie's Aria-Bronhill; Beatnik Love Affair-Stubbs, Richard; Mad About the Boy-Cleo Laine

NOTES: This great four hour event was Martin Tickner's idea aided by Mrs. and Mrs. Flint-Shipman, owners of the Phoenix. When the evening was over and Coward was on the stage he said, "Thank you for making this obviously the most moving theatrical moment in my life."

P-175 *Blithe Spirit* (revival) Globe Theatre, London July 23, 1970 (204 performances)

Revival of **Noël Coward's comedy**. Produced by H.M. Tennent Ltd. by arrangement with Arthur Cantor and The Yvonne Arnaud Theatre. Directed by Nigel Patrick. Sets by Pamela Ingram. Lighting by Joe Davis.

CAST: Patrick Cargill (Charles Condomine), Phyllis Calvert (Ruth Condomine), Beryl Reid (Madame Arcati), Amanda Reiss (Elvira), John Hart Dyke (Dr. Bradman), Daphne Newton (Mrs. Bradman), Sylvia Brayshay (Edith)

SYNOPSIS: See P-97.

REVIEWS:
London Times, July 20, 1970: "Coward's technique in this play is a simple yet effective one: he grafts all the frenzied jealousies and petty deceits of the standard adultery comedy on to a deliciously unlikely story of a novelist plagued by his first wife's ghost. He himself described the piece as an improbable farce and my one reservation about Nigel Patrick's production is that it treats it instead as a believable comedy with too much emphasis on the verbal subtlety and not enough whirlwind pace."

P-176   *Hay Fever* (revival) Helen Hayes Theatre, NY Nov. 9, 1970 (24 performances)

Revival of **Noël Coward's comedy.** Directed by Arvin Brown. Produced by Leonard Sillman. Sets and Lighting by Ben Edwards. Costumes by Jane Greenwood.

CAST: Shirley Booth (Judith Bliss), John Williams (David Bliss), Roberta Maxwell (Sorel Bliss), Sam Waterston (Simon Bliss), Marian Mercer (Myra Arundel), Michael McGuire (Richard Greatham), Carole Shelley (Jackie Coryton), John Tillinger (Sandy Tyrell), Sudie Bond (Clara)

SYNOPSIS: See P-38.

REVIEWS:
New York Times, Nov. 10, 1970: "Noël Coward's *Hay Fever* is almost a classic — which is about as good as being almost a virgin. Coward's play is brilliantly written but poorly crafted. The writing is nothing but a delight, but the play itself is too thin. It contains an idea rather than tells a story. *Hay Fever* must be high comedy if it is anything at all, and here high comedy it isn't."

New York Daily News, Nov. 10, 1970: "One is impressed to discover that, after all these years, Noël Coward's early comedies can still be entertaining. But although last night's revival at the Helen Hayes of this earliest success in this vein, the 1925

Hay Fever, has its merry moments and one truly hilarious scene, it is only spasmodically effective."

New York Post, Nov. 10, 1970: "Noël Coward's gift for writing polite comedies about impolite people is shown delightfully in his early *Hay Fever*, which was revived last night...*Hay Fever* is not one of Mr. Coward's best comedies, but it is almost steady fun, and it is always a pleasure to see a play of his again."

P-177   *Tonight At 8* (revival) Hampstead Theatre Club, London Dec. 21, 1970

Revival of 3 of **Noël Coward's one act plays**: *We Were Dancing, Red Peppers* and *Family Album*. Directed by Gillian Lynne. Sets and Costumes by John Halle.

CAST: *We Were Dancing*: Richard Cornish (Ippaga), George Camiller (George Davies), Diana Beevers (Eva Blake), Millicent Martin (Louise Charteris), Gary Bond (Karl Sandys), Joyce Grant (Clara Bethel), Alan MacNaughton (Hubert Charteris), Oliver Ford-Davies (Major Blake); *Red Peppers*: Millicent Martin (Lily Pepper) Gary Bond (George Pepper), Richard Cornish (Alf), Alan MacNaughton (Bert Bentley), Oliver Ford-Davies (Mr. Edwards) Joyce Grant (Mabel Grace); *Family Album*: Gary Bond (Jasper Featherways), Millicent Martin (Jane, his wife), Sally Home (Harriet Winter), Oliver Ford-Davies (Charles Winter), Diana Beevers (Emily Valance), George Camiller (Edward Valance), Richard Cornish (Richard Featherways), Joyce Grant (Lavinia Featherways), Alan MacNaughton (Burrows)

REVIEWS:
London Times, Jan 21, 1971: "Of the three, *We Were Dancing* still looks emphatically the best. *Red Peppers*, Coward's hymn to the tatty world of twice-nightly variety, also works simply because the action is carefully rooted in a vanished theatrical past. Only *Family Album*, blending mild satire on Victorian hypocrisy with candid exploitation of the period's sentimentality now looks as if it's being kept alive by the cast's and the director's artificial respiration."

NOTES: Focusing on the musical plays, the title was changed from 8:30 to 8, presumably because that was when the show began.

P-178   *The Grand Tour* Sadler's Wells, London May27-June 12, 1971. Tried out at Theatre Royal, Norwich Feb. 10, 1971.

A ballet with **music by Noël Coward** (freely adapted and orchestrated by

Hershy Kay) Produced and performed by The Royal Ballet. Choreographed by Joe Layton. Decor by John Conklin. Lighting by John B. Read.

SYNOPSIS: An American lady on a luxury cruise has a romantic flirtation with a Steward. Other people on the ship include Noël Coward, Gertrude Lawrence, Mary Pickford, Theda Bara, George Bernard Shaw, Alice B. Toklas, Gertrude Stein and Douglas Fairbanks.

REVIEWS:
Sunday London Times, Feb. 28, 1971: "There can be no doubt that the compsoer of "I'll See You Again" and "Someday I'll Find You" is among the immortals."

New York Times, Feb. 27, 1971: "Mr. Layton has been clever in choosing dances with the appearance and manner for the various roles and even more so in coaxing relaxed amusing performances from them."

NOTES: This ballet contained old Coward songs arranged for dancing and was done in repertory with *Apollo, Beauty and The Beast, Checkpoint, Danses Concertants, Diversions* and *Field Figures*. Joe Layton had worked with Coward on *Sail Away* (P-154 & 156), *The Girl Who Came to Supper* (P-160) and *Androcles and The Lion* (T-45).

P-179   *Private Lives* (revival) Queens and Globe Theatres, London Sept. 21, 1972 (517 performances)

Revival of **Noël Coward's comedy.** Produced by H.M. Tennent Ltd. by arrangement with Arthur Cantor. Directed by John Gielgud. Designed by Anthony Powell. Costumes by Beatrice Dawson. Lighting by Joe Davis.

CAST: Polly Adams (Sybil Chase), Robert Stephens (Elyot Chase), James Villiers (Victor Prynne), Maggie Smith (Amanda Prynne), Cari Hedderwick (Louise)

SYNOPSIS: See P-61.

NOTES: When Robert Stephens, who was married to Maggie Smith left due to divorce, he was replaced by John Standing.

P-180   *Oh Coward!* The New Theatre, NY Oct. 4, 1972 (294 performances)

A revue with words and music by Noël Coward. Devised and directed by Roderick Cook. Produced by Wroderrick Productions. Sets by Helene

Pond and Herbert Senn. Musical direction and arrangements by René Wiegert. Lighting by James Nisbet Clark. Additional musical arrangements by Herbert Helbig and Nicholas Deutsch.

CAST: Barbara Cason, Roderick Cook & Jamie Ross

MUSICAL NUMBERS: Something To Do With Spring; Bright Young People; Poor Little Rich Girl; Ziegeuner; Let's Say Goodbye; This Is A Changing World; We Were Dancing; Dance Little Lady; Room With A View; Sail Away; The End of The News; The Stately Homes of England; London Pride; Aunt Jessie; Uncle Harry; Chase Me Charley; Saturday Night At the Rose And Crown; Island of Bolamazoo; What Ho Mrs. Brisket; Has Anybody Seen Our Ship; Men About Town; Why Do The Wrong People Travel?; The Passengers Always Right; Mrs. Worthington; Mad Dogs and Englishmen; A Marvelous Party; You Were There; Three White Feathers; Mad About The Boy; Nina; A Bar On The Piccolo Marina; Let's Do It; Finale: Where Are the Songs We Sung?, Someday I'll Find You, I'll Follow My Secret Heart, If Love Were All, I'll See You Again

REVIEWS:
New York Post, Oct. 5, 1972: "Sir Noel is such a fine actor that it is always a shame not to see him in his own work, but Barbara Cason, Roderick Cook and Jamie Ross, who obviously understand and appreciate the Coward tradition, handle their numbers excellently. There are no dull moments in *Oh Coward!*, all of the many songs are a pleasure to listen to, and the result is a worthy tribute to one of the great men of the modern theatre."

NBC-TV, Oct. 5, 1972: "What comes through in *Oh Coward!* is not the music, but the words. Sour, urbane, funny and knowing, with a sudden twist or pause, and surprising off-beat ending."

Time Magazine, Oct. 23, 1972: "Coward is a word wizard, but his subtlest gift is inflection, and he was master of the pause before Pinter was born. This sometimes defeats actors, but not the impeccably polished trio in this show. They sing and deliver their lines with sly, artful perfection. They help to make *Oh Coward!* the most marvelous party in town."

NOTES: This production began in Toronto (470 performances) and toured to Chicago and Boston before becoming the New York version. It was transferred to television twice (see T-64, T-72). For recording see D-135.

P-181   *Cowardy Custard* Mermaid Theatre, London July 10, 1972

An entertainment featuring **words and music of Noël Coward.** Devised by

Gerald Frow, Alan Strachan & Wendy Toye. Directed by Toye and the Cast. Designed by Tim Goodchild. Orchestrations by Keith Amos. Musical direction by John Burrows.

CAST: Olivia Breeze, Geoffrey Burridge, Jonathan Cecil, Tudor Davies, Elaine Delmar, Laurel Ford, Peter Gale, John Moffatt, Patricia Routledge, Anna Sharkey, Una Stubbs & Derek Waring

MUSICAL NUMBERS: Medley: If Love Were All, I'll See You Again, Time and Again, Has Anybody Seen Our Ship?, Try To Learn To Love, Kiss Me, Go Slow Johnny, Tokay, Dearest Love, Could You Please Oblige Us With a Bren Gun?, Come the Wild Wild Weather, Spinning Song, Parisian Pierrot; Play Orchestra Play, You Were There, Any Little Fish, In A Boat On A Lake, A Room With A View, When You Want Me, Specially For You, Beatnik Love Affair, I'm Mad About You, Poor Little Rich Girl, Louisa, Mad About The Boy, The Stately Homes of England, I Went To A Marvelous Party, Mrs. Worthington, Why Must the Show Go On?, Sequence: London Pride, London Is A Little Bit Of All Right, What Ho Mrs. Brisket, Don't Take Our Charlie For the Army, Saturday Night At the Rose and Crown, London At Night; There Are Bad Times Just Around The Corner, Alice Is At It Again, The Passenger's Always Right, Useful Phrases, Mad Dogs and Englishmen, Why Do The Wrong People Travel, Nina, I Like America, Bronxville Darby and Joan, I Wonder What Happened to Him?, Twentieth Century Blues, Miss Mouse, Let's Do It (music by Cole Porter), Medley: Nothing Can Last Forever, Would You Like To Stick A Pin In My Balloon?, Mary Make-Believe, Dance Little Lady, Men About Town, Forbidden Fruit, Sigh No More, Younger Generation, I'll Follow My Secret Heart, If Love Were All

REVIEWS:
London Observer, July 16, 1972: "Beautifully staged by Wendy Toye, the show is a matter of pure enjoyment."

London Sunday Times, July 16, 1972: "By setting the famous songs and gloriously impertinent retorts of his affectionate but combative nature against memories of his life *Cowardy Custard* becomes a piece of creative criticism."

Variety, July 26, 1972: "*Cowardy Custard* starts slowly, runs overlong, but otherwise offers sparkling proof of Coward's vast and eclectic talent."

New York Newsday, Sept. 10, 1972: "*Cowardy Custard* is a delight of London's current stage."

NOTES: For recording see R-134. Goodspeed Opera House in Connecticut produced the American premiere of the show under the title of *Noël* on April 8,

1981. The cast was headed by Millicent Martin and Jeremy Brett and staged by Ned Sherrin with musical direction by Glen Roven.

P-182 *Gala performance of Oh, Coward!*. The New Theatre, NY. Jan. 14, 1973

    See P-180.

REVIEWS:
New York Daily News, Jan. 18, 1973: "During the performances, Coward was completely absorbed by the three clever performers on stage alternately applauding, nodding smiling approval and grinning happily."

New York Times, Jan. 15, 1973: "The occasion suggested three of his best know titles, for he has been a blithe spirit in this century and *Oh Coward!* afforded him a brief encounter with his past, one that must certainly have seemed bittersweet."

NOTES: This proved to be Sir Noël's last public appearance. He died in Jamaica on March 26, 1973.

P-183 *Service of Thanksgiving*. St. Martin-in-the-Fields, England. May 24, 1973

    A memorial service for **Sir Noël Coward**. Laurence Olivier, Yehudi Menuhin, and John Gielgud participated.

P-184 *Noël Coward New York Memorial*, The New Theatre, NY May, 1973

NOTES: In her book *Radie's World*, columnist and Coward friend Radie Harris recalled the memorial that she, Roderick Cook, Geoffrey Johnson and Margalo Gillmore organized. "Helen Hayes read a poem that Noël had written on the occasion of her daughter's eighth birthday. Cyril Ritchard described his appearance in Noël's musical *Sigh No More*, in which he sang two numbers, "Nina" and "Whatever Happened to Him?" One of Cyril's couplets was 'Whatever happened to Lord Keeling? I heard that he got back from France, frightened three nuns in a train at Darjeeling by suddenly waving his lance!' Cyril said, 'I had told Noël that I though that couplet about three nuns was vulgar, especially offensive to me. You see, I have an aunt who is a nun.' 'Oh, he said, in that case we'll make it four.'" Glynis Johns and Cathleen Nesbitt also appeared. There were greetings from Jack Benny, Bob Hope, Cole Leslie and Graham Payn.

P-185 *Relative Values* (revival) Westminster Theatre, London Sept. 6, 1973

    Revival of **Noël Coward's comedy**. Directed by Charles Hickman. Produced by Henry Sherwood. Sets by Geoffrey Scott. Costumes by

Anthony Holland.

CAST: Margaret Lockwood (Felicity, Countess of Marshwood) John Stone (Crestwell), Heather Bell (Alice), Gwen Cherrell (Moxie), Margaret Gibson (Lady Hayling), Bryan Stanion (Peter Ingleton), Derek Ensor (Sir John Hayling), Joyce Blair (Miranda Frayle), Kenneth Fortescue (Nigel), Drewe Henley (Don Lucas)

SYNOPSIS: See P-124.

REVIEWS:
The Stage, Sept. 13, 1973: "As an example of Coward's skill as a playwright, this play finds him in 'pot boiler' mood and though the characters occasionally have some witty lines the dialogue bears little relationship to real people and merely hints at class conscious values."

London Sunday Times Sept. 16, 1973: "*Relative Values* was first done in 1951, but its tone is redolent of 1931, not to say 1911."

Variety Sept. 19, 1973: "*Relative Values* is one of his later comedies written when he was supposed to be in creative decline and generally out of fashion with critics and audiences. It is evident that the author had indeed staled by then for the show isn't in the same league with some of his earlier pieces. Much of the dialogue is droll but the plot is strained to provide fun and wit."

NOTES: Charles Hickman also directed Anna Neagle (the star of the first film version of *Bitter-Sweet*) in 1983 at Connaught Theatre in Worthington on Sussex in the role of the Countess. Neagle in turn had played the role in April 1978 at the Vienna English Theatre under the direction of Cyril Frankel. The play had it New York premiere at the Equity Library Theatre Sept. 25, 1986.

P-186   *Design For Living* (revival) Phoenix Theatre, London Nov. 21, 1973

Revival of **Noël Coward's comedy**. Produced by H.M. Tennent Ltd. in association with Robert Regester on behalf of Earnest Entertainment Enterprises, Inc. Directed by Michael Blakemore. Designed by Michael Annals. Lighting by Robert Bryan.

CAST: Vanessa Redgrave (Gilda), Peter Bayliss (Ernest Friedman), Jeremy Brett (Otto), John Stride (Leo), Hazel Hughes (Miss Hodge), Mark Dowse (Photographer), Neil Wilson (Mr. Birbeck), Yolande Turner (Grace Torrence), Connie Booth (Helen Carver), Christopher Malcolm (Henry Carver), Willie Jonah (Matthew)

SYNOPSIS: See P-71.

P-187   *Noël Coward In Two Keys* Ethel Barrymore Theatre, NY Feb. 28, 1974 (140 performances)

Broadway Premiere of **two of Noël Coward's plays** from *Suite In Three Keys: Come Into The Garden Maud & A Song At Twilight.* Produced by Richard Barr and Charles Woodward. Directed by Vivian Matalon. Sets and lighting by William Ritman. Costumes by Ray Diffen. Hair Styles by Ray Iagnocco.

PLAYS AND CASTS: *Come Into The Garden Maud*: Jessica Tandy (Anna-Mary Conklin), Thom Christopher (Felix, a waiter), Hume Cronyn (Verner Conklin), Anne Baxter (Maud Caragnani),; *A Song At Twilight*: Jessica Tandy (Hilde Latymer), Thom Christopher (Felix, a waiter), Hume Cronyn (Hugo Latymer), Anne Baxter (Carlotta Gray)

SYNOPSIS: See P-165

REVIEWS:
New York Daily News, March 1, 1974: "*Noël Coward In Two Keys*, last night's twin bill at the Barrymore, is an exceedingly attractive way to mark finis to a brilliant career. The plays, both comedies of a sort, are pure theatre and written with a flourish, and they are being consummately acted by a small cast. The late playwright would have been pleased with the evening, I feel sure, and you should be too. In it, the Cronyns, Hume and Jessica, seem like transfigured Lunts, and Miss Baxter makes an admirable companion."

New York Post, March 1, 1974: "The two plays were wonderfully entertaining in themselves, but they have the important additional value of showing the scope of Sir Noël's talent as a dramatist. As we all knew, he had a brilliantly civilized wit and could toss off sparkling dialogue with apparent ease. But *A Song at Twilight* shows he was equally skillfull with serious drama. What a tragedy to the theatre the death of Noël Coward was!"

NOTES: The American production of *Suite In Three Keys* cut *Shadows of The Evening*, played them in one evening and retitled the piece *Noël Coward In Two Keys*. Coward died on March 26, 1973 and he probably knew about the plans to produce his last works in America. It was chosen as one the season's Best Plays.

P-188   *Oh Coward!* Criterion Theatre, London

West End premiere of the revue utilizing the **words and music of Noël**

Coward. See P-180.

CAST: Roderick Cook, Jaimie Ross, Geraldine McEwan

P-189   *Private Lives* (revival) Forty Sixth Street Theatre, NY Feb. 6, 1975 (92 performances)

Revival of **Noël Coward's comedy**. Directed by John Gielgud. Produced by Arthur Cantor by arrangement with H.M. Tennent, Ltd. Sets by Anthony Powell. Costumes by Germinal Rangel & Beatrice Dawson. Lighting by H.R. Poindexter. Production Manager: Mitchell Erickson.

CAST: Niki Flacks (Sybil Chase), John Standing (Elyot Chase), Remak Ramsay (Victor Prynne), Maggie Smith (Amanda Prynne), Marie Tommon (Louise)

SYNOPSIS: See P-61.

REVIEWS:
New York Times, Feb. 7, 1975: "Noël Coward's *Private Lives* is not only so very durable but remarkable. The fact that is also screamingly funny has also probably never hindered it. How perfect the play is. It is satisfyingly obvious and satisfyingly complete. The curtains fall on each act with a happy plop of fulfullment. A gorgeous, enchanting play."

New York Daily News, Feb. 7, 1975: "I've come to the no doubt rash conclusion that Noël Coward's *Private Lives*, which is a mere 45 years old, is an immaculate comedy. It seems to get funnier each time I see it, and last night at the 46th Street Theatre it was the funniest ever. Too bad the author himself isn't around anymore. I'm sure he would have loved this *Private Lives*. So should you."

NOTES: Playing concurrently was *A Musical Jubilee,* which featured Tammy Grimes (the last Broadway Amanda) singing Coward's "Poor Little Rich Girl."

P-190   *Present Laughter* (revival) Kennedy Center, Washington D.C. March 29, 1975. Also played Forrest Theatre, Philadelphia, PA Sept., 1975

Revival of **Noël Coward's comedy**. Produced by The John F. Kennedy Center For The Performing Arts. Directed by Stephen Porter. Sets by Oliver Smith. Costumes by Nancy Potts. Lighting by John Gleason.

CAST: Douglas Fairbanks Jr. (Garry Essendine), Lindsay Crouse (Daphne), Paddy Croft (Miss Erikson), Bruce Heighley (Fred), Ilka Chase

(Monica), Jane Alexander (Liz Essendine), George Pentecost (Roland Maule), Richard Neilson (Henry), Roy Cooper (Morris Dixon), Diana Van Der Vlis (Joanna Lyppiatt), Dorothy Blackburn (Lady Saltburn)

SYNOPSIS: See P-100

NOTES: At the Forrest Theatre Daphne was played by Cecilia Hart, Miss Erickson by Kathleen Roland, Fred by Paul Collins, Liz by Angela Thornton, Morris by Richard Clarke, Joanna by Katherine McGrath and Lady Saltburn by Enid Rodgers.

P-191   *Blithe Spirit* National Theatre, Lyttleton Theatre, London June 24, 1976

Revival of **Noël Coward's comedy.** Directed by Harold Pinter. Sets by Eileen Diss. Costumes by Robin Fraser Paye. Lighting by Richard Pilbrow.

CAST: Richard Johnson (Charles Condomine), Elizabeth Spriggs (Madame Arcati), Rowena Cooper (Ruth), Maria Aitkin (Elvira), Geoffrey Chater (Dr. Bradman), Joan Hickson (Mrs. Bradman), Susan Williamson (Edith)

P-192   *Semi-Monde* Citizen's Theatre, Glasgow. Sept. 11, 1977

First professional production of a **play by Noël Coward** written in 1926. Directed and designed by Philip Prowse.

SYNOPSIS: A kind of *Grand Hotel*, taking place in the lobby of a Paris hotel and concerning the comings and goings of many characters, several of them homosexual.

REVIEWS:
London Financial Times, Sept. 12, 1977: "Every now and then there is a moment of vintage Coward. The characters talk about returning to London, being homesick for the South of France, living for the moment...The young cast, all thirty of them, project an idea of world weary insouciance rather than its emdodiment."

The Guardian, Sept. 12, 1977: "As so often with Coward, it is not so much the people themselves that grip you as his own equivocal attitude towards them. The whole point of Coward in the mid-twenties was that he was uneasy without being prophetic."

NOTES: This play was written in 1920 and not produced, perhaps due to the frankness of characters. It received its first production here by the Citizen's Theatre Company.

P-193   *Look After Lulu* (revival) Theatre Royal Haymarket, London Oct. 9, 1978 (9 wks. of performances) Tried out at the Chichester Festival.

Revival of **Noël Coward's farce.** Produced by Duncan C. Weldon and Louis I. Michaels for Triumph Theatre Productions Ltd. Directed by Patrick Garland. Designed by Carl Toms. Lighting by Mick Hughes.

CAST: Geraldine McEwan (Lulu), Martin Milman (Bomba), Tom Karol (Valery), Michael Hughes (Emile), Kate Percival (Yvonne), Shelley Borkum (Paulette), Janice Halsey (Chantal), John Haden (Simon), Gary Raymond (Philippe de Croze), Martin Chamberlain (Adonis), George Howe (Gigot), Fenella Fielding (Claire), Clive Francis (Marcel Blanchard), Paul Hardwick (General Koschnadieff), Nigel Stock (Herr Van Putzeboum), Michael Hughes, John Haden (Florist's Boys), Peter Bowles (Prince of Salestria), Yvette Milman (Rose), Martin Milman (Oudatte), Tom Karol (Cornette), Robert Perceval (Mayor), Michael Hughes (Photographer), Nigel Stock (Inspector of Police)

REVIEWS:
London Times, July 26, 1978: "Noël Coward's adaptation of Feydeau had the bad luck to be caught in the crossfire of the radical theatre campaign when the Royal Court staged it in 1959. Brought in as a sure fire West End hit to keep the Court in business, it failed to do the trick. All of which was most unfair to Coward, who was only guilty of adapting Feydeau for Britian some years before the arrival of the Feydeau boom. I only wish there had been more jokes and that Coward had entirely transformed the play instead of merely tinkering with it."

P-194   *Present Laughter* (revival) Kennedy Center, Washington D.C. Nov., 1978

Revival of **Noël Coward's comedy.** Directed by Roderick Cook. Produced by Ed Mirvsch's Royal Alexandra Theatre Company. Costumes by Hilary Corbett. Sets and lighting by John Jensen.

CAST: Peter O'Toole (Garry Essendine), Maureen McRae (Daphne), Maggie Asley (Miss Erikson), James B. Douglas (Fred), Marie Kean (Monica), Jackie Burroughs (Liz Essendine), Peter Dvorsky (Roland Maule), Claude Bede (Henry), Rod Menzies (Morris Dixon), Barbara Gordon (Joanna Lyppiatt), Sheila Haney (Lady Saltburn)

SYNOPSIS: See P-100

NOTES: Peter O'Toole did a television production of the play. See T-45.

P-195   *Fallen Angels* (revival) Roundabout Stage Two Theatre, NY April 22, 1980
(104 performances)

Revival of **Noel Coward's comedy**. Produced by the Roundabout Theatre
(Gene Feist & Michael Fried). Directed by Stephen Hollis. Sets by Roger
Mooney. Costumes by Andrew B. Marlay. Lighting by Norman Coates.

CAST: Jo Henderson (Julia Sterroll), John Clarkson (Frederick Sterroll),
Beulah Garrick (Saunders), Jim Osyter (William Banbury), Carol Teitel
(Jane Banbury), Stephen Schnetzner (Maurice Duclos)

SYNOPSIS: See P-36.

REVIEWS:

New York Times, July 11, 1980: "Noel Coward may have had a talent to amuse, but
he also had a remarkable gift for utter inanity. Nowhere, perhaps is this more
apparent than in *Fallen Angels*. The evening is not without its charms, however
minor and trivial they may be. Though *Fallen Angels* is one of Coward's worst
plays, it offers a paradoxically appealing portrait of the wasteful artist as a young
man."

New York Post, July 11, 1980: "This is a funny, ebullient exercise in style. It does
not rank among Coward's best two or three plays, yet it has a dash of its own, a
sense of fun and a mordent manner that really does remind you happily perhaps
of those olden days when there really was something shocking."

NOTES: Jo Henderson was succeeded by Valeri French and Jim Osyter by Don
Perkins.

P-196   *An Evening with The Lyrics of Noël Coward* 92nd Street YM-YWHA, NY
May 11 & 12, 1980 (2 performances)

A celebration of **Noël Coward's lyrics** presented as part of an ongoing
series which began in 1970 and is still going strong. Artistic director:
Maurice Levine. Director, Music Department: Hadassah B. Markson.
Pianist: Uel Wade.

CAST: Roderick Cook, Christine Andreas, Keith Baker and Hermione
Gingold.

P-197   *Private Lives* (revival) Duchess Theatre, London April 16, 1980 - Jan. 10, 1981. Transferred from the Greenwich Theatre.

Revival of **Noël Coward's comedy**. Directed by Alan Strachan. Produced by John Gale.

CAST: Maria Aitken (Amanda), Michael Jayston (Elyot)

P-198   *Present Laughter* (revival) The Vaudeville Theatre, London March 17, 1981-Dec. 5, 1981. Tried out at the Greenwich Theatre Jan. 29, 1981-March 7, 1981

Revival of **Noël Coward's comedy**. Directed by Alan Strachan. Sets and Costumes by Peter Rice. Produced by John Gale. Lighting by John A. Williams.

CAST: Donald Sinden (Garry Essendine), Belinda Lang (Daphne), Sheila Mitchell (Miss Erikson), Colin Spaull (Fred), Gwen Watford (Monica), Dinah Sheridan (Liz Essendine), Julian Fellows (Roland Maule), Ian Gardner (Henry), Michael Fleming (Morris Dixon), Polly Adams (Joanna Lyppiatt), Jill Johnson (Lady Saltburn)

SYNOPSIS: See P-100.

REVIEWS:
London Financial Times, Jan 30, 1981: "I've always thought *Present Laughter* the best of Noël Coward's plays, and this production beautifully directed by Alan Strachan, shows my reasons clearly. Garry Essendine is a part that a good actor can make his own with no tribute to anyone, and Mr. Sinden's version, while absolutely faithful to the play, is also a comple Sinden performance. It is a total success."

Punch (London), March 18, 1981: "Here, as in his 1980 revival of Coward's *Private Lives*, Strachan has recognised a very funny play about fundamentally very sad people; though *Private Lives* said a lot between its clipped and clenched lines about Coward's relationhip off-stage with Gerturde Lawrence, *Present Laughter* says a lot more about his private life and the people who made it work. In that sense it is at certain times one of the most autobiographical of all his plays, though Donald Sinden sensibly avoids all the perils of an impersonation."

NOTES: This production was taped for British television. See T-32.

P-199 *Noël and Gertie* May Fair Theatre, London April, 1981

> An entertainment devised by Sherdan Morley from the **words and music of Noël Coward** as a benefit for the Combined Theatrical Charities Council.

NOTES: Sheridan Morley, author of the first of the Coward bios and son of Robert Morley, became the literary conservator of the Coward estate after Sir Noël died. This was his first attempt at theatrical 'Noël mining'.

P-200 *Oh Coward!* (revival) On Stage, NY May 24, 1981 (37 performances)

> Revival of the revue using **music and lyrics by Noël Coward**. Produced by Barbara Darwall and John Montagnese in association with Talent to Amuse. Same credits as P-180, except Musical direction by Russell Walden, Lighting by F. Mitchell Dana, Costumes by Jack McGroder, Musical Staging by Clarence Teeters.

> CAST: Terri Klausner, Russ Thacker, Dalton Cathey, Kay Walbye

REVIEWS:
New York Times, July 11, 1981: "The public figure that Noel Coward presented as singer and actor — very crisply British, waspishly witty and highly sophisticated — lingers so firmly in the mind that it can still come as somewhat of a shock to realize how broadly his creative talents ranged."

New York Post, June 6, 1981: "I really recommend this show-it demonstrates Coward as a Cowardly lion, and Cook has dome some great cuisine."

Women's Wear Daily, May 27, 1981: "This never version comes across as a fast-moving, handsomely staged entertainment, but it might well be subtitled 'Where's Coward?' for a lot of Coward's genius and sentiment gets lost."

P-201 *Tonight At 8:30* (revival) Lyric Theatre, London August 11, 1981- Sept. 12, 1981. Tried out in Birmingham, June 1981.

> Revival of **three of Noël Coward's one act plays:** *Shadow Play, Hands Across The Sea* and *Red Peppers*. Produced by Eddie Kulukundis and John Wallbank for Knightsbridge Theatrical Productions Ltd. Directed by Jonathan Lynn. Choreographed by David Toguri. Designed by Saul Radomsky. Costumes by Bob Ringwood. Lighting by Mark Pritchard. Music orchestrated and directed by Ian Hughes. Sound by Paul Farrah.

CAST: *Shadow Play*: Victoria Duncan (Lena) Estelle Kohler (Victoria Gayforth), Zulema Dene (Martha Cunningham), John Standing (Simon Gayforth), John Lester (Hodge), Tim Brown (Michael Doyle), Susie Blake (Sybil Heston), Malcolm Mudie (A Young Man), Hugh Lloyd (George Cunningham); *Hands Across The Sea*: Victoria Duncan (Walters) Estelle Kohler (Piggie), (Her husband), Tim Brown (Alastair Corbett), Susie Blake (Mrs. Wadhurst), Hugh Lloyd (Mr. Burnham), Zulema Dene (Clare Wedderburn), Malcolm Mudie (Bogey); *Red Peppers:* Estelle Kohler (Lily Pepper) John Standing (George Pepper), Tim Brown (Alf), Hugh Lloyd (Bert Bentley), Malcolm Mudie (Mr. Edwards) Zulema Dene (Mabel Grace);

REVIEWS:
Birmingham Post, June 24, 1981: "From *Red Peppers* with its sardonic view of a third rate music hall song and patter act, through *Hands Across The Sea* to *Shadow Play* the lines dance across the evening like a string of diamonds and the whole production should be a resounding success when it transfers to the West End."

London Daily Express, August 12, 1981: "All in all, it's an entertaining evening. But it reminds us that it still needs courage to tackle this kind of Coward."

Sunday London Telegraph, August 15, 1981: "Noël Coward's *Tonight at 8:30* is like a dinner at which each of the three courses consists of crackers spread with caviar. One can hardly complain, but nonetheless one leaves feeling vaguely unsatisfied."

P-202 *Present Laughter* (revival) Circle in the Square Theatre, NY July 15, 1982
       (175 performances)

Revival of Noël Coward's comedy. Produced by the Circle in The Square (Theodore Mann & Paul Libin). Directed by George C. Scott. Sets by Marjorie Bradley Kellogg. Costumes by Ann Roth. Lighting by Richard Nelson.

CAST: George C. Scott (Garry Essendine) Kate Burton (Daphne), Bette Henritze (Miss Erikson), Jim Piddock (Fred), Dana Ivey (Monica), Elizabeth Hubbard (Liz Essendine), Nathan Lane (Roland Maule), Richard Woods (Henry), Edward Conery (Morris Dixon), Christine Lahti (Joanna Lyppiatt), Georgine Hall (Lady Saltburn)

SYNOPSIS: See P-100.

REVIEWS:
New York Post, July 16, 1982: "This is a most civilized play. Coward used the

English language with a deftness that had not been heard since Oscar Wilde. He can dazzle with the commonplace. He can make strange English place names, such as Uckfield or Stoke Poges, extravagantly funny. With climactic timing he can bring the house down with a line like "What a day for Cunard!" Genius."

New York Daily News, July 16, 1982: "How welcome Noël Coward is on a summer night, sending gales of laughter swirling through the Circle in the Square with his *Present Laughter.* And the evening might be said to be atypical Coward, at that. George C. Scott has taken this very fragile comedy and pointed it in the direction of knockabout farce while still trying to retain some semblance of Cowardian style. And fragile though it is, the play is somehow resilient enough to sustain such treatment and provide enormously funny entertainment."

P-203 *Private Lives* (revival) The Lunt-Fontanne Theatre, NY May 8, 1983 (63 performances)

> Revival of **Noël Coward's comedy.** Produced by The Elizabeth Theatre Group (Zev Bufman & Elizabeth Taylor). Directed by Milton Katselas. Sets by David Mitchell. Costumes by Theoni V. Aldredge. Lighting by Tharon Musser. Additional music by Stanley Silverman. Sound by Jack Mann.

> CAST: Elizabeth Taylor (Amanda), Richard Burton (Elyot), John Cullum (Victor), Kathryn Walker (Sybil), Helena Carrol (Louise)

SYNOPSIS: See P-61.

REVIEWS:
New York Times, May 9, 1983: "That play, the seeming inconsequentiality of its dialogue notwithstanding, is a wise and painful statement about both the necessity and the impossibility of love. In this version, whose billed director is Milton Katselas, there's no attempt to mine the gold beneath the text – or to make the most of the on-the-surface dross. Instead we get an intermittent effort by the stars to create the fan-magazine fantasy that their own offstage private lives dovetail neatly with Coward's story. But life doesn't imitate art in this *Private Lives* – it obliterates it."

New York Daily News, May 9, 1983: "The Elizabeth Taylor-Richard Burton revival of Noël Coward's dancing comedy *Private Lives* is more spectacle than a theatrical performance. It's LIZ AND DICK TOGETHER AGAIN!"

NOTES: This was the first production of what was planned to be the ongoing Elizabeth Production Company. After the distaster of this and the next show, *The*

Corn Is Green starring Cicely Tyson, the Elizabeth Company was no more.

P-204   *Noël & Gertie* Kings Head Theatre, London May 9, 1983 - June 4, 1983

> The second incarnation of Sheridan Morley's **tribute to Noël Coward** and Gertrude Lawrence, utilizing the **words and music of Noël Coward.** Directed by Alan Strachan. Choreographed by Kenn Oldfield. Decor by Norman Coates. Costumes by David Shilling. Pianist: William Blezard.

> CAST: Simon Cadell, David McAlister (Noël), Joanna Lumley, Gillian Bevan (Gertie), Sheridan Morley (Narrator)

REVIEWS:
London Daily Telegraph, May 10, 1983: "Considerable talent and a load of affection have gone into *Noël & Gertie.*"

P-205   *Design For Living* (revival) The Globe Theatre, London August 4, 1983 Originally produced at the Greenwich Theatre June 21, 1982 before transferring to the West End.

> Revival of **Noël Coward's comedy.** Directed by Alan Strachan. Produced by Duncan C. Weldon with Paul Gregg and Lionel Becker for Triumph Apollo Productions Ltd. Designed by Finlay James. Miss Aitken's costumes by Yuki.

> CAST: Maria Aitken (Gilda), Ian Oglivy (Leo), Gary Bond (Otto), Roland Curra (Ernest), Marilyn Cutts (Helen Carver), Andrew Francis (Matthew), Jeff Harding (Photographer), Helen Horton (Grace Torrence), Julia McCarthy (Miss Hodge), Nicholas Tudor (Mr. Birbeck), Jaime Sturgeon (Henry Carver)

SYNOPSIS: See P-71.

REVIEWS:
Punch, June 22, 1982: "Of all the major comedies *Design For Living* is perhaps least known and the most interesting. It's a play about license and order, about untidiness of the bed and of the heart and about the corruption of popularity and the triumph of Alan Strachan's new production is the awareness that it's also about the history of the 1930's."

London Times, August 5, 1983: "Sexual manners may have caught up with the play in the 1960's, but its popularity now may have more to do with a new generation clutching for the style of the 1930's...It becomes a play about liberations in matters other than sexual."

P-206   *Hay Fever* (revival) The Queen's Theatre, London Oct. 26, 1983

Revival of **Noël Coward's comedy**. Directed by Kim Grant. Produced by Peter Baldwin by arrangement with Stoll Moss Theatres Ltd. and Pencon Productions Ltd. Designed by Carl Toms. Lighting by Joe Davis.

CAST: Penelope Keith (Judith Bliss), Moray Watson (David Bliss), Rosalyn Landor (Sorel Bliss), Mark Payton (Simon Bliss), Susan Bovell (Myra Arundel), Donald Pickering (Richard Greatham), Abigail McKern (Jackie Coryton), David Delve (Sandy Tyrell), Elizabeth Bradley (Clara)

SYNOPSIS: See P-38.

REVIEWS:

Punch (London), Oct. 27, 1983: "As Judith Bliss, there's little doubt that Penelope Keith is the most perfect casting we've seen since the war: far closer to the right age than Edith Evans, who was a whole generation too old when she did the famous National Theatre revival of 1964. Miss Keith also has precisely the right mix of ruthlessness and charm, one that curiously eluded the infinitely vaguer Celia Johnson in the last (1968) revival."

London Spectator, Oct. 27, 1983: "Those of us who saw the author's production at the Old Vic in 1964 were, admittedly, spoiled. As Coward wrote, he had a company 'that could play the Albanian telephone directory.' Kim Grant's production fails to impose style. The play comes across as meringue left in the tin for too long, and made me yearn for Wilde or Orton."

London Daily Mail, Oct. 27, 1983: "*Hay Fever is* an unstoppable comedy not of manners as much as bad manners. Yet as with all Coward's seemingly effortless concoctions, there's always far more beneath the surface than meets the eye – a reason why each character behaves as he does, which makes them instantly recognisable and acceptable from generation to generation."

P-207   *A Celebration and Unveiling of a Memorial Stone* Westminster Abbey, London March 28, 1984   11:30 AM

Songs by the Ambrosian Singers, directed by John McCarthy. Orchestrations by Robert Docker and John McCarthy.

Songs included: London Pride, If Love Were All, I'll See You Again, Sail Away,

I'll Follow My Secret Heart, Someday I'll Find You, Play Orchestra Play, Has Anyone Seen Our Ship?, Sigh No More, Come the Wild Wild Weather

NOTES: Sir John Gielgud read Coward's poem "When I Have Fears," Derek Jacobi recited "The War Years," and Penelope Keith did the Toast from *Cavalcade*.

P-208   *Design For Living* (revival) Circle in the Square Theatre, NY June 1, 1984
(245 performances)

Revival of **Noël Coward's comedy.** Produced by Circle in the Square (Theodore Mann & Paul Libin). Directed by George C. Scott. Sets by Thomas Lynch. Cosutmes by Ann Roth. Lighting by Marc B. Weiss.

CAST: Jill Clayburgh (Gilda), Richard Woods (Ernest Friedman), Frank Langella (Otto), Raul Julia (Leo), Helene Carroll (Miss Hodge), Lisa Kirk (Grace Torrence), Anne Swift (Helen Carver), Robertson Carricart (Henry Carver), Arthur French (Matthew)

SYNOPSIS: See P-71

REVIEWS:
New York Daily News, June 21, 1984: "The revival is neither ideally cast nor directed. But then, how could it be. For this utterly scandalous, yet strangely sexless comedy was created by the author expressly as a vehicle for himself and the Lunts. And who could ever possibly top, or come close to that combination. It can't match the earlier *Private Lives* in craftsmanship or wit."

New York Post, June 21, 1984: "With a glance of wit, a dazzle of merriment and a finesse of style, Noël Coward's *Design For Living* finally returned to Broadway last night. As ever, where Coward shows the staying power of greatness is in his ability to invest the most ordinary phrase with, in its own context, a gurglins humor."

NOTES: Jill Clayburgh, Frank Langella, Raul Julia, Lisa Kirk and Anne Swift were replaced by Anne Swift, Frank Converse, John Glover, Louise Troy and Cecilia Hart respectively.

P-209   *Cavalcade* (revival) Chichester Festival Theatre, UK May 1, 1985

Revival of **Noël Coward's play.** Directed by David Gilmore. Decor by Roger Glossop. Costumes by Rebecca Neil. Choreography by Lindsay Dolan. Musical Direction by Colin Sell. Lighting by Bill Bray. Sound by Tim Oliver and Matthew Gale.

CAST: Joanna McCallum (Jane Marryot), Lewis Fiander (Robert Marryot), Elizabeth Estensen (Ellen Bridges), Berwick Kaler (Alfred Bridges), Janet Behan (Margaret Harris), Claire Fox (Edith Harris), Greg Saunders (Edward Marryot), Alastair Brett (Joe Marryot), Abigail Painter (Fanny Bridges), Sally Cooper (Mirabelle), Tom Fahy (Lt. Edgar), Sophia Winter (Ada/Rose Darling) Robert Demeger (Tom Jolly/George Grainger), Jane Salter (Cook), Jenny Michelmore (Annie), Shirley Stelfox (Mrs. Snapper/Marion Christie), Charmain Gradwell (Connie Crawshay), Alex Jennings (Tim Bateman), Simon Green (Douglas Finn/Uncle George), Brett Fancy (Uncle Harry), Michael Simkins (Uncle Dick/Lord Martlett), Michael Grandage (Uncle Jim/Stage Manager), Jaye Griffiths (Gladys) All other roles played by members of the community.

SYNOPSIS: See P-67.

REVIEWS:
London Observer, May 5, 1985: "The biggest surprise about Coward's *Cavalcade* is that it should prove so pitifully thin. Feeble and repetitive little domestic scenes alternate with mob appearances by a large part of Chichester's population, with their sisters and their cousins and their aunts. *Cavalcade* is solemn and meretricious crap."

London Daily Mail, May 2, 1985: "Anyone remotely interested in the stage, or simply wanting to be hit in the eye and heart by emotional spectacle, ought to hitchhike there, if necessary, because there's nothing remotely like *Cavalcade* anywhere else. It make a wonderful night of theatre. Challenges and complications are risen to so efficiently that Coward himself might have been impressed. As for the the audience, they loved it."

Punch (London), May 8, 1985: "This is an epic devoted to the much wider concept of duty that runs through most of his work, and somewhere in *Cavalcade* you can find almost everything that mattered about Coward as a dramatist and as a man: the strong sense of the immediate past, the concept of duty and decent behaviour as about all else, the brisk edginess of a love scene on the Titanic, and overall a cascading sense of sheer theatre."

NOTES: The ending of the play was altered to include two hundred people singing Jerusalem, rather than the chaos of the 1929 nightclub.

P-210   *Hay Fever* (revival) Music Box Theatre, NY Dec. 12, 1985 (124 performances)

Revival of **Noël Coward's comedy**. Produced by Roger Peters in association with MBS Co. Directed by Brian Murray. Sets by Michael H. Yeargan. Costumes by Jennifer Von Mayrhouser. Lighting by Arden Fingerhut. New song by Kander and Ebb.

CAST: Rosemary Harris (Judith Bliss), Roy Dotrice (David Bliss), Mia Dillon (Sorel Bliss), Robert Joy (Simon Bliss), Carolyn Seymour (Myra Arundel), Charles Kimbrough (Richard Greatham), Deborah Rush (Jackie Coryton), Campbell Scott (Sandy Tyrell), Barbara Bryne (Clara)

SYNOPSIS: See P-38.

REVIEWS:
New York Times, Dec. 13, 1985: "In the unlikely event that you stop laughing and start thinking at the sparkling new Broadway revival of *Hay Fever,* you may notice that Noël Coward's comedy has skin-deep characters, little plot, no emotional weight or redeeming social value and very few lines that sound funny out of context. All of which goes to show that some plays defy the laws of theatrical gravity. In this now 60 year old jape, Coward demonstrates that pure fluff also rises: *Hay Fever* is a classic spun out of the thinnest and most dizzying of air."

New York Daily News, Dec. 13, 1985: "Like the armful of flowers she saunters in with from the garden at her first entrance, Rosemary Harris carries Noël Coward's comedy conceit with an airy grace that never once falters. And *Hay Fever*, a wafer-thin play with nothing on its mind but the nimble jesting, demands no less. It is all style and this very stylish production is a lark."

NOTES: Besides being an almost perfect revival of the play, audiences were treated to a new song by Kander and Ebb in the style of the Master.

P-211   *Blithe Spirit* (revival) Vaudeville Theatre, London Jan. 30, 1986

Revival of **Noël Coward's comedy**. Produced by Avenue Productions Ltd. (Martin Tickner). Directed by Peter Farago. Designed by Carl Toms. Lighting by Leonard Tucker. Music by Richard Addinsell.

CAST: Simon Cadell (Charles Condomine), Jane Asher (Ruth Condomine), Marcia Warren (Madame Arcati), Joanna Lumley (Elvira), Roger Hume (Dr. Bradman), Rachel Herbert (Mrs. Bradman), Imogen Bain (Edith)

SYNOPSIS: See P-97

REVIEWS:

London Daily Mail, Jan. 31, 1986: "The play is and remains a minor masterpiece, a triumph of style, technique and theatrical daring."

London Financial Times, Jan. 31, 1986: "First class, bright, intelligent and thoroughly enjoyable revival."

Punch (London), Feb. 12, 1986: "This impressive company seems to have understood that Coward never really works unless he is played for real insead of for laughs. An eminently well made comedy has been given a production of rock solid craftsmanship and tremendous affection."

NOTES: In the pre-West End tour Madame Arcarti was played by Lila Kedrova.

P-212 *Noël and Gertie* Donmar Warehouse, London Aug. 28-Sept. 20, 1986

> Revision of the entertainment devised by Sheridan Morley with **words and music by Noël Coward**. Produced by Avenue Productions Ltd. and The Salisbury Playhouse. Directed by David Horlock. Decor by Carl Toms. Lighting by Peter Hunter. Choreography by Jonathan Howell. Musical direction by William Blezard.

> CAST: Lewis Fiander (Noël), Patricia Hodge (Gertie)

REVIEWS:
Sunday London Daily Mail, Aug. 31, 1986: "The show focuses happily on their adult partnership, dovetailing a neatly varied selection of Coward's songs with excerpts from the plays and revues in which they both appeared."

London Listener, April 9, 1986: "Like Sondheim, Noël Coward tends to be underestimated purely as a composer. Long overdue is a reassessment of the Master's contribution of popular song, as is a peep behind his self-image. But Sheridan Morley's biographical revue *Noël and Gertie* seems to take at face value the myths Coward cultivated around both his own personality and his professional partnership with Gertrude Lawrence."

P-213 *Oh Coward!* (revival) Helen Hayes Theatre, NY Nov. 17, 1986
      (56 performances)

> Broadway premiere of the revue utilizing **words and music by Noël Coward** (played off-Broadway originally). Lighting by Mitchell Dana. Costumes by David Toser. Musical direction by Dennis Buck. Executive producer: Richard Seader. Produced by Raymond J. Greenwald. Other credits same as P-180.

CAST: Roderick Cook, Catherine Cox, Patrick Quinn

REVIEWS:
New York Times, Nov. 18, 1986: "In the years since Mr. Cook first put his revue together, the show has not been appreciably altered. On Broadway or off, this remains basically a cabaret show. As in the author's self-description, the evening is 'so nonchalant and frightfully debonair.' *Oh Coward!* scrupulously minds its manners."

New York Daily News, Nov. 18, 1986: "Everything about this production is so stiff, so arch, that you come away with the image of Coward he had a the low point of his career, in the aftermath of World War II."

P-214 *Blithe Spirit* (revival) Neil Simon Theatre, NY March 31, 1987 (103 performances)

Revival of **Noël Coward's comedy**. Produced by Karl Allison, Douglas Urbanski, Sandra Moss in association with Jerome Minskoff and Duncan C. Weldon. Directed by Brian Murray. Sets by Finlay James. Costumes by Theoni V. Aldredge. Lighting by Richard Nelson. Music arranged by Marvin Hamlisch.

CAST: Richard Chamberlain (Charles Condomine), Judith Ivey (Ruth Condomine), Geraldine Page (Madame Arcati), Blythe Danner (Elvira), William LeMessena (Dr. Bradman), Patricia Connolly (Mrs. Bradman), Norah Cavendish (Edith)

SYNOPSIS: See P-97.

REVIEWS:
New York Times, April 1, 1987: "Four first rate actors, all except Blythe Danner miscast, none in top form, struggle for three acts to find the light touch that might make this lark, written in less than a week in 1941, take flight."

New York Daily News, April 1, 1987: "Noël Coward plays ought to be handled as if they were the very best champagne, which, when properly chilled sparkles perfectly. The current production of *Blithe Spirit*, though full of fizz, has been mounted by people who think you have to shake the bottle. There are laughs, but it's Cold Duck, not Mumms."

Newsweek, April 13, 1987: "In *Blithe Spirit* Coward retained his fabled 'talent to amuse', but a streak of gentility softens the genius of *Private Lives* and *Design For Living*. Still, Coward's beautiful bitcheries are enough in evidence to remind us that he was precursor of playwrights like Harold Pinter and Joe Orton."

NOTES: This was to be Geraldine Page's final performances. On June 13, 1987 she died. Patricia Conolly played Madame Arcati until the show closed.

P-215   *Easy Virtue* (revival) The Garrick Theatre, London April 21, 1988
Originally performed at the Kings Head Theatre Dec. 31, 1987.

Revival of **Noël Coward's play**. Produced by Tandemstar, Dan Crawford and Mark Burns by arrangement with Louis Benjamin for Stoll Moss Theatres Ltd. and Jolly Good Productions Ltd. Directed by Tim Luscome. Sets by Bruce Snyder. Lighting by Leonard Tucker. Costumes by Tim Heywood.

CAST: Mabel Terry-Lewis (Mrs. Whittaker), Marda Vanne (Marion), Halliwell Hobbes (Colonel Whittaker), Joan Clement Scott (Hilda), Lionel Hogarth (Furber), Robert Harris (John), Jane Cowl (Larita), Joyce Carey (Sarah Hurst), Vernon Kelso (Charles Burleigh), Peter Carpenter (Philip Bordon), William Podmore (Mr. Harris), Gipsy O'Brien (Nina Vansittart), Peter Macfarlane (Hugh Petworth), C. Bailey Hick (Bobby Coleman), Constance Best (Lucy Coleman), Wallace Wood (Henry Furey), Grace Hampton (Mrs. Hurst), Nancy B. Marsland (Mrs. Phillips), Marlon Evensen (Mary Banfield)

REVIEWS:
London Daily Mail, April 22, 1988: "The evening is nothing short of a triumph. That it remains one of Coward's least known and rarely revived plays is astonishing. The play is a deadly and radical assault on all the deep seated prejudices and smug moral certainties with which the middle class have defended themselves against anything they fail to understand."

London City Limits, April 22, 1988: "The best evening of Coward the West End has seen in years."

Punch (London), May 6, 1988: "No writer of his generation ever went more directly to the jugular of the moralistic but fundamentally hypocritical society of the 1920's."

NOTES: This was the first major revival of the play. At the King's Head Mrs. Wittaker was played by Avril Angers, Furber by Noël Hill, Sarah by Julie Dawne Cole, Charles by Eric Carte, Philip by Richard Stirling, Hugh by Sean Patterson, Nina by Louise Sanderson, Rev. Henry Furley by Andrew Short, Lucy by Amelia

Blacker, Mrs. Phillips by Janet Hargreaves, Mary by Amelia Blacker.

P-216   *Bitter Sweet* (revival) Sadler's Wells Theatre, London Feb. 23-Mar. 19, 1988

> Revival of **Noël Coward's operette**. Produced by the New Sadler's Wells Opera, director Joseph Karaviotis in association with The Theatre Royal, Plymouth and with investment from The Arts Council. Directed by Ian Judge. Score revised and musically supervised by Michael Reed. Sets by Russell Craig. Costumes by Deidre Clancy. Choreography by Lindsay Dolan. Lighting by Nick Chelton. Musical Direction by Stuart Hutchinson. Orchestrations by Robert Stewart and Michael Reed. Additional orchestrations by Ted Brennan and Alexander Faris.

> CAST: Ann MacKay or Valerie Masterson (Sarah Millick), Martin Smith (Carl Linden), Rosemary Ashe (Manon), Gordon Sandison or Ian Platt (Capt. Auguste Lutte), Tom Griffin (Singer & Footman), Sara Weymouth (Dolly Chamberlain & Lotte), David Kinder (Lord Henry Jekyll & Footman), Clive Walton (Vincent T. Howard & Footman), Michael Chance (Frank, Footman & Lt. Tranisch), Lorraine Vaughan (Helen & Hansi), Claire Hayes (Jacky & Gloria), Clare Welch (Mrs. Millick), Rupert Vansittart (Hugh Devon), Lucy Fenwick (Lady Devon), Alec Bregonzi (Sir Arthur, Herr Schlick & The Marquis of Shayne), Fiona Lamont (Harriet), Susan Stubbs (Honor), Sally-Anne Middleton (Victoria), Carol Lesley-Green (Effie), Anne O'Neill (Jane), Tom Griffin (Mr. Proutie), Michael Fitchew (The Marquis of Steere), Robert Jon (Lord Edgar James), Ian Platt (Lord Sorrel), David Dyer (Mr. Vale), Donald Jones (Mr. Bethel), Lucy Fenwick (Freda), Rachel Izen (Gussi)

SYNOPSIS and MUSICAL NUMBERS: See P-58.

REVIEWS:
London Daily Mail, Feb. 25, 1988: "For those of us still numbed by the tastelessness of *Carrie*, the RSC's answer to period musicals, the revival of *Bitter-Sweet* comes as a reviving antitdote. What is surprising, when we are all taught that it was Rodgers and Hammerstein who first married plot and score together seamlessly, is how nearly Noël Coward beat them to it by almost twenty years."

London Independent, Feb. 27, 1988: "With so much third rate Coward currently plodding around the country, it is reassuring to find proof that at his best he led the field – at least in British Musical Theater."

London Observer, Feb. 28, 1988: "Much of what in 1928 was received as affectionate and genuine homage to the popular theatre of fifty years earlier looks doubly synthetic now."

NOTES: This revival was recorded, making it the first complete version of *Bitter-Sweet* to hit the record stores. See D-120.

P-217   *The Vortex* (revival) The Garrick Theatre, London Jan. 26, 1989. Tried out at the Citizen's Theatre, Glasgow Jan., 1988.

Revival of **Noël Coward's play**. Produced by Josephine Hart Productions Ltd. in association with Stagescreen Productions Ltd. and Dramatis Personae by arrangement with Louis Benjamin for Stoll Moss Theatres Ltd. Directed and designed by Philip Prowse. Lighting by Gerry Jenkinson. Choreographed by Imogen Claire.

CAST: Jill Fenner (Preston), Anne Lambton (Helen Saville), Tristram Jellinek (Pauncefort Quentin), Fidelis Morgan (Clara Hibbert), Maria Aitken (Florence Lancaster), Martyn Stanbridge (Tom Veryan), Rupert Everett (Nicky Lancaster), Stephen MacDonald (David Lancaster), Yolanda Vazquez (Bunty Mainwaring), Derwent Watson (Bruce Fairlight)

SYNOPSIS: See P-35.

P-218   *Blithe Spirit* (revival) Lyric Theatre, Hammersmith, London June 12, 1989

Revival of **Noël Coward's comedy**. Produced by Lee Dean & Robert Kennedy for Gallery Productions by arrangement with the Churchill Theatre, Bromley. Directed by John David. Designed by Terry Parsons. Lighting by Richard Caswell.

CAST: Neil Stacy (Charles Condomine), Deborah Grant (Ruth Condomine), Peggy Mount (Madame Arcati), Rula Lenska (Elvira), Michael Knowles (Dr. Bradman), Eira Griffiths (Mrs. Bradman), Lynette Mc-Morrough (Edith)

SYNOPSIS: See P-97.

P-219   *Noël and Gertie* Comedy Theatre, London Dec. 12, 1989 (206 performances). Tried out at Yvonne Arnaud Theatre, Guildford Nov. 28, 1989.

West End premiere of the entertainment devised by Sheridan Morley with the **music and lyrics of Noël Coward**. Directed by Alan Strachan. Produced by Independent Theatrical Productions Ltd., Zoë Dominic for Avenue Productions Ltd. and Bill Freedman. Musical direction by Jonathan Cohen. Designed by Carl Toms. Choreographed by David Toguri. Lighting by Leonard Tucker.

CAST: Simon Cadell (Noël), Patricia Hodge (Gertie), Jonathan Cohen (Pianist)

MUSICAL NUMBERS: Play Orchestra Play, Some Day I'll Find You, Any Little Fish, Mrs. Worthington, Parisian Pierrot, Dance Little Lady, We Were Dancing, You Were There, Then, Has Anybody Seen Our Ship?, Men About Town, I Travel Alone, Sail Away, Why Must The Show Go On?, Come The Wild, Wild Weather, I'll Remember Her, I'll See You Again.

REVIEWS:
Variety, Jan. 3, 1990: "The enormous affection Noël Coward and Gertrude Lawrence had for each other and the theatre is elegantly and touchingly evoked by Sheridan Morley in *Noel & Gertie*. Morley's stylish material has a smooth flow and is at its most disarming and lyrical when evoking Coward's devotion to Lawrence."

NOTES: This is a completely new revision of P-212.

P-220   *Private Lives* (revival) Aldwych Theatre, London Sept. 19, 1990

Revival of **Noël Coward's Comedy**. Produced by Michael Codron. Directed by Tim Luscombe. Designed by Carl Toms. Lighting by Leonard Tucker.

CAST: Sara Crowe (Sybil Chase), Keith Baxter (Elyot Chase), Edward Duke (Victor Prynne), Joan Collins (Amanda Prynne), Mary Pegler (Louise)

NOTES: Sara Crowe won the Olivier Award for Best Supporting Actress.

P-221   *The Vortex* (revival) Ahmanson at the Doolittle Theatre, Los Angeles. Jan. 17, 1991-Mar. 31, 1991

Revival of **Noël Coward's play.** Directed by Robert Allan Ackerman. Produced by Center Theatre Group/Ahmanson Theatre (Gordon Davidson, producing director) in association with Josephine Hart Prods. Ltd. Sets by Hugh Landwehr. Costumes by Robert Wojewodski based on 1988 designs by Phillip Prowse for the Citizens Theatre of Glasgow. Lighting by Arden Fingerhut. Sound by Jon Gottlieb. Choreographed by Dana Landers.

CAST: Babbie Green (Preston), Brian Wallace (Barker), Suzanne Bertish (Helen Saville), Ian Abercrombie (Pauncefort Quentin), Erica Rogers (Clara Hibbert), Stephanie Beacham (Florence Lancaster), Simon Templeman (Tom Veryan), Rupert Everett (Nicky Lancaster), George Innes (David Lancaster), Molly Hagan (Bunty Mainwaring), Julian Barnes (Bruce Fairlight)

SYNOPSIS: see P-35.

REVIEWS:
Variety Jan. 28, 1991: "Theatre lovers are advised to leap into *The Vortex*. Coward depicts charming people who are victims of their own selfishness and their hectic, misplaced values. It's not surprising that the play was shocking when it debuted, but what's startling and a little disconcerting is how relevant it is today. The elegant, theatrical play remains entertaining even at its starkest."

NOTES: This production was Broadway bound, but never arrived.

P-222 *Cole & Coward* Kaufman Theatre, NY Nov. 14, 1991

One women show consisting of Cole Porter and **Noël Coward songs**. Produced by Martin Kaufman.

CAST: Julie Wilson, William Roy

P-223 *Noël & Gertie* Duke of York Theatre, London Nov. 28, 1991-Jan. 25, 1992

Limited holiday engagement of the entertainment devised by Sheridan Morley with **words and music by Noël Coward**. Produced by Independent Theatrical Productions Ltd, Zoe Dominic for Avenue Productions Ltd., Bill Freedman Ltd. and Eddie Kulukundis for Knightsbridge Theatrical Productions Ltd. A co-production with Churchill Theatre Bromley of the original West End production. Directed by Sean Mathias. Designed by Carl Toms. Choreography by Eleanor Fazan. Lighting by Leonard Tucker.

CAST: Susan Hampshire (Gertie), Edward Petherbridge (Noël), Jason Carr (Pianist)

P-224   *Private Lives* (revival) Broadhurst Theatre, NY Feb. 20, 1992 (37 performances) Extensive pre-Broadway national tour of 11 cities in 16 weeks beginning in Denver, CO and including Dallas, TX.

Revival of **Noël Coward's comedy**. Directed by Arvin Brown. Produced by Charles H. Duggan/PACE Theatrical Group. Sets by Loren Sherman. Costumes by William Ivey Long. Lighting by Richard Nelson.

CAST: Jill Tasker (Sybil Chase), Simon Jones (Elyot Chase), Edward Duke (Victor Prynne), Joan Collins (Amanda Prynne), Margie Rynn (Louise)

SYNOPSIS: See P-61.

REVIEWS:
Theatre Week (New York), Nov. 25, 1991: "What was happening on the road early on was a fearsome flatness that left the show, to borrow from the script, 'breathlessly lovely and completely unexciting.'"

The New Yorker, Feb. 21, 1992: "In a play renowned for style, one would expect an actress renowned for glitz to fall flat on her face. Actually, Miss Collins does just fine as Amanda. She doesn't reinvent the role, or anything, but she has her moments. And if her voice could be a little more variable and her timing a little sharper and her curtain call a little more gracious toward her co-star, Simon Jones — well, what the hey?"

New York Post, Feb. 21, 1992: "If you haven't seen the play before you'll enjoy the evening more than if you have, particularly if you also have a natural curiosity to see Miss Collins in the flesh."

Associated Press, Feb 21, 1992: "Noël Coward's *Private Lives* is usually thought of as one of those indestructible plays, a classic romantic comedy. That assessment is sorely tested at the Broadhurst Theatre where Joan Collins and company nearly batter the life, and humor, out of Coward's best-known work."

NOTES: This production toured the country before coming to Broadway and foul notices.

P-225   *Post-Mortem* The King's Head Theatre, London Sept. 29-Nov. 8, 1992

Professional stage premiere of **a play by Noël Coward** (written in 1930). Produced by the King's Head Theatre. Directed by Richard Stirling. Designed by Mark Friend. Costumes by Tim Heywood.

CAST: Avril Angers, Harry Burton, Max Gold, Walter Hall, Carol Holt, Will Knightley, Ian Michie, Susannah Morley, Steven Pacey, Neil Roberts, Roy Sampson, Sylvia Syms

SYNOPSIS: In 1917 John Cavan is on the front lines of WWI. Surrounded by his companions, he listens to their hopes and fears the future they are fighting for. And then he is wounded. The action jumps ahead to England 1930. Lady Cavan sits at her window playing patience. Her son John appears, dressed in his uniform. He visits with his family, Monica the woman he loved and the survivors of the 1917 bunker.

NOTES: After appearing in *Journey's End* in Singapore, Coward was inspired to write his own anti-war play. Coward wrote in his Introduction to *Play Parade, Vol I*: "*Post-Mortem* was not actually written for the theatre. But I put it into play form, for the simple reason that I felt more at home in that than in any other. It has not yet been produced, although one day perhaps it will be. I think it might probably be quite effective, provided that it is expertly directed and acted." The text was first published by Heinemann, London in 1931.

P-226   *Noël and Gertie* The Theatre at Saint Peter's Church, NY Nov. 24-Dec. 20, 1992 (27 performances)

New York premiere of the entertainment devised by Sheridan Morley **with the words and music of Noel Coward**. Directed by Brian Murray. Produced by The York Theatre Company (Janet Hayes Walker, producing director, Molly Pickering Grose, managing director) Scenic design by James Morgan, Costumes designed by Barbara Beccio. Lighting by Mary Jo Dondlinger. Choreogaphy by Janet Watson.

CAST: Jane Summerhayes (Gertie), Michael Zaslow (Noel)

P-227   *Hay Fever* (revival) Albery Theatre, London Nov. 26, 1992. Tried out at Theatre of Comedy Oct. 10, 1992.

Revival of **Noël Coward's comedy**. Produced by the Theatre of Comedy Company. Directed by Alan Strachan. Set and costumes by Anthony Powell. Lighting by Mick Hughes.

CAST: Abigail Cruttenden (Sorel Bliss), Nick Waring (Simon Bliss), Maria Charles (Clara), Maria Aitken (Judith Bliss), John Standing (David Bliss), Richard Garnett (Sandy Tyrell), Carmen Du Sautoy (Myra Arundel), Christopher Godwin (Richard Greatham), Sara Crowe (Jackie Coryton)

SYNOPSIS: See P-38.

REVIEWS:
London Daily Mail, Nov. 27, 1992: "For the appeal of this play to have survived across the decades there is obviously a great deal more going for it than mere high camp and high jinks. Something much deeper and enduring must bind it to our collective consciousness. Alan Strachan's wildly inventive revival succeeds brilliantly on both levels."

London Daily Telegraph, Nov. 30, 1992: "This is the theatre of cruelty played for laughs, and as you listen to the deadly precision of the dialogue, you realise with a shock what a large debt Harold Pinter owes to Coward. Coward made spectacular use of the pregnant pause, most notably in the marvellous tea party scene."

Sunday London Times, Nov. 29, 1992: "This is a sadistically funny revival: and it confirms my long-held view that Noël Coward was the Harold Pinter of the Jazz Age. *Hay Fever* is a comedy of menace."

Noël Coward and Gertrude Lawrence perform "Has Anybody Seen Our Ship?" from *Red Peppers*, one of the one act plays that make up *Tonight at 8:30* (1936).
Photo courtesy of Photofest.

Florence Henderson, José Ferrer, Herman Levin (producer) and Noël Coward try out the score of *The Girl Who Came To Supper* (1964).
Photo courtesy of Photofest.

Filmography

This section details the film appearances of Noël Coward, the film adaptations of his plays, the original films he wrote and/or directed and produced, the films containing his music and one film featuring Coward as a character. These entries are preceded by the letter "F."

F-1   *Hearts of the World*   World Pictures 1918

A silent film produced, written and directed by D.W. Griffith.

CAST: Lillian Gish, Dorothy Gish, Robert Harron, Kate Bruce, **Noël Coward**

NOTES: Noël Coward made his film debut at age 17 as an extra in D.W. Griffith's film starring Lillian and Dorothy Gish. Paid a pound a day, he wheeled a wheelbarrow up and down a village street in Worcestershire with Lillian Gish. In Gish's 1969 Prentiss-Hall autobiography, *The Movies, Mr. Griffith & Me*, she tells of "a darling seventeen-year-old English boy, whom Mother promptly added to her brood. He had an original mind and a sense of theatre. In one scene the French girl I was playing packed her possessions and left home...This young actor was supposed to help me by pushing the loaded wheelbarrow down the street. At his own suggestion the boy pushed the wheelbarrow toward the camera instead of away from it. The boy was Noël Coward and this film was his first."

F-2   *The Queen Was In The Parlour*   Gainsborough Pictures, England 1927

Film version (silent) of Noël Coward's play. Screenplay and Direction by Graham Cutts. First shown in London at the Avenue Pavilion Feb., 1928.

CAST: Lili Damita (Nadya), Paul Richter (Sabien), Harry Leichke (Prince Keri), Rosa Richards (Zana), Klein Rogges (General Krish), Trude Hesterberg (Grand Duchess Emilie of Zalgar)

SYNOPSIS: see P-45.

F-3   *The Vortex* Gainsborough Pictures, England 1928

Film version (silent) of Noël Coward's play. Screenplay by Eliot Stannard. Directed by Adrian Brunel.

CAST: Dorothy Fane (Helen Saville), Kinsey Peile (Pauncefort Quentin), Willette Kershaw (Florence Lancaster), Alan Hollis (Tom Veryan), Ivor Novello (Nicky Lancaster), Sir Simeon Stuart (David Lancaster), Frances Doble (Bunty Mainwaring), Julie Suedo (The Dancer)

SYNOPSIS: see P-35.

REVIEWS:
Kine Weekly: "Noël Coward's play has been filtered, and a mother's vanity and clinging to her faded looks quite well presented. Considering the difficulties of the story, which is hardly suitable for screen purposes, Adrian Brunel has done very well."

The Bioscope: "Excellent as this production is in many details, it is another proof that the most successful of stage plays is not necessarily a fit subject for the screen."

NOTES: At about the same time Hitchcock was coping with the film of *Easy Virtue*. (F-4) Realising that his plays were difficult film material, Michael Balcon asked Coward to write an original screen story. Coward concurred and wrote *Concerto*. It was never filmed, but became the plot of *Bitter-Sweet* (P-58).

F-4   *Easy Virtue* Gainsborough Pictures, England 1928

Film version (silent) of Noël Coward's play. Produced by Michael Balcon. Directed by Alfred Hitchcock. Screen adaptation by Eliot Stannard. First show in London at the Stoll, March, 1928.

CAST: Isabel Jeans (Larita), Franklyn Dyall (Her Husband), Violet Farebrother (Mrs. Whittaker), Dacia Deane (Marion), Frank Elliot (Colonel Whittaker), Dorothy Boyd (Hilda), Robert Irvine (John), Eric Bransby-Williams (The Co-respondent), Ian Hunter (Plaintiff's Council), Enid Stamp-Taylor (Sarah Hurst)

SYNOPSIS: see P-43.

F-5   *Show of Shows* Warner Brother, Vitaphone 1930

NOTES: Beatrice Lillie's number by **Noël Coward,** "The Roses Have Made Me Remember" (from *Charlot's Revue of 1924* P-34) was filmed, cut and later released as a short. Miss Lillie unsuccessfully sued Warner Brothers for releasing the short without her permission.

F-6   *Private Lives* Metro-Goldwyn-Mayer, US 1931

> **Film version of Noël Coward's comedy.** Directed by Sidney Franklin. Screen adaptation by Hans Kraly, Richard Schayer and Claudine West.
>
> CAST: Una Merkel (Sybil Chase), Robert Montgomery (Elyot Chase), Reginald Denny (Victor Prynne), Norma Shearer (Amanda Prynne), Jean Hersholt (Oscar), George Davis (Page)

SYNOPSIS: see P-61.

REVIEWS:
New York Times, Dec. 19, 1931: "Noël Coward's stage comedy *Private Lives* has blossomed into a motion picture. Sidney Franklin's direction is excellent and Norma Shearer as Amanda Prynne gives an alert, sharp portrayal. She appears to be inspired by the scintilating dialogue. This is a swift and witty picture and even though it cannot boast of the effective presence of the author in the part of Elyot, it is one of the most intelligent comedies to come to the screen."

NOTES: Although Noël Coward and Gertrude Lawrence screen-tested, the lead parts went to others. After filming their one and only film *The Guardsman*, it was reported in the July 1931 *Vanity Fair* that the Lunts had agreed to appear in the film, but they instead opted to return to the stage.

F-7   *Tonight Is Ours* Paramount Pictures, US 1932

> **Talkie remake of Noël Coward's play** *The Queen Was In The Parlour.* Directed by Stuart Walker. Screen adaptation by Edwin Justus Mayer.
>
> CAST: Claudette Colbert (Nadya), Fredric March (Sabien), Paul Cavanaugh (Prince Keri), Ethel Griffies (Zana), Arthur Byron (General Krish), Alison Skipworth (Grand Duchess Emilie of Zalgar), Clay Clement (Seminoff), Warburton Gamble (Alex), Edwin Maxwell (Delegate)

SYNOPSIS: see P-45.

REVIEWS:
New York Times, Jan. 23, 1933: "Quite a pleasant entertainment."

F-8   *Cavalcade* Fox Film Company, US 1932

Film version of Noël Coward's play. Directed by Frank Lloyd. Screen adaptation by Reginald Berkeley. First shown in NY at the Gaiety Theatre, Jan. 5, 1933.

CAST: Diana Wynyard (Jane Marryot), Clive Brook (Robert Marryot), Una O'Conner (Ellen Bridges), Herbert Mundin (Alfred Bridges), Irene Browne (Margaret Harris), Margaret Lindsay (Edith Harris), John Warburton (Edward Marryot), Frank Lawton (Joe Marryot), Ursula Jeans (Fanny Bridges), Sheila MacGill (Edith as a child), Dick Henderson Jr. (Edward as a child), Douglas Scott (Joe as a child), Bonita Granville (Fanny as a child), Beryl Mercer (Cook), Merle Tottenham (Annie Grainger), Tempe Piggot (Mrs. Snapper), Bill Bevan (George Grainger)

SYNOPSIS: see P-67.

REVIEWS:
New York Times, Jan. 6, 1933: "It is a most affecting and impressive picture that Fox has produced from Noël Coward's stage panarama, *Cavalcade*."

Photo Play date n/a: "Very rarely a film succeeds in presenting not only a poignant human story, but also in conveying the sweep and power of world events against which the humans work out their lives. It is this rare achievement which makes *Cavalcade* so outstanding."

New York Sun, Jan. 6, 1933: "Something of an event, a distinguished, important contribution to the screen, justifying all that had been expected of it."

Daily News, Jan. 6, 1933: "*Cavalcade* is exquisitely pictured with gaiety, laughter and songs intermingling with the tragedy of the tale. We love it and so will you."

Noël Coward, Jan. 12, 1933: "I have just seen the *Cavalcade* picture and it is quite unbelievably good. It really is a glorious achievement in every respect."

NOTES: The film won the Academy Award for Best Picture and for Frank Lloyd's direction. William S. Darling also won an Oscar for Best Art Direction. The stage production was filmed at the Drury Lane as a guide for the film. The film is available on video from MGM.

F-9   *Bitter-Sweet* British and Dominion Films, England. 1933

Film version of Noël Coward's operette. Directed by Herbert Wilcox. Screen adaptation by Herbert Wilcox and Moncton Hoffe. **Music and lyrics by Noël Coward.** First shown in London at the Carlton, Haymarket, Sept., 1933. First show in NY at the Rivoli Theatre Aug. 23, 1933.

CAST: Anna Neagle (Sarah Millick), Ferdinand Graavey (Carl Linden), Norma Walley (Mrs. Millick), Esme Percy (Hugh Devon), Ivy St. Helier (Manon), Miles Mander (Captain Auguste Lutte), Clifford Heatherley (Herr Schlick), Kay Hammond (Gussi), Stuart Robertson (Lt. Tranisch), Pat Paterson (Dolly), Patrick Ludlow (Henry), Hugh Williams (Vincent Howard), Gibb McLaughlin (The Footman)

SYNOPSIS: See P-58

REVIEWS:
New York Times, Aug. 24, 1933: "It is an artistic production and its scenes are set forth with gratifying elegance and sober fluency to the frequent accompaniment of tuneful music and singing."

NOTES: The film cut Act III of the stage version completely. Numbers retained include: "The Call of Life," "If You Could Only Come Away," "I'll See You Again," "Tell Me What Is Love," "Ladies of The Town," "If Love Were All," "Dear Little Cafe," "Tokay," "Kiss Me." The film is most important for preserving the magical performance of Ivy St. Helier as Manon.

F-10   *Design For Living* Paramount Pictures, US 1933

Film version of Noël Coward's comedy. Directed by Ernst Lubitsch. Screen adaptation by Ben Hecht. First shown in NY at Criterion Theatre Nov. 22, 1933.

CAST: Fredric March (Tom Chambers), Gary Cooper (George Curtis), Miriam Hopkins (Gilda), Edward Everett Horton (Max Plunkett), Franklin Pangborn (Mr. Douglas), Isabel Jewell (Lisping Stenographer), Harry Dunkinson (Mr. Egelbaucer), Helean Phillips (Mrs. Egelbaucer), James Donlin (Fat Man), Vernon Steele (First Manager), Thomas Braidon (Second Manager), Jane Darwell (Housekeeper), Armand Kaliz (Mr. Burton), Adrienne d'Ambricourt (Proprietress of Cafe), Wyndham

Standing (Max's Butler), Emile Chautard (Conductor), Nora Cecil (Tom's Secretary)

SYNOPSIS: see P-71.

REVIEWS:
New York Times, Nov. 23, 1933: "Notwithstanding the fact that Mr. Coward's clever lines were tossed to the four winds and that the whole action of the story is materially changed, Mr. Lubitsch, who knows his motion picutre as few others do, has in this offering, fashioned a most entertaining and highly sophisticated subject, wherein his own sly humor is constantly in evidence."

NOTES: Screenwriter Ben Hecht proudly declared that there was one line of Coward's dialogue left in the film. Coward wasn't able to find it. This film is available on video.

F-11   *The Scoundrel* Paramount Picture (filmed in Astoria), NY 1934

A film written and directed by Ben Hecht and Charles MacArthur. Originally entitled *Miracle in 49th Street*. Opened at Radio City Music Hall in New York May 2, 1935. Opened at the Plaza, London May 23, 1935.

CAST: **Noël Coward** (Anthony Mallare), Julie Haydon (Cora Moore), Hope Williams (Mathilde), Alexander Woollcott (Vandeveer Veyden), Stanley Ridges (Paul Decker), Martha Sleeper (Julia Vivian), Ernest Cossart (Jimmy Clay), Everly Gregg (Mildred Landwiler), Rosita Moreno (Carlotta), Edward Ciannelli (Maurice Stern), Richard Bond (Howard Gillette), Helen Strickland (Mrs. Rollinson), Lionel Stander (Rothstein)

SYNOPSIS: Anthony Mallare, a successful and heartless book publisher, meets and publishes an innocent, young poetess, Cora, and he falls in love with her, taking her away from her pompous fiancé. As always before, the affair runs its course and Mallare leaves Cora and her now alcoholic ex-fiancé to fend for themselves and goes about his life as it was. When he is killed in a plane crash, none of his so called friends mourn for him. Mallare returns to earth with the mission of finding someone who will shed a tear for him. He finds Cora taking care of Paul, her ex-fiancé. When Paul shoots himself, Mallare is able to pray for his life. When Mallare saves Paul, Cora shed the tears and Mallare is finally able to rest in peace.

REVIEWS:

New York Times, May 3, 1935: "Mr. Coward is so perfectly atttuned to the part that we cannot help suspecting that he contributed to the dialogue. He is a master at delivering the barbed epithet. You have to hear him reciting a line like 'It reeks with morality' — stressing the r's so as to make it exquisitely funny — to know how good he can be."

New York Sun, May 3, 1935: "A singulary adult picture, a most devastating study of a group of New York literary celebrities. Builds to an end as emotional, as mystic and as forceful as any motion pictures have yet offered us. Coward, as the gaunt, deliberating, cynical publisher unwilling to let himself feel deep emotion, as the drowned man strangely sent back for his one chance at peace, he has an uncanny quality. It is not a performance easily forgotten."

New York Herald Tribune, May 12, 1935: "Coward's British ability at underplaying on stage turns out to be eminently well suited for the more intimate scale of the screen close up."

NOTES: Coward accepted the film, his first as star, with the understanding that Helen Hayes, MacArthur's wife, would play opposite him. When he wound up with Julie Haydon, he was not pleased. Before the picture was released, advance publicity predicted that Coward would give Gary Cooper a run for his money. He didn't. The film won an Academy Award for Best Original Story and became a cult classic to up and coming writers such as Betty Comden, Adolph Green and Leonard Bernstein.

F-12   *Les Amants Terribles* (*Private Lives*), France 1936

   French film version of Noël Coward's comedy. Directed by Marc Allegret.

   CAST: Andre Luguet (Elyot Chase), Gaby Morlay (Amanda Prynne)

SYNOPSIS: see P-61.

F-13   *Bitter-Sweet* Metro-Goldwyn-Mayer, US 1941

   Technicolor Hollywood re-make of Noël Coward's operette. Directed by W.S. Van Dyke II. Screen adaptation by Lesser Samuels. **Music and lyrics by Noël Coward.** Produced by Victor Saville.

   CAST: Jeanette MacDonald (Sarah Millick), Nelson Eddy (Carl Linden), Fay Holden (Mrs. Millick), Veda Ann Borg (Manon), George Sanders (Baron Von Tranisch), Sig Rumann (Herr Schlick), Ian Hunter (Lord Shayne), Felix Bressart (Max), Edward Ashley (Harry Daventry), Curt Bois (Ernst), Dianna Lewis (Jane), Lynne Carver (Dolly), Janet Beecher

(Lady Daventry), Charles Judels (Herr Wyler), Herman Bing (Market-Keeper), Greta Meyer (Mama Luden)

SYNOPSIS: see P-58.

REVIEWS:
New York Times, Nov. 22, 1940: "A stock story patched together our of Mr. Coward's tender and fragile work. The prologue and epilogue of the original, which established the heroine as a gentle, nostalgic old English lady, have been casually dropped by the way."

NOTES: Not one of Coward's favorite films, to say the least. This was another in the line of MacDonald-Eddy films and not quite as successful as the rest. Available on Video MGM-UA.

F-14   *We Were Dancing* Metro-Goldwyn-Mayer, US 1942

Film version of Noël Coward's one act play contained in *Tonight At 8:30*. Directed by Robert Z. Leonard. Screen adaptation by Claudine West, Hans Rameau & George Froeschel. First shown in US at Radio City Music Hall, April 30, 1942.

CAST: Norma Shearer (Vicki Wilomirska), Melvyn Douglas (Nicki Prax), Gail Patrick (Linda Wayne), Lee Bowman (Hubert Tyler), Marjorie Main (Judge Sidney Hawkes), Reginald Owen (Major Tyler-Blane), Alan Mowbray (Grand Duke Basil), Florence Bates (Mrs. Vanderlip), Heather Thatcher (Mrs. Tyler-Blane), Connie Gilchrist (Olive Ransome), Nella Walker (Mrs. Bentley), Florence Shirley (Mrs. Charteris), Russell Hicks (Mr. Bryce-Carew), Norma Varden (Mrs. Bryce-Carew)

REVIEWS:
New York Times, May 1, 1942: "According to the credits, it is based on a couple of one-act plays by Noël Coward. And indeed it does have a brittle quality characteristic of that author's work."

NOTES: The film bears little resemblance to the original play beyond the title.

F-15   *In Which We Serve* Two Cities, England. 1942

Original film **produced and written by Noël Coward. Directed by Noel Coward** and David Lean. **Music by Noël Coward.** Photographed by Ronald Neame. Art Director: David Rawnsley. Art Supervision: G.E. Calthrop. Opened in US at the Capitol, NY Dec. 22, 1942. Opened at the

Gaumont, Haymarket and the Marble Arch Pavilion (simultaneously)
Sept. 27, 1942

CAST: **Noël Coward** (Captain "D"), John Mills (Shorty Blake), Bernard
Miles (Walter Hardy), Celia Johnson (Alix), Joyce Carey (Mrs.
Hardy), Kay Walsh (Freda Lewis), Derek Elphinstone (Number One), Michael
Wilding (Flags), Robert Sanson (Guns), Philip Friend (Torps), James
Donald (Doctor), Ballard Berkeley (Engineer Commander), Chimmon
Branson (Snotty), Kenneth Carten (Sub Lt.), George Carney (Mr. Blake),
Kathleen Harrison (Mrs. Blake), Wally Patch (Uncle Fred), Richard
Attenborough (Young Stoker), Penelope Dudley Ward (Maureen Fen-
wick), Hubert Gregg (Pilot), Frederick Piper (Edgecombe), Caven Wat-
son (Brodie), Johnnie Schofield (Coxswain), Geoffrey Hibbert (A.B. Joey
Mackridge), John Boxer (A.B. Hollett), Leslie Dwyer (Parkinson), Walter
Fitzgerald (Colonel Lumsden), Gerald Case (Capt. Jasper Fry), Dora
Gregory (Mrs. Lemmon), Lionel Grose (Reynolds), Norman Pierce (Mr.
Scatterthwaite), Ann Stephens (Lavinia), Daniel Massey (Bobby), Jill
Stephens (May Blake), Eileen Peel (Mrs. Farrell), Barbara Waring (Mrs.
Macadoo), Kay Young (Barmaid), Juliet Mills (Freda's Baby)

SYNOPSIS: The story of the destroyer, Torrin, from the building to her eventual
sinking in battle in May of 1940. When the ship is sunk and the crew is clinging to
the wreckage, we see several flashbacks relating to the various stages of war and
the ship's part in it: including the rescue from Dunkirk and several battles against
German destroyers. When some of the men are rescued, the Captain makes his
farewell speech, declaring that the spirit of the Torrin will go on inspiring them till
victory is won. The last shots are of the Captain in command of new ship, steaming
out to a fresh battle.

REVIEWS:
New York Times, Dec. 24, 1942: "One of the most eloquent motion pictures of these
or any other times had its American premiere last night. The great thing which
Mr. Coward has accomplished in this film is a full and complete expression of
national fortitude. Mr. Coward himself is somewhat cryptic and attitudinized in
the role of the ships commander. For all his depth and sincerity, he still plays Mr.
Coward."

NOTES: Dissatisfied by Hollywood's treatment of his work, Coward put together
a film company to produce his own works. This was the first of several films
produced by Two Cities. Knowing that he would need expert help directing,
Coward gave film editor David Lean his big break. According to Lean, Coward
grew bored quickly and only directed the scenes in which he was an intergral part
and Lean had his chance to direct the rest. Coward won a special Academy Award

for his outstanding production achievement for this film. The working title was of the screenplay was *White Ensign*. A piano suite from the incidental music by Coward (arranged by Elsie April) was published by William Chappell in 1942.

F-16   *This Happy Breed* Cineguild for Two Cities, England, 1943

> **Film version of Noël Coward's play. Produced and adapted by Noël Coward.** Directed by David Lean. First shown at the Gaumont, Haymarket & the Marble Arch Pavilion, London May 29, 1944. First shown in the US at the Little Carnegie, NY. April 13, 1947.
>
> CAST: Robert Newton (Frank Gibbons), Celia Johnson (Ethel), Alison Leggatt (Sylvia), Stanley Holloway (Bob Mitchell), John Blythe (Reg), Kay Walsh (Queenie), Eileen Erskine (Vi), Amy Veness (Mrs. Flint), Guy Verney (Sam), Betty Fleetwood (Phillis Blake), Merle Tottenham (Edie), John Mills (Billy)

SYNOPSIS: see P-101.

REVIEWS:
New York Times, April 14, 1947: "Noël Coward's notable affection for the people of the British Isles and his particular talent for holding a theatrical mirror up to them are again most nicely demonstrated in the film made from his play. It has a quiet charm and gentle penetration of human nature which should give it wide appeal."

NOTE: This time Lean alone retained direction credit. The film is available on video.

F-17   *Blithe Spirit* Gineguild for Two Cites, England, 1944-45

> **Film version of Noël Coward's comedy. Screen adaptation by Noël Coward.** Directed by David Lean. Incidental music by Richard Addinsell. First shown at the Odeon, Leicester Square, London, April, 1945. First shown in US at the Winter Garden Theatre, NY Oct. 3, 1945.
>
> CAST: Rex Harrison (Charles Condomine), Constance Cummings (Ruth Condomine), Margaret Rutherford (Madame Arcati), Kay Hammond (Elvira), Hugh Wakefield (Dr. Bradman), Joyce Carey (Mrs. Bradman), Jacqueline Clark (Edith)

SYNOPSIS: see P-97.

REVIEWS:
New York Times, Oct. 4, 1945: "Like most Coward works, *Blithe Spirit* is essentially a conversation piece. The dialogue is generally sharp and witty and though toned down a bit in the trip from stage to screen, there is enough innuendo left to preserve the brittle sophistication of the play."

NOTES: Coward, who was out of the country when this film was shot, was not satisfied with the results and felt the film stage bound. Time and repeated television showing have proved him wrong. The film won an Academy Award for Best Special Effects for Thomas Howard.

F-18   *Brief Encounter* Cineguild, England 1945

Film version of Noël Coward's one act play *Still Life* from *Tonight At 8:30*. Directed by David Lean. **Produced by Noël Coward. Screen adaptation by Noël Coward.**

CAST: Trevor Howard (Alec Harvey), Celia Johnson (Laura Jesson), Everly Gregg (Dolly Messiter), Sydney Bromley (Johnny), Margaret Barton (Beryl Waters), Dennis Harkin (Stanley), Edward Hodge (Bill), Stanley Holloway (Albert Godby), Joyce Carey (Myrtle Bagot), Cyril Raymond (Fred Jesson), Valentine Dyall (Stephen Lynn), Marjorie Mars (Mary Norton), Nuna Davey (Mrs. Rolandson), Irene Handle (Organist), Wilfred Babbage (Policeman), Avis Scott (Waitress), Henrietta Vincent (Margaret), Richard Thomas (Bobbie), George V. Sheldon (Clergyman), Wally Bosco (Doctor), Jack May (Boatman)

SYNOPSIS: see P-83.

REVIEWS:
New York Times: "The whole thing has been presented in such a delicate and affecting way — and with such complete naturalness in characterization and fidelity to middle class detail — that those slight discrepancies in logic may be easily allowed."

NOTE: The play was expanded and became a classic film, certainly the most successful of the Two Cities films and David Lean's directorial career was solidified. The film is available on video.

F-19   *The Astonished Heart* Gainsborough Pictures, England 1949-50

Film version of Noël Coward's one act play contained in *Tonight At 8:30*. Directed by Terence Fisher and Anthony Darnborough. **Screen adapta-**

tion and incidental music by Noël Coward. Distributed by J. Arthur Rank. First show in NY at the Park Avenue Feb. 14, 1950. Released by Universal International.

CAST: **Noël Coward** (Christian Faber) Celia Johnson (Barbara Faber), Joyce Carey (Susan Birch), Graham Payn (Tim Verney), Michael Horden (Ernest), Alan Webb (Sir Reginald), Margaret Leighton (Leonora Vail), Alice Smith (Amy Veness), Philip Lucas (Ralph Michael), Patricia Glyn (Helen), Everly Gregg (Miss Harper), John Salew (Soames), Gerald Anderson (Waiter), John Warren (Barman), Mary Ellis (Patient)

SYNOPSIS: see P-83.

REVIEWS:
New York Times, Feb. 15, 1950: "Mr. Coward is capable of doing better, though there are moments when the dialogue lets off caustic sparks. The writing and acting of the lead role by Mr. Coward himself are equally austere. His manner is too cool and reserved. *The Astonished Heart* is sluggish entertainment."

NOTES: Despite lovely performances by Celia Johnson and Margaret Leighton, the film was not a success and is seldom seen today. It is one of the rare film appearances of Coward's lover, Graham Payn. A symphonic suite from the incidental music by Noël Coward was published by William Chappell, 1950.

F-20   *Meet Me Tonight: Red Peppers, Fumed Oak, Ways and Means* Anthony Havelock Allan Productions, US 1952.

Film version of three of Noël Coward's one act plays from *Tonight At 8:30*. Directed by Anthony Pelissier. **Screen adaptation by Noël Coward**. First shown at the Odeon, Leicester Square, London Sept., 1952. Distributed by J. Arthur Rank. Called *Tonight At 8:30* in US and distributed by Continental Distributors. First show at the Baronet, NY May 26, 1953.

CAST: *Red Peppers*: Kay Walsh (Lily Pepper) Ted Ray (George Pepper), Ian Wilson (Alf), Bill Fraser (Bert Bentley), Fran Pettingel (Mr. Edwards), Martita Hunt (Mabel Grace), Toke Townley (Stage Manager), Frank's Fox Terriers (Performing Dog Act), The Young China Troupe (Chinese Jugglers); *Fumed Oak*: Stanley Holloway (Henry Gow), Betty Ann Davies (Doris Gow), Dorothy Gordon (Elsie), Mary Merrall (Mrs. Rocket); *Ways and Means*: Nigel Patrick (Toby Cartwright), Valerie Hobson (Stella Catwright), Mary Jerrold (Nannie), Jack Warner (Murdock), Yvonne Ferneau (Elena), Jessie Royce Landis (Olive) Michael Trubshaw (Lord Chapworth), Jacques Cey (The Fence)

SYNOPSIS: see P-83.

REVIEWS:
New York Times, May 26, 1953: "The selection is typical Coward, a tri-partite set of observations shot through with compassion, humor and an intimate knowledge of ways of life at three different levels. *Tonight At 8:30* is in short a varied entertainment short on excitement but funny and trenchant enought for many tastes."

NOTES: Very faithful and charming renderings of Coward's plays did not guarantee success. The film, which tried to cash in on the success of the Somerset Maugham omnibuses, *Trio* and *Quartet*, had its US TV debut on Nov. 10, 1956 under the title of *Tonight At 8:30*.

F-21   *Around The World In 80 Days* United Artist. Todd A-O, Great Britain, 1955

A film produced by Michael Todd. Screenplay by S. J. Perelman. Based on Jules Verne's novel. Music by Victor Young. Directed by Michael Anderson. First shown at the Rivoli Theatre, NY Oct. 17, 1956

CAST: David Niven (Fogg), Cantiflas (Passepartout), Robert Newton (Mr. Fix), Shirley MacLaine (Princess Aouda), **Noël Coward** (Hesketh-Baggot) Among the cameos were: Bea Lillie, Marlene Dietrich, Frank Sinatra, Sir John Gielgud and many others.

REVIEWS:
New York Post, Oct. 18, 1956: "Running down the list of notable moments-I find Noël Coward as manager of an employment agency."

NOTES: The film won Academy Awards for Best Picture, Best Screenplay (adapted), Best Cinematography (Color), Best Film Editing, and Best Music Score. Coward's role, though larger than most of the cameos, lasted for one scene for which he wrote his own dialogue. Ironically, Yul Brynner won his Best Actor Oscar for *The King and I* that year in a role originally turned down by Coward on the stage. The film is available on video.

F-22   *Our Man In Havana* Columbia Pictures, Great Britain, 1959

A film written by Graham Greene. Produced and directed by Carol Reed. Columbia Pictures. 107 minutes. First shown in NY Jan. 27, 1960.

CAST: **Noël Coward** (Hawthorne), Alec Guiness (Jim Warmold), Ernie

Kovacs (Captain Segura), Burl Ives (Dr. Hasselbacker), Maureen O'Hara (Beatrice), Jo Morrow (Millie), Ralph Richardson ("C"), Paul Rogers (Carter)

REVIEWS:
New York Times, Jan 28, 1960: "It is not until the delightfully crocky Noël Coward, lips pursed primly and umbrella cocked upon his arm has bullied a timid Mr. Guiness into the washroom of a famous bar and ordained him a spy for the British Secret Service that you realize a comedy is underway. Mr. Coward is beautifully brazen as a bumbling bureaucrat."

NOTES: This was perhaps Coward's best performance on film and one of the few film successes in which he had a large role.

F-23   *Surprise Package* Columbia Pictures, US 1960

A film written by Harry Kurnitz. Based on a book by Art Buchwald. Produced and directed by Stanley Donen. 99 minutes.

CAST: **Noël Coward** (King Pavel II), Mitzi Gaynor (Gabby Rogers), Yul Brynner (Nico March), Eric Pohlmann (Stephan Miralis), George Coulouris (Dr. Panze)

REVIEWS:
New York Times, Oct. 15, 1960: "Noël Coward, of all incredible people, plays the exiled King whose hobby is collecting full grown nymphets with the air of an aging high priest of Tibet."

NOTES: The only film in which Coward can be seen to sing and dance. In a few years time Coward and screen writer, Harry Kurnitz, would work together again, but as collaborators on the musical, *The Girl Who Came To Supper* (P-160)

F-24   *The Grass Is Greener* Universal-International, US 1960

A film directed and produced by Stanley Donen. **Music by Noël Coward**, from his old song hits. (Including a new title song). Screenplay by Hugh and Margaret Williams.

CAST: Cary Grant (Victor), Deborah Kerr (Hilary), Jean Simmons (Hattie), Robert Mitchum (Charles), Moray Waters (Sellars)

REVIEWS:
New York Times, "From a stage play by Hugh and Margaret Williams, it is very

much watered-down Noël Coward, with none of that popular playwrights old sparkle but with several of his familiar tunes, such as "Mad About The Boy" and "I'll Follow My Secret Heart" woven into the musical score."

F-25   *Paris When It Sizzles* Paramount Pictures, US 1964

A film written by George Axelrod. Directed by Richard Quine. Produced by Axelrod and Quine. 110 minutes.

CAST: **Noël Coward** (Alexander Meyerheimer), Audrey Hepburn (Gabrielle Simpson), William Holden (Richard Benson), Tony Curtis

REVIEWS:
New York Times, April 9, 1964: "Noël Coward is seen in Cannes as one of the most improbable film producers on record. *Paris When It Sizzles* is a rockhard chestnut that is hard to savor or swallow."

F-26   *Bunny Lake Is Missing* Columbia Pictures, US 1965

A film produced and directed by Otto Preminger. Screenplay by John and Penelope Mortimer. Based on a novel by Evelyn Piper. First shown in NY Oct. 3, 1965.

CAST: **Noël Coward** (Wilson), Laurence Olivier (Inspector Newhouse), Carol Lynley (Ann), Keir Dullea (Steven), Martita Hunt (Ada Ford), Anna Massey (Elvira), Clive Revill (Andrews), Lucie Mannheim (Cook), Finlay Currie (Doll Maker)

REVIEWS:
New York Times, Oct. 4, 1965: "A couple of obvious red herrings are elaborately dragged through the film by Noël Coward as a weirdo landlord. A specious and unconvincing picture."

NOTES: The most memorable line to come out of the film was when Coward turned to Keir Dullea on the set and muttered "Keir Dullea, gone tomorrow."

F-27   *A Matter of Innocence* Universal Pictures, US 1968

Film version of Noël Coward's short story, *Pretty Polly Barlow.* **Directed by Guy Green. Produced by George W. George and Frank Granat. Screenplay by Keith Waterhouse and Willis Hall. Music by Michel Legrand. First shown in NY on Feb. 26, 1968. 102 minutes.**

CAST: Hayley Mills (Polly), Trevor Howard (Robert Hook), Shashi Kapoor (Amaz), Brenda de Banzie (Mrs. Innes-Hook), Dick Patterson (Preston), Kalen Lui (Lorelei), Patricia Routledge (Miss Gudgeon), Peter Bayliss (Critch), Dorothy Alison (Mrs. Barlow), David Prosser (Ambrose)

REVIEWS:
New York Times, Feb. 27, 1968: "It is entertaining in a way bad movies are."

NOTES: In the early planning stages of the film Coward agreed to not only write a title song but to appear in a bit role. He did neither. The story was adapted more successfully on British television (T-43) See B-57 for original publication of *Pretty Polly Barlow*.

F-28   *Boom* Universal Pictures, US 1968

Film version of Tennessee William's play *The Milk Train Doesn't Stop Here Anymore*. Formerly titled *Go-Forth*. Direced by Joe Losey. Produced by John Heyman and Norman Pigeon. Opened in NY May 26, 1968. 110 minutes.

CAST: **Noël Coward** (The Witch of Capri), Elizabeth Taylor (Flora Goforth), Richard Burton (Chris Flanders), Joanna Shimkus (Blackie), Michael Dunn (Rudy), Romolo Valli (Dr. Lullo), Fernado Piazza (Etti), Veronica Wells (Simonetta), Howard Taylor (Jounalist), Claudye Ettori (Manicurist)

REVIEWS:
New York Times, May 29, 1968: "The one unequivocable success is a brief appearance by Noël Coward as the Witch of Capri, Mrs. Goforth's wickedly gossipy friend."

NOTES: Coward's role was played by Mildred Dunnock on the stage and unchanged except for gender. According to director, John Waters in *Premiere Magazine*, August, 1992, Katherine Hepburn turned down the role, insulted to have been asked. Waters sights the lunch scene between Coward as the Witch and Taylor as Goforth as his favorite in the film.

F-29   *Star!* 20th Century Fox Pictures, US 1968

Film biography of Gertrude Lawrence. Directed by Robert Wise. Produced by Saul Chaplin. Screenplay by William Fairchild. **Songs by Noël Coward**, Cole Porter, George and Ira Gershwin and others. Musical numbers staged by Michael Kidd. First seen in US at the Rivoli Theatre,

NY Oct. 22, 1968.   174 mins.

CAST: Julie Andrews (Gertrude Lawrence), Daniel Massey (Noël Coward), Richard Crenna (Richard Aldrich), Michael Craig (Sir Anthony Spencer), Robert Reed (Charles Fraser), Bruce Forsyth (Arthur Lawrence), Beryl Reid (Rose)

REVIEWS:
New York Times, Oct. 23, 1968: "Daniel Massey acts beautifully as a kind of warmed Noël Coward and the film, which gets richer and better as it goes along, has a nice scene from *Private Lives*. People who liked Gertrude Lawrence had better stick with their record collections and memories."

NOTES: Coward was portrayed by Massey, who was not only his Godson, but had appeared as Coward's son in *In Which We Serve*. Much Coward material was used in this not-quite-true bio-flick, including the premiere of "Forbidden Fruit," the balcony scene from *Private Lives* (including "Someday I'll Find You"), "Parisian Pierrot," and a scene from *Red Peppers* (including "Has Anyone Seen Our Ship?"). Strangly enough Beatrice Lillie, who was one of Lawrence's best friends, was not portrayed in the film, but a ficticious women named Billie Carlton took her place in Lawrence's life. Coward thought the whole enterprise ridiculous, feeling that "Gertie's life wasn't the stuff of drama." The critics agreed. The film was one of the last big road show bombs to come out of 20th Century Fox and put a halt to big musicals and Julie Andrews career. It was severely cut and re-released as *Those Were The Happy Days*.

F-30   *The Italian Job* Paramount Pictures, US 1969

A Film directed by Peter Collinson. Screenplay by Troy Kennedy Martin. Produced by Michael Deeley. 101 mins.

CAST: **Noël Coward** (Mr. Bridger), Michael Caine (Charlie Croker), Maggie Blye (Lorna), Benny Hill (Prof. Simon Peach), Tony Beckley (Freddie), Raf Vallone (Altabarie), Rossano Brazzi (Beckerman)

REVIEWS:
New York Times, Oct. 9, 1969: "Noël Coward, apparently not in the pink of health is the syndicate chief who oversees the plan (to steal 4 million dollars) from a London prison. Although the movie means to be kind to Coward, it exploits him in vaguely unpleasant ways, including decor. His prison cell is decorated with pictures of the royal family that in real life has never seen fit to Knight him."

NOTES: The above review was made moot when in 1970 Coward became Sir Noël

Coward. This was his last film. Although there is talk of film versions of *Hay Fever*, *Private Lives* and several other plays, none have been released as of publication date.

Noël Coward broadcasting "Don't Let's Be Beastly To the Germans" on BBC radio (1943). Photo courtesy of Photofest.

Radio Broadcasts

This section will detail the radio appearances of Noël Coward and the radio adaptations of his work. These entries will be preceeded by an "R." This list is not intended to be conclusive, but representative of Coward's radio work. Please note that, during WWII from 1940-45, Coward broadcast from all over the world. It is impossible to know exactly how many of these broadcasts were done.

R-1   *The Swiss Family Wittlebot* BBC-Radio. Oct. 26, 1924
        A sketch by **Noël Coward.**

NOTE: This was Noël Coward's writing debut on radio. Although he did not appear in the broadcast, his sketch did.

R-2   *Noël Coward Sings his songs at the piano* 2LO-Radio, London. Aug. 5, 1925

NOTE: This was Noël Coward's radio debut as performer.

R-3   *My Programme by George Grossmith* 2LO-Radio. Dec. 11, 1926
        Noël Coward wrote *The Last Resource,* a one act sketch especially for the broadcast.   It was performed by Heather Thatcher and Harry Hilliard.

R-4   *The Fleischmann Hour* NBC-Radio. Oct. 13, 1932 (1 hr.)
        Otto Kruger and Madge Kennedy (they replaced Coward and Lawrence on Broadway) did a scene from *Private Lives*.

R-5   *The Fleischmann Hour* NBC-Radio. Jan. 19, 1933 (1 hr.)
        G. Kerr did a scene from **Noël Coward's play** *Cavalcade.*

R-6   *The Fleischmann Hour* NBC-Radio. Mar. 30, 1933 (1 hr.)
       Peggy Wood (original London star) did a scene from **Noël Coward's
       operette** *Bitter-Sweet*.

R-7   *The Fleischmann Hour* NBC-Radio. July 27, 1933 (1 hr.)
       Robert Montgomery (star of the film version) did a scene from **Noël
       Coward's comedy** *Private Lives*.

R-8   *The Fleischmann Hour* NBC-Radio. Nov. 23, 1933 (1 hr.)
       Gary Cooper (star of the film version) did a scene from **Noël Coward's
       play** *Design For Living*.

R-9   *Henry Hall's Guest Night* BBC-Radio, CBS-Radio, WABC & WJZ
       Oct. 27, 1934 (6-6:30PM)

       Noël Coward appeared as guest and plugged *Conversation Piece,* which
       was on Broadway and sang two new songs: "I Travel Alone" and "Most of
       Every Day."

REVIEWS:
Variety, Oct. 30, 1934: "Coward's singing voice offers little in the way of harmony,
still being rather harsh. The Coward songs will probably make the grade with the
legion of Coward fans."

R-10   *Rudy Vallee Show* NBC-Radio Jan. 3, 1936 (1 hr.)
       Noël Coward was a guest on the popular crooners show.

R-11   *Bitter-Sweet* Lux Radio Theatre CBS-Radio. May 11, 1936
       60 minute radio adaptation of **Noël Coward's operette** starring Irene
       Dunne as Sari Linden.

R-12   *Cavalcade* BBC-Radio. June 24 & 26, 1936
       Radio adaptation of **Noël Coward's play**. Directed by Val Gielgud.

       CAST: Mary O'Farrell (Jane), Martin Lewis (Robert), Joyce Barbour,
       Lesley Wareing, Eliot Makeham, Jack Clayton (Edward), Murial Pavlow
       (Edith), Robert Holland (Joe), Doreen Lotinga (Fanny)

REVIEWS:
London Times, June 25, 1936: "Here at last is a broadcast play which can be
enjoyed without a single reservation. Mr. Noël Coward's spectacle is in many ways
a model broadcast play."

R-13   *The Royal Gelatin Hour* NBC-Radio Aug. 20, 1936 (1 hr.)
A scene from **Noël Coward's comedy** *Private Lives* was presented on this show hosted by Rudy Vallee.

R-14   *Conversation Piece* Lux Radio Theatre CBS-Radio. Nov. 16, 1936 (1 hr.)
Radio adaptation of **Noël Coward's operette** starring Lily Pons (Melanie), Adolph Menjou (Duc), George Sanders (Lord Sheere), Marjorie Gatson (Lady Julia), Hosted by Cecil B. DeMille.

NOTES: George Sanders had played (though not in this role) in the original West End and Broadway cast. This adaptation only kept "I'll Follow My Secret Heart" and "Nevermore" for Melanie and added a classical piece for Miss Pons to sing in the party scene. Fifteen some odd years later Lily Pons would record the role of Melanie with Coward in his original West End role of the Duc for Columbia Records (D-96).

R-15   *Red Peppers* The Royal Gelatin Hour NBC-Radio. Dec. 3, 1936
Noël Coward and Gertrude Lawrence performed **Noël Coward**'s one act play from *Tonight At 8:30* on Rudy Vallee's show.

REVIEWS:
New York Post, Dec. 4, 1936: "The clipped precision of their delivery made the most of this bit of bright foolishness for the microphone."

Variety, Dec. 9, 1936: "The skit held together brightly and was steadily interesting as a novelty to American listeners. Well adapted to radio.

R-16   *Cavalcade* Lux Radio Theatre CBS-Radio. Dec. 28, 1936 (1 hr.)
Radio adaptation of **Noël Coward**'s play. Narrated by Cecil B. DeMille.

CAST: Herbert Marshall (Robert Marryot), Madeleine Carroll (Jane Marryot), Una O'Connor (Ellen Bridges), David Niven (Edward Marryot), Elsa Buchanan (Edith), Douglas Scott (Edward as a boy). **Noël Coward** appeared as an intermission guest.

NOTES: Coward appeared live from his dressing room at the National Theatre in NY, where he was appearing in *Tonight at 8:30*. He tells the radio audience how he came to write and direct *Cavalcade* and he gives a toast (rather like the one in *Cavalcade*) to America.

R-17   *Hay Fever* BBC-Radio July 14, 1937
Radio adaptation of **Noël Coward's play**.

CAST: Dame Marie Tempest (Judith Bliss), Frank Cellier (David Bliss), Joan Henley (Sorel Bliss), Glen Byam Shaw (Simon Bliss), Valerie Taylor (Myra Arundel), Norman Shelley (Richard Greatham), Ann Trevor (Jackie Coryton), Lawrence Hardman (Sandy Tyrell), Polly Emery (Clara)

REVIEWS:
London Times, July 15, 1937: "Mr. Coward's comedy might almost have been designed expressly for broadcasting."

NOTES: Dame Marie Tempest created the role of Judith in the original West End production and it was for her talents that Coward fashioned the role.

R-18   *Your Hit Parade* NBC-Radio. Sept. 29, 1937
         Noël Coward sang his song, "Mad Dogs and Englishman" on this popular show.

R-19   *Shadow Play* The Royal Gelatin Hour NBC-Radio. July 26, 1938 (1 hr.)
         Radio adaptation of **Noël Coward**'s one act musical from *Tonight At 8:30* featuring the original star, Gertrude Lawrence.

R-20   *The Circle* NBC-Red Network. Jan. 29, 1939
         Ronald Coleman was the host of this Kellogg's sponsored show. **Noël Coward** talked about disliking long runs and sang from the newly opened *Set To Music* accompanied by Robert Emmet Dolan's orchestra. Groucho and Chico Marx were also featured as were Carole Lombard and Cary Grant in an adaptation of Coward's *Red Peppers*. Dolan played Bert Bentley. Coward reportedly made 5,000 dollars for his appearance and an additional 1,500 dollars for a rewrite of the material.

R-21   *Private Lives* Campbells Playhouse CBS-Radio. April 21, 1939
         Radio adaptation of **Noel Coward**'s play. Produced by D. Taylor. Directed by Orson Welles, John Houseman and Paul Stewart. Script adapted by Orson Welles, John Houseman and Howard Koch. Announced by E. Chappell. Orchestra conducted by Bernard Herrmann.

         CAST: Gertrude Lawrence (Amanda), Orson Welles (Elyot), Edgar Barrier (Hotel Manager), Naomi Campbell (Sybil), Robert Speaight (Victor).

NOTES: A fairly faithful and nicely played radio adaptation with Coward's original star Gertrude Lawrence in top form. Miss Lawrence was also interviewed.

R-22   *We Were Dancing* Screen Guild Theatre WABC, CBS Radio (7:30-8:00)

Radio adaptation of **Noël Coward**'s one act play from *Tonight At 8:30* Starring Robert Montgomery, Adolph Menjou, Binnie Barnes, Hedda Hopper, Roger Pryor and the Oscar Bradley orchestra.

R-23   **Noël Coward** spoke from London on the NBC Red Network on July 18, 1940 from 6:15-6:22 PM. He discussed the morale of Englishmen as they await the attack by Germany.

R-24   *London Topical Talk* BBC-Radio July 19, 1940

   Noël Coward appeared as guest.

R-25   *Australia Visited* Series of Broadcasts BBC-Radio. 1940

   Noël Coward broadcasted on the state of the troops in Australia.

R-26   *Private Lives* Great Moments From Great Plays CBS-Radio June 13, 1941 Radio adaptation of **Noël Coward**'s play featuring Alan Reed. Produced, adapted, directed and hosted by Charles Martin. Orchestra conducted by Ray Bloch.

R-27   *Treasury Hour* BBC Radio and NBC-Radio, US. Oct. 21, 1941 **Noël Coward** appeared on this show from London sponsored by Bendix Corporation in US.

R-28   *Henry Morgenthau Broadcasts,* NY Dec. 25, 1943 **Noël Coward** told of his War experiences.

R-29   *In Which We Serve* Philip Morris Playhouse CBS-Radio. April 2, 1943 Radio adaptation of **Noël Coward**'s screenplay by Charles Martin featuring Sir Cedric Hardwicke. Orchestra conducted by Ray Bloch.

R-30   *In Which We Serve* Lux Radio Theatre CBS-Radio. June 21, 1943 Radio adaptation of **Noël Coward**'s screenplay.

R-31   *Noel Coward Songs, Music and Recitation.* BBC-Radio. July 19, 1943 Accompanied by Billy Ternents orchestra **Noël Coward** sang "London Pride" and "Don't Let's Be Beastly To The Germans." He also recited his poem "Lie In The Dark and Listen." The orchestra played his incidental music from *In Which We Serve* and a medley from *Bitter-Sweet.*

REVIEWS:

Variety, Aug. 11, 1943: "Coward has a sure sense of the theatre, well worth 20 minutes of anybody's listening."

NOTES: When the British public heard the sardonic irony of "Don't Let's Be Beastly To The Germans" they evidently took the lyric literally and wrote hundreds of letters of protest to the BBC.

R-32   *NY As A Drama Center* WNYC-Radio. Jan. 13, 1943
  Noël Coward and Elmer Rice were interviewed by Mayor LaGuardia on the eve of the opening of Gertrude Lawrence in the City Center Revival of *Susan and God*. City Center had just opened that Saturday night.

R-33   *Blithe Spirit* Everything For the Boys NBC-Radio. May 16, 1944
  30 minute radio adaptation of **Noel Coward**'s play starring Ronald Coleman (Charles), Loretta Young (Elvira), Edna Best (Ruth) and Mercedes McCambridge.

NOTES: Although most of the play was gone (it was done in under 20 minutes) there was some fun left in the fact that NBC saw fit to change the Condomines to the Kents (perhaps a tribute to their home). A remote broadcast had Coleman, Young and Best talking to the boys overseas and sending messages from home.

R-34   *14th Army Broadcast* BBC-Radio. Nov., 1944
  Noël Coward reported on the courage of the 14th Army.

R-35   *Shadow Play* Textron Theatre CBS-Radio. Nov. 10, 1945
  Radio adaptation of **Noël Cowards one act musical** from *Tonight At 8:30* starring Helen Hayes & Alfred Drake. Directed by Lester O'Keefe. Music directed by W. Selinsky. Announced by Frank Gallup.

R-36   *Bitter-Sweet* BBC-Radio. 1946
  Radio adaptation of **Noël Coward's operette** starring Evelyn Laye (the original Broadway star).

R-37   *Brief Encounter* Academy Award Theatre CBS-Radio. Nov. 20, 1946 (1 hr.)
  Radio adaptation of **Noël Coward**'s film version of his one act play *Still Life* from *Tonight At 8: 30*

R-38   *Blithe Spirit* Theatre Guild On The Air ABC-Radio. Feb. 23, 1947 (1 hr.)
  Radio condensation of **Noël Coward's comedy**. Directed by Homer Fickett. Musical Direction by Harold Levey. Adapted for radio by Robert Cenedella. Narrated by Roger Pryor.

CAST: Clifton Webb (Charles), Leonora Corbett (Elvira), Mildred Natwick (Madame Arcati), Cathleen Cordell (Ruth), Betty Breckenridge (Daisy), Robert Chisholm (Dr. Bradman), Valerie Cossart (Mrs. Bradman)

NOTES: This live and pretty faithful presentation from the Vanderbilt Theatre in NY was to have included the entire original Broadway cast, but Peggy Wood was indisposed and replaced by Kathleen Cordell. The show used a flashback format with Charles narrating from a ship to America and Edith the maid underwent a name change to Daisy.

R-39   *Still Life* Theatre Guild On The Air ABC-Radio . April 6, 1947
Radio condensation of **Noël Coward**'s one act play from *Tonight At 8:30*. Adapted for radio by Erik Barnouw. Directed by Homer Fickett. Produced by Carol Irwin. Muiscal direction by Harold Levey. Narratored by Roger Pryor.

CAST: Ingrid Bergman (Laura), Peggy Wood (Mary), Sam Wannamaker (Alec), David Anderson (Bobby), Romney Brent (Fred), Jimsey Somers (Cathy), Betty Breckenridge (Counter Girl), Robert Dryden (P.A. Voice), Barbara Weeks (Movie Heroine), Peter Capell (Villain), Cameron Prud'homme (Conductor), Carl Frank (Stephen)

R-40   *Brief Encounter* Lady Esther Screen Guild Players CBS-Radio. May 12, 1947
Radio adaptation of **Noël Coward**'s screenplay from his one act play *Still Life* from *Tonight At 8:30*. Produced and directed by Bill Lawrence. Adapted by Harry Kronman. Music conducted by Wilbur Hatch.

CAST: Herbert Marshall (Alec Harvey), Lillie Palmer (Laura Jesson) and Eric Snowdon (Fred Jesson).

R-41   *Hay Fever* Studio One CBS-Radio. Jun 3, 1947
Radio condensation of **Noël Coward**'s comedy. Adapted and directed by Fletcher Markle. Music by Alexander Semmler.

CAST: Evelyn Varden (Judith Bliss), Everett Sloan (David Bliss), Anne Burr (Sorel Bliss), William Woodson (Simon Bliss), Joan Alexander, Susan Douglas, Donald Buka

R-42   *The Noel Coward Show* BBC-Radio. July, 1947
Series of 13 shows featuring **Noël Coward** singing and talking.

R-43   *Brief Encounter* The Camel Screen Guild Players CBS -Radio. Jan 26, 1948
30 minute radio adaptation of **Noël Coward**'s one act play *Still Life* and the
film version of it.

CAST: Irene Dunne (Laura Jesson), Herbert Marshall (Alec Harvey),
Tom Conway (Fred Jesson)

NOTES: An almost identical version as R-37.

R-44   *Brief Encounter* Lux Radio Theatre CBS Radio Nov. 29, 1948
Radio adaption of **Noël Coward's film version of his one act play** from
Tonight at 8:30.

CAST: Greer Garson (Laura), Van Heflin (Alec)

R-45   *Bitter-Sweet* The Railroad Hour WJZ (ABC)-Radio . Jan. 31, 1949
Radio adaptaion of **Noël Coward**'s operette starring Jeanette MacDonald
(star of 2nd film version) and Gordon MacRae. Adapted by Jean Holloway. Orchestra directed by Carmen Dragon. Choir directed by Norman
Luboff.

R-46   *Brief Encounter* Electric Theatre CBS-Radio. May 1, 1949
Radio adaptation of **Noël Coward's film version of his one act play** from
Tonight At 8:30 featuring Helen Hayes.

R-47   *Still Life* Theatre Guild On The Air ABC-Radio. Nov. 13, 1949
Radio adaptation of **Noël Coward's one act play** from *Tonight at 8:30.*
Adapted for radio by Erik Barnouw. Directed by Homer Fickett. Narrated
by Roger Pryor.

CAST: Helen Hayes (Laura), David Niven (Alec), Carl Frank (Fred),
Butch Cavell (Bobby), Jimsey Somers (Cathy), Wesley Addy (Stephen),
Barbara Weeks (Mary), Betty Breckenridge (Counter Girl), Robert
Dryden (P.A. Voice), Roger Pryor (Waiter), Peter Capell (Villain)

R-48   *Bitter-Sweet* The Railroad Hour NBC-Radio. Jan. 9, 1950
Half hour radio version of **Noël Coward's operette** starring Gordon Mac-
Rae and Dorothy Kirsten.

R-49   *Ace of Clubs Broadcast* BBC-Radio. Oct., 1950
Noël Coward appeared with the cast (see P-117) in this salute to bolster
attendence of show.

R-50   *Brief Encounter* Lux Radio Theatre CBS-Radio. May 14, 1951
Radio adaption of **Noël Coward's film version of his one act play** from
Tonight at 8:30.
CAST: Olivia De Havilland (Laura), Richard Basehart (Alec)

R-51   *A Star Danced* NBC-Radio. June 2, 1951
Noël Coward appeared in the cast of this tribute to his friend and colleague
Gertrude Lawrence.

R-52   *Blithe Spirit* Best Plays NBC-Radio. Aug. 31, 1952
One hour radio adaptation of **Noël Coward's comedy** starring John Loder
and original Broadway cast member, Mildred Natwick as Madame Arcati.
Hosted by John Chapman.

R-53   *Bitter-Sweet* The Railroad Hour NBC-Radio. Feb. 23, 1953
Half hour radio version of **Noël Coward's operette** starring Gordon Mac-
Rae and Dorothy Warenskjold.

R-54   *Tonight At 8:30* Best Plays NBC-Radio. Aug. 30, 1953
One hour radio version of **Noël Coward's plays.**

R-55   *Stage Struck* CBS-Radio. Mar. 14, 1954
Noël Coward appeared as guest on this one hour series produced in
cooperation with the League of NY Theatres. Mike Wallace was the host.
Produced by Howard G. Barnes. Directed by Bruno Zirato Jr. Written
and researched by Robert Corcoran.

NOTES: The series, which featured backstage chats and performances with many
of Broadway's stars and creators, premiered Oct. 2, 1953 with Lilo and Gwen
Verdon doing numbers from *Can-Can*, Rosalind Russell doing a bit from *Wonderful Town* and Basil Rathbone, and Shirley Booth. The show was introduced by
composer Arthur Schwartz (then president of the League)

R-56   *Stage Struck* CBS-Radio . May 2, 1954
Noël Coward again appeared as guest. (see R-55)

R-57   *Sunday With Garroway* NBC-Radio. Aug. 29, 1954
Noël Coward appeared as a guest of Dave Garroway.

R-58   *After The Ball Broadcast* BBC-Radio, London. Nov. 12, 1954
One hour salute to *After The Ball* to bolster the audience. Vanessa Lee
sang "Sweet Day" and "This Is A Changing World" and **Noël Coward** did

several other songs. The broadcast had little effect on business. *After The Ball* closed on Dec. 20, 1954.

R-59   *Anthology* NBC-Radio. Jan. 2, 1955
       Noël Coward appeared as a guest.

R-60   *Biographies In Sound: "I Knew Gertrude Lawrence"* NBC-Radio. Jan. 23, 1955
       Noël Coward was heard on tape and in recorded excepts from *Private Lives, Shadow Play*, and *Red Peppers*.

R-61   *Brief Encounter (Still Life)* BBC-Radio. May 4, 1955
       Radio version of **Noël Coward**'s film version of his one act play from *Tonight At 8:30*. Adapted by Maurice Horspool.

       CAST: Wendy Hiller (Laura Jesson), James McKechnie (Alec Harvey)

R-62   *Film Critics Award Dinner* NBC-Radio. Jan. 18, 1958
       Noël Coward appeared in a segment live from Sardi's Restaurant in NY.

R-63   *Noël Coward: Talking On Theatre* BBC-Radio. Sept. 19, 1961

R-64   *Personal Closeup* CBS-Radio. Mar., 1963
       Noël Coward was interviewed by Mike Wallace

R-65   *Invitation To Learning* CBS-Radio. Aug. 24, 1964
       Noël Coward was a guest on this 5 minute show discussing *Design For Living*.

R-66   *Noël Coward On Acting* BBC-Radio. Mar. 12, 1966

R-67   *"The Master" at 70* BBC-Radio 4. Dec. 11, 1969
       Gale Pedrick assessed, with assistance from **Noël Coward**'s music and the recorded view of those who had known him over the years, the achievements of Noel Coward at 70 years of age. Produced by Denys Gueroult.

R-68   *The Music of Noël Coward* BBC-Radio 4. Dec. 13, 1969
       A tribute to Noël Coward's music and lyrics including selections from *Conversation Piece, Operette, Sigh No More, Bitter-Sweet, Private Lives, Tonight at 8:30* and featuring on disc, Coward and Lawrence in a scene from *Red Peppers*. Produced by Alan Owen. Hosted by Hubert Gregg.

CAST: Rae Woodland, Cherry Lind, Leslie Fyson, Robert Docker, BBC Chorus, BBC Concert Orchestra lead by Arthur Leavins and conducted by Marcus Dods.

R-69   *Private Lives* Saturday Night Theatre BBC-Radio 4. Dec. 13, 1969
Radio version of **Noël Coward's comedy.** Adapted for radio by Cynthia Pughe. Produced by Norman Wright.

CAST: Gudrun Ure (Sybil Chase), Edward De Souza (Elyot Chase), Peter Tuddenham (Victor Prynne), Moira Lister (Amanda Prynne), Lorna Philippe (Louise)

R-70   *Noël Coward at 70* Woman's Hour BBC-Radio 2. Dec. 16, 1969
A birthday tribute for Noël Coward introduced by Marjorie Anderson.

CAST: Richard Attenborough, Celia Johnson, Evelyn Laye, Daniel Massey and Sir Laurence Olivier.

R-71   *Noël Coward Talks* BBC-Radio. Jan. 27, 1972
Noël Coward was interviewed by Edgar Lustgarten.

R-72   *The Life and Times of Noël Coward* BBC-Radio 12 part radio documentary Narrated by Sheridan Morley.

R-73   *The Girl Who Came To Supper* BBC-Radio 4. Sept. 19, 1979
Radio version of **Noël Coward's musical.** (See P-160) Adapted by Alan Melville.

CAST: Keith Michel (Regent), Peggy Ashcroft (Queen Mother), Doris Hare (Ada Cockle), Edward Hardwicke (Northbrook), Stephen Bone (The King), Deborah Fallender (Mary)

R-74   *Private Lives* BBC-Radio
Radio version of **Noël Coward's play.**

CAST: Patricia Routledge (Amanda), Paul Scofield (Elyot), John Rye (Victor), Miriam Margolies (Sybil)

R-75   *Hay Fever* BBC-Radio
Radio version of **Noël Coward's play.**

CAST: Peggy Ashcroft (Judith Bliss), Tony Britten (Simon Bliss), Millicent Martin (Myra), Julia Foster (Jackie), Maurice Denham (David Bliss), Betty Bascomb (Clara)

R-76   *Noël Coward In Two Keys* National Public Radio. Jan. 3, Jan. 10 and Jan 17, 1993.
Radio versions of **Noel Coward's plays,** *Come Into The Garden Maud* and *A Song At Twilight*. Produced by the New England Stage Company. Rosemary Lamb and Frances Bragdon, producers. Directed by Ken Oxman.

CAST: *Come Into The Garden Maud*: James Elwood (Verner), Susan Riskin (AnnaMary), Rosemary Lamb (Princess Maud); *A Song At Twilight*: Michael Allinson (Hugo), Sian Philips (Lady Hylda), Rosemary Lamb (Carlotta), J. DeSouiza (Felix)

Noël Coward as Frank Gibbons in the May 5, 1956, television broadcast of *This Happy Breed*. Photo courtesy of Photofest.

Mary Martin and Noël Coward rehearse at his home in Bermuda for their television spectacular, *Together With Music* (1956).
Photo courtesy of Photofest.

Television Productions and Appearances

This section details Noël Coward's television appearances and television adaptations of his works. It is hoped that this, being the most complete listing of Coward's TV work here and abroad, will show how his plays have transferred from one medium to the next. Entries are preceded by the letter "T."

T-1   *Hay Fever* NBC-RCA TV, NY Aug. 1, 1939.

      80 minute television version of **Noël Coward's comedy**.

      CAST: Isobel Elson (Judith Bliss), Dennis Hoey (David Bliss), Virginia Campbell (Sorel Bliss), Montgomery Clift (Simon Bliss), Nancy Sheridan (Myra Arundel), Lowell Gilmore (Richard Greatham), Barbara Leeds (Jackie Coryton), Carl Harbord (Sandy Tyrell), Florence Edney (Clara)

SYNOPSIS: See P-38.

REVIEWS:
Variety, Aug. 2, 1939: "Program was mildly diverting and that's about the rating *Hay Fever* always had, the Noël Coward trifle however being used considerably in stock, although it was hardly a Broadway success. *Hay Fever* was under a partial handicap because one of the three cameras required was out of order."

NOTES: The young Montgomery Clift appeared in this experimental TV version.

T-2   *Hay Fever*   WRGB, Schenectady, NY. 1943

SYNOPSIS: See P-38.

NOTES: This experimental television station broadcasted a local production of **Noël Coward**'s comedy.

T-3   *Blithe Spirit*   NBC-TV, NY   May 12, 1946

TV version of **Noël Coward's comedy**. Produced, adapted and directed by Edward Sobel. Technical Directorion by Albert Protzman. Sets by Robert Wade.

CAST: Philip Tonge (Charles Condomine), Carol Goodner (Ruth), Leonore Corbett (Elvira), Estelle Winwood (Madame Arcati), Alexander Clark (Dr. Bradman), Valerie Cossart (Mrs. Bradman), Doreen Lang (Edith)

SYNOPSIS: See P-97.

REVIEWS:
Variety, May 13, 1946: "By every standard, video has demonstrated with this production of *Blithe Spirit* that it can equal the best of stage and screen entertainment. From the technical viewpoint, *Blithe Spirit* was transferred with polish, fluency and compactness. Only one word can describe the show's thesping: superlative. This is television as it should be.

NOTES: Leonore Corbett was the original Broadway Elvira and Philip Tonge, who had a long history with Coward beginning in 1911 in *Where The Rainbow Ends* (P-4), had appeared in that production as Dr. Bradman, a role he repeated in the 1956 Coward TV version (T-11). Both Valerie Cossart and Doreen Lang played their roles in the original Broadway cast.

T- 4   *Blithe Spirit*   BBC TV, London   1948

Television version of **Noël Coward's comedy**.

CAST: Marian Spenser (Ruth), Ronald Squire (Charles), Beryl Measor (Madame Arcati), Betty Ann Davies (Elvira)

SYNOPSIS: See P-97.

T-5   *Red Peppers* NBC Comedy Hour NBC-TV, NY   Mar. 18, 1951

TV version of **Noël Coward's one act play** from *Tonight At 8:30*

CAST: Rex Harrison (George Pepper), Beatrice Lillie (Lily Pepper)

T-6   *Still Life* Schlitz Playhouse of Stars CBS-TV, NY Oct. 26, 1951

TV version of **Noël Coward**'s one act play from *Tonight At 8:30*. Executive Producer: Felix Jackson. Produced and directed by Frank Telford. Script adapted by Robert Anderson.

CAST: Margaret Sullavan (Laura), Wendell Corey (Alec), Henry Jones (Albert), Bibi Osterwald (Myrtle), Ruth Gilbert (Beryl), Fred Wayne (Stanley)

SYNOPSIS: See P-83.

REVIEWS:
Variety, Oct. 31, 1951: "TV version, while it necessarily couldn't have as much scope as the film [*Brief Encounter*], projected just as much mood and emotion."

T-7   *Toast of the Town* CBS TV, NY Feb. 22, 1953

Ed Sullivan presented a scene from **Noël Coward**'s play *Cavalcade* featuring John Forsyth and Maria Riva (Marlene Dietrich's daughter). They did the famous Titanic scene.

T-8   *Tonight At 8:30* Producer's Showcase NBC-TV, NY Oct. 18, 1954.

TV adaptations of *Red Peppers, Still Life, & Shadow Play* by F. Hugh Herbert. Produced by Fred Coe. Directed by Otto Preminger. Music supervised by Carmen Dragon. Executive producer: Jack Rayel. Costumes by Rose Bogdanoff. Sets by William Molyneux. Choreographed by Dick Barstow. Scenic design by William C. Molyneux. Miss Rogers costumes by Travilla.

CAST: Ginger Rogers (Lily Pepper, Laura Jesson, Victoria Gayforth), Martyn Green (George Pepper), Trevor Howard (Alec Harvey), Gig Young (Simon Gayforth), Estelle Windwood (Mabel Grace), Louis Hector (Mr. Edwards), Ilka Chase (Dolly), Lucie Lancaster (Mrs. Bagot), Philip Coolidge (Bert Bentley), Dermot McNamara (Alf), Philip Bourneuf (Albert), Robert Shawley (Boy), John Baragrey (Michael), Gloria Vanderbilt (Sibyl), Margaret Hayes (Martha), David Poleri (Gondelier), Bert Thorn (George), Francis Bethencourt (Young Man), Diana Herbert (Lena)

SYNOPSIS: See P-83.

REVIEWS:
Variety, Oct. 19, 1954: "Ginger Rogers had a personal triumph. No mean accomplishment as she changed mood and characters in three diverse roles."

NOTES: This was the very first Producers Showcase and premiered a series that included *Peter Pan, Our Town, The Petrified Forest, Dodsworth* and other gems of TV's golden age. This was also the television debut of Ginger Rogers and Trevor Howard (repeating his role from the film *Brief Encounter*) See P-83, P-85 for original productions

T-9   *Cavalcade* The 20th Century Fox Hour CBS-TV, NY. Oct. 5, 1955

An adaptation of **Noël Coward's play** by Peter Packer. Directed by Lewis Allen. Photographed by Lloyd Ahern. Produced by Otto Lang. Art direction by Mark-Lee Kirk.

CAST: Michael Wilding (Robert Marryot), Merle Oberon (Jane Marryot), Marcia Henderson (Edith Harris), Caroline Jones (Fanny Bridges), Noel Drayton (Bridges), Nora O'Mahoney (Ellen), Doris Lloyd (Mrs. Snapper), Victoria Warde (Margaret Harris), Richard Lupino (Joey Maryot), John Irving (Edward Marryot)

SYNOPSIS: See P-67.

REVIEWS:
Variety, Oct. 6, 1955: "Certainly the show had a polish and pictorial quality that auguered well for the future and reflected a thorough understanding of the unique and different needs of the TV screen."

NOTES: Also know as *Heart of A Woman*, this was a 44 minute version of the play (see P-67). It was the premiere production of the series and was produced on film and shown in cinemas in Great Britain in 1956. The show was introduced by Joseph Cotten.

T-10   *Together With Music* Ford Star Jubilee CBS-TV, NY. Oct. 22, 1955

A 90 minute **entertainment written and directed by Noël Coward.**

Directed for Televison by Jerome Shaw. Produced by Richard Lewine. Lighting Director: Bob Barry. Technical Director: John Koushouris. Musical Director and Orchestrations by Tutti Camarata and Peter Matz. Miss Martins Gowns by Mainbocher.

CAST: Mary Martin & Noël Coward

MUSICAL NUMBERS (by Noël Coward): *Together With Music-Both; Uncle Harry, Nina, Mad Dogs & Englishmen-Coward; *90 Minutes Is A Long Long Time-Both; I'll See You Again, Dance Little Lady, Poor Little Rich Girl, Someday I'll Find You, I'll Follow My Secret Heart, If Love Were All, Play Orchestra Play-Coward; World Weary, *What's Going To Happen To The Tots?-Coward; London Pride-Martin

REVIEWS:
New York World-Telegram & Sun, Oct. 23, 1955: "In terms of artisty, wit and sheer excitement, I dought that there has ever been a more satisfying television show than the Mary Martin-Noël Coward act, *Together With Music.* It will stand as a landmark."

Hollywood Daily Variety, Oct. 23, 1955: "90 minutes was a sheer delight and a remarkable feat of sustained entertainment."

New York Times, Oct. 23, 1955: "The reward were unusual and varied, a bravura display of extaordinary personalities and talents."

New York Daily News, Oct. 23, 1955: "It was Noel's TV debut, and he may write off the occasion as one of the triumphs of his career. During ninety minutes, less time out for commercials, the Britisher and Mary, alone and together, faced the inexorable cameras and present the brightest, most intelligent, and most captivating musical revue I have ever seen on video. It was a knockout of a show."

NOTES: * These songs were written for the telecast. Noël Cowards TV debut was a triumph. Two numbers were intended and cut: a Cowardization of Gilbert and Sullivan's "Tit Willow" and "The Party's Over Now." For recordings see D-104, D105, D-106.

T-11   *Blithe Spirit* Ford Star Jubilee, CBS-TV, Hollywood. Jan. 14, 1956

TV adaptation of **Noël Coward's comedy. Adapted and directed by Noël Coward.** Produced by Richard Lewine and Lance Howard. TV direction by Frederick DeKordova.

CAST: **Noël Coward** (Charles), Lauren Bacall (Elvira), Claudette Colbert (Ruth), Mildred Natwick (Madame Arcati), Brenda Forbes (Mrs. Bradman), Philip Tonge (Dr. Bradman), Marion Ross (Edith)

SYNOPSIS: See P-97.

REVIEWS:
Variety, Jan. 16, 1956: "Coward's timing, inflections and nuances were as triumphant as his direction."

New York Daily News, Jan. 16, 1956: "*Blithe Spirit* brings ghostly laughter to TV. Light as thistledown and merry as an epigram tossed off in a glittery drawing room. A frothy delight. Debonaire and suave as ever, Coward made Charles a scintillating character."

Time Magazine, Jan. 23, 1956: "Viewers last night were treated to the raciest and most profance language that has ever been heard on TV. The show itself was one of the highlights of a drama-studded week."

Cue Magazine, Jan. 28, 1956: "Very nearly the best comedy that's ever come to our TV screen. From the super-enameled quality of this and his other TV venture [*Together With Music*], it's patent that Mr. Coward, who played the harried author takes his television work as seriously as he's taken all the other creative tasks to which he's affixed his name. It's a joy to have him around."

NOTES: Coward loathed the Hollywood experience and vowed to only do televison that originated from New York from now on. He and co-star Claudette Colbert did not get along. When it was apparent that she did not know her lines (a cardinal Coward sin) she plaintively told the master, "But Noël, just last night I knew those lines backwards." "And that is how you are saying them today," he replied. Another Coward witicism attributed to this relationship: "I would wring her neck, if I could find it."

T-12   *Person To Person*   CBS-TV, NY.   April 27, 1956

Noël Coward appeared as one of two segments (the other was Dr. Vannevar Bush, atomic scientist!) on the popular Friday night interview show that made effective use of televisions technological advances. Produced by Edward R. Murrow, Jesse Zousmer & John Aaron.

REVIEWS:
Variety, May 2, 1956: "Coward came through with several sharp lines and in general played his role of the sophisticated with consummate skill, just like a character

in one of his plays."

NOTES: Noel Coward was interviewed from Charles Russell and Lance Hamilton's apartment and discussed the opening of *South Sea Bubble* (P-143) two nights previously and read a telegram from its star Vivien Leigh. He wittily touched on rehearsals for the upcoming TV production of *This Happy Breed* (T-13), his painting (he called the style "touch and Gaugin"), his taste in books and poetry and his likes and dislikes as related to America. According to Coward's diaries he was proud of the fact that he was relaxed and nonchalant.

T-13   *This Happy Breed*   Ford Star Jubilee, CBS-TV, NY. May 5, 1956

Color TV version of **Noël Coward**'s play. Adapted and directed by **Noël Coward**. Produced by Richard Lewine. TV direction by Ralph Nelson.

CAST: **Noël Coward** (Frank Gibbons), Norah Howard (Mrs. Flint), Edna Best (Ethel), Beulah Garrick (Sylvia), Guy S. Paull (Bob Mitchell), Robert Chapman (Reg), Patricia Cutts (Queenie), Joyce Ash (Vi), Rhoderick Walker (Sam), Sally Pierce (Phillis Blake), Very Marshall (Edie), Roger Moore (Billy)

SYNOPSIS: See P-101.

REVIEWS:
New York Daily News, May 7, 1956: "Not top drawer Coward. It didn't have the entertainment content of virtuousity of his lighter plays. Cowards production and direction were smooth and the cast was of high quality. Noël seemed in some of his emotional moments a bit too casual but, on the whole he gave a lovable and solid portrayal of as un-Cowardania character as you can imagine."

Variety, May 9, 1956: "*This Happy Breed* made rewarding viewing if only for Coward's performance. Divorcing himself completely from the white tie and tail identity, Coward was the sincere father and the perfect husband with all the middle class virtues and standards indelibly portrayed. It was a capital performance."

New York World Telegram, May 5, 1959: "This is one of Noël Coward's best works. CBS is sparing no pains and no pennies to give it a first rate production."

NOTES: As opposed to his previous Hollywood experience, Coward loved working on this play and with Edna Best.

T-14   *Ed Sullivan Show*   CBS-TV, NY. April 8, 1956

Noël Coward appeared on the popular Sunday night variety show. He and Kostalanetz performed a cut version of *Carnival of Animals* and Coward sang "Mad Dogs & Englishmen."

REVIEWS:
Variety, April 11, 1956: "A suave debonaire Coward threw off the witty rhymes with great flair."

T-15   *South Sea Bubble* BBC, London Sept. 14, 1956

Act II, Scenes 1 & 2 of **Noël Coward's play** were televised from the theatre before an invited audience. By this time Vivien Leigh had left the show. See P-143 for production.

T-16   *Nude With Violin* BBC, London Dec 11, 1956.

A condensed version of the end of Act I and both scenes of Act II of **Noël Coward's play** were televised from the Globe Theatre, London with the cast noted in P-144.

T-17   *Ed Sullivan Show* CBS-TV, NY. Dec. 8, 1957

Noël Coward sang his Medley of Hits and "What's Going To Happen To The Tots?." Also appearing that night were Kirk Douglas, Tony Curtis, Ernest Borgnine, Janet Leigh and The Platters.

REVIEWS:
Variety, Dec. 11, 1957: "The sophisticates' 'dream boy,' Noël Coward should carefully consider future offers to do TV. The charm and wit he has in theatres and night clubs for some reason has failed to come across on the Ed Sullivan TV showcase."

NOTES: Following Noël Coward was contralto Jean Madeira singing his "Zigeuner" from *Bitter-Sweet*.

T-18   *Small World* CBS-TV, NY Mar. 22, 1959 & Mar. 29, 1959.

A sunday afternoon public affairs program hosted by Edward R. Murrow in which he conversed with three guests. Produced by Murrow and Fred W. Friendly. **Noël Coward** apppeared on the same program as James Thurber and Siobhan McKenna.

T-19   *What's My Line?* CBS-TV, NY Mar. 1, 1959

Noël Coward was the mystery guest and he plugged *Look After Lulu*

T-20   *Private Lives* A.T.V., England. Jan. 16, 1959.

TV adaptation of **Noël Coward's play**. Directed by Lionel Harris.

CAST: Maxine Audley (Amanda), Peter Gray (Elyot), Yolande Turner (Sybil), Gordon Chater (Victor)

SYNOPSIS: See P-61.

T-21   *Nude With Violin* BBC, England. 1959

TV adaptation of **Noël Coward**'s comedy.

SYNOPSIS: See P-144.

T-22   *Noel Coward Interview Show,* Oct., 1959

Hosted by **Noël Coward**. Directed by Dennis Vance. Produced by Howard Connell. Written by Jock Gourlay. Coward shot a pilot in Paris for a proposed series of interviews with great men of the world. He interviewed Darryl Zanuck, but ultimately did not do the series.

T-23   *Red Peppers* Three In One (Art Carney Show) Feb. 8, 1960 Friday

Television adaptation of **Noël Coward's one act play** from *Tonight at 8:30*. Directed by Marc Daniels. Produced by David Susskind.

CAST: Elaine Stritch (Lily Pepper), Art Carney (George Pepper), Myron McCormick, Zamah Cunningham (Mabel Grace), Fran Conroy, William Hickey

SYNOPSIS: See P-83.

REVIEWS:
Variety, Feb. 10, 1960: "The real value of the plays in terms of this program is that they provided juicy roles for Carney. Miss Stritch worked only in the last one, but hers was a sparkling contribution."

NOTES: The other one act plays on this show were Sean O'Casey's *Pound On*

Demand and Eugene O'Neill's *Where The Cross Is Made*.

T-24   *The Vortex*   BBC, England 1960

TV version of **Noël Coward's play**.

CAST: Ann Todd (Florence), David McCallum (Nicky), Ann Castle (Helen), Patience Collier (Clara)

SYNOPSIS: See P-35.

T-25   *Hay Fever*   Play of The Week BBC, England May 24, 1960

Television version of **Noël Coward's comedy**. Directed by Casper Wrede.

CAST: Dame Edith Evans (Judith Bliss), Richard Wattis (Richard Greatham), George Devine (David Bliss), Maggie Smith (Jackie), Pamela Brown (Myra)

SYNOPSIS: See P-38.

REVIEWS:
London Times, May 25, 1960: "It was by natural right that Dame Edith Evans dominated this production of what, even on critical reexamination, still seems Mr. Noël Coward's best play and one of the most perfectly engineered comedies of the century. This was acting in the grand manner."

Variety, June 1, 1960: "Maybe the chief credit should go to Noël Coward for this revival proved that in *Hay Fever* he created one of the few dateless comedies since Oscar Wilde."

NOTES: Four years later both Dame Edith Evans and Maggie Smith would both star in the National Theatre's production of *Hay Fever*, which brough Coward back into prominence.

T-26   *Tonight Show with Jack Paar*   NBC-TV, US Feb. 28, 1961.

Noël Coward appeared as a guest on this popular late night talk show.

REVIEWS:
Variety, Mar. 1, 1961: "Coward's self possession, casualness and sophisticated glibness was a dandy show biz fillip. He was just Coward and that's a big asset."

T-27   *Brief Encounter*   NBC-TV Dinah Shore Show Chevy Show Mar. 26, 1961

TV adaptation of **Noël Coward's film version of his one act play** from *Tonight at 8:30.* Adapted by Joseph Schrank. Directd by Dean Whitmore & Bob Finkel. Produced by Bob Finkel. Executive producer: Henry Jaffe. Musical direction by Harry Zimmerman. Assistant to the producer: Carolyn Raskin. "Brief Encounter" theme by W. Earl Brown.

CAST: Dinah Shore (Laura Jesson), Ralph Bellamy (Alec Harvey), Howard St. John (Albert Godby), Colette Lyons (Myrtle Bagot), Arte Johnson (Stanley), Jacqueline De Wit (Dolly), Bennye Gatteys (Beryl Waters)

SYNOPSIS: See P-83.

NOTES: This was Dinah Shore's TV dramatic debut. The local and time of the play was moved from contemporary England to Boston in 1908. It is eroniously reported in several Noël Coward books that Coward himself played Alec in this version.

T-28   *This Happy Breed*   BBC-TV, London April 8, 1962

TV version of **Noël Coward's play.**

SYNOPSIS: See P-101.

T-29   *Today Show*   NBC-TV, NY Oct. 3, 1963 7-9am. Taped Sept. 16, 1963

Two hour salute to **Noël Coward**. Produced by Al Morgan.

CAST: Beatrice Lillie, Skitch Henderson, Sally Ann Howes, **Noël Coward**

REVIEWS:
NY Herald Tribune, Oct. 2, 1963: "A must for Coward fans, who have seen the Master in too few TV appearances. Outstanding are a grand selection of Coward songs including "Mad Dogs and Englishmen" and "I'll See You Again" sung by Sally Ann Howes and played by Skitch Henderson and orchestra. A bonus comes when Mr. Coward calls an arrangement of "I'll Remember Her" "too skittish," has it replayed legato and then sings along enthusiastically and sentimentally."

NOTES: Beatrice Lillie sang a rare Noël Coward song entitled "The Spinning Song."

T-30   *Fallen Angels* BBC-TV, London Oct. 23, 1963 Wednesday 60 minutes

Television version of **Noël Coward's comedy.** Directed by Alan Bromley.
Produced by Peter Luke.

CAST: Moira Redmond (Jane), Ann Morrish (Julia), Ann Beach (Maid),
Richard Thorpe, James Villiers, David Ritch.

SYNOPSIS: See P-36.

REVIEWS:
Variety, Oct. 23, 1963: "Noël Coward's *Fallen Angels* from the 20's seemed a
perverse choice. Set in period and the thesps encouraged to gush and attitudinize
in a highly artificial manner. It pointed up the historic flavor of Coward's conception, instead of toning it down for comtemporary consumption."

T-31   *Sunday* NBC TV, NY Dec. 8, 1963

Noël Coward appeared and discussed *The Girl Who Came To Supper* with
entertainment editior William Zinser.

T-32   *Ed Sullivan Show* CBS-TV, NY Dec. 25, 1963 (sunday night)

Tessie O'Shea and the company performed the entire "London Sequence"
from **Noël Coward's musical** *The Girl Who Came To Supper*.

REVIEWS:
Variety, Dec. 25, 1963: "One of the more ambitious undertakings was the presentation of 'London Is A Little Bit Of Alright' with Tessie O'Shea in the lead spot.
It had color, pace and an authoratative performance by Miss O'Shea. This
sequence from Noël Coward's *The Girl Who Came To Supper* was a bit too long
for video needs but was nonetheless entertaining."

T-33   *What's My Line?* CBS -TV, NY Jan. 12, 1964.

Noël Coward appeared as a mystery guest.

T-34   *A Choice of Coward: Present Laughter* Granada Television Aug. 10, 1964

Noël Coward introduced each of the television versions of his plays.
Directed by Joan Kemp-Welch. Adapted by Peter Wildeblood.

CAST: Peter Wyngarden (Garry Essendine), Ursula Howell (Liz), Jennie Linden (Daphne), Joan Benham (Monica), Barbara Murray (Joanna), James Bolan, Danvers Walker, Ruth Pocher, Edwin Apps, Jane Eccles

SYNOPSIS: See P-100.

REVIEWS:
Variety, Aug. 19, 1964: "This comedy shows Coward dashing dexterity and flippant dialogue at the top of its craft and made a speedily entertaining contribution to the schedules."

T-35   *A Choice of Coward: Blithe Spirit* Granada Television Aug. 17, 1964

TV version of **Noël Coward's comedy.** See T-34.

CAST: Helen Cherry (Ruth), Griffith Jones (Charles), Hattie Jacques (Madame Arcati), Joanna Dunham (Elvira)

SYNOPSIS: See P-97.

T-36   *A Choice of Coward: The Vortex* Granada Television.Aug. 24, 1964

TV version of **Noël Coward's comedy.** See T-34.

SYNOPSIS: See P-35.

T-37   *A Choice of Coward: Design For Living* Granada Television. Aug. 31, 1964

TV version of **Noël Coward's comedy.** See T-34.

SYNOPSIS: See P-71.

T-38   *90 Years On: Churchill's 90th Birthday Tribute* BBC-TV, London & WOR-TV, NY Nov. 29, 1964

Written by Terrence Rattigan. **Narrated by Noël Coward.**

T-39   *Golden Hour of Drama* ATV Aug. ,1965

Noël Coward did an introduction to this spectacular.

T-40   *Great Acting* BBC-2-TV 50 minutes. Mar. 12, 1966

Noël Coward was interviewed by Michael MacOwan. Produced by Hal Burton.

REVIEWS:
Variety, March 25, 1966: "Full of illuminating insights about Coward's methods and attitudes. A full scale protrait of a dedicated artist."

T-41   Norwegian Broadcasting Company 1966

Noël Coward was interviewed.

T-42   *Eamonn Andrews Show* BBC-TV, London May 22, 1966

Noël Coward was a guest along with Dudley Moore, Lucille Ball and Cassius Clay (Mohammed Ali).

T-43   *Pretty Polly Barlow* Armchair Theatre BBC-TV, London Aug. 10, 1966 Sat.

TV adaptation of **Noël Coward's short story** by William Marchant. Directed by Bill Bain. Produced by Leonard White.

CAST: Lynn Redgrave (Polly), Donald Houston (Robert Hook), Zia Mohyeddin (Amaz), Dandy Nichols (Mrs. Innes-Hook), Poulet Tu (Lorelei), Stuart Cooper, Leon Sinden, Derek Smee, Lillias Walker.

REVIEWS:
Variety, Aug. 10, 1966: "It made easy and beguiling entertainment for those who could suspend disbelief, it's flaw being Coward's curious attitude to the modern world, which he seems to think hasn't changed much since the 20's. But the playing was so deft and William Marchant's buoyant adaptation maintained such a lively air of flippancy that it diverted thoughout."

NOTES: This story also was adapted to film as *A Matter of Innocence* (F-27)

T-44   *Blithe Spirit* NBC-TV, NY Hallmark Hall of Fame Dec. 7, 1966

90 minute television adaptation of **Noël Coward's comedy**. Adaptation by Robert Hartung. Produced and directed by George Shaefer. Sets by Ed Wittstein. Costumes by Noel Taylor.

CAST: Dirk Bogarde (Charles), Rosemary Harris (Elvira), Rachel Roberts (Ruth), Ruth Gordon (Madame Arcati), Geoffrey Lumb (Dr. Bradman), Joan White (Mrs. Bradman), Mildred Tarras (Edith)

SYNOPSIS: See P-97.

REVIEWS:
New York Times, Dec. 8, 1966: "Mr. Schaefer's direction lacked the light touch that was clearly needed and the play's formidable quotient of pure slapstick was not endowed with many beguiling touches. The ingredients of the author's astral cocktail were more determinedly shaken up than drolly stirred."

Variety, Dec. 14, 1966: "*Blithe Spirit* proved both durable and adaptable in this sprightly rendition of Noël Coward's bit of WWII whimsy."

T-45   *Present Laughter* I.T.V. England Mar. 15, 1967 Thurs. & ABC-TV, US Feb. 28, 1968 as Theatre Night.

Television version of **Noel Coward's comedy**. Directed by Gordon Flemyng. Sets by Henry Graveney. Music arranged by Derek Scott from Noël Coward.

CAST: Peter O'Toole (Garry Essendine), Honr Blackman (Liz), Avice Landon (Monica), Marie Lohr (Lady Saltburn), Isla Blair, Tim Preece (Roland Maule), William Dexter, Sheila Keith, Edward Hardwicke, Tony Selby (Valet), Yolande Turner (Joanna)

REVIEWS:
Variety, March 15, 1967: "Though inevitable cuts in the original text interrupt the flow somewhat (Coward's craft was too exact to permit easy tampering) the play was put across with as much visual variety as could be wished from an essentially set bound piece."

T-46   *Look After Lulu* BBC-TV, London 1967

TV version of **Noël Coward's farce**.

T-47   *Androcles and the Lion* NBC-TV, NY Nov. 15, 1967

A television musical with book by Peter Stone. Music and lyrics by Richard Rodgers. Based on the play by George Bernard Shaw. Directed by Joe Layton. Sets by Tom John. Costumes by Theoni Aldredge. Lighting by Phil Hymes. Music direction by Jay Blackton. Orchestrations by Robert Russell Bennett. Dance Arrangments by David Baker.

CAST: **Noël Coward** (Caesar), Geoffrey Holder (Lion), Patricia Routledge (Megaera), Norman Wisdom (Androcles), John Cullum (Captain),

Inga Swenson (Lavinia), Brian Bedford (Lentulus), Clifford David (Metellus), Ed Ames (Ferrovius), William Redfield (Pintho), Kurt Kasznar (Manater of Gladiators), George Mathews (Roman Centurion), Bill Hickey (Keeper of the Lions), Bill Star (Retiarius & Lion), George Reeder (Secutor & Lion), Steve Bookvar (Lion)

SYNOPSIS: Androcles, a lover of animals finds a lion with a thorn stuck in his paw and removes it. Later, because he is a Christian, he is taken to the arena to be torn to bits by the lions as Caesar watches. When the lion he helped recognizes him he is saved and becomes Caesar's animal keeper.

REVIEWS:
Variety, Nov. 22, 1967: "Noël Coward, absent too long from American home screens, played Caeser, with the blithest possible spirit. His rapid speech, however, was not always captured by the mikes."

NOTES: Noël Coward sang two numbers: "The Emperor's Thumb" and "Don't Be Afraid of An Animal" (duet with Wisdom) and made a very Noël Cowardish Caesar. For recording of score see D-112. On July 31, 1967, according to the *NY Daily News*, Coward was out of the production due to illness.

T-48   *Mrs. Capper's Birthday* BBC-TV, London

Adaptation of **Noël Coward's short story** by William Marchant. Produced by Leonard White.

T-49   *Star Quality* Playhouse Aug. 14, 1968 Monday

TV adaptation of **Noël Coward's short story** by William Marchant. Produced by Leonard White. Directed by Guy Varney. Decor by David Marshall.

CAST: Glynis Johns (Lorraine Barry), Robert Hardy (Ray Malcolm), Arne Gordon (J.C. Roebuck), Jim Norton (Bryan Snow), Joyce Barbour, Tandy Cronyn, Barry Justice (Tony Orford), Mona Bruce (Marian)

REVIEWS:
Variety, Aug. 14, 1968: "It is fair to say that only a professional as imbued in the world of theatre as Noël Coward could have inspired *Star Quality* and only a man who loves it as well as Coward could have so accurately pinpointed it's excitements, frustrations, virtues, faults, glamour, and mean trickeries. The result is a play of complete fascination to all who are stage struck and of more than passing interest to the outsider."

T-50   *Don't Count The Candles* BBC-TV, UK 1968 & CBS-TV, US Mar. 26, 1968.

Film by Lord Snowdon about aging featurning **Noël Coward**.

T-51   *David Frost Show* ITV and WNEW, NY Sept. 16, 1968.

Noël Coward was interviewed by David Frost.

T-52   *Post-Mortem* The Jazz Age Drama Series BBC-TV Sept. 17, 1968

First presentation of **Noël Coward**'s 1930 play. Directed by John Mac-Kenzie

T-53   *Saturday Special: The Words and Music of Noël Coward* ITV , London 1968

T-54   *Hay Fever* Play of the Month BBC1, London Aug. 11, 1968

90 minutes television version of **Noël Coward's comedy**. Produced by Cedric Messina. Directed by John Gorie. Designed by Richard Henry.

CAST: Celia Johnson (Judith Bliss), Dennis Price (David Bliss), Lucy Flemming (Sorel Bliss), Ian McKellen (Simon Bliss), Anna Massey (Myra Arundel), Charles Gray (Richard Greatham), Vickery Turner (Jackie Coryton), Richard Briers (Sandy Tyrell), Hazel Hughes (Clara)

SYNOPSIS: See P-38.

REVIEWS:
Variety, Aug. 14, 1968: "This specially produced TV version provided a polished, jolly peak hour entertainment, with an able cast giving full value to Coward's witty dialogue and exaggerated by amusingly outrageous characters."

NOTES: Celia Johnson had just done a successful revival of the play in the West End. She also replaced Dame Edith Evans in the National Theatre production.

T-55   *Marvelous Party!* London Weekend Televisison, London. Jan. 10, 1969.

A musical tribute to **Noël Coward's words and music**. Produced and choreographed by Gillian Lynne. Direced by Piers Haggard.

CAST: Laurence Harvey, Cleo Laine, Betty Marsden, Ronnie Stevens,

Ray Davis, Caryl Little, Valerie Masterson, Virginia Mason, Paddy Mc-Intire

REVIEWS:
Variety, Jan. 22, 1969: "A feast for Coward fans, this one hour potpourri of some of the maestro's better and lesser items was otherwise a shade too one tracked for the average viewer."

London Daily Telegraph, Jan. 11, 1969: "This was hardly the fairest way to celebrate the great man. His derivative and genteel music is the least memorable part of his output."

T-56   *Omnibus: Noël Coward: Playwright* BBC-1 Dec. 6, 1969.

Produced by Hal Burton. Designed by Michael Porter. Introduced by Ronald Bryden.

NOTES: **Noël Coward** was interviewed by Patrick Garland. Excerpts from *The Vortex, Hay Fever, Blithe Spirit, This Happy Breed* and *Star* were shown. Coward said on this program, "I think writing is an art and a craft and if you can combine the two you make a living out of it."

T-57   *The Vortex* BBC-1, London The Wednesday Play Deb. 10, 1969

Television version of **Noël Coward's play.** (P-35) Directed by Philip Dudley. Produced by Graeme McDonald. Designed by Tony Abbott

CAST: Richard Warwick (Nicky), Margaret Leighton (Florence), Alan Melville (Pawnie), Patrick Barr (David Lancaster), Jennifer Daniel (Helen Saville), Barry Justice (Tom Veryan), Felicity Gibson (Bunty Mainwaring), Nancie Jackson (Clara Hibbert), David McKail (Bruce Fairlight), Patricia Mort (Preston)

REVIEWS:
London Observer, Dec. 14, 1969: "The brittle jokes seemed genuinely funny. The drugs are surely a substitute for homosexuality. Richard Warwick's Nicky was all the better for avoiding any temptation to imitate the master. Margaret Leighton played his mother with courageous panache."

Variety, Dec. 17, 1969: "The play is now outmoded in its content and impact after 46 years. But the BBC version though necessarily truncated, proved that even then Coward was suavely witty, had a feeling for the big punchy scene and for characters, however foolish they may now seem, were never passengers."

T-58   *This Happy Breed* BBC-2, London Dec. 11, 1969

Television version of **Noel Coward's play**. Directed by Donald Mc-Whinnie. Produced by Ronald Travers. Designed by Richard Wilmot. Script edited by James Brabazon. Lighting by Jim Richards. Pianist: Patrick Harvey.

CAST: Dandy Nichols (Mrs. Flint), Gillian Martel (Ethel), Gillian Raine (Sylvia), Frank Finlay (Frank Gibbons), Christopher Hancock (Bob Mitchell), Robert Cook (Reg), Tamara Hinchco (Queenie), Vivien Heilbron (Vi), Terence Edmond (Sam), Mary Larkin (Phillis Blake), Sara-Jane Ladbrook (Edie), Andrew Ray (Billy)

T-59   *The Marquise* BBC1, London Play of the Month Dec. 14, 1969

Television version of **Noël Coward's play**. Directed by Alan Gibson. Produced by Cedric Messina. Designed by Eileen Diss. Script edited by Rosemary Hill. Costumes by Charles Knode. Lighting by Dennis Channon. Music arranged by Douglas Gamley.

Richard Vernon (Comte Raoul de Vriaac), Clara Madden (Adrienne), Nigel Terry (Jaques Rijar), Philip Latham (Esteban), David Griffin (Miquel), Wensley Pithey (Father Clement), Alan MacNaughtan (Hubert), Celia Johnson (The Marquise Eloise de Kestournel), Barbara New (Alice)

T-60   *Red Peppers* BBC1, London Dec. 15, 1969

Television version of **Noël Coward's interlude with music** from *Tonight at 8:30*. Produced by Michael Mills. Designed by Brian Tregidden. Wardrobe by Raymond Hughes. Makeup by Pamela Burns. Musical direction by Dennis Wilson. Musical numbers arranged by John Heawood.

CAST: Dora Bryan (Lily Pepper), Bruce Forsyth (George Pepper), Cyril Cusack (Bert Bentley), Anthony Quayle (Mr. Edwards), Edith Evans (Mabel Grace), Freddie Foot (Alf)

T-61   *Noël Coward's Birthday Party* BBC1, London Dec. 16, 1969

Birthday party taking place at the Lancaster Room at the Savoy. 300 of **Noël Coward's** closest friends were present. Lord Mountbatten and Sir Laurence Olivier were among the after dinner speakers. The program was

introduced by Richard Attenborough. The commentator was Sheridan Morley.
Produced by John Vernon.

NOTES: Lord Mountbatten made a list of Noël Coward's talents: "There may be
better singers, pianists, dancers, painters, etc., etc., etc., but there would have to
be fourteen different people. There is only one Noël Coward and he combines
the attributes of all fourteen."

T-62   *Songs of Coward* BBC-TV, London Dec. 26, 1969.

T-63   *Dick Cavett Show* ABC-TV, NY Feb. 10, 1970. repeated June 1, 1970.

> **Noël Coward** appeared with Alfred Lunt and Lynn Fontanne on the talk
> show.

NOTES: In *Cavett* by Dick Cavett and Christopher Porterfield (Harcourt, Brace
Jovanovich 1974) Cavett tells of one of his most thrilling shows, "The one show
that people seem to recall with a slight catch in the throat and hush in the voice is
the one with the Lunts and Noël Coward. Jack Paar called the day after to say it
was the best thing he'd ever seen on television." Cavett goes on to talk about his
nerves when "Coward, whose devastating ability to get a laugh with one syllable
and thereby fire the ball back into you court got me off balance for a moment or
two. But there is a kind of warm security about being onstage with a truly great
professional that took over quickly and made me quite comfortable."

T-64   *David Frost Show* WNEW-TV, NY Feb. 19, 1970 90 minutes.

> **Noël Coward** was the guest along with Margaret Mead. Sergio Franchi
> sang a Coward song before the Master appeared.

REVIEWS:
NY Daily News, Feb. 20, 1970: "What Noël Coward proved again is that nothing is
more fascinating or entertaining than civilized conversation."

T-65   *Tony Awards* ABC-TV , NY April 19, 1970.

> The annually televised awards were presented live at the Mark Hellinger
> Theatre, NY. Produced by Alexander Cohen. **Noël Coward** was given a
> special Tony Award for Distinguished Achievement in the Theatre. After
> he descended the Cecil Beaton staircase of the *Coco* set to great applause
> and was presented the award by his old friend, Cary Grant. (The Lunts
> also received the honor), he said "This is my first award, so please be kind."

T-66   *Oh Coward!* CBC-TV, Toronto, Canada. Feb. 16, 1971

A 60 minute TV version of the current Toronto revue based on **Noël Coward's words and music.** Produced and directed by Paddy Sampson. Adapted by Roderick Cook.

CAST: Roderick Cook, Tom Kneebone, Dinah Christie

REVIEWS:
Variety, Feb. 17, 1971: *"Oh Coward!* was excellent fun. Familiar Coward and unfamiliar Coward blended into a first rate TV hour."

T-67   *Tribute to Sir Noël Coward* BBC1, London

A tribute to the late **Sir Noël Coward** featuring film clips and speeches from Olivier, Richard Attenborough, John Mortimer and Alan Melville.

T-68   *This Is Noël Coward* 1973. Shown on ITV, London April 8, 1973 as a tribute to the late Sir Noel Coward. Shown on WNET-TV, NY Oct, 1974 and repeated on Dec. 11, 1974.

A 90 minute musical TV biography of **Sir Noël Coward**. Written, produced and directed by Charles Castle. Edited by Martin Bohan. Cartoon designed by Osbert Lancaster. Assistant to producer: Judith Harris.

CAST: **Noël Coward**, Sir John Gielgud, Maurice Chevalier, Richard Burton, David Niven, Lilli Palmer, Joan Sutherland, Yul Brynner, John Mills, Dame Edith Evans, Hermione Gingold, Brian Aherne, Cecil Beaton, Dame Anna Neagle, Dame Sybil Thorndike, Dame Gladys Good, Joyce Grenfell, Adrianne Allen, Binkie Beaumont, Gladys Calthrop, Joyce Carey, Zena Dare, Peter Daubeny, Celia Johnson, Danny LaRue, Cole Lesley, Michael MacLiammoir, Graham Payn, Ginette Spanier, Herbert Wilcox, Googie Withers, The Earl Mountbatten of Burma

REVIEWS:
New York Times, Dec. 11, 1974: "A marvelously stylish blend of entertainment and straightforward biographical information. *This Is Noël Coward* is deliciously witty, surprisingly moving."

T-69   *Brief Encounter* NBC-TV Hallmark Hall of Fame Dec. 11, 1974

Adaptation of **Noël Coward's play** *Still Life* and the film *Brief Encounter.* Directed by Alan Bridges. Executive producer: Carlo Ponti & Duane C.

Bogie. Produced by Cecil Clarke. Teleplay by John Bowen. Edited by Peter Weatherly. Music by Cyril Orndel. Photographed by Arthur Ibetson. Art direction by Peter Roden.

CAST: Sophia Loren (Anna Jesson), Richard Burton (Alec Harvey), Jack Hedley (Graham Jesson), Ann Firbank (Melanie Harvey), Rosemary Leach (Mrs. Gaines), Gwen Cherrell (Dolly), Jon LeMessurier (Stephen), Benjamin Ednay (Alistair Jesson)

T-70   *Mad About the Boy: Noël Coward - A Celebration* Camera 3 CBS-TV, NY Feb. 22, 1976 & Feb. 29, 1976 Two 1/2 hour shows.

Produced and directed by Sheldon Larry. Musical direction and accompaniment by Ken Nurock.

CAST: George Rose, Jean Marsh, Carole Shelley, Kristopher Tabori

REVIEWS:
NY Times, Feb. 27, 1976: "The bulk of the two 1/2 hours is marvelously witty and entertaining. It would have doubtlessly pleased the man who one advised young playwrights to 'consider the public...above all never, never bore the hell out of it.'"

NOTES: The progams contained scenes from Coward's plays including *Tonight At 8:30, The Vortex, Design For Living, South Sea Bubble* and *A Song At Twilight.* It also featured songs including "You Were There," "London Is A Little Bit of All Right," "20th Century Blues," "Play Orchestra Play" and "Why Must the Show Go On." The entertainment was linked by Coward's own words from poems and autobiography.

T-71   *Private Lives* BBC-TV , London Dec. 28, 1976

Adaptation of **Noël Coward's play**. Directed by John Gorrie. Produced by Cedric Messina. Designed by Stuart Walker. Costumes by Robin Fraser Paye.

CAST: Penelope Keith (Amanda), Alec McCowen (Elyot), Polly Adams (Sybil), Donald Pickering (Victor), Francoise Pascal (Louise)

T-72   *Design For Living* BBC1, London May 12, 1979

Television adaptation of **Noël Coward's comedy**.

CAST: Rula Lenska (Gilda), Dandy Nichols (Maid)

REVIEWS:
London Observer, May 13, 1979: "Somewhere in one of the better decorated lower regions, Noël Coward is stretched out on a chaise-longue. *Design For Living* has barely begun. Suddenly there is a snapping sound. Coward has just bitten through the stem of his ebony cigarette holder. What the Hell have they done to his play?"

T-73   *Present Laughter* BBC-TV, London 1981. Arts Cable Network, US

TV version of the revival of **Noël Coward's comedy.** Taped at the Vaudeville Theatre. Directed by Alan Stachan. Sets and Costumes by Peter Rice. Produced by John Gale. Produced for Television by Keith Williams. Directed for Television by Rick Gardner.

CAST: Donald Sinden (Garry Essendine), Belinda Lang (Daphne), Sheila Mitchell (Miss Erikson), Colin Spaull (Fred), Gwen Watford (Monica), Dinah Sheridan (Liz Essendine), Julian Fellows (Roland Maule), Ian Garndner (Henry), Michael Fleming (Morris Dixon), Elizabeth Councell (Joanna Lyppiatt), Jill Johnson (Lady Saltburn)

SYNOPSIS: See P-100.

T-74   *Song By Song By Coward* ITV, London & WNET, NY 1980

A one hour salute to **Noel Coward**'s lyrics as part of a BBC-PBS TV series. Produced and directed by Ned Sherrin. Finale Medley by Caryl Brahms and Peter Greenwell. Orchestrations by Peter Knight. Musical adaptations by Peter Greenwell. Staged by Irving Davies. Additional material by Neil Shand. Directed by Vernon Lawrence.

CAST: Cleo Laine, David Kernan, Gemma Craven, Ned Sherrin & Ian Carmichael

MUSICAL NUMBERS: Play Orchestra Play, London Pride, Let's Do It (Music by Porter), Three White Feathers, Poor Little Rich Girl, The Stately Homes of England, Mrs. Worthington, I Wonder What Happened to Him?, Medley: I'll Follow My Secret Heart, Someday I'll Find You, I'll See You Again; Come the Wild Wild Weather, A Bar On The Piccalo Marina, If Love Were All, Finale: Where Are The Songs We Sung?, Dance Little Lady, Mad About The Boy, He Never Did That To Me, Matelot, Sail Away, Has Anybody Seen Our Ship, Mad Dogs, Why Do The Wrong People Travel?, I Travel Alone, Chase Me Charlie, Alice Is At It Again, You Were There, This Is A Changing World, Room With A View, World Weary, 20th Century Blues, Auntie Jessie, Something Very Strange, Ziegeuner, Any Little Fish

T-75   *Oh Coward!* CBC, Toronto & Broadway on Showtime , US July, 1980.

TV version of 10th anniversary production of revue of **Noël Coward's words and music** (P-180). Executive producers: Richard Seader and Maurice Levine. Produced by Russell Moore. Directed by Seymour Berns. Sets by Nancy Robertson. Lighting by Marney Stewart. Distributed by Columbia Pictures Televison Canada. Other credits same as P-180.

CAST: Roderick Cook, Jaimie Ross, Pat Galloway

NOTES: A cut version was shown on Showtime.

T-76   *Mike Wallace Special* , CBS-TV, NY Dec. 25, 1981

A segment on **Noël Coward**'s career and life appeared.

T-77   *South Bank Show: Laurence Olivier: A Life* LWT, London Oct. 17, 1982

Noël Coward appeared in a interview taped by the BBC in the 1960's.

T-78   *Suite In Three Keys* BBC, London 1983

TV version of **Noël Coward**'s last play.

CAST: Deborah Kerr, Paul Scoffield

T-79   *A Private Life* BBC1, London April 8, 1983

A documentary about **Noël Coward**.

T-80   *Star Quality: Noël Coward Stories* BBC 1985. & PBS TV,WGBH TV Boston & Arts and Entertainment 1987. Produced by Masterpiece Theatre and Quintet Films.

A series of dramatizations of **Noël Coward's stories**. Produced by Allan Shallcross. Executive Producer: Victor Glynn. The plays include:

Star Quality BBC1, London Nov. 10, 1985, WNET-TV, NY April 5, 1987

Screenplay by Stanley Price. Directed by Alan Dossor. Lighting by Clive Thomas. Costumes by Irene Whilton. Music by John Altman.

CAST: Susannah York (Lorraine Barry), Peter Chelsom (Bryan Snow), Ian Richardson (Ray Malcolm), David Yelland (Tony Orford), Pam Ferris (Marian), David Swift (J.C. Roebuck), Neville Barber (Gerald Wentworth), Tim Bannerman (Chales Hawkins), Ben Aris (Eric Larch), Jo Kendall (Linda Copeland), Amanda Donohoe, Bill Ritchie (Understudies), Sidney Livingston, Jonathan Lacey, Lucy Hancock (Stage Managers), Aubrey Woods (Adrian Gurney), Maggie Ollerenshaw (Usherette)

SYNOPSIS: Young playwright Bryan Snow's first play is to be produced on the West End and directed by the great Ray Malcolm. When Lorraine Barry, star of stage, screen and everything else comes on board the fun begins. Lorraine is a terror and insists on having an incompetent costar and one of her toady friends in a large role. Lorraine and Malcolm lock horns and agree on only one thing, the need for a rewritten ending to the play. By the opening night, Bryan learns many of the theatre's toughest lessons and Lorraine finally exhibits what make her unique: her star quality.

REVIEWS:
New York Times, March, 28, 1987: "Elegantly brittle, terribly sophisticated on top and very sentimental below. *Star Quality* is acted brightly enough to launch this latest Masterpiece Theatre with a kind of verve Coward himself would have appreciated."

NOTES: The character of Lorraine Barry was thought by many to be based on Gertrude Lawrence. This story was also adapted in 1968 (see T-49)

T-81   *Mrs. Capper's Birthday* WNET-TV, NY April 19, 1987

Screenplay by Jack Rosenthal. Directed by Mike Okrent. Music by Chris Walker. Designed by Colin Shaw. Costumes by Rita Reeke.

CAST: Patricia Hayes (Mrs. Capper), Avis Bunnage (Alice), Paula Wilcox (Maureen), Max Wall (Mr. Godsall), Kathryn Pogson (Audrey), Gary Waldhorn (Jack), Paddie O'Neil (Arlene), Hugh Laurie (Bob), John Bard (Maurice), Roger Sloman (David), Danyse Alexander (Mrs. Bertram), Mark Boyton (Newspaper Boy), Sandra Hale (Laura), Sue Carpenter (Mrs. Burgess), Chris Walker (Pianist), Peter McMichael (Soldier), Elaine Lordan (Girlfriend), Andrew Paul (Young Drunk)

SYNOPSIS: Taking place on one summery Sunday in 1972, Mrs. Capper's birthday is seen from morning to night. The old charwoman rises, greets the day and her long dead husband's picture (she speaks to her husband throughout) and goes off to the flat of two of her favorite clients. She finds a large mess there, not including the kitchen. The mistress has another man in her bed and the master also slept elsewhere. Mrs. Capper is rewarded for keeping mum with a lovely diamond clip for her birthday. When she gets home to the lodgings she rents from Alice, Alice's elderly beau Mr. Godsall brings Mrs. Capper a gift and makes a play for her. Alice is far from amused. The evening finally arrives and Mrs. Capper's daughter and son in law take the old ladies out for a birthday celebration, first to a french restaurant and then to Mrs. Capper's favorite pub, where she sings "I'll Be Seeing You." The birthday end where it began with Mrs. Capper tucked in her bed and saying goodnight to her beloved dead husband.

NOTES: This too was adapted for TV in the 1960's (T-48)

T-82   *Me and The Girls* WNET-TV, NY April 19, 1987

Screenplay by Ken Taylor. Directed by Jack Gold. Designed by Olivei Bayldon, Music arranged by Francis Shaw. Costumes by Irene Whilton. Choreographed by Linsay Dolan.

CAST: Tom Courtenay (George), Nichola McAuliffe (Mavis), Robert Glenister (Harry), Philip Voss (Prof. Lembach), Tessa Pritchard (Bonny), Catherine Rabett (Sally), Andre Maranne (Dr. Pierre), Philip Voss (Prof. Lembach), Nancy Nevinson (Sister Dominique), Oliver Pierre (Michel), Trace Booth (Sue), Harry Fowler (Ted Bentley), Malcolm Sinclair (Ronnie), Adam Robertson (Police Constable), Julie-Anne Blythen (Irma), Maria Friedman (Lily Man), Jayne and Michelle Jordan (The Martin Twins), Colette Stevenson (Moira), Chrissie Kendall (Gloria), Annie Wensak (Elsie)

SYNOPSIS: George, a middle aged Gay song and dance man, heads up a second rate European tour along with his "Bombshells.". When George collapses during a performance, he is taken to hospital, where he remembers key elements in his adult life: the formation of the act, meeting Harry-Boy (the love of his life), and Harry-Boy's death. When his memories are done, so is he. George dies peacefully in bed and in death performs one last time.

REVIEWS:
New York Times, April 5, 1987: "The series reaches its high point with *Me and the Girls* perfectly pulled together by the writer Ken Taylor and the director Jack Gold. *Me and the Girls* takes the Coward strengths and weaknesses and wraps them up into a memorable little drama."

T-83 *Mr. & Mrs. Edgehill* WNET-TV, NY April 5, 1987

Screenplay by T.R. Bowen. Directed by Gavin Millar. Music by Stanley Meyers.

CAST: Ian Holm (Eustace Edgehill), Judi Dench (Dorrie Edgehill), Rachel Gurney (Cynthia Marchmont), Alan MacNaughtan (Sir Humphrey), Daphne Goddard (Eloise), Amanda Pays (Vivienne), Raymond Francis (Admiral Sir Arthur), John Harding (Neville Stern), Madge Hindle (Bett Howell), Robert Blythe (Charlie Howell), Shane Rimmer (Brod Sarnton), John Horsley (Sir Mostyn), Henry Moxon (John Petrie), Martin Wimbush (Henry Ceran), Pat Star (Irma Handley), Jay Ruparella (Ippaga)

SYNOPSIS: Just as failed pineapple growers, Mr. and Mrs. Edgehill are about to leave Samola, Mr. Edgehill is appointed British Resident of a small desert island that the English think will be very instrumental in the coming second world war. After some hesitation on Mrs. Edgehill's part, they take up residency and are joined on the island by the Americans. When the Japanese begin to get too close, the Americans withdraw, but the Edgehills, having no word from their superiors, stay to meet their fate.

REVIEWS:
Chicago Sun Times, April, 3, 1987: "Mr. and Mrs. Edgehill is a touching, poignant story about lost lives, lost loves and rediscovery proving that television can serve as a forum for material that is both intellectually rewarding and enjoyable entertainment."

T-84 *Bon Voyage* WNET-TV, NY Aril 26, 1987

Screeplay by Stanley Price. Directed by Mike Vardy. Music by Francis Shaw. Designed by Richard Morris.

CAST: Judy Parfitt (Lola Widmeyer), Nigel Havers (Roddy Buchanan), Helen Horton (Irma Turnbull), Michael Aldridge (Sir Colin Bland), Ursula Howells (Lady Mary Bland), Ed Devereau (Henry Teitelbaum), Doreen Mantel (Nancy Teitelbaum), Michael Fitzpatrick (Orwin Wendell), Tara Ward (Lisa Wendell), Jerry Harte (Capt. Berringer), Takashi Kawahara (Kito), Janene Possell (Mavis), Gay Baynes (Helen), Ray Knight (Reiner), Santiago Varela (Peppo), Zane Stanley (Steward)

SYNOPSIS: A luxury cruise ship heading to Hawaii and Japan carries middle aged American writer Lola Widmeyer and British playboy Roddy Buchanan. Despite the difference in their ages, the have a ship board romance and fall in love. Seated with them at the Captain's Table (the original title of the story) is an insufferable gossip, Mrs. Turnbull, Lord and Lady Bland and a middle aged American couple, the Teitlebaums. At the end of the cruise Mr. Teitlebaum has a heart attack and dies, while Lola and Roddy decide to marry.

NOTES: The story bears some similarities to the plot of *Sail Away*.

T-85   *What Mad Pursuit?* Art & Entertainment Network, NY

Screenplay by Stanley Price. With acknowledgements to *Long Island Sound* by Noël Coward. Directed by Tony Smith. Musical Direction by Tony Britten. Costumes by Juanita Waterson. Designed by Cecilia Brereton.

CAST: Carol Baker (Louise Steinhauser), Paul Daneman (Evan Lorrimer), Neil Cunningham (Lester Gage), Philip Joseph (Don Wilson), Jane Carr (Irene Marlow), Clive Swift (Bonwit Steinhauser), Sandra Dickenson (Delia Hughes-Hitchcock), Jacqueline Pearce (Luella Rosen), Hadyn Gwynne (Shirley Benedict), Helen Buzard (Leone Crane), David Roper (Hughes Hughes-Hitchcock), Britt Walker (Aesop), Imogene Bickford-Smith (Bright Eyes), David Gillian (Dwight Vacadoo), Bradley Lavelle (Tim Murphy), Nicholas Pritchard (Suki), Ted Maynard (Neuman Block), Helen Horton (Mrs. Loomis), Pamela Mandell (Woman Questioner)

SYNOPSIS: Evan Lorrimer, famed British novelist in the US for a lecture tour, accepts Louise Steinhauser's invitation for a quiet, restful weekend in her home on Long Island. It turns out to be anything but. Forced to share a bathroom with Broadway star, Lester Gage seems small potatoes after the hoards of famous people descend on the house, pour martinis in to Evan and drag him to other, larger parties. The weekend ends with Lorrimer making his escape back to the city through a second story window. After he loses footing and falls, he is brought back from the hospital to recover in this restful and quiet house.

NOTES: This story, which was not presented on Masterpiece Theatre, was based on truth. Coward was in exactly the same situation in the late 1930's. Read Clifton Webb for Lester Gage, Cobina Wright for Louise Steinhauser, Grace Moore for Irene Marlow etc. Coward, himself, adapted the story into a play, *Long Island Sound*. It was never produced, but seems to be the basis of this teleplay.

T-86-94*Tonight At 8:30* BBC April 14, 1991 and A&E 1992 (entitled *Collins Meets Coward* on A&E. Premiered March 31, 1992 with *Ways and Means, The Astonished Heart and Still Life.*)

Eight **Noël Coward one act plays** from *Tonight at 8:30* plays were presented in slightly edited 1/2 hour formats by the Joan Collins Repertory Company. Costumes by Colin Lavers & Bill Taylor. Produced for BBC by Knaves-Acres Productions. Lighting by Clive Thomas. Designed by Graham Lough and George Kyriakides. Adapted and produced by Bryan Izzard. Associated producer-Joan Collins. Camera supervised by Roger Fenn. Sound supervised by Alan Stokes. Video edited by Chris Wadsworth. Musical direction by Burt Rhodes. Choreography by Roger Hannah. *The Astonished Heart, Ways and Means & Hands Across The Sea* directed by Paul Annett. *Still Life* directed by Sidney Lotterby. *Family Album, Shadow Play & Fumed Oak* directed by John Genister. *Red Peppers* directed by Bryan Izzard.

PLAYS AND CASTS: *The Astonished Heart:* Sian Phillips (Barbara Faber), Jessica Martin (Susan Birch), Edward Duke (Tim Verney), Edward Jewesbury (Sir Reginald), Joan Collins (Leonora Vail), John Alderton (Christian Faber); *Red Peppers*: Joan Collins (Lily Pepper) Anthony Newley (George Pepper), Richard Dempsey (Alf), Reg Varney (Bert Bentley), Henry McGee (Mr. Edwards), Moyra Fraser (Mabel Grace); *Hands Across The Sea*: Vera Jakob (Walters) Joan Collins (Piggie), John Nettles (Her husband), Edward Duke (Alastair Corbett), Miriam Margolies (Mrs. Wadhurst), Bernard Cribbins (Mr. Wadwurst) Richard Dempsey (Mr. Burnham), Sian Phillips (Clare Wedderburn), Nicholas Grace (Bogey); *Fumed Oak*: Anthony Newley (Henry Gow), Joan Collins (Doris Gow), Prudence Oliver (Elsie), Joan Sims (Mrs. Rocket); *Shadow Play*: Kate O'Sullivan (Lena) Joan Collins (Victoria Gayforth), Jean Anderson (Martha Cunningham), Simon Williams (Simon Gayforth), Michael Meadmore (Michael Doyle), Carrie Ellis (Sybil Heston), Edward Duke (A Young Man), Edward Jewesbury (George Cunningham); *Family Album*: Denis Quiley (Jasper Featherways), Jessica Martin (Jane, his wife), Liza Sadovy (Harriet Winter), Charles Collingwood (Charles Winter), Bonnie Langford (Emily Valance), Dominic Jephcott (Edward Valance), Richard Kane (Richard Featherways), Joan Collins (Lavinia Featherways), John Alderton (Burrows); *Ways and Means*: John Standing (Toby Cartwright), Joan Collins (Stella Catwright), Miriam Margolies(Nannie), Kate O'Sullivan (Elena), Harold Innocent (Gaston), Tony Slattery (Stevens), Sian Phillips (Olive), Edward Duke (Lord Chapworth); *Still Life*: John Alderton (Alec Harvey), Jane Asher (Laura Jesson), Moyra Fraser (Dolly Messiter), Stephen Simms (Johnny), Diane

Langton (Beryl Waters), Steve Nicholson (Stanley), Brian McCardie (Bill), Norman Rossington (Albert Godby), Joan Collins (Myrtle Bagot)

T-95   *Coward* South Bank Show LWT, London Feb. 1992 and Bravo, NY March 21, 1992

One hour documentary about **Noël Coward**'s life and career from Iambic Productions for LTW. Distributed by RM Associates. Produced and directed by Chris Hunt. Edited and presented by Melvyn Bragg. Associate producer: Cas Gorham. Sets by Alison Humphries. Costumes by Janet Benge. Makeup by Jenny Sharpe.

CAST: **Noël Coward**, Daniel Massey, Philip Hoare, John Osborne, Lord Laurence Olivier, Graham Payn, Ned Sherrin, Sir John Mills, John Lahr, Sir David Lean, Sir John Gielgud, Maria Aitkin, Alex Jennings, Michael Jayston

NOTES: Using archival footage of Coward interviews from the 1960's and early 70's and interviews with the above named, this documentary tried to explore Coward's sexuality as well as his work. Clips from the 1960 TV *Hay Fever,* silent film of a dress rehearsal of the original *Design For Living,* clips of Coward singing in *Together With Music,* films clips from *Brief Encounter, In Which We Serve, The Astonished Heart,* and specially enacted scenes from *The Vortex, Present Laughter* and *A Song At Twilight* filled out the program.

Discography

The section on 78's and Long Playing Recordings will be divided into three sections, the first containing recordings by Noël Coward as artist, the second original cast recording of works composed by Noël Coward, and the third just recordings of works by Noël Coward. All except one recording were issued first in England. The single exception will come at the end of the first section. Unless indicated the music and lyrics are by Noël Coward. These entries will be preceeds by the letter "D."

78's Part I: Noël Coward as Performer

D-1   "Room With A View" from *This Year of Grace!*
        "Mary Make Believe" from *This Year of Grace!* with orchestra conducted
        by Carroll Gibbons
        H.M.V. Records #B2719. Recorded 1928.

D-2   "Try To Learn To Love" from *This Year of Grace!*
        "Dance, Little Lady" from *This Year of Grace!* with orchestra conducted
        by Carroll Gibbons
        H.M.V. Records #B2720. Recorded 1928.

D-3   "Lorelei" from *This Year of Grace!*
        "A Dream of Youth" with piano accompaniment by Carroll Gibbons.
        H.M.V. Records #B2737. Recorded 1928.

NOTE: "A Dream of Youth" was later re-labelled with the correct title, "The Dream Is Over."

D-4   "Ziegeuner" from *Bitter-Sweet*
"World Weary" from *This Year of Grace!* (US version) with piano accompiment (uncredited)
H.M.V. Records #B3158. Recorded 1929.

NOTE: This recording was issued in the US as Victor #24772.

D-5   *Private Lives*-Love Scene, Act I containing the song "Some Day I'll Find You."
Private Lives-Scene, Act II including Noël Coward and Gertrude Lawrence indulging in musical reminiscences at the piano
H.M.V. #C2043. 12 inch Plum Label. Recorded 1930.

NOTE: This recording was issued in the US as Victor #36034.

D-6   "Half-caste Woman" from *Cochran's 1931 Revue*
"Any Little Fish" from *Cochran's 1931 Revue* with orchestra conducted by Ray Noble.
H.M.V. Records #B3794. Recorded 1931.

NOTE: Issued in America by the RCA Victor Company as #22819

D-7   "Lover of My Dreams" from *Cavalcade* with orchestra conducted by Ray Noble.
"Twentieth Century Blues" from *Cavalcade* New Mayfair Novelty Orchestra with vocal by uncredited singer (Al Bowlly)
H.M.V. Records #B3794. Recorded 1931.

NOTE: "Lover of My Dreams" was coupled with "Mad Dogs and Englishmen" (D-11) and issued in the US as Victor #24332.

D-8   "Cavalcade Suite" from *Cavalcade*. New Mayfair Orchestra with Prologue and Epilogue spoken by Noël Coward.
H.M.V. Records #C2289 (2 parts, 12 inch). Recorded 1931.

D-9   *Cavalcade*-Vocal Medley from *Cavalcade* with orchestra conducted by Ray Noble.
H.M.V. Records #C2431 (2 parts, 12 inch). Recorded 1932.

NOTE: The Medley consists of "Soldiers of the Queen," "Goodby, Dolly," "Lover of My Dreams," "I Do Like to Be Beside The Seaside," "Goodbye My Bluebell," "Alexander's Ragtime Band," "Everybody's Doing It,"

"Lets All Go Down The Strand," "If You Were The Only Girl," "Take Me Back To Dear Old Blighty," "There's A Long Long Trail," "Keep The Homefires Burning" and "Twentieth Century Blues." All but the last named not by Coward.

D-10   *Noël Coward Medley* containing "Parisian Pierrot" from *London Calling!*, "Poor Little Rich Girl" from *On With The Dance,* "Room With a View" from *This Year of Grace!*, "Dance Little Lady" from *This Year of Grace!* on Part I and "Some Day I'll Find You" from *Private Lives*, "Any Little Fish" from *Cochrans' 1931 Revue*, "If You Could Once Come With Me" from *Bitter-Sweet* and "I'll See You Again" from *Bitter-Sweet* on Part II with orchestra conducted by Ray Noble.
H.M.V. Records #C2450 (2 parts, 12 inch). Recorded 1932.

NOTE: This recording was issued in the US as Victor #39002.

D-11   "Let's Say Goodbye" from *Words and Music*
"Mad Dogs and Englishmen" from *Words and Music* with orchestra conducted by Ray Noble.
H.M.V. Records #B4269. Recorded 1932.

D-12   "Something To Do With Spring" from *Words and Music*
"The Party's Over Now" from *Words and Music* with orchestra conducted by Ray Noble.
H.M.V. Records #B4270. Recorded 1932.

D-13   *Noël Coward Sings* consisting of two parts. The first entitled Poor Little Rich Girl includes "Poor Little Rich Girl" (orchestra only), "Zigeuner," "Dear Little Cafe" (orchestra only), "Call of Life," "Ladies of The Town" (orchestra only)(All songs but the first from *Bitter-Sweet*). The second part was entitled *Bitter-Sweet* and includes "Tokay" (orchestra only) "World Weary," "Caballero" (orchestra only), "Green Carnations," "I'll See You Again" (orchestra only). With Leo Reisman and his orchestra.
Victor #36239, 12 inch. Recorded April 11, 1933

D-14   "I Travel Alone"
"Most of Ev'ry Day" with uncredited piano accompaniment.
H.M.V. Records #B8234. Recorded 1934.

D-15   "Fare Thee Well" (by Sam Coslow)
"Love in Bloom (by Robin and Rainger) with uncredited piano accompaniment.
H.M.V. Records #B8237. Recorded 1934.

D-16   "I'll Follow My Secret Heart" (2 parts) from *Conversation Piece* sung by Yvonne Printemps with Noël Coward's assistance with the Theatre Orchestra conducted by Reginald Burston.
H.M.V. Records #DA1363, 10 inch Red Label. Recorded 1934.

D-17   Finale Act II of *Conversation Piece* including "Melanie's Aria" (2 parts) performed by Yvonne Printemps, Noël Coward and Company with the Theatre Orchestra conducted by Reginald Burston.
H.M.V. DA1366, 10-inch Red Label. Recorded 1934.

NOTE: The above two recordings are part of the *Conversation Piece* score. For the others see D-53-55.

D-18   "Mrs. Worthington"
"We Were So Young" (by Kern and Hammerstein) with orchestra conducted by Percival Mackay.
H.M.V. Records #B8369. Recorded 1935.

NOTE: This record was issued in the US as Victor #25230.

D-19   "Parisian Pierrot" from *London Calling!*
"We Were Dancing" from *Tonight at 8:30* with the Phoenix Theatre Orchestra conducted by Clifford Greenwood.
H.M.V. Records #B8414. Recorded 1936.

D-20   *Red Peppers* (a shortened version of the play from *Tonight at 8:30*) including two numbers: "Has Anybody Seen Our Ship?" and "Men About Town" with Gertrude Lawrence.
H.M.V. #C2815, 12 inch Plum Label.

D-21   *Shadow Play* (a shortened version of the play from *Tonight at 8:30*) including the numbers: "Then," "Play, Orchestra Play" and "You Were There" with Gertrude Lawrence.
H.M.V. #C2816, 12 inch Plum Label.

NOTE: This recording was issued in the US as Victor #36191.

D-22   *Family Album* (a shortened version of the play from *Tonight at 8:30*) including the numbers: "Here's A Toast," "Let's Play a Tune on the Music Box" and "Hearts and Flowers" with Gertrude Lawrence and company.
H.M.V. #C2817, 12 inch Plum Label.

NOTE: This recording was issued in the US as Victor #36192.

D-23   "Dearest Love" from *Operette*
"Gipsy Melody" from *Operette* with His Majesty's Theatre Orchestra conducted by Frank Collinson.
H.M.V. Records #B8721. Recorded 1938.

D-24   "The Stately Homes of England" from *Operette*
"Where Are the Songs We Sung?" from *Operette* with His Majesty's Theatre Orchestra conducted by Frank Collinson.
H.M.V. Records #B8722. Recorded 1938.

D-25   "Dearest Love" from *Operette*
"I'll See You Again" from *Bitter-Sweet* with uncredited piano accompaniment.
H.M.V. Records #B8740. Recorded 1938.

D-26   "Just Let Me Look At You" (by Kern and Fields)
"Poor Little Rich Girl" from *On With The Dance* with uncredited piano accompaniment.
H.M.V. Records #B8772. Recorded 1938.

D-27   "The Last Time I Saw Paris" (by Kern and Hammerstein)
"London Pride" with orchestra conduced by Carroll Gibbons.
H.M.V. Records #B9198. Recorded 1941.

D-28   "Could You Please Oblige Us With A Bren Gun?"
"There Have Been Songs In England" with orchestra conducted by Carroll Gibbons.
H.M.V. Records #B9204. Recorded 1941.

D-29   "Imagine the Duchess's Feelings"
"It's Only You" (by Carroll Gibbbons) with piano acccompaniment by Carroll Gibbons.
H.M.V. Records #B9210. Recorded 1941.

D-30   "Don't Let's Be Beastly To the Germans"
"The Welcoming Land (recitation written by Clemence Dane) with piano accompaniment by Robb Stewart.
H.M.V. Records #B9336. Recorded 1943.

D-31   "I Wonder What Happened To Him" from *Sigh No More* with uncredited piano accompaniment.
"Sigh No More" from *Sigh No More* with the Piccadilly Theatre Orchestra.
H.M.V. Records #B9433. Recorded 1945.

D-32   "Nina" from *Sigh No More*
"Matelot" from *Sigh No More* with the Piccadilly Theatre Orchestra.
H.M.V. Records #B9434. Recorded 1945.

D-33   "Never Again" from *Sigh No More,* London; *Set To Music,* US with the
Piccadilly Theatre Orchestra.
"Wait A Bit, Joe" from *Sigh No More* with uncredited piano accompaniment.
H.M.V. Records #B9435. Recorded 1945.

D-34   "This is a Changing World" from *Pacific 1860*
"Uncle Harry" from *Pacific 1860* with uncredited orchestra.
H.M.V. Records #B9532. Recorded 1947.

D-35   "Bright Was The Day" from *Pacific 1860*
"His Excellency Regrets" from *Pacific 1860* with uncredited orchestra.
H.M.V. Records #B9533. Recorded 1947.

D-36   "Josephine" from *Ace of Clubs*
"Three Juvenile Delinquents" from *Ace of Clubs* (not sung by Coward, but
by the original artists) with the Cambridge Theatre Orchestra conducted
by Mantovani.
H.M.V. Records #B9946. Recorded 1950.

D-37   "Sail Away" from *Ace of Clubs* (later used in *Sail Away*) with orchestra
conducted by Frank Cantell.
"Don't Make Fun of The Fair" from *The Lyric Revue* with piano accompaniment by Norman Hackforth.
H.M.V. Records #B10119. Recorded 1951.

D-38   *Cabaret Medley* containing "Dance, Little Lady," "Poor Little Rich Girl,"
"Room With A View," "Any Little Fish," "You Were There," "Some Day
I'll Find You," "I'll Follow My Secret Heart," "If Love Were All," "Play,
Orchestra Play" with uncredited orchestra.
Columbia Records #DB3009, Dark Blue Label. Recorded 1952

D-39   "I Like America" from *Ace of Clubs*
"Why Does Love Get In The Way?" from *Ace of Clubs* with the Cafe de
Paris orchestra conducted by Sidney Simone and piano by Norman Hackforth.
Columbia Records #DB3078, Dark Blue Label. Recorded 1952

D-40   "Time and Again"
"There Are Bad Times Just Around the Corner" from *The Globe Revue* with the Cafe de Paris orchestra conducted by Sidney Simone and piano by Norman Hackforth.
Columbia Records #DB3107, Dark Blue Label. Recorded 1952

D-41   "A Room With a View" from *This Year of Grace!*
"Mad Dogs and Englishmen" from *Words and Music* with Wally Stott and his Orchestra.
Philips Records #BB2001, 10 inch. Recorded 1954.

D-42   "Poor Little Rich Girl" from *On With The Dance*
"Uncle Harry" from *Pacific 1860* with Wally Stott and his Orchestra.
Philips Records #BB2002, 10 inch. Recorded 1954.

78's Part II: Original Cast Recordings listed by show; Noël Coward as Composer/Lyricist

London Calling! (1923):

D-43   "There's Life in the Old Girl Yet"
"What Loves Means to Girls Like Me" performed by Maisie Gay with orchestra conducted by Philip Braham.
H.M.V. #B1805, 10-inch Plum Label.

D-44   "Carrie" performed by Gerturde Lawrence
Decca Records #D512 recorded 1926

D-45   "Russian Blues" performed by Gertrude Lawrence
Decca Records #D514 recorded 1926

NOTE: D-44 and D-45 was recorded in conjunction with its use in *Charlot's Revue of 1926* with "A Cup of Coffee A Sandwich and You" (not by Coward) on the B side of D-45 and Jack Buchanan singing "Gigolette" (not by Coward) on the B side of D-45. For Noël Coward's recording of "Parisian Pierrot" see D-10 (part of Medley) & D-19.

On With The Dance (1925):

D-46   "Poor Little Rich Girl" performed by Alice Delysia with the London Pavilion Orchestra conducted by J.B. Hastings
H.M.V. #B2070, 10-inch, Plum Label.

NOTE: "That Means Nothing To Me" (also from the show) by Worton David and Godfrey was on the flip side. For Noël Coward's recording on Poor Little Rich Girl see D-10 (part of Medley), D-26, D-38 (part of medley), D-42

Charlot's Revue of 1926:

D-47   "Poor Little Rich Girl" performed by Gertrude Lawrence.
        Decca Records #D513

NOTE: "Susannah's Squeaking Shoes" (not by Coward) sung by Beatrice Lillie on the B side.

This Year of Grace! (1927):

    See D-1, D-2, D-3, D-4

Bitter-Sweet (1929):

D-48   "If Love Were All" performed by Ivy St. Helier with orchestra
        "Zigeuner" performed by Peggy Wood with piano
        H.M.V. #B3144, 10-inch Plum Label. Recorded 1929.

D-49   "If You Could Only Come With Me"/"I'll See You Again"
        "Dear Little Cafe" performed by Peggy Wood and George Metaxa with orchestra.
        H.M.V. #C1746, 12-inch Plum Label. Recorded 1929.

D-50   "I'll See You Again"
        "Zigeuner" performed by Evelyn Laye (US star) piano accompaniment by Gordon Whelan.
        Columbia #DB1870, 10-inch Dark Blue Label. Recorded 1940.

NOTE: For Noël Coward's recordings see D-10, D-38.

Private Lives (1930):

D-51   "Some Day I'll Find You" performed by Gertrude Lawrence with orchestra.
        Decca #M400, 10 inch Red Label. Recorded N/A

NOTE: Flip side is the non-Coward "My Sweet" from the film "Aren't We All?"

D-52   "Some Day I'll Find You" performed by Gertrude Lawrence with

orchestra.
Brunswick #05001, 10-inch Black Label. Recorded N/A

NOTE: Flip side is the non-Coward "Limehouse Blues" from *A to Z*
See D-5 for Coward and Lawrence recordings.

Words and Music (1931):

D-53   "Three White Feathers" performed by Doris Hare with orchestra conducted by Ray Noble.

NOTE: For Coward recordings see D-11, D-12, D-41.

Conversation Piece (1934):

D-54   "Charming, Charming"
        "Dear Little Soldiers" performed by Yvonne Printemps, Heather Thatcher, Moya Nugent and Maidie Andrews with the Theatre Orchestra conducted by Reginald Burston.
        H.M.V. #DA1364, 10-inch Red Label.

D-55   "English Lesson" performed by Yvonne Printemps
        "Nevermore" performed by Yvonne Printemps with Louis Hayward, with the Theatre Orchestra conducted by Reginald Burston.
        H.M.V. #DA1365, 10-inch Red Label.

D-56   "Regency Rakes" performed by Sidney Grammer, George Sanders, Pat Worsley, Anthony Brian with the Theatre Orchestra conducted by Reginald Burston.
        "There's Always Something Fishy About the French" performed by Heather Thatcher and Moya Nugent with the Theatre Orchestra conducted by Reginald Burston.
        H.M.V. #DB8133, 10-inch Plum Label.

NOTES: See D-16 & D-17 for "I'll Follow My Secret Heart" and "Melanie's Aria."
Also see D-96 for full studio cast recording.

Tonight at 8:30 (1936):

See Side B of D-19, D-20, D-21, D-22.

Operette (1938):

D-57   "Operette" performed by Fritzy Massary and Sextet with His Majesty's
Theatre Orchestra conducted by Benjamin Frankel.
"Countess Mitzi" performed by Fritzy Massary and Chorus with His
Majesty's Theatre Orchestra conducted by Benjamin Frankel.
H.M.V. #B8738, 10-inch Plum Label.

D-58   "Where Are The Songs We Sung?"
"Dearest Love" performed by Peggy Wood with His Majesty's Theatre
Orchestra conducted by Benjamin Frankel.
H.M.V. #B8739, 10-inch Plum Label.

D-59   "The Stately Homes of England" (2 parts) performed by Hugh French,
Ross Landon, John Gatrell and Kenneth Carten with His Majesty's
Theatre Orchestra conducted by Benjamin Frankel.
H.M.V. #B8741, 10-inch Plum Label.

NOTE: For Coward's recordings see D-23, D-24, D-25.

Set To Music (1939):

D-60   "Mad About The Boy" (Shop Girl version)
"Mad About The Boy" (Cockney Maid version) performed by Beatrice
Lillie
Liberty Music Shop #L249, 10-inch.

D-61   "Weary Of It All" performed by Beatrice Lillie
Liberty Music Shop #L250, 10 inch.

NOTE: "I Hate Spring" (not by Coward) is on the flip side.

D-62   "Three White Feathers" performed by Beatrice Lillie with Hugh French.
Liberty Music Shop #L251, 10 inch.

NOTE: "Get Yourself A Geisha" (not by Coward) is on the flip side.

D-63   "Marvellous Party" performed by Beatrice Lillie
Liberty Music Shop #L252, 10 inch.

NOTE: "The Gutter Song" (not by Coward) is on the flip side. For Noël Coward's
recordings see D-33.

Sigh No More (1945):

D-64 "The End of The News" performed by Joyce Grenfell with Mantovani and his orchestra.
Decca #F8561, 10-inch Blue Label.

NOTE: "Oh, Mr. Du Maurier" (not by Coward) is on the flip side.

D-65 "Matelot"
"Sigh No More" performed by Graham Payn with Mantovani and his orchestra.
Decca #F8562, 10-inch Blue Label.

NOTE: Payn and Grenfell also recorded together on D-82, with Payn repeating the same titles. For Noël Coward's recording see D-31-33.

Pacific 1860 (1946):

D-66 "His Excellency Regrets" performed by Members of the Company
"If I Were A Man" and "Uncle Harry" performed by Pat McGrath, Graham Payn and Sextet with the Drury Lane Orchestra conducted by Mantovani.
Decca #K1590, 12-inch Red Label.

D-67 "Dear Madame Salvador" and "My Horse Has Cast A Shoe"
"Bright Was The Day" performed by Mary Martin and Graham Payn with the Drury Lane Orchestra conducted by Mantovani.
Decca #K1591, 12-inch Red Label.

D-68 "One, Two, Three" and "I Never Knew"
"I Saw No Shadow" performed by Mary Martin with the Drury Lane Orchestra conducted by Mantovani.
Decca #K1592, 12-inch Red Label.

D-69 "Invitation to the Waltz" performed by Members of the Company
"I Wish I Wasn't Quite Such A Big Girl" performed by Daphne Anderson and Sextet with the Drury Lane Orchestra conducted by Mantovani.
Decca #K1593, 12-inch Red Label.

D-70 "Pretty Little Bridesmaids" performed by Sextet and "Mother's Lament" performed by Rose Hignell, Maidie Andrews and Gwen Bateman.
"This Is A Changing World" performed by Sylvia Cecil with the Drury Lane Orchestra conducted by Mantovani.
Decca #K1594, 12-inch Red Label.

D-71   "Fumfumbolo" performed by Graham Payn and Company and "This Is A Night For Lovers" performed by Sylvia Cecil, Maria Perilli and Winefride Ingham.
"The Toast Music" and "Finale" performed by Graham Payn and Mary Martin with the Drury Lane Orchestra conducted by Montovani.
Decca #K1595, 12-inch Red Label.

NOTE: For Noël Coward's recording see D-34, D-35, D-42.

Ace of Clubs (1950):

D-72   Vocal Gems Part I containing: "Nothing Can Last Forever" performed by Syvia Cecil, "I'd Never, Never Know" performed by Pat Kirkwood, "Something About A Sailor" performed by Graham Payn, "My Kind of Man" performed by Pat Kirkwood, "This Could Be True" performed by Pat Kirkwood and Graham Payn, "Josephine" performed by Pat Kirkwood. With the Cambridge Theatre Orchestra conducted by Mantovani.
H.M.V. #C7796, 12-inch Plum Label.

D-73   Vocal Gems Part II containing: "Sail Away" performed by Graham Payn, "Why Does Love Get In The Way?" performed by Pat Kirkwood, "In A Boat" performed by Pat Kirkwood and Graham Payn, "Chase Me, Charlie" performed by Pat Kirkwood, "Evening In Summer" performed by Sylvia Cecil, "I Like America" performed by Graham Payn. With the Cambridge Theatre Orchestra conducted by Mantovani.
H.M.V. #C7797, 12-inch Plum Label.

D-74   "Juvenile Delinquents" performed by Peter Tuddenham, Colin Kemble and Norman Warwick with the Cambridge Theatre Orchestra conducted by Mantovani.
H.M.V. #B9946, 10-inch Plum Label.

NOTE: For Noël Coward's recordings, see D-36, D-37, D-39.

78's Part III: Non-Cast Recordings; Music and Lyrics by Noël Coward

D-75   "Tokay"
"Dear Little Cafe" performed by Nelson Eddy (star of second film version of *Bitter-Sweet*) COL #4263-M

D-76 "Call of Life"
"If You Would Only Come With Me" performed by Nelson Eddy (star of second film version of *Bitter-Sweet*) COL #4264-M

D-77 "Romantic Melodies by Jeanette MacDonald" 78 Victor Album #MO-1217. Contains MacDonald's (star of second film version of *Bitter-Sweet*) renditions of "Zigeuner" and "I'll See You Again"

D-78 "*Bitter-Sweet* Medley" performed by Jack Hylton Orchestra with uncredited Vocal VIC #36908

D-79 "The Dream Is Over" performed by Anna Neagle HMV #B4365.

D-80 *Conversation Piece* Orchestra Medley HMV (E) #C-2654

D-81 *Tonight At 8:30.* Medley from *Family Album* and "You Were There." Vocals by Sam Browne with the original orchestra from the London production conducted by Clifford Greenwood HMV (E) #B-5019

D-82 *Noël Coward Vocal Gems* (4 parts) HMV #C3635 & C3636 12-inch Plum Label 1947
Part 1 contains: "I'll See You Again" performed by the orchestra conducted by Harry Acres, "One Two Three" performed by Joyce Grenfell, "The Stately Homes of England" performed by the orchestra, "Dearest Love" performed by Anne Ziegler. Part 2 contains: "Room With A View" performed by Graham Payn and Joyce Grenfell, "London Pride" performed by Joyce Grenfell, "Ladies of The Town" performed by the orchestra, "Dance Little Lady" performed by Graham Payn. Part 3 contains: "Mad About The Boy" performed by Joyce Grenfell, "Sigh No More" performed by Graham Payn, "Zigeuner" performed by the orchestra, "I'll Follow My Secret Heart" performed by Anne Ziegler. Part 4 contains: "Parisian Pierrot" performed by Joyce Grenfell, "Some Day I'll Find You" performed by the orchestra, "Matelot" performed by Graham Payn, "I'll See You Again" performed by Anne Ziegler.

NOTE: Both Grenfell and Payn were original in *Sigh No More*. Payn re-recorded his versions of "Matelot" and "Sigh No More." See D-65.

Long Playing Recordings

This section of long playing records is divided into two sections: Coward as performer and composer/lyricist and Coward as composer/lyricist.

LP's Part I: Coward as Performer and Composer/Lyricist

D-83   *Noël Coward-I'll See You Again* Philips Records 10" (E) BBR-8028

A recital of his great successes with Wally Stott and his orchestra. Liner notes taken from Coward's annotations in *The Noël Coward Song Book* (B-66).

Songs: A Room With A View, Don't Put Your Daughter On The Stage, Mrs. Worthington, World Weary, Alice, Someday I'll Find You, Mad Dogs and Englishmen, Poor Little Rich Girl, Uncle Harry, I'll See You Again.

NOTE: Four songs from this 10" long playing album were released on 78 RPM. See D-41, D-42.

D-84   *Marlene Dietrich at the Cafe de Paris, London* Philips Records 10" (E) BBR-8006 recorded June 21, 1954

NOTE: Noël Coward introduces Marlene Dietrich with a verse of his own about her.

D-85   *Le Carnival des Animaux* Philips Records   NBR6001, UK, Columbia Records US

Contains Saint-Saens' *Carnival of Animals* with new verses by Ogden Nash spoken by Noël Coward with the Andre Kostelanetz Orchestra. Leonid Hambro and Jascha Zayde, pianists. See P-142 for live rendering of material.

D-86   *Noël and Gertie and Bea* Parlophone(E) 7135, US & EMI Records PMC 7135, UK

LP reissue of 78's sung by Noël Coward, Gertrude Lawrence and Beatrice Lillie. Includes Side B of D-4, D-21, Side B of D-18

D-87   *Noël and Gertie* RCA LCT-1156, US & EMI Records CLP 1050, UK

LP reissue of 78's sung by Noël Coward and/or Gertrude Lawrence. Includes Side A of D-4, D-5, Side A of D-6, Side B of D-11, D-15, D-17, Side A of D-18, D-19, D-20, Side B of D-24

D-88 *Noël Coward and Gertrude Lawrence- "We Were Dancing"* Monmouth Evergreen MES/7042
LP reissues of D-5, D-19, D-20, D-21, D-18,

NOTES: Also included is Gertrude Lawrence and Douglas Fairbanks Jr. in *Moonlight Is Silver* by Clemence Dane and Richard Addinsell (HMV #C 2710)

D-89 *Noël Coward-The Revues* World Records SHB44

D-90 *Noël Coward's Greatest Hits Vol. One* Stanyan Records SR 10025

D-91 *Noël Coward* (1899-1973) Stanyan Records SR 10068

LP reissues of D-1, Side A of D-33, D-32, D-38, D-22, Side B of D-23, Side B of D-36, Side A of D-35, Side A of D-34, Side A of D-40

D-92 *Cavalcade of London Theatre* Decca Records D140D1/4

4 LP reissue of over 50's show cuts from the 20's to the mid 70's beginning and ending with Noël Coward and including Part 2 of Side B of D-66, Gertrude Lawrence's recording of "Someday I'll Find You," Joyce Grenfell doing "That Is The End of The News" and Beatrice Lillie's version of "Piccolo Marina" from D-149. Coward's opening and closing remarks are taken from D-114 and he tells that theatre is for entertainment. "I will accept anything in the theatre...provided it amuses or moves me. But if it does neither, I want to go home."

NOTE: Besides the Coward shows represented, this compilation includes cast recordings from such shows as *Anything Goes, Belle, Cinderella, Come Spy With Me, Divorce Me Darling, Half A Sixpence, Irene, Joseph, Maggie May, No Strings, Oliver, Perchance To Dream, Show Boat, Streamline, Trawlawny, Zip Goes A Million* and many others.

D-93 *A Voice To Remember* EMI Records EMSP-75

LP reissue of 78's including one Coward cut: Side B of D-11

D-94   *A Broadcast Tribute To British Stage and Screen Royalty* Magna Records 2289

LP reissue of 78's including Side B of D-11.

D-95   *Nostalgia's Greatest Hits Vol. 1* Stanyan Records 10055

Contains LP reissue of Side B of D-2.

D-96   *Conversation Piece* Columbia Records SL-163, reissued as ASl-163.

A 2 record studio cast recording of Noël Coward's operette (now called a musical play) starring Lily Pons, Noël Coward, Cathleen Nesbitt, Ethel Griffies, Norah Howard, Richard Burton, Rex Evans, Eileen Turner, Dorothy Johnson, Rosalind Nadell, Ellen Faull and a Childrens Chorus. Orchestrations by Carol Huxley. Orchestra Directed by Lehman Engel. Produced by Goddard Lieberson.

D-97   *Noël Coward At Las Vegas* Columbia Records ML 5063

Recorded in actual performance at Wilbur Clark's Desert Inn. With Carlton Hayes and His Orchestra. Piano Accompaniment and Arrangements by Peter Matz. See P-140 for musical numbers and details of Las Vegas engagement.

D-98   *Noël Coward In New York* Columbia Records ML 5163

An album of Noël Coward singing his own songs. Orchestra directions, piano accompaniment and arrangements by Peter Matz.

Songs: I Like America, Louisa, Half-Caste Woman, I Went to a Marverlous Party, Time and Again, Why Must The Show Go On?, New York Medley: Let's Say Goodbye, Teach Me To Dance Like Grandma, We Were Dancing, Sigh No More, Zigeuner, You Were There, I'll See You Again, Mad Dogs & Englishmen; What's Going To Happen To The Tots?, Sail Away, Wait a Bit, Joe, 20th Century Blues, I Wonder What Happened to Him (Indian Army Officer), The Party's Over Now

REVIEWS:
New York Sunday News, Feb. 24, 1957: "It is always diverting to hear Coward sing his own songs."

D-99   *The Noël Coward Album* Columbia Records MG 30088
Reissue of D-97 and D-98 in a two record set with a deluxe foldout cover.

D-100   *Peter and The Wolf & Carnival of Animals* Columbia Records CL 720

Side B of this record is a reissue of D-85.

D-101   *Command Performance* DRG Archive DARC1-1106. Released as a 1979
LP.

Includes exerpts for the *Night of 100 Stars* at the London Palladium June
28, 1956 including "Three Theatrical Dames" by Coward performed by
Peter Ustinov, Laurence Harvey and Paul Scofield as Dames Rosie,
Margaret and Laura respectively. The recording also includes a live
recording of Beatrice Lillie performing "I've Been To A Marvelous Party"
and a live recording of Coward performing his lyric to Cole Porter's "Let's
Do It" (possibly from the *Night of 100 Stars* in July, 1958). This lyric differs
from the Las Vegas version with references to Mrs. Humphrey Ward, T.S.
Eliot and Fry, Hildegarde and Hutch, girls from the RADA, BBC personel, House of Commons & McCarthy.

D-102   *Joan Sutherland Sings Noël Coward* (with guest appearance of Noël
Coward) London Records OS 25992. 1966. Orchestrations by Douglas
Gamley.

With an orchestra conducted by her husband Richard Bonynge, Joan
Sutherland sings "I'll Follow My Secret Heart" (with Noël Coward's
appearance), "Never More," "Melanie's Aria," "Charming, Charming"
(with Margreta Elkins, Elizabeth Robinson and Morag Beaton), "I'll See
You Again" (with John Wakefield), "Zigeuner" (with John Leach on
cembalon), "Dearest Love" (with Noël Coward's assistance), "Where Are
The Songs We Sung?," "Countess Mitzi," "I Knew That You Would Be
My Love," "Bright Was The Day" & "This Is A Changing World."

D-103   *Together With Music* AMR Records AMR-303
This early pirated version contains "The Party's Over Now" which was cut
from the live TV show. This is perhaps a tape of one of the dress rehearsals
and thus different from the DRG release of the same title.

D-104   *Together With Music* No Label XTV-24162/3

Another pirated version of TV soundtrack.

D-105   *Together With Music* DRG Records DARC-2-1103

Official and complete TV soundtrack recording of the 1955 TV special starring Noël Coward and Mary Martin (See T-8)

D-106   *Noël Coward & Margaret Leighton in Noël Coward Duologues* Camden Records TC 1069 1956.
Contains a complete adaptation of *Brief Encounter*, Act II, Scene 1 of *Blithe Spirit* and Act II, Scene 1 of *Present Laughter*

D-107   *The Apple Cart & Poems by Noël Coward* Camden Records TC 1094
Contains Noël Coward and Margaret Leighton in the Interlude from Bernard Shaw's *The Apple Cart* (see P-131 for Coward's appearance in the play) and the following poems by Noël Coward recited by Coward and Leighton: The Boy Actor, Nothing Is Lost, Honeymoon, Mrs. Mallory, A Question of Values, Do I Believe?, Letter For the Seaside, 1880, 1901, A Lady At A Party & Opera Notes.

D-108   *Sail Away* Capitol Records SW-1667

Noël Coward Sings the Score of his musical.

REVIEWS:
New York Times, Feb. 18, 1962: "It is a revelation. Suddenly this seemingly routine score glows and sparkles."

D-109   *Noël Coward Sings His Score For The Girl Who Came To Supper* DRG Records SL 5178
Contains Coward's demo of the score of his 1964 musical. Included are several cut songs including: Time Will Tell, Long Live The King (If He Can), I'm A Lonely Man, What's The Matter With A Nice Beef Stew & Just People.

D-110   *High Spirits* PYE Records (45 RPM, EP) NEP-24196

Noël Coward sings four songs (Something Tells Me, If I Gave You, Home Sweet Heaven & Forever and a Day) from from the musical with orchestra conducted by Peter Knight. See D-115 for LP reissue, D-177 for CD.

D-111   *Androcles and The Lion* RCA Records LSO-1141

Cast album of Richard Rodgers' TV score. See T-47 for details.

D-112 *Back to Back*

Recording of poems, with John Betjeman

D-113 *Theatre* Arogo Records PLP 1138

D-114 *Talking About Theatre* Decca Records

D-115 *A Special Event/Noël Coward* DRG Records SL 5180

LP reissue of D-129, D-110, and the first commercial release of a recording made as an opening night present by Noël Coward and Joe Layton for the cast of Sail Away: Bronxville Darby and Joan and This Is A Night For Lovers sung by Coward and Layton.

D-116 *The Best of Marlene Dietrich* Columbia Records C32245

Compilation featuring some of D-86 including Coward's poem.

LP's Part II: Noël Coward as Composer/Lyricist

D-117 *Noël Coward: The Great Shows* Monmouth Evergreen Records MES/7062-3, US

Contains LP reissues of D-48, D-49, D-50, D-54, D-55, D-56, D-16, D-17, D-57, D-58, D-59, D-72, D-73, D-74, D-9.

D-118 *The Golden Age of Noel Coward* EMI Records GX2502 1883

LP reissue of 78 material.

D-119 *Alice Delysia* World Record Club (E) 164

LP reissue of D-46

D-120 *Bitter-Sweet* TER Classics. TER 2 1160.

First complete recording of Coward's operette. Mostly original cast album of 1988 West End revival. Directed by Ian Judge. Chorus and Orchestra of The New Sadler's Wells Opera conducted by Michael Reed.

CAST: Valerie Masterson (Sari), Martin Smith (Carl), Rosemary Ashe (Manon), *Donald Maxwell (Capt. Lutte), Tom Griffin (Singer),

NOTES: *Did not appear in production. This recording includes the first ever recordings of "The Opening/That Wonderful Melody," "Polka," "The Last Dance," "Finale: Act I," "Opening Chorus (Life in the Morning)," "Bitter Sweet Waltz," "Officers' Chorus (We Wish to Order Wine)," "Ta-Ra-Ra-Boom-De-Ay," "Alas, The Time Is Past," "Finale."

D-121 *Bitter-Sweet* Angel Records. S 35814.

Studio Cast featuring Vanessa Lee, Roberto Cardinall, Julie Dawn, Rita Williams, Jean Alister, Mary Thomas, Dorothy Dorow, John Hauxvell, The Rita Williams Singers, Michael Collins and his Orchestra.

REVIEWS:
The Theatre, June, 1960: "After many years a recording company has finally decided to record Noël Coward's famous operetta, *Bitter-Sweet*. The result includes a batch of lilting melodies, lush orchestrations, and an able cast headed by Vanessa Lee. Certainly *Bitter-Sweet* has a sort of creaking charm and boasts such lovely songs as "I'll See You Again" and "Ziguener," but I fail to see what qualities make it better or different than the American operettas of Herbert and Romberg. Most noticeable is the absence of Mr. Coward's famous wit from this piece of work. Also, though Angel did a nice job on the songs they recorded, this new album omits almost one third of the musical's score. In closing I must add that Julie Dawn's wispy and meaningful rendition of the lyrics of "If Love Were All" almost makes the record a good buy."

D-122 *Bitter-Sweet* Music For Pleasure (E) 1091 & World Records. WRC TP80.

Studio Cast featuring Adele Leigh, Susan Hampshire, James Pease, and the Linden Singers. Conducted by Kenneth Alwyn.

D-123 *Bitter-Sweet* Readers Digest. 46-N3.

Studio Cast featuring Rosalind Elias, Jeanette Scovotti and John Hauxvell. Conducted by Lehman Engel.

NOTE: This is coupled with a recording of *Countess Maritza* (not by Coward)

D-124 *Bitter-Sweet* Bright Tight Discs. B151377.

Recording of tracks from film version featuring Nelson Eddy and Jeanette MacDonald.

D-125 *Bitter-Sweet* Columbia Records COL (E) TWO-273

Studio Cast featuring June Bronhill, Neville Jason, Julia d'Alba, Leslie Fyson and Chorus. Orchestrated and conducted by Johnny Douglas.

D-126 *Pacific 1860* AMR Records 300

Pirated reissue of 78's. See D-66-71 for details.

D-127 *Pacific 1860* That's Entertainment Records TER 1040

The first legal LP issue of D-66-71. See P-109 for more details.

D-128 *After The Ball* Philips (E) BBL-7005

Original Cast Album. See P-135 for cast and songs. Due to contractual obligations, Lord Darlington's songs are not included in the album.

D-129 *London Morning* Decca Records LW 5254 10" recording.

Recording of Coward's score for the 1960 ballet. The London Philharmonic Ochestra conducted by Geoffrey Corbett. Orchestrated by Gordon Jacob. See P-152 for production details.

D-130 *Sail Away* Capitol Records SWAO-1643

Original Broadway Cast Album. See P-154 for details.

D-131 *Sail Away* Stanyan Records 10027

Original London Cast Recording. See P-156 for details.

D-132 *Girl Who Came To Supper, The* Columbia Records KOS-2420

Original Broadway Cast Album. See P-160 for details.

D-133 *High Spirits* ABC Records SOC-1

Original Broadway Cast Recording. See P-161 for details.

D-134 *High Spirits* PYE Records (E) NPL 18100

Original London Cast Recording. See P-163 for details.

D-135 *Oh, Coward!* Bell Records 9001

Original Cast Recording of off-Broadway entertainment based on Noël Coward's words and music. See P-180 for details.

D-136 *Cowardy Custard* RCA Records 5656/7

Original Cast Recording of London entertainment based on Noël Coward's words and music. See P-181 for details.

D-137 *Noël and Gertie* That's Entertainment Records TER 1117

Cast album of P-219.

D-138 *Forty Years of English Musical Comedy* Rococo (C) 4007

LP reissue of 78's including: Side A of D-43

D-139 *Revue 1912-1918* Parlophone(E) 7145

LP Reissue of Side A of D-43.

D-140 *Revue 1919-1929* Parlophone (E) 7150

LP reissue of 78's including: Side A of D-43

D-141 *Revue 1930-40* Parlophone (E) 7154

LP Reissue of 78's including D-53.

D-142 *Musical Comedy Medleys 1928-34* JJA Records 1977-6

Contains period Medley from *This Year of Grace* performed by the London Pavillion Orchestra (original orchestra) conducted by Ernest Irving.

D-143 *A Nostalgia Trip To The Stars 1920-1950 Vol. 1* Monmouth Evergreen 7030

LP reissue of 78's including D-79

D-144   *Movie Star Memories* World Records (E) SH-217

LP reissue of 78's including D-79

D-145   *Beatrice Lillie Sings* JJC Records M 3003

LP reissue of 78's including D-60, Side A of D-61, D-62, D-63.

D-146   *Thirty Minutes with Beatrice Lillie* Liberty Music Shop 10" 1002

10" reissue of 78's including D-60, Side A of D-61, D-62, D-63.

D-147   *A Marvelous Party With Beatrice Lillie* AEI Records 2103

includes D-61-64.

D-148   *Legendary Musical Stars* Time/Life P-15637

includes Beatrice Lillie singing Mad About The Boy

D-149   *An Evening With Beatrice Lillie* London Records (E) 5212

D-150   *Beatrice Lillie: Auntie Bea* London Records (E) 5471

D-151   *Queen Bea A Musical Autobiography* DRG Records DARC-2-1101

Reissue of two Beatrice Lillie albums *An Evening With Beatrice Lillie* (D-147) and *Auntie Bea* (D-148) and six sides made in 1961. Coward numbers include the rarely heard "Spinning Song," "The Irish Song," "Weary of It All," "Piccolo Marina" and "The Party's Over Now."

D-152   *The Star Gertrude Lawrence* Audio Fidelity Records AFLP 709

Contains LP reissues of Lawrence 78's including D-51, "Parisian Pierrot" from London Calling and a solo version of "You Were Meant For Me" (not by Coward) from *London Calling.*

D-153   *"A Bright Particular Star"* Gertrude Lawrence Decca Records DL 74940

Contains later version of "Someday I'll Find You" from *Private Lives.*

D-154   *Gertrude Lawrence Souvenir Album* Decca Records 10" 5418

D-155   *Gertrude Lawrence, A Remembrance* Decca Records 8673

D-156   *Nelson Eddy's Greatest Hits* Columbia Records CS 9481

> Contains Eddy's (star of second film version of *Bitter-Sweet*) rendition of "I'll See You Again."

D-157   *Jeanette MacDonald-Smilin' Through* Camden 325

> Contains MacDonald's (star of second film version of *Bitter-Sweet*) rendition of "Zigeuner." See D-78

D-158   *The Entrancing Evelyn Laye* Music For Pleasure (E) 1162

> Contains Laye's (original Broadway star of *Bitter-Sweet*) renditions of "Zigeuner" and "I'll See You Again."

D-159   *CUT! Out Takes From Hollywood's Greatest Musicals Vol. 2* Out Take Records OFT-2

> Contains Jeanette MacDonald & Nelson Eddy performing "The Call of Life," which was cut from the second film version of *Bitter-Sweet.*

D-160   *Choice Cuts, Vol 1* Choice Cuts Records ST-500/1

> Contains Jeanette MacDonald performing "If Love Were All" from the second film version of *Bitter-Sweet.*

D-161   *The Music of Noël Coward* London Records LL 1062
Frank Chasfield and His Orchestra play lush arrangements of "A Room With A View," "Dear Little Cafe," "20th Century Blues," "Zigeuner," "You Were There," "Dearest Love," "I'll Follow My Secret Heart," "Dance Little Lady," "Tokay," "Mad About The Boy," "Someday I'll Find You," "Mirabelle Waltz," "Sigh No More," "I'll See You Again."

D-162   *The Famed Songs of Noël Coward and Ivor Novello* Dot Records 3047

> Conducted by John Gregory. Vocals by John Hanson, Doreen Hume, Dick Bentley, Jean Campbell, Vanessa Lee, Bruce Trent

D-163 *Noël Coward Revisited* MGM Records MGM 4430, Painted Smiles Records PS 1355

From the Ben Bagley series this tribute to the little known Coward songs contains vocals by Dorothy Loudon, Hermione Gingold, Nancy Andrews, Laurence Harvey and Edward Earle with musical direction and arrangments by Norman Paris. The songs on the album are: London At Night (*After The Ball*), Evening in Summer (*Ace of Clubs*), The Wife of an Acrobat (*Words and Music*), Nothing Can Last Forever (*Ace of Clubs*), Green Carnations (*Bitter-Sweet*), That is the End of the News (*Sign No More*), May I Have The Pleasure & The Waltz (*After The Ball & Pacific 1860* respectively), Housemaid's Knees (*Words and Music*), You Were There (*Tonight At 8:30*), He Never Did That To Me, If Love Were All (*Bitter-Sweet*), Don't Let's Be Beastly To The Germans, Chase Me Charlie (*Ace of Clubs*), Never Again (*Set To Music*) and a Finale.

Note: If Love Were All sung by Loudon was recorded for the Painted Smiles reissue and is not included on the MGM issue. For CD reissue with more material see D-180.

D-164 *Mad About The Man-The Songs of Noël Coward* Stanyan Records SR 10115

Arranged and conducted by Jack Pleis. Carmen McRae-vocals

Songs include: I'll See You Again, Zigeuner, Someday I'll Find You, A Room With a View, World Weary, Any Little Fish, Mad About The Boy, Poor Little Rich Gird, I'll Follow My Secret Heart, If Love Were All, Why Does Love Get In The Way?, Never Again.

D-165 *The King's Singers Sing Flanders and Swann and Noël Coward* Moss Music Group MMG-1120

D-166 *Bobby Short is Mad About Noël Coward* Atlantic Records SD 2-607

Bobby Short on piano and vocal with Beverly Peer on bass and Richard Sheridan on drums with some arrangenments and piano by William Roy. Contains the following Noël Coward songs: The Younger Generation, Medley: You Were There/Then, Matelot, A Room with a View, Nina, Any Little Fish, World Weary, We Were Dancing, Never Again, Josephine, If Love Were All, Let's Fly Away (music by Cole Porter), Something To Do With Spring, Someday I'll Find You, Imagine the Duchess's Feelings, Poor

Little Rich Girl, Medley: Where Are the Songs We Sung?/Dear Little Cafe/Hearts and Flowers, Wait A Bit Joe, I Travel Alone, I'll See You Again

D-167 *Star!* 20th Century Fox Records DTCS 5102

> The soundtrack album of Gertrude Lawrence's biopic contains "Parisian Pierrot," "Has Anybody Seen Our Ship?," "Someday I'll Find You" sung by Julie Andrews and Daniel Massey.

Cassettes Only

D-168 *Paul Scofield and Cast present Private Lives and Present Laughter* Audio Partners 20132 (1987-2 cassettes)

> Two plays presented aurally with Patricia Routledge

D-169 *Star Quality* Audio Partners 20343 (1988-2 cassettes)

> Denholm Elliot reading *Star Quality* and *Traveler's Joy*

D-170 *Star Quality* Old Greenwich, CT Listening Library CXL536 (6 casts)

> Denholm Elliot and Julia McKenzie read *Mrs. Capper's Birthday*, *Traveler's Joy* and *Aunt Tittie*

Compact Discs

D-171 *The Noël Coward Album* Sony Masterworks MDK 47253

> CD reissue of D-98, D-99, D-100

NOTE: Buyer beware! The first half of the CD, which represents Noël Coward at Las Vegas cuts the final song ("The Party's Over Now") and the second half (Noël Coward in New York) cuts the entire New York Medley and "I Wonder What Happened To Him."

D-172 *Noël Coward Classic Recordings 1928-1938* Conifer CDHD 168

> CD reissue of the A side of D-1, the B side of D-2, the A side of D-6, the A side of D-7, the B side of D-11, the A side of D-12, the A side of D-14, D-17, D-22, the A side of D-23, the B side of D-24, D-25 & Play Orchestra Play from D-20 (with Gertrude Lawrence)

D-173 *Compact Coward* CDP7 92802

> CD reissue of the B side of D-1, D-5, the B side of D-6, the B side of D-7, D11, the B side of D-12, D-14, D 16, The A side of D-18, D-27, the A side of D-28,the A side of D-31, D38 & the A side of D39

D-174 *More Compact Coward* CDP7 921572

> CD reissue of the A side of D-1, the B side of D-2, D-4, the A side of D-6, the A side of D-12, D-21, D-22, the B side of D-25, the A side of D24, the A side of D-25, the B side of D-26, the A side of D-30, D-32, the B side of D-33, the B side of D-34 & the A side of D-37

D-175 *The Complete Noël Coward* 4 CDs

D-176 *High Spirits* DRG 13107

> CD reissue of D-110 and D-134.

D-177 *High Spirits* MCA

> CD reissue of D-133.

D-178 *The Girl Who Came To Supper* Sony Discs SK48210

> CD reissue of D-132.

D-179 *Sail Away* Broadway Angel

> CD reissue of D-130.

D-180 *Noël Coward Revisited* Painted Smiles PSCD-110

> CD reissue of D-163 with the following additional material: Operette, When My Ship Comes In, Hall of Fame, Most of Every Day, & Let's Live Dangerously sung by Myvanyn Jenn, Arthur Siegel, Barbara Lea and Ann Hampton Calloway.

D-181 *A Marvelous Party with Beatrice Lillie* AEI-CD006

> CD reissue of D-147.

D-182 *The Marlene Dietrich Album* Sony MDK 47254

CD reissue of D-84 with extra material.

D-183 *Bitter-Sweet* TER Classics. CDTER 2 1160.

CD issue of D-120.

D-184 *Bitter-Sweet* TER Classics. CDTER01001.

Highlights of D-183.

Awards and Honors

The following is a short list of awards, nominations, honors and degrees received by Noel Coward. Since it is impossible to catalogue all honors, this list hits the highlights and is representative of his great achievements in an age before there were awards for everything. These entries are preceded by the letter "A."

A-1   President of Actor's Orphanage from April 1934 through June 1956.

A-2   Honorary Academy Award (Oscar) for Outstanding Production Achievement for *In Which We Serve*. 1942.

A-3   Nomination for Best Original Screenplay for *In Which We Serve*. 1942.

A-4   New York Drama Critics Circle Award for *Blithe Spirit* 1942.

A-5   Award of the Year from the Plumber's Association of America (for saying on TV that good plumbing was one of the most important things in life.) 1956.

A-6   Tony nomination for Best Book of a Musical for *The Girl Who Came To Supper*. An odd nomination, since only Harry Kurnitz is credited with writing the Book. 1964.

A-7   Tony nomination for Best Director of a Musical for *High Spirits*. 1964.

A-8   Sun. Dec 14, 1969 began with National Film Theatre showing *In Which We Serve* at the Prince of Wales Theatre, London.

A-9   Special Tony Award. 1970.

A-10   Fellow of the Royal Society of Literature. 1970.

A-11   Knighted by Queen Elizabeth. 1970.

A-12   Noël Coward Bar opened at the Phoenix Theatre, London. 1970.

A-13   Doctor of Literature. University of Sussex, Brighton. 1972.

A-14   Memorial stone at Westminster Abbey Mar. 28, 1984 presented by
       The Queen Mother.

A-15   *The Noël Coward Murder Mystery* by George Baxt published, 1992.

Miscellaneous Projects

This section features plays, books and projects that for one reason or another are left unrealized or unproduced. These include unproduced plays, unreleased recordings, etc. Of course it is impossible to know what unfulfilled ideas lurk inside the mind of an artist, but Coward's diaries give a hint to the plans that remained unmaterialized. Each entry is preceded by the letter "M."

M-1   *The Last Trick*. Written in 1918. Unproduced and unpublished play.

M-2   *The Impossible Wife*. Written in 1918. Unproduced and unpublished play.

M-3   *Barriers Down*. Written in 1920. Unproduced and unpublished play.

M-4   *A Young Man's Fancy*. Written in 1922. Unproduced and unpublished play.

M-5   *Julian Kane*. Written in 1930. Unpublished novel.

M-6   *Time Remembered*. Written in 1941. Unproduced and unpublished play.

M-7   *Long Island Sound*. Written in 1947. Unproduced and unpublished play. Used as a basis for the television version of *What Mad Pursuit?*. (See T-85) According to Coward's diaries, he talked to Cukor about a film of this property on Feb. 9, 1948 in Hollywood.

M-8   A film version of *The Marquise* with Bette Davis. According to Coward's diaries, he talked with MCA on Feb. 2, 1948 about this idea. He also thought of making it into a musical for Dame Maggie Teyte.

M-9   A recording of *Design For Living* with the Lunts was in the planning stages at Columbia Records.

M-10   A recording of *Bitter-Sweet* was made by Goddard Lieberson under the baton of Lehman Engel and starring Portia Nelson, but was never released.

M-11   Coward was considering starring in a television play of *The Final Test* by Terrence Rattigan in 1951

M-12   *The Young Idea*, according to his diaries, Coward thought of a musical version of his play on July 27, 1958. He meant it to star Daniel and Anna Massey and for the setting to be changed to to Long Island.

M-13   *Past Conditional*. Unfinished third volume of memoirs. Finally published incomplete, as part of *Autobiography*.

Annotated Bibliography

This bibliography is intended to be a respresentative sampling of the books and press surrounding the life and career of Noël Coward. It includes all publications of his writing and a sampling of other people's writing about him spanning the decades from the 1920's to the present (1993). If one were to catalogue all of the newspaper items that appeared about Noël Coward in both the US and the UK, they would take many more books, so this is a selected bibliography. The entries are preceeded with the letter "B."

B-1   Adams, Samuel Hopkins. *A. Woollcott: His Life and His World*. Reynal & Hitchcock, NY. 1945.
        Coward, one of Woollcott's friends, is mentioned throughout the book.

B-2   Adams, Val. "Ford Cancelling Coward's Third Show." *New York Times*. Feb. 12, 1956.
        After sponsoring Cowards first two TV forays, Ford decided that the ratings did not warrent sponsoring the third show which was to be either *Present Laughter* or *Peace In Our Time*.

B-3   _____. "Coward Has CBS Bring Show East." *New York Times*. April 9, 1956.
        After Ford changed it's mind and was sponsering *This Happy Breed*, Coward convinced CBS to do the show from NY rather than Hollywood, which he hated during his *Blithe Spirit* TV experience.

B-4   Agate, James. "The Ingenium of Noël Coward." *My Theatre Talks*. Blom, NY. 1971. pp. 185-92.

B-5   _____. *The Contemporary Theatre*. Chapman and Hall, London. 1925.

Coward wrote a Preface on criticism.

B-6   _____. *A Short View of The English Stage*. Herbert Jenkins, London. 1927. "The Naughty Playwrights. Chapter on Coward, Lonsdale, Arlen etc.

B-7   Albee, Edward. "Notes for Noël About Coward." Introduction to *Three Plays by Noël Coward*. Grove, NY. 1965. pp. 3-6.

B-8   Amory, Cleveland and Bradlee, Frederic. Editors. *Vanity Fair: A Cavalcade of the 1920's and 1930's*. Viking Press, NY. 1960. pp. 56-57.
This oversize volume includes several pictures of Coward and an article published in Vanity Fair in 1921 entitled *Memoirs of Court Favorites*. These would appear in book form as *A Withered Nosegay*.

B-9   Atkinson, Brooks. *Broadway*. Macmillan Company, NY. 1970.
Coward is referred to several times in this history of Broadway.

B-10   Baer, Atra. "Coward Fires Rocket at TV." *New York Journal-American*. April 6, 1956.
Coward talked about TV and censorship, "What you need is a new code of censorship. Some of your taboos are fairly ridiculous."

B-11   Baxter, Beverly. "A Cavalcade of Noël Coward." *New York Times*. Dec. 11, 1949.
An interview with the 50 year old Coward. After several flops, Coward says that he is sure that he can regain his pre-war touch.

B-12   Beerbohm, Max. *Heroes and Heroines of Bitter Sweet*. Leadlay, Ltd., London. 1931.
A collection of caricatures of Coward and the cast of *Bitter-Sweet*.

B-13   Bennett, Arnold. Introduction to *The Plays of Noël Coward*. Doubleday, Doran, NY. 1928. pp. v-xi.

B-14   Berkman, Edward O. *The Lady and The Law: The Remarkable Story of Fanny Holtzman*. Little, Brown, Boston-Toronto. 1976. pp. 109-118.
Berkman relates the story of how Coward's lawyer Holtzman sold the film rights to *Cavalcade* for a hefty sum and helped to create a classic Academy Award winning film.

B-15   Bolitho, William. "In The Egg." *The New York World*. Feb. 7, 1929.

A profile on Coward concludes with "insincerity and a certain imitative-ness, both of them a form of indolence, probably will be his hard corners."

B-16   Bolt, Robert. "Mr. Coward Had the Last of the Wine." *Sunday London Times*. Jan. 29, 1961.
A reply to Coward's attack on the new wave theatre.

B-17   Bolton, Whitney. *Morning Telegraph*. March, 28, 1959.
Coward blamed the failure of *Look After Lulu* on the critics and their reactions. Bolton took exception to this thesis and blamed the play.

B-18   Bordman, Gerald. *American Operetta*. Oxford University Press, NY. 1981. pp. 131-133.
Bordman praises *Bitter-Sweet* and tells why it is one of the greatest scores in the history of operetta.

B-19   Braybrooke, Patrick. *The Amazing Mr. Noël Coward*. Denis Archer, London. 1933.
Written early in Coward's career, this book is useful in providing a picture of the almost idolatrous regard in which Coward was held by many in the early '30's. It was reprinted in a limited edition of 100 copies by Folcroft Library, PA in 1974.

B-20   Breit, Harvey. "Talk With Noël Coward." *New York Times*. Feb. 25, 1951
Coward, in town to celebrate the advent of another of his books of short stories called *Star Quality* and, to record *Conversation Piece* with Lily Pons for Columbia. When asked about television (this was before his debut) he replied, "I loathe television." When queried about his film performance in *The Scoundral*, he said with wit, "I though I was very good in the parts I was dead."

B-21   Briers, Richard. *Coward & Company*. Robson Books, London. 1987.
A book of anectodes about and by Coward by an actor with whom he was vaguely acquainted. Not much that isn't told elsewhere, and better. The only saving grace are the cartoons that accompanied reviews of Coward's shows in *Punch*.

B-22   Brown, Jared. *The Fabulous Lunts*. Atheneum, NY. 1986. pp. 204-211, 217-20, 337-345.
In his remarkably complete volume, Brown gives a full accounting of the Lunts collaboration with Coward in *Design For Living, Point Valaine* and

Quadrille. He also tells about their business partnership, Transatlantic Productions and of course their deep affection for one another. Coward was to write a farewell play for the Lunts entitled "Swan Song" or "Rehearsal Period," but it never got past the planning stage.

B-23   Brown, John Mason. *Dramatis Personae*. Viking, NY. 1963. pp. 159-190. Two pieces, the first written in 1935 entitled "Richard Brinsley Sheridan to Noël Coward" was an imaginary letter of admiration and warning from Sheridan to Coward. The second, written in 1946 is entitled "English Laughter-Past and Present." This piece takes off from the the the unriveting performance the author saw of the Broadway cast of *Present Laughter* starring Clifton Webb and goes on from there to wish that Coward had been there on the stage to make his not-so-funny lines seem funny and witty.

B-24   _____. "English Laughter — Past and Present." *The Saturday Review of Literature, XXIX*. November 23, 1946. pp. 24-28. Short piece discussing Wilde, Maugham and Coward as social historians.

B-25   Buchwald, Art. "Noël's War With The Critics." *Los Angeles Times*. 1957. Coward was vocal in this article about his disaffection with theatre parties and the power of NY theatre critics, especially Kerr and Atkinson.

B-26   Burton, Hal, (ed.). *Great Acting*. Hill and Wang, NY. 1967. pp. 164-77. From a BBC-TV series of interviews on great acting including Olivier, Sybil Thorndike, Ralph Richardson, Peggy Ashcroft, Michael Redgrave, Edith Evans, John Gielgud and Coward. See T-40.

B-27   Calder, Robert. *Willie: The Life of W. Somerset Maugham*. St. Martin's Press, NY. 1989. Coward, one of Maugham's friends is mentioned throughout this engrossing biography.

B-28   Casson, John. *Lewis & Sybil*. Collins, St. James's Place, London. 1972. p.98. This biography of Dame Sybil Thorndike and Lewis Casson (they appeared in Coward's *Waiting in the Wings* in 1960) by their son contains a reminicence of the family's first meeting with Noël Coward. "After he left Sybil said: 'Isn't he a darling? He's a young actor and he's brilliant. He writes music and writes songs and he'll be a terrific success one day. He's called Noël Coward.'"

B-29   Castle, Charles. *Noël*. Doubleday, NY. 1973
A companion book to Castle's film documentary, *This Is Noël Coward*. It includes all that is in the film and many longer interviews with Coward and his colleagues such as Gielgud, Gingold, Celia Johnson, Dame Sybil Thorndike, David Niven etc. See T-68.

B-30   Coe, Richard. "Noël Coward Has 70 Years Of A Perfect Life."
Washington Post. Nov. 16, 1969
Coe recounts the high spots in Coward's career and writes about the plans for his 70th birthday celebration in London which include BBC-TV revivals of *Blithe Spirit, Hay Fever* and *Bitter-Sweet*. The National Theatre was to show the film *In Which We Serve* and offer a revival of *Private Lives* with Lynn Redrave and Michael Caine. The imminent publication of Sheridan Morley's bio *A Talent To Amuse* is also mentioned.

B-31   Comden, Betty & Green, Adolph. "Noël Coward." *Double Exposure*. ed. Roddy McDowall. Delacorte, NY. 1966. pp. 33-35.

B-32   "Coward At Home." *The Sketch*, London. 1925.
A pictorial showing Coward in his dressing gown dictating music to his secretary, standing in his library and going through his plays.

B-33   Coward, Noël Pierce. *A Withered Nosegay*. Christopher, London. 1922. Boni and Liveright, NY. 1922. (under the title *Terribly Intimate Portraits*). A short book of burlesque historical memoirs. Illustrated by Lorn Lorraine. Several parts sold to Vanity Fair.

B-34   _____. *Chelsea Buns*. Hutchinson, London. 1925.

B-35   _____. "Coward Talks of Jazz." *Telegraph*. Nov. 15, 1925.
Coward writes that he loves Tin Pan Alley and feels that Jazz is purely American. "Poor Little Rich Girl" is his favorite of his songs.

B-36   _____. Letter to the Editor. *New York American*. Feb. 14, 1926.
Coward wrote to the editor, "in my humble opinion *The Great God Brown* is not only by far the greatest play Mr. O'Neill has written, but one of the greatest plays that has ever been written." He also expressed the desire to do the play in London. He never did.

B-37   _____. "The Truth About Us Moderns." *Theatre World, V*. March, 1927. p. 13.

An essay by Coward.

B-38   _____. "Mr. Coward Goes To The Play." *London Daily Mail.* Mar. 13, 1927.
Coward tells of loving the US and American Theatre. He is most impressed by *Beyond the Horizon* by O'Neill, *Daisy Mayme* by George Kelly, *Chicago* by Maurine Watkins and *Saturday's Children* by Maxwell Anderson.

B-39   _____. "Off Stage Views of Stage People." *The World.* Oct. 5, 1927.
Coward contributed a brief autobiography to date.

B-40   _____. *Collected Sketches and Lyrics of Noël Coward.* Hutchinson and Company Ltd., London & NY. 1931.

B-41   _____. *A Spangled Unicorn.* Doubleday, Doran and Company Ltd., Garden City, NY. 1933.
A very satirical book of poetry.

B-42   _____. *Present Indicative.* Doubleday, Doran and Co., Garden City, NY. 1937.

B-43   _____. *To Step Aside.* Doubleday, Doran and Company, Inc., NY. 1939.
This first collection of short stories contains: *The Wooden Madonna, Traveller's Joy, Aunt Tittle, What Mad Pursuit, Cheap Excursion, The Kindness of Mrs. Radcliffe* and *Nature Study.*

B-44   _____. *Curtain Calls.* Doubleday, Doran and Company, Inc. 1940.
Collection containing *Tonight at 8:30, Conversation Piece, Easy Virtue, Point Valaine,* and *This Was a Man.*

B-45   _____. *Australia Visited.* William Heinemann Ltd., London. 1941
Coward's radio addresses.

B-46   _____. "Lie In The Dark and Listen." *Atlantic Monthly, LCXXII.* October, 1943. p. 98.
Coward's poem about the war.

B-47   _____. "Lines to an American Officer." *The Saturday Review of Literature,* XXVI. October 16, 1943. p. 63.

Coward's poem about the war.

B-48   _____. *Middle East Diary*. Doubleday, Doran and Company, Garden City, NY. 1944.

B-49   _____. *Star Quality*. Doubleday and Company, Inc. Garden City, NY. 1951.
This collection contains *A Richer Dust, Mr. and Mrs. Edgehill, Stop Me If You've Heard It, Ashes of Roses, This Time Tomorrow* and the title story.

B-50   _____. "Noël Coward — and the Sea." *New York Herald Tribune*. Oct. 7, 1951.
"Much of what I consider my best work has been done near or on salt water. For example, *Private Lives* was conceived on board a ship in the China Seas; *Cavalcade* I wrote at Goldenhurst; *Design For Living* in a freighter between Peru and Mexico and *Blithe Spirit* on the coast of Wales."

B-51   _____. "In The Days of My Youth." *Punch*. July 8, 1953.
A piece about light music from the Edwardian era through Ivor Novello.

B-52   _____. "Coward Upsets His Apple Cart." *Theatre Arts Magazine*. Sept. 1953.
A charming article about Coward's performance in Shaw's *The Apple Cart*. He sums up the experience of playing a King: "I am not at all certain that in the future when I write a part I shall not write myself a king: it really is so satisfactory having all the other characters standing up so often."

B-53   _____. *Future Indefinite*. Doubleday, Doran and Co., Garden City, NY. 1954.

B-54   _____. "A Spotlight On The Lunts." *New York Herald Tribune*. Jan. 1, 1956.
A love letter to his friends and colleagues (*Design For Living, Point Valaine, Quadrille*). "They are perfect actors."

B-55   _____. *Pomp and Circumstance*. Doubleday and Company, Inc., Garden City, NY. 1960.
Coward's only full length novel. And a funny one.

B-56   _____. *The Collected Short Stories*. William Heinemann Ltd, London. 1963.

B-57   _____. *Pretty Polly Barlow and other stories*. Doubleday and Company, Inc., Garden City, NY. 1965
This collection of short stories contains *Mrs. Capper's Birthday, Me and The Girls* and the title story.

B-58   _____. "Echo of Laughter." *McCalls, XCIII*. February 1966. pp. 98-99.
This short story was published in *Bon Voyage* under the title of *Mrs. Ebony*.

B-59   _____. *Bon Voyage*. William Heinemann Ltd., London. 1967.
This collection of short stories contains *Solaili, Mrs. Ebony, Penny Dreadful* and *Bon Voyage*.

B-60   _____. *Not Yet The Dodo*. Methuen, London & NY. 1967.
A collection of Coward's poetry.

B-61   _____. *The Lyrics of Noël Coward*. William Heinemann Ltd., London. 1965. Overlook Press, Woodstock, NY. 1973.

B-62   _____. *The Noël Coward Diaries*. Payn, Graham and Morley, Sheridan (ed.). Weidenfeld and Nicolson, London. 1982.

B-63   _____. *Collected Verse*. Methuen, London & NY. 1984. Edited by Graham Payn and Martin Tickner.

B-64   _____. *Noël Coward Autobiography*. Methuen London. 1986.
Reissues of *Present Indicative* and Future Indefinite put together in chronological order and including the unfinished third volume of autobiography entitled *Past Conditional*, which recalls the period between the other two books.

B-65   _____. *The Collected Short Stories of Noël Coward*. E.P. Dutton, NY. 1986.
This was reissued under the title *Star Quality* by Obelisk to coincide with the television productions of several of the stories.

B-66   _____. *The Noël Coward Song Book*. Joseph, London. 1953.
Coward wrote introductions and annotations to his song book.

B-67   _____. *Coward Plays: One*. Methuen, London. 1979 (first of five volumes)
This volume contains: *Hay Fever, The Vortex, Fallen Angels, Easy Virtue.*

B-68   _____. *Coward Plays: Two*. 1979.
This volume contains: *Private Lives, Bitter-Sweet, The Marquise, Post-Mortem.*

B-69   _____. *Coward Plays: Three*. 1979.
This volume contains: *Design For Living, Cavalcade, Conversation Piece,* 3 plays from *Tonight At 8:30.*

B-70   _____. *Coward Plays: Four*. 1979.
This volume contains: *Blithe Spirit, Present Laughter, This Happy Breed,* 3 plays from *Tonight At 8:30.*

B-71   _____. *Coward Plays: Five*. 1983.
This volume contains: *Relative Values, Look After Lulu, Waiting In The Wings, Suite In Three Keys.*

B-72   _____. *Three Plays*. Ernest Benn, London. 1925.
Contains *The Rat Trap, The Vortex and Fallen Angels*. Also contains a piece by Coward "Author's Reply to His Critics."

B-73   . *The Plays of Noël Coward*. Doubleday, Doran and Company, Inc., NY. 1928.
Contains *Home Chat, Sirocco* and *This Was A Man*. This was published in England as *Three Plays With A Preface* by Secker. 1928.

B-74   _____. *Play Parade Volume I* . William Heinemann Ltd., London. 1934; Doubleday, Doran and Company, Inc. 1933.
All volumes of the Play Parade series contain introductions by Noël Coward. This volume was the only one published by Doubleday in the US and contains *Design For Living, Cavalcade, Private Lives, Bitter-Sweet, Post-Mortem, The Vortex* and *Hay Fever.*

B-75   _____. *Play Parade Volume II*. William Heinemann Ltd., London. 1950.
This volume contains *This Year of Grace!, Words and Music, Operette, Conversation Piece, Fallen Angels* and *Easy Virtue.*

B-76   _____. *Play Parade Volume III*. William Heinemann Ltd., London. 1950.
This volume contains *The Queen Was in the Parlous, I'll Leave It To You, The Young Idea, Sirocco, The Rat Trap, This Was a Man, Home Chat,* and *The Marquise.*

B-77   _____. *Parade Volume IV*. William Heinemann Ltd., London. 1954.
This volume contains all the plays in *Tonight at 8:30, Present Laughter* and *This Happy Breed.*

B-78   _____. *Play Parade Volume V*.   William Heinemann Ltd., London. 1958.
This volume contains *Pacific 1860, Peace In Our Time, Relative Value, Quadrille* and *Blithe Spirit.*

B-79   _____. *Play Parade Volume VI*. William Heinemann Ltd., London. 1962.
This volume contains *South Sea Bubble, Nude With Violin, Waiting In The Wings, Ace of Clubs* and *Point Valaine.*

B-80   _____. *Bitter-Sweet*. Secker, London. 1929. Samuel French. 1932.

B-81   _____. *Bitter-Sweet and Other Plays*. Doubleday, Doran and Company, Inc., Garden City, NY. 1932.
Collection contains *Easy Virtue, Hay Fever* and the title piece.

B-82   _____. *Blithe Spirit*. Doubleday, Doran and Company, Garden City, NY. 1941. William Heinemann Ltd., London. 1942.

B-83   _____. *Cavalcade*. Daily Mail (serialized) Dec. 10-23, 1931. William Heinemann Ltd., London. 1932.; Doubleday, Doran and Company, Garden City, NY. 1933.

B-84   _____. *Conversation Piece*. William Heinemann Ltd., London. 1934. Chappell Music. 1934 (Vocal Score).

B-85   _____. *Design For Living*. Doubleday, Doran and Company, Garden City, NY. 1933. William Heinemann Ltd., London. 1933.

B-86   _____. *Fallen Angels*. Benn, London. 1924. (Contemporary British

Dramatists Series No. 25)

B-87   _____. *Easy Virtue*.   Benn, London. 1925 (Contemporary British Dramatists series No. 26)

B-88   _____. *Hay Fever*.   Benn, London. 1925 (Contemporary British Dramatists series No. 26).   Harper, NY. 1925.   Samuel French.   1927. Doubleday, Doran and Company, Garden City, NY. 1935.

B-89   _____. *Home Chat*.   Secker, London. 1927.

B-90   _____. *I'll Leave It to You*.   Samuel French, London. 1920.

B-91   _____. *Look After Lulu*.   William Heinemann Ltd., London. 1959.

B-92   _____. *Marquise, The*.   Benn, London.   1927 (Contemporary British Dramatists series No. 53).

B-93   _____. *Nude With Violin*.   Plays and Players, London.   Dec. 1956 & Jan. 1957.   William Heinemann Ltd., London. 1957.   Doubleday and Company. Garden City, NY. 1958.   Samuel French, NY. 1958.

B-94   _____. *Operette*.   William Heinemann Ltd., London. 1938.   Chappell Music. 1938 (Vocal Score).

B-95   _____. *Pacific 1860*. Chappell Music. 1947 (Vocal Score)

B-96   _____. *Peace In Our Time*.   William Heinemann Ltd., London. 1947. Doubleday and Company, Inc. 1948.Samuel French, NY. 1949.

B-97   _____. *Point Valaine*.   Doubleday, Doran and Company, Inc. 1935. William Heinemann Ltd., London. 1935.

B-98   _____. *Post-Mortem*.   Doubleday, Doran and Company, Inc. 1931. The play was published even though it was not to be performed professionally until 1992.

B-99   _____. *Present Laughter*.   William Heinemann Ltd., London. 1943. Samuel French, NY 1949.

B-100   _____. *Private Lives*. William Heinemann Ltd., London. 1930.
Samuel French, NY 1947.

B-101   _____. *Quadrille*. William Heinemann Ltd., London. 1935. Samuel
French, NY. 1954. Doubleday, Doran and Company, Inc., Garden City,
NY. 1955

B-102   _____. *Queen Was In The Parlour, The*. Benn, London. 1926
(Contemporary British Dramatists series No. 50).

B-103   _____. *Rat Trap, The*. Le Roy Phillips, Boston. 1924. Benn, London.
1924

B-104   _____. *Relative Values*. William Heinemann Ltd., London. 1952.

B-105   _____. *Sirocco*. Secker, London. 1927.

B-106   _____. *South Sea Bubble*. William Heinemann Ltd., London. 1956.

B-107   _____. *Suite In Three Keys*. William Heinemann Ltd., London. 1966.
Doubleday and Company, Inc., Garden City, NY. 1967.   Samuel French,
NY. 1967.
Contains *A Song at Twilight, Shadows of the Evening* and *Come Into The
Garden Maud*.

B-108   _____. *This Happy Breed*. William Heinemann Ltd., London. 1943.
Samuel French, NY. 1945. Doubleday and Company, Inc., Garden City,
NY. 1947.

B-109   _____. *This Was A Man*. Secker, London. 1926. Harper, NY. 1926.

B-110   _____. *This Year of Grace*. Chappell Music, London. 1928
(Vocal Score).

B-111   _____. *Tonight At 8:30*. The Sun Dial Press, New York. 1936.
William Heinemann Ltd., London. 1936. (3 volumes)

B-112   _____. *Vortex, The*. Benn, London. 1927 (Contemporary British
Dramatists series No. 19).

B-113   _____. *Waiting in the Wings*. William Heinemann Ltd., London.

1960. Doubleday, NY. 1960. Samuel French, NY. 1960.

B-114 _____. *Words and Music*. Chappell Music, London. 1932 (Vocal Score).

B-115 _____. *Young Idea, The*. Samuel French, NY. 1924.

B-116 _____. *Olivier*. Gourlay, Logan (ed). Stein and Day, NY. 1974. pp. 42-43.
Coward contributed a two page bouquet to Olivier along with many of his other colleagues. Coward calls Oliver the greatest actor of our time and recalls directing him in *Private Lives, Theatre Royal* and *Biography*.

B-117 _____. "Coward Seconds Hayes." *Variety*. Mar. 19, 1958.
Coward agreed with Helen Hayes' complaints about the burgeoning theatre- party market, which charged inflated prices for dinner and a show, the extra proceed which went to a charity. Coward remarked, "In three months in NY I had only 6 or 8 audiences that I considered good. You can't play comedy to people who resent paying $50.00 for a pair of tickets to see you. They defy you to be funny."

B-118 Crosby, John. "Noël Coward, Three Shows Later." *New York Herald-Tribune*. April 20, 1956.
Noël told Crosby what he learned from his experience in television.

B-119 Curtis, Anthony, ed. *The Rise and Fall of the Matinee Idol: Past Deities of the Stage and Screen, Their Roles, Their Magic, and Their Worshippers*. St. Martin's Press, NY. 1974. pp. 89-98.
Compiled from various contributor's recollections, this volume gives an idea of the appeal of such stars as Lily Elsie, George du Maurier, Gladys Cooper, Gertrude Lawrence, Jack Buchanan, Ivor Novello, Lillian Gish and Noël Coward.

B-120 Damase, Jacques. *Les Folies du Music Hall*.
Coward wrote the forward to this book on french music halls.

B-121 Darlington, W.A. "Mastery of Coward." *London Daily Telegraph*. Jan. 14, 1974.

B-122 Davies, Hunter. "Noël's Facinated by Noël." *New York Sunday Times*. Dec. 28, 1969.

An interview at Noël's Swiss Chalet about his 70th birthday and the attendant celebrations and of course his career.

B-123   Dean, Basil. *Seven Stages: An Autobiography 1888-1927*. Hutchinson, London. 1970.
Dean directed many of Coward's early plays.

B-124   Delaney, Kevin. "Noël Coward's TV Appeal Limited?." *New York World Telegram*. Mar. 13, 1956.
One of many articles about the cancellation of Coward's third show for Ford (it was telecast).

B-125   Dorin, Rube. "Comedy Lack Irks Coward." *Morning Telegram*. Sept. 15, 1950.
Coward bemoans 'message' plays and 'not enough comedy on Broadway.'

B-126   Dunn, Douglas. "Pity The Poor Philosopher: Coward's Comic Genius." *Encounter*. Oct., 1980.
Dunn discusses Coward's plays up to 1941.

B-127   Earley, Mary D. *Stars of the '20's*. Photographs by James E. Abbe. Viking Press, NY 1975. pp. 41-45.
Earley provides a brief biographical sketch accompanying a nice collection of theatrical portraits by Abbe, including Coward.

B-128   Elsom, John. *Post-War British Theatre*. Routledge, London. 1976. pp. 25-34.
Elsom discusses Coward as an actor.

B-129   Emerson, Gloria. "Queen's Honors List Changes Name On The Marquee to Sir Noël Coward." *New York Times*. Jan. 1, 1970.
Emerson reported on Coward's impending Knighthood.

B-130   Engel, Lehman. *This Bright Day*. MacMillan, NY. 1974.   pp. 191-193.
Musical director/conductor Engel recalls the preparation and recording of the studio cast album of *Conversation Piece* starring Lily Pons and Coward (see D-96).

B-131   Ervine, St. John. "The Plays of Mr. Noël Coward." *Queen's Quarterly, XLIII*. Spring 1935.
A survey of Coward's work up to 1935.

B-132 Fields, Sidney. "Only Human." *New York Daily Mirror.* May 4, 1956.
Coward spoke about his upcoming television production of *This Happy Breed* and television in general: "I'm impressed not with the amount of brains, but of brawn which handleds the amazing techical achievements. But the brain is coming up."

B-133 Fisher, John. *Call Them Irreplaceable.* Elm Tree Books, London. 1976.
Contains a tribute to Coward as an entertainer.

B-134 Forbes, Alastair. "Memories of the Master." *The London Spectator.*
Sept. 11, 1982.
A review of Coward's Diaries.

B-135 Furnas, J.C. "The Art of Noël Coward." *Fortnightly Review, CXXXIV.*
Dec., 1933.
A tribute to Coward's versatility, with regret for his lack of moral vision.

B-136 Gallico, Paul. *The Revealing Eye: Personalities of the 1920's.* Photos by Nickolas Muray. Atheneum, NY. 1967. pp 80-81.
Gallico and Muray attempt to describe the 1920's through the artists who created the essense of the era including George Abbott, Judith Anderson, the Astaires, Bankhead, Ethel Barrymore, Irene Bordoni, Porter, Lawrence, Le Gallienne, Loos, O'Neill, and Coward.

B-137 Ganzl, Kurt & Lamb, Andrew. *Ganzl's Book of Musical Theatre.*
The Bodley Head, London. 1988.
In the section profiling London's Musical theatre, Ganzl and Lamb include information and synopses of *Bitter-Sweet* and *Conversation Piece.*

B-138 Gehman, Richard. "The Impeccable Skipper of *'Sail Away.'* *Theatre Arts Magazine.* September 1961. pp. 8-11, pp. 72-74.
Background piece with pictures (Coward made the cover) on the upcoming musical, *Sail Away,* and how Coward wrote and cast it. He loves the people involved and tells of his future plans, which include a trip to the Far East and the third volume of his autobiography, *Past Perfect* (never completed).

B-139 Gelb, Arthur. "News of The Rialto." *New York Times.* Sep. 17, 1961.
Gelb reported that Coward planned a "Coward Cavalcade" on Broadway, like "A Thurber Carnival" after he opened *Sail Away.* This never materialized.

B-140   Gielgud, John. *Early Stages*. The Macmillan Company, NY. 1939. pp. 96-101, 116-120, 207-208.
Gielgud, Coward's understudy and replacement in *The Vortex* and *The Constant Nymph* writes of his experiences in following the master in the roles.

B-141   _____. *Gielgud, An Actor and His Time, A Memoir*. Sidgwick and Jackson Ltd., London. 1979. Clarkson N. Potter, Inc., NY. 1980. pp. 61-63.
Gielgud understudied and replaced Coward in *The Vortex* and *The Constant Nymph*. He tells of Coward's habit of knowing all the lines at the first rehearsal.

B-142   Gilbert, Douglas. "Noël Coward Kliegs As A Bathing Beauty In His Maiden Mugging." *New York World-Telegram*. 1935.
Coward, on the set of *The Scoundrel* faces the photographers.

B-143   Godbout, Oscar. "Notes On A Ballad Singer and A British Star Now Working On the West Coast." *New York Times*. Jan. 8, 1956.
An article about the preparations for the Hollywood telecast of *Blithe Spirit*.

B-144   Gordon, Max. *Max Gordon Presents*. Bernard Geis Associates. 1963. pp. 152-156, 165-170
Gordon, who produced Coward's *Design For Living*, tells of his introduction to Coward and how he became the producer of one of his biggest successes.

B-145   Gotram, Mike. "Those Naughty Songs They Didn't Let Noël Coward Sing On TV." *Hush Hush*. May, 1956.
Hilarious article about how much dirtier Coward's lyrics were in Vegas. "...and some of his ditties were too risque even for sex-mad Las Vegas!" Hush Hush got a private recording of Coward's British version of Cole Porter's 'Let's Do It' with references to McCarthy. They further went on to say "most Americans who have followed Noël's career are aware that he's a bit queer. But they would consider it in poor taste for him to flaunt his peculararities in public. And he's too smart for that."

B-146   Graham, Trey. "Noël Coward: A Figment Of His Own Imagination." *The Washington Blade*. October 23, 1992.
Basically a review of Clive Fisher's biography.

B-147   Gray, Frances. *Noël Coward*. St. Martins, NY. 1987.
Like Lahr's *Coward The Playwright*, Gray attempts a critical study of
Coward as a dramatist. She chooses his five great comedies (*Hay Fever,
Private Lives, Present Laughter, Blithe Spirit* and *Design For Living*) and
does an in depth study of them.

B-148   Greacen, Robert. *The Art of Noël Coward*. Hand and Flowers Press. 1953.

B-149   Green, Blake. "Keeper of The Legend of Noël and Gertie." *New York
Newsday*. December 11, 1992.
Interview with Sheridan Morely (Coward's literary executor and biog-
rapher) on the occasion of Coward's 93rd birthday and the New York
premier of *Noël and Gertie*.

B-150   Gross, Ben. "Looking And Listening." *New York Sunday News*. Nov. 13,
1955.
At a cocktail party with Tennessee Williams, Ruth Chatterton and Coward,
Coward commented on his preference for an average audience over an
audience of sophisticates. He also announced that he'd do *Peace In Our
Time* on television. He did *This Happy Breed* instead.

B-151   Gussow, Mel. "Remembered Laughter." *New York Times Book
Review*. Nov. 28, 1976.
A review of Cole Lesley's bio.

B-152   Hadfield, John (ed.). *A Last Encore*. Little, Brown, NY. 1973.
A coffee table book using the Coward's words and illustrations of his life
and times.

B-153   Harris, Radie. *Radie's World*. G.P. Putnam's Sons, NY. 1975. pp. 11-12
& 256-273.
Beginning with the forward and ending with a chapter entitled "Noël and
Gertie," Hollywood Reporter columnist Radie Harris writes of her
friendship with Coward which lasted until his death.

B-154   Hawkins, William. "Tonight at Seven-Thirty." *Theatre Arts Magazine*.
September 1954. p. 75.
A short piece with pictures about the opening of *After The Ball* in London.
Hawkins reported that Americans had been writing for tickets for the
opening for months. He also said that the show itself was "lovely to look

at and lovely to hear, though a bit uneven in its efforts to amalgamate the Oscar Wilde immediacy and the Coward retrospect."

B-155 Heimer, Mel. "TV's Sophisticated Sentimentalist." *New York Journal- American's Pictorial TViews*. June 24, 1956.
A piece about Coward's three TV shows to date.

B-156 "Heureux Noël." *The New Yorker*. Jan. 19, 1929.
A profile of Coward to date.

B-157 Higham, Charles and Moseley, Roy. *Cary Grant: The Lonely Heart*. Harcourt Brace Jovanovich, NY. 1989.
Coward is written about as a friend of Grant's and his intelligence work during WWII is explored.

B-158 Hirschhorn, Clive. "England? It's Impossible To Live Here, Says Noël Coward." *London Sunday Express*. May 23, 1965.
Coward, at 65 years of age, recalls his career and tells why he couldn't possibly ever live in modern England.

B-159 Hobson, Harold. "Sir Noël Coward: Playwright-Actor Who Was Master of Comedy." *The London Times*. Mar. 27, 1973.

B-160 Hulbert, Jack. *The Little Woman's Always Right*. W.H. Allen, London. 1975.
Hulbert's book about his career and that of his more famous wife, Cicely Courtneidge, recalls Coward understudying him in *The Light Blues* as "very young and very pimply, pompous and precocious, which was exactly the part, and he was very good, which rather annoyed me as I didn't like him." In the 1960's Coward supervised Courtneidge in the musical adaptation of his play *Blithe Spirit*.

B-161 Huggett, Richard. *Binkie Beaumont. Eminence Grise of the West End Theatre 1933-1973*. Hodder & Stoughton, London. 1989. pp. 204-208, 229-232, 238-39, 265-268, 317-319, 453-455, 482-483, 491-508, 512-513, 518-521.
Since many of Coward's plays were produced by Binkie Beaumont for H.M. Tennent, beginning with the smash hit *Blithe Spirit* and ending with Coward's last West End appearance in his own *Suite In Three Keys*, Coward is heavily featured in this detailed study of Beaumont's life and career. It

is also coincidental that the two theatrical comrades died within one day of each other.

B-162 "I Worked With Noël Coward." *Picturegoer Weekly*. Mar. 27, 1935.
An anonymous journalist interviewed Coward on the set of *The Scoundrel* and even got to be an extra (along with The Lunts, Edna Ferber and George Jean Nathan) in a scene in a theatre lobby. Coward was quoted about why he finally fell to the cinema's lure after having failed a dual screen test with Gertrude Lawrence: "What really induced me to try films was that I wanted the experience. I was interested in doing *Miracle in 49th Street* (*The Scoundrel*) because Hecht and MacArthur, whom I admire enormously are producing and directing it and because it's being made in NY."

B-163 Kiernan, Robert F. *Noël Coward*. Unger, NY. 1986
An academic study of Coward's works.

B-164 Kurnitz, Stanley J. and Howard Haycraft. *Twentieth-Century Authors: A Biographical Dictionary of Modern Literature*. H.W. Wilson, NY. 1942. pp. 319-320.
Biographical sketchs of English authors including Agate, Bagnold, Barrie and Coward.

B-165 Laffey, Bruce. *Beatrice Lillie-The Funniest Woman in the World*. Wynwood Press, NY. 1989. pp. 247-255.
Accounts of all of Lillie's associations with Coward, including *This Year of Grace, Set To Music* and more deeply *High Spirits*. Whereas Lillie's autobiography (really written by her lover, John Philip) credits Noël with cruelty, this more objective bio puts the blame on that same Mr. Philip, who apparently was a maniac.

B-166 Lahr, John. *Coward the Playwright*. Methuen, London. 1982.
A good analysis of most of Coward's plays, with a keen eye on the hitherto unwritten about private life of Sir Noël. Explores how his homosexuality affected his writing.

B-167 _____. "Noël Coward." *Automatic Vaudeville: Essays on Star Turns*. Knopf, NY. 1984. pp. 22-40.
Mostly taken from the introduction of *Coward the Playwright*.

B-168 Lawrence, Gertrude. *A Star Danced*. Doubleday, Doran, Garden City,

NY. 1945.
Not very truthful, as Coward was quick to tell.

B-169   Lerner, Alan Jay. *The Musical Theatre, A Celebration*. McGraw-Hill Book Company, NY. 1986. pp. 109-114.
In one chapter of Lerner's fun, but far from indepth celebration, he salutes Coward as 'Destiny's Tot': "His ballads were literate, graceful, and glistened with the polish of Coward's readily identifiable language. His comedy lyrics were the funniest of anyone to come down the lyrical pike, be they witty, silly in the best sense, outrageous or glibly cynical. Of Noël, the pure and simple fact is he was the most original composer/lyricist to emerge in England during the post-war years." This from one of the greatest lyricists of all time.

B-170   Lesley, Cole. *The Life of Noël Coward* (*Remembered Laughter* in US). Jonathan Cape Ltd, London; Knopf, NY. 1976.

B-171   _____, Payn, Graham, & Morley, Sheridan. *Noël Coward and His Friends*. Weidenfeld & Nicholson Ltd, London; Morrow, NY 1979

B-172   Levin, Milton. *Noël Coward*. Twayne Publishers, Inc., NY. 1968.
An academic study of Coward's plays.

B-173   Lillie, Beatrice. (aided and abetted by John Philip, written with James Brough) *Every Other Inch A Lady*. Doubleday, NY. 1972. pp. 202-205, pp. 349-356.
Lady Peel, who did Coward material throughout her career, tells about co-star, Coward in his *This Year of Grace* and then ends with the fights and feuds that accompanied his direction of her in *High Spirits*.

B-174   Lyons, Leonard. "Lyon's Den." *New York Post*. June 20, 1958.
Lyon's gives report on being a house guest at Somerset Maugham's Villa Maurosque along with Coward. He quotes Coward on dancing: "I even hate walking. I resent having to put one foot in front of the other.", and on marriage: "There are many reasons why you should marry—for love or for money—and many why you shouldn't."

B-175   Macdonnell, A.G. "The Plays of Noël Coward." *The Living Age, XCI*. Jan. 1932. pp. 439-46.
Sees most of Coward's work before *Private Lives* and *Post-Mortem* as false starts, but looks hopefully to his future development.

B-176   Mandelbaum, Ken. *Not Since Carrie: 40 Years of Broadway Flops*. St. Martins, NY. 1991. pp. 120-123, 259-262.
In his amusing and astute examination of Broadway flop musicals, Mandelbaum concludes that despite some good points, *The Girl Who Came To Supper* was "a blatant attempt to copy 'My Fair Lady' and never equaled its predecessor's quality." In Chapter 7, entitled 'Not Bad,' Mandelbaum tells of *Sail Away*'s gestation and concludes that "it was a highly enjoyable evening that did not pretend to be anything more than light, revuelike entertainment. The score was delightful."

B-177   Mander, Raymond and Mitchenson, Joe. *Theatrical Companion to Coward*. Rockliff, London; Macmillan, NY. 1957

B-178   Marchant, William. *The Privilege of His Company: Noël Coward Remembered*. Bobb-Merrill Co., NY. 1975
A very personal memoir of the time spent by Marchant with Coward from 1950 on. Marchant adapted several of Coward's short stories for BBC in the 1960's. He tells the real story behind *What Mad Pursuit* (short story) and the out of town dish on *Sail Away*. Although short on facts, it is long on heart.

B-179   Martin, Mary. *My Heart Belongs*. William Morrow and Company, Inc. NY. 1976; Quill, NY 1984. pp. 129-142.
Under the chapter "Some Royal Occasions and a King-size Fight," Martin tells of her invitation by Coward to play in *Pacific 1860* and the subsequent fights that ensued during the production. She also tells about the TV special the two performed, *Together With Music*.

B-180   Massey, Raymond. *A Hundred Different Lives*. Little, Brown, Boston, Toronto. 1979. pp. 73-79, pp. 119-123, pp. 169-173.
Massey, who was good friends with Coward (his son Daniel is Coward's Godson), recalls working with Coward in *The Second Man*. When Coward came to the first rehearsal letter perfect (as he demanded of everyone in his plays), Massey feared that he, not knowing his words, would surely be fired. Massey wasn't and the play proved a great success.

B-181   Maugham, Somerset. Introduction to *Bitter-Sweet and Other Plays* by Noël Coward. Doubleday, Doran, NY. 1929. pp. v-xiii.

B-182   Maxwell, Elsa. "Elsa's Log." *New York Journal-American*. Jan. 21, 1956.

Elsa mentions Coward and the television production of *Blithe Spirit* and comments on cursing on television.

B-183   _____. "Elsa Maxwell's Midweek Memo." *New York Journal -American*. Aug. 6, 1958.
Elsa, the party giver, reported on a party in Monte Carlo at Rosita Winston's to which Coward attended. He told Maxwell that he was having his portrait painted by Jim Shoop and that he wasn't allowed to see it until it was done.

B-184   McCabe, John. *George M. Cohan: The Man Who Owned Broadway*. Doubleday and Company, Garden City, NY. 1973. pp. 258-260.
McCabe relates that Cohan thought of Coward as his only peer. "As far as is known, Noël Coward is the only person in the theatre ever to receive a fan letter from George M. Cohan." Coward remembered it being after Cohan saw him and Gertrude Lawrence in *Tonight at 8:30*.

B-185   McCord, Bert. "Coward Returning As Actor For First Time In 20 Years." *New York Herald Tribune*. Mar. 24, 1954.
It was announced that Coward would be doing two different plays in repertory on Broadway the next season.

B-186   McCoy, Tex & Falkenburg, Jinx. "NY Closeup." *New York Herald Tribune*. Feb. 23, 1950.
The duo congratulated Coward on his film version of *The Astonished Heart* and a typical Coward interview follows.

B-187   Millstein, Gilbert. "Mr. Coward Dissects Las Vegas." *New York Times* Magazine. June 26, 1955.
Coward, having opened in his curiously triumphant cabaret act in Las Vegas comments on the desert resort with pictures.

B-188   _____. *Short Stories, Short Plays and Songs by Noël Coward*. Dell, NY. 1955.

B-189   Morehouse, Ward. "Broadway After Dark." *New York Sun*. Feb. 2, 1931.
An interview with Coward taking place in his dressing room at the Times Square Theatre, where he was appearing in *Private Lives*. Coward spoke of travel in general and his recent Eastern trip with Jeffrey Amhearst in particular. He also referred to his desire to write another novel. He had already written three and had one published. "All were lousy," said Co-

ward. He mentioned his NY apartment at the Wyndham, which he shared with his secretary, John Wilson.

B-190 _____. "Dear Noël On Love and Marriage." *Theatre Arts*. Nov. 1956. pp. 17-19, 84.
Coward is quoted on the subject: "Speaking as a bachelor and as an author, loving is more important that being in love. As for myself, I've sometimes thought of marrying — and then I've thought again."

B-191 _____. "Noël Coward-The Cosmopolitan of The Month." *Cosmopolitan Magazine*. June 1944.
This profile of Coward concludes with, "Noël like having a good time. He like garden parties. He like swimming and he likes lying on the beach or on a rock in the sun. But he enjoys himself most when he is acting. More travel is predictable for Noël just as marriage is not."

B-192 Morley, Sheridan. *A Talent To Amuse*. Heinemann, London; Doubleday, NY 1969, Little Brown, Boston. 1985.

B-193 _____. *Gertrude Lawrence*. McGraw Hill, NY 1981.

B-194 _____. *Out In The Midday Sun The Paintings of Noël Coward*. Philosophical Library, London 1988.

B-195 Mosel, Tad & Macy, Gertrude. *Leading Lady*: The World and Theatre of Katherine Cornell. Little Brown and Company, NY. 1978.
Coward, one of Cornell's friends is mentioned throughout this biography of the great stage star.

B-196 Nathan, George Jean. "Mr. Coward." *Passing Judgements*. Fairleigh Dickinson University Press, NJ. 1970. pp. 147-58.
About *Design For Living*.

B-197 _____. "Noël Coward." *The Theatre of The Moment: A Journalistic Commentary*. Knopf, NY. 1936.
About *Point Valaine*.

B-198 Newman, Shirlee P. *Mary Martin On Stage*. Westminster Press, Philadelphia. 1969. pp. 57-58.
In this almost children's book Newman touches on Coward's problems with Martin and *Pacific 1860*.

B-199   Nichols, Beverly. "Celebrities in Undress: XLIX-Noël Coward." *The Sketch*, London. March 2, 1927.
Mr. Nichols explored the Coward legend, which he found on the negative side. He called Coward "clovenhoofed" and "a sentimantalist terrified of being found out — by himself." Perhaps a true assessment.

B-200   Noble, Peter. *Ivor Novello, Man of the Theatre*. The Falcon Press, London. 1951. pp. 121-125, 132-133.
The distasterous opening night of *Sirocco* is dissected and the filming of *The Vortex* with Novello in Coward's role is also examined in this interesting biography of Coward's theatrical rival and friend.

B-201   "Noël's Just A Big Coward As He Ducks Tax Collector." *New York Journal*. May 17, 1956.
One of the many items about Coward's move from England to Bermuda for tax purposes.

B-202   "Noël Coward Firm On Taxes." *New York Herald Tribune*. May 25, 1956.
Another item about Coward's tax exile. Coward was quoted, "It's just not worth it" to live in England.

B-203   "Noël Coward Tells Why He's Happy With American TV." TV Guide. July 14, 1956.
Coward said, "The Mary Martin show was great fun, the Hollywood experience (*Blithe Spirit*) was an unhappy one, but I adore my work with Ed Sullivan and my visit from Ed Murrow.   But best of all I liked doing *This Happy Breed*, a happy show from the word 'go.'"

B-204   "Noël Coward To End Self Imposed Exile." *New York Times*. March 27, 1957.
Coward returned to England after two years in tax exile. He sailed on the Queen Elizabeth with the Lunts to direct Michael Wilding, who was replacing John Gielgud in *Nude With Violin* on June 22, 1957. At the end of August he was to go to Hollywood to supervise a production of *Relative Values* directed by Charles Russell. Gladys Cooper was to repeat her London role with Mildred Natwick and John Williams.

B-205   "Noël Coward Too Busy For Palace Engagement." *New York Herald* Tribune. July 14, 1957.
Coward cancelled plans to do his cabaret act at the Palace Theatre. It had been announced that he would be booked into the Vaudeville theatre

following Liberace.

B-206 O'Brian, Jack. *New York Journal-American*. Oct. 29, 1955.
Coward's nervousness about his television debut with Mary Martin
(*Together With Music*) last Saturday was reported on.

B-207 _____. "TV's New Blithe Spirit." *New York Journal-American*. 1956.
Within a color cover of the Pictorial TView, O'Brian emphatically states,
"we would like to say here that Noël Coward is a new and lively and
welcome hand in TV's creative corral. He works like a longshoreman at
his sprawling craft, which encompasses virtually anything in the spoken,
written or acted English work, occasionally a little in french."

B-208 O'Casey, Sean. "Coward Codology." *The Green Crow*. Braziller, NY.
1956. pp. 87-115.

B-209 O'Connor, Jim. "Noël Offers Kay Kendall 'Bubble' Lead." *New York
Journal*. Sept. 27, 1956.
Coward wanted Kay Kendall to play the lead in the Broadway production
of *South Sea Bubble*. (The production never happened and Kendall died
soon after). He was also interested in Louis Jourdan and Michael Wilding
for other leading roles. It was announced that CBS would be the angel for
the production in return for the television rights.

B-210 O'Hara, John. "Appointment With O'Hara." *Colliers Magazine*. Jan. 20,
1956.
O'Hara, renowned novelist, wrote a particularly nasty diatribe against
Coward's criticisms of current novels. He even wrote a little verse, trying
to beat Coward at his own racket.

B-211 Parish, James. *The Jeanette MacDonald Story*. Mason/Charter, NY. 1976.
pp. 123-124.
Parish writes about MacDonald's involvement in the second film version
of *Bitter-Sweet*. Parish reveals that MacDonald was considered for the first
film version that went to Anna Neagle.

B-212   Raymond, John. "Play Orchestra Play!." *New Statesman, LVI*. October 25, 1958. pp. 563-64.
The publication of Play Parade, Vol. V (B-78) is discussed and reviewed.

B-213   Richards, Dick (ed.). *The Wit of Noël Coward*. Leslie Frewin, London. 1968.

B-214   Robb, Inez. "So Noël Now Sees Daylight." *New York Journal-American*. April 20, 1940.
A snotty article about Coward's Paris war job and how he now has to get to a desk by 9AM.

B-215   Rodgers Richard. *Musical Stages*. WH Allen, London. 1975.   pp. 76-78,
Composer Rodgers tells about his first introduction to Coward in 1925, when Coward was appearing in *The Vortex*. Rodgers loved the play, but was most impressed with the moment in the second act when Coward sat down at the piano and played one of Rodger's least known songs, "April Fool." He took it as a tremendous compliment. The two met in person a couple of days later and formed a mutual admiration society. Rodgers puts down the Coward nay-sayers: "Even one of his lesser-known operettas, *Conversation Piece*, contains more charm, skill and originality than fifty musical plays put together by men specializing in particular fields."

B-216   Rogers, Ginger. *Ginger, My Story*. Harper, Collins, NY. 1991. pp. 333-334.
Ginger tells about starring in the TV version of *Tonight At 8:30*.

B-217   Rogers, John G. "Noël Coward on Noël Coward." *New York Magazine, NY Herald Tribune*. Dec. 8, 1963. p. 35
Typical interview, revealing Coward as a warm optimist.

B-218   Saki. *The Complete Works*.
Coward wrote the introduction.

B-219   Salter, Marjorie & Allen, Adrianne. *Delightful Food*. Sidgwick and Jackson, London. 1957.
Coward wrote the Foreward for this book.

B-220   Senior, Evan. "A Talent To Amuse-Noël Coward at 60." *Plays and Players*. Dec. 1959.
Coward comments on being 60 years old.

Spirit, Ford pulled out and it was announced that *This Happy Breed* would be produced on Playhouse 90.

B-222 _____. "Coward Put Back In Ford TV Show." *New York Times*. March 24, 1956.
Ford changed its mind and decided to sponsor *This Happy Breed*.

B-223 Short, Earnest. *Theatrical Cavalcade*. Eyre & Spottiswoode, London. 1942. pp. 188-193.
In Short's chapter on Play Production and the Play Producer; The Actor-Dramatist, Coward's writing and its effect on other actors is discussed. The author suggests that Coward is far from flippant and not without social values.

B-224 Shulman, Milton. "Noël Coward - A New Look at the Old Master." *London Evening Standard*. April 29, 1966.
An indepth four part series on Coward's career to date.

B-225 Sillman, Leonard. *Here Lies Leonard Sillman, Straightened Out At Last*. Citadel Press, NY. 1959. pp. 263-282.
In a chapter entitled "The Greatest" Sillman tells of his introduction to Coward.

B-226 Smith, Milburn. "Noël Coward Rehearses a New Musical 'Sail Away.'" *The Theatre*. August 1961. pp. 16-17.
The background piece tells of an afternoon rehearsal and the background of the show. It was "inspired by a song he wrote for Beatrice Lillie, 'A Bar on The Piccolo Marina,' in which a staid English widow goes slightly off her nut during a stay in Capri." He had originally conceived of the show as a vehicle for a single female star and decided on the title "Later Than Spring." All that was changed and became *Sail Away*.

B-227 Snider, Rose. *Satire in the Comedies of Congreve, Sheridan, Wilde and Coward*. Orono: University of Maine Press. 1937.
Scholarly examination of the satirical elements in Coward's plays, concluding that Coward's comedy represents "a reversion to the freedom of the Restoration."

B-228 Sobel, Louis. "What's In A Name?." *New York Journal-American*. June 28, 1956.
Sobol reports that Coward went backstage at the Latin Quarter to say hello

B-228   Sobel, Louis. "What's In A Name?." *New York Journal-American*. June 28, 1956.
Sobol reports that Coward went backstage at the Latin Quarter to say hello to Johnny Ray. Ray enticed him the see the show. When the captain showed Coward, party of one, to his table, he said "I hope you enjoy the show, Mr. Cohen."

B-229   Spitzer, Marian. "The Real Noël Coward." *The New York World*. Oct. 11, 1925.
This article disclaims Coward's Cinderella legend and examines the hard work that goes into his career. Coward speaks about being misunderstood by the critics: "Take *Fallen Angels*, for instance. All I tried to do was write a French comedy in English and back home they went on about it as though I had ruined the entire social fabric of the British Empire. *The Vortex* they said was an attempt to show up English society and *Hay Fever* I heard from some quarters was an expose of the acting profession. It's utterly maddening." He also reveals that the title *Hay Fever* means nothing and was a last minute replacement for the original title, *Still Life*, which later became the title of the one act play that was filmed as *Brief Encounter*.

B-230   Stansbury, H.H. "New Romance Diana Smiles." *New York American*. March 31, 1926.
Lady Diana Manners refused to comment on reports of her engagement to Noël Coward. Coward did comment: "It is a charming suggestion, but there are insurmountable difficulties, as it appears that Lady Diana is now the wife of Alfred Duff, member of Parliment."

B-231   Stokes, Sewell. "Noël Coward." *Theatre Arts Magazine*. January 1944.
An in depth look at Coward's career to date concluding with "if theatrical historians attempt to understand Coward through the medium of his films, they will fail." Sewell felt that he had to be seen to be understood.

B-232   Teichmann, Howard. *Smart Aleck*. William Morrow and Company, Inc., NY. 1976.
This bio of Alexander Woollcott includes references to Coward throughout.

B-233   Titterton, W.R. "Noël Coward." *Theatre World, VII*. Dec. 1927. p. 24.
Possibly the earliest attempt to do more than gossip about Coward's life and plays. Calls Coward "among the prophets," sounding the "note of protest."

B-234   Torre, Marie. "Coward Will Stay Despite Raps." *New York Herald Tribune*. April 10, 1956.
The article tells about the bad notices for *This Happy Breed* TV production and how it was almost cancelled by Ford, but that Coward still intends to do more TV.

B-235   _____. "Coward: 'I Shall Return.'" *New York Herald Tribune*. July 25, 1957.
Undaunted by low ratings and bouts with the censors, Coward, then appearing on Broadway in *Nude With Violin*, vows to do more television: "It might be a good idea to bring *Nude With Violin* to television after the Broadway run. I think the play will get by the Bible Belt without stress. There isn't a damn in the whole thing."

B-236   Trewin, J.C. "Tap-Tap." *Dramatists of Today*. London: Staples Press. 1953. pp. 151-61.
Discussion of Coward's work.

B-237   Traubner, Richard. *Operetta, A Theatrical History*. Doubleday & Co., Garden City. 1983. pp. 339-347.
This history of operetta places Coward's work in the field in perspective and Traubner has high regard for the scores of *Bitter-Sweet, Conversation Piece, Operette, Pacific 1860, Ace of Clubs* and *After The Ball*, if not for their libretti. Traubner gives especially high marks for Coward's lyrics, ranking him as Gilbert's successor.

B-238   Tuck, Jay Nelson. "Ford Gives Coward The Air-Too Sophisticated for TV." *New York Post*. Mar. 13, 1956.
Coward's third show to be sponsored by the Ford Motor Company is cancelled (it was eventually reinstated). The show was to be a cut version of *Present Laughter* to be retitled *Twinkle Twinkle Little Star*. The article revealed that Coward's contract was not with Ford, but CBS.

B-239   Tynan, Kenneth. "A Tribute to Mr. Coward." *A View of the English Stage, 1944-63*. Poynter, London. 1975. pp. 135-37.

B-240   _____. "In Memory of Mr. Coward." *The Sound of Two Hands Clapping*. Cape, London. 1975. pp. 58-63.

B-241   _____. "Let Coward Flinch." *London Observer*. Jan. 22, 1961.
Tynan writes in response to Coward's two scathing articles abouth the new

breed in the theatre. "The bridge of a sinking ship, on feels, is scarcely the ideal place from which to deliver a lecture on the technique of keeping afloat."

B-242   Walkley, A.B. "Sex Plays and Noël Coward." *Vanity Fair*. November 1925.
Walkley examines *Fallen Angels* and *The Vortex*.

B-243   Watts, Richard. "Mr. Coward and Message Plays." Two On The Aisle column. *New York Post*. Sept. 24, 1950.
Coward made a speech at a luncheon of local drama reporters in NY and spoke against 'message' plays.

B-244   Webster, Margaret. *Don't Put Your Daughter On The Stage*. Alfred A. Knopf, NY. 1972. pp. 311-321.
Webster, who directed Coward's *Waiting In The Wings* tells about the casting, rehearsal and performances of the play. Since Coward was not at rehearsal (due to his tax exile), he hasn't written about the production of this play and this is the most detailed account.

B-245   Weintraub, Stanley, (ed.). *Modern British Dramatists 1900-1945*, 2 vols. Dictionary of Literary Biography, Vol. X.   Gale Research Company, Detroit. 1982. pp. 116-129.
Various writers contributes biographical and critical essays on British playwrights including Auden, J.M. Barrie, Arnold Bennett, Oscar Wilde, Shaw, O'Casey and Coward.

B-246   Whiting, John. "Coward Cruising." *The London Magazine*, II. 8/62. pp. 64-66. & *John Whiting on Theatre*. Ross, London. 1966. pp. 101-08.
Argues that although Coward may also write about the middle classes, his true talent lies in the aristocratic world.

B-247   Williams, Emlyn. *George*. Hamish Hamilton, London. 1961.

B-248   _____. Emlyn. Viking Press, NY. 1974.

B-249   Wilson, John S. "International Romance." *New York Times*.
Reporting on the upcoming Philadelphia tryout of *The Girl Who Came To Supper*, the piece points out that it would be ending its run at the O'Keefe Theatre in Toronto and moving to Philly. Coward tells why he was convinced to write just the score (he usually wrote book & score) for *Supper*,

"I always thought 'The Sleeping Prince' was made for a musical. It's very light. It was charming in London with Larry and Vivien. And 1911 is a very good period. It was the year I first went on the stage and it's full of the sort of music that I was brought up on." The Noël Coward renaissance is touched on and the upcoming production of *High Spirits*. Coward ends with a quote, "'My Fair Lady' was written for me originally and so was 'The King and I.' It would have been exciting to do them. But if I had, I wouldn't have written the things that I've been doing."

B-250   Wilson, Sandy. *Ivor*. Michael Joseph Ltd., London. 1975
Show writer, Wilson's coffee table tribute to Ivor Novello includes his appearances in such Coward pieces as *Sirocco* and *The Vortex*.

B-251   Wood, Peggy. "Why Actors Respect Noël Coward As A Stage Director: No Hanky Panky." *Variety*. Jan. 7, 1970.
Renowned actress Wood writes of her 61 years of friendship with Noël and their work together in *Bitter-Sweet* and *Blithe Spirit*.

B-252   _____. *Arts And Flowers*. William Morrow and Company, NY. 1963.
Wood's autobiography includes *Bitter-Sweet* and *Blithe Spirit*.

B-253   Woodbridge, Homer E. "Noël Coward." *The South Atlantic Quarterly*, XXXVII. July 1938. pp. 239-51.
General resume of Coward's work through 1937, focusing on the serious plays. Woodbridge predicts rather ominously that "he will never write better plays than he has written."

B-254   Woollcott, Alexander. *The Letters of Alexander Woolcott*. The Viking Press, NY. 1944. Edited by Beatrice Kaufman and Joseph Hennessey.
Many of the letters contained are either to or refer to Coward.

B-255   Zolotow, Sam. "Coward Reports Two Shows In the Offing." *New York Times*. Dec. 7, 1949.
Coward announced the completion and imminent production of *Home and Colonial* (later *Island Fling* in US & *South Sea Bubble* in UK) hopefully to star Gertrude Lawrence. He also announced his new musical, *Ace of Clubs*.

B-256   Zolotow, Maurice. *Stagestruck, The Romance of Alfred Lunt and Lynn Fontanne*. Harcourt, Brace & World, NY. 1965.

Index

A to Z, D-52
Aaron, John, T-12
Abbey, Harold, P-77
Abbott, George, P-14, B-136
Abbott, Tony, T-57
Abercrombie, Ian, P-221
Ace of Clubs, 21, 24, P-117,
 R-49, D-36, D-37, D-38, D-39,
 D-164, B-79, B-236, B-256
Ackerman, Robert Allan,
 P-221
Acres, Harry, D-82
Actor's Fund Benefit, P-72
Adam, Timothy Forbes, P-129
Adams, Polly, P-179, P-198,
 T-71
Adams, Ruth, P-77
Adams, Samuel Hopkins, B-1
Adams, Tony, P-156
Addinsell, Richard, P-211,
 F-17, D-88
Addy, Wesley, R-47
Adler, Murray, P-16
Admire, Jere, P-154
Adrian, Max, P-151
After The Ball, 22, P-135,
 R-58, D-128, D-164, B-154,
 B-237
Agate, James, B-4, B-5, B-6
Ahern, Lloyd, T-9
Aherne, Brian, P-139, T-68
Ainsworth, John, P-145, P-147
Aitken, Maria, P-191, P-197,
 P-205, P-217, P-227, T-95
Albee, Edward, B-7
Albery, Bronson, P-24
Alderman, John, P-150
Alderton, John, T-86-94
Aldin, Cecil, P-17

Aldredge, Theoni V., P-203,
 P-214, T-47
Aldridge, Michael, T-84
Alexander, Arthur, P-58
Alexander, Chris, P-108
Alexander, Danyse, T-81
Alexander, Joan, R-41
Alford, Bobby, P-145
Algar, Robert, P-56, P-58
Alison, Dorothy, P-27
Alister, Jean, D-121
All Clear, P-92
Allan, Patrick, P-174
Allegret, Marc, F-12
Allen, Adrianne, 12, P-47,
 P-61, P-62, P-26, T-68
Allen, Bobby, P-154
Allen, Ivan, P-160
Allen, Lewis, T-9
Allison, Karl, P-214
Allison, Michael, P-129, R-76
Altman, John, T-80
Alwyn, Kenneth, D-122
Alyn, Glen, P-1224
Ambient, Mark, P-15
Ambrosian Singers, P-207
Ames, Ed, T-47
Ames, Gerald, P-36
Amherst, Jeffrey, 12, P-60,
 B-190
Amos, Keith, P-181
And Now Noël Coward, P-170
Anderson, Clifford, P-4
Anderson, Daphne, P-109,
 P-174, D-69
Anderson, David, P-39
Anderson, Gerald, F-19
Anderson, J. Grant, P-88
Anderson, Jean, T-86-94

Anderson, Judith, B-136
Anderson, Marjorie, R-70
Anderson, Maxwell, B-38
Anderson, Michael, F-21
Anderson, Robert, T-6
Andreas, Christine, P-196
Andrews, Julie, F-29
Andrews, Maidie, P-67, P-75,
 P-78, P-90, P-109, P-153, D-54
Andrews, Nancy, D-164
Andrews, Robert, P-38, P-126,
 D-164
Androcles and The Lion,
 P-178, T-47, D-111
André, Yvonne, P-105
Angel, Adrienne, P-161
Angers, Avril, P-174, P-215,
 P-225
Annals, Michael, P-186
Annett, Paul, T-86-94
Anstee, Paul, P-144
Anthology, R-59
Anthony, Michael, P-111
Apollo, P-178
Apple Cart, The, 22, P-131,
 P-134, D-107, B-52
Apps, Edwin, T-34
Appleby, Basil, P-112
Archer, William, P-9
Aris, Ben, T-80
Armchair Theatre, T-43
Armstrong, Will Steven, P-167
Arnold, Sydney, P-156
*Around The World In
 80 Days*, 23, F-21
Art Carney Show, The, T-23
Arthur, Carol, P-161
Ash, Joyce, T-13
Ashcroft, Peggy, R-73, R-75

Ashe, Rosemary, P-216, D-120
Asher, Jane, P-211, T-86-94
Ashley, Edward, F-13
Ashworth, Stephen, P-156
Asley, Maggie, P-194
Astaire, Fred, 7, P31, P-32,
    B-136
Astar, Ben, P-112
Astonished Heart, The, 17, 21,
    P-83, F-19, T-86-94, T-95,
    B-186
Atherton, Effie, P-64, P-70
Atkinson, Don, P-154
Attenborough, Richard,
    P-174, F-15, R-70, T-61, T-67
Aubrey, Madge, P-56
Audley, Maxine, P-164, T-20
Audre, P-146
Aunt Tittie, D-171
Australia Visited, R-25, B-46
Autumn Idyll, An, 3, P-6
Averty, Brenda, P-157
Axelrod, George, F-25
Aylward, Derik, P-111

Babbage, Wilfred, F-18
Bacall, 22, T-10
Baddeley, Angela, 22, P-124
Baddeley, Hermione, 8, P-24,
    P-37, P-116
Badel, Alan, P-111
Bagley, Ben, D-164
Bain, Bill, T-43
Bain, Imogen, P-211
Baker, Carol, T-85
Baker, David, T-47
Baker, George, P-150
Baker, Hylda, P-171
Baker, Josephine, P-103
Baker, Keith, P-196
Baker, Lionel, P-109
Balaber, Syndee, P-161
Balcon, Michael, 11, F-3, F-4
Baldwin, Peter, P-206
Ball, Lucille, T-42
Bankhead, Tallulah, 8, 24,
    P-36, P-114, P-172, B-136
Banks, Leslie, P-30
Bannerman, Margaret, 8
Bannerman, Penryn, P-75,

    P-78
Bannerman, Tim, T-80
Bannister, Leslie, P-59
Baptise, Thomas, P-144
Baravalle, Victor, P-78
Barbour, Joyce, P-32, P-70,
    P-74, P-82, R-12, T-49
Bard, John, T-81
Barkdull, Les, P-167
Barker, Phyllis, P-95
Barker-Bennet, Edith, P-44
Barkworth, Peter, P-143
Bernard, Ivor, P-35
Barnes, Binnie, p-67, R-22
Barnes, Howard, G., R-55
Barnes, Jean, P-75, P-88
Barnes, Julian, P-221
Barnett, Nancy, P-59
Barnett, Sylvia, P-59
Barnett, Wilson, P-95
Barnouw, Erik, R-39, R-47
Barr, Richard, P-141, P-169,
    P-187
Barr, Patrick, T-57
Barratt, Watson, P-77
Barrett, Sean, P-165
Barrett, Ray, P-174
Barrett, Wilson, P-69
Barrie, Amanda, P-174
Barrie, J.M., P-12, B-244
Barrier, Edgar, R-21
Barron, Marcus, P-44
Barrow, Janet, P-111
Barry, Jean, P-56
Barrymore, Ethel, P-72, B-136
Barstow, Richard, P-113, T-8
Barton, Margaret, F-18
Barton, Mary, P-24
Bascomb, Betty, P-168, R-75
Basehart, Richard, R-50
Bassie, Joan, P-167
Bateman, Gwen, P-109
Bates, Florence, F-14
Bates, Michael, P-151
Batley, Dorothy, P-124
Batty, Archibald, P-131
Bauersmith, Paula, P-154
Baxley, Barbara, P-114
Baxter, Anne, P-187
Baxter, Keith, P-220

Bayldon, Olivei, T-82
Bayliss, Peter, P-131, P-186,
    F-27
Beach, Ann, T-30
Beacham, Stephanie, P-221
Beamish, Silvia, P-135
Beaton, Brian, P-163
Beaton, Cecil, P-129, P-139,
    P-150, T-65, T-68
Beaton, Morag, D-102
Beauchamp, Beatrice, P-2
Beaumont, Binkie, 24, 25,
    T-68, B-161
Beaumont and Fletcher, P-24
Beaumont, Dianna, P-44
Beauty and The Beast, P-178
Beccio, Barbara, P-226
Becker, Lionel, P-205
Beckley, Tony, F-30
Bede, Claude, P-194
Bedford, Brian, P-172, T-47
Beecher, Janet, F-13
Beerbohn, John, P-67
Beerhohn, Max, B-12
Beevers, Diana, P-177
Behan, Janet, P-209
Behrman, S.N., 10, 15, P-76
Bell, Diana, P-157
Bell, Gatenby, P-69
Bell, Heather, P-185
Bell, Stanley, P-36
Bellamy, Ralph, T-27
Bellew, Dyrle, P-23
Benda, G.K., P-34
Benefit For Negro Actor's
    Guild, P-89
Benge, Janet, T-95
Benham, Joan, P-95, T-34
Benjamin, Louis, P-215,
    P-217
Bennett, Arnold, B-13, B-245
Bennett, Richard Rodney,
    P-174
Bennett, Robert Russell,
    P-160, T-47
Benny, Jack, 22, P-14, P-184
Benson, Goerge, P-174
Bentley, Dick, D-163
Berenson, Beatrice, P-77
Berger, Bill, P-150

Berman, Ingrid, R-39
Beringer, Esmé, P-23
Berkeley, Ballard, F-15
Berkeley, Reginald, 16, F-8
Berlin, Irving, P-39
Berlyn, Ivan, P-24
Bernette, Sheila, P-174
Berns, Seymour, T-75
Bernstein, Leonard, F-11
Bertish, Suzanne, P-221
Best, Constance, P-43, P-215
Best, Edna, 8, P-27, P-36, P-46,
    P-124, P-139, R-33, T-13
Bethencourt, Francis, T-8
Betjeman, John, D-112
Better Half, The, P-29
Bevan, Bill, F-8
Bevan, Gillian, P-204
Bevan, Ilsa, P-58, P-59
Bevans, Philippa, P-150
Beyond The Horizon, B-38
Bickford-Smith, Imogene,
    T-85
Bilrook, Lydia, P-3
Bing, Herman, F-13
Bine, Ronald, P-117
Biographies In Sound, R-60
Biography, P-76,B-116
Bishop, Anne, P-151
Bishop, Ward, P-71
Bitter-Sweet, 11, 12, 15, 16, 18,
    19, 27, P-58, P-59, P-77, P-186,
    P-216, F-3, F-8, R-6, R-11, R-
    31, R-45, R-48, R-53, R-68, T-
    17, D-4, D-10, D-13, D-25,
    D-75, D-76, D-77, D-78, D-120,
    D-121, D-122, D-123, D-124,
    D-125, D-157, D-158, D-159,
    D-160, D-161, D-164, D-184,
    D-185, B-12, B-18, B30, B-68,
    B-74, B-80, B-81, B-137, B-181,
    B-237
Black, Phyllis, P-30
Blacker, Amelia, P-215
Blackman, Honor, P-171
Blackton, Jay, P-160, T-47
Blair, Anthony, P-67
Blair, Joyce, P-174, P-185
Blake, Beulah, P-77
Blake, Eubie, P-32

Blake, Susie, P-201
Blakemore, Michael, P-186
Blane, Ralph, P-161
Blaney, Norah, P-153
Blayney, May, P-20
Blezard, William, P-204, P-212
Blithe Spirit, 4, 19, 20, 22, 24,
    25, 26, 27, P-15, P-97, P-98, P-
    99, P-124, P-161, P-163, P-175,
    P-191, P-211, P-214, P-218, F-
    17, R-33, R-38, R-52, T-3, T-4,
    T-11, T-35, T-44, T-56, D-106,
    B-3, B-30, B-70, B-78, B-82, B-
    143, B-147, B-161, B-182, B-
    203, B-221
Bloch, Ray, R-26, R-29
Bloom, Leslie, P-155
Blye, Maggie, F-30
Blythe, Robert (Bobby), P-67,
    T-83
Blythe, Dorothy, P-129
Blythe, John, F-16
Blythen, Julie-Anne, T-82
Bogarde, Dirk, P-126, T-44
Bogart, Humphrey, 22
Bogdanoff, Rose, T-8
Boggetti, Victor, P-84
Bogie, Duane, C. T-69
Bohan, Martin, T-68
Bois, Curt, F-13
Bolan, James, T-34
Bolger, Ray, P-14
Bolton, Guy, P-27
Bon Voyage, T-84, B-59
Bond, Gary, P-174, P-177,
    P-205
Bond, Richard, F-11
Bond, Sudie, P-176
Bone, Stephen, R-73
Bonynge, Richard, D-102
Boom, F-28
Bookvar, Steve, T-47
Booth, Connie, P-186
Booth, Janie, P-159
Booth, Roger, P-159
Booth, Shirley, P-176, R-55
Booth, Trace, T-82
Bordon, Ethel, P-71
Bordoni, Irene, B-136
Borg, Veda Ann, F-13

Borgnine, Ernest, T-17
Borkum, Shelley, P-193
Bosco, Wally, F-18
Boucicault, Dion, P-12
Boucicault, Nina, P-51
Boulter, Rosalyn, P-87
Boulton, Guy Pelham, P-46
Bourchier, Arthur, P-23
Bourneuf, Philip, T-8
Bovell, Susan, P-206
Bowden, Charles, P-141
Bowen, Dennis, P-135
Bowen, John, T-69
Bowen, T.R., T-83
Bowles, Peter, P-193
Bowlly, Al, D-7
Bowman, Lee, F-14
Bowman, Nellie, P-34
Boxer, John, F-15
Boyd, Dorothy, P-58, F-4
Boyd, Margot, P-153
Boyd, Ruth, P-80
Boyer, Carol, P-77
Boyer, Martha, P-77
Boyle, Billy, P-174
Boyne, Peter, P-120
Boyton, Mark, T-81
Brabazon, James, T-58
Bradley, Buddy, P-70
Bradley, Elizabeth, P-206
Bradley, Oscar, R-22
Bragdon, Frances, R-76
Bragg, Melvyn, T-95
Braham, Philip, P-22, P-32,
    P-37
Brahms, Caryl, T-74
Braidon, Thomas, P-39, F-10
Braithwaite, Lilian, 7, P-35,
    P-39, P-41
Brand, Lena, P-67
Brandon, Dorothy, P-18
Bransby-Williams, Eric, F-4
Branson, Chimmon, F-15
Braswell, Charles, P-154
Bray, Bill, P-209
Brayshay, Sylvia, P-175
Brazzi, Rossano, F-30
Breckenridge, Betty, R-38,
    R-39, R-47
Breeze, Alan, P-171

Breeze, Olivia, P181
Bregonzi, Alec, P-216
Brennan, Ted, P-216
Brent, Romney, 14, P-70, R-39
Brererton, Cecilia, T-85
Bressart, Felix, F-13
Brett, Alastair, P-209
Brett, Jeremy, P-174, P-181,
    P-186,
Brian, Anthony, P-58, P-75,
    P-78, D-56
Brickerton, J.P., P-39
Brief Encounter, 18, 20, F-18,
    R-37, R-44, R-46, R-50, R-61,
    T-6, T-8, T-27, T-69, T-95, D-
    106
Briers, Richard, P-164, P-174,
    T-54
Brigadoon, 21
Bring On The Girls, P-27
Britton, Florence, P-90
Britton, Tony, P-174, R-75,
    T-85
Bromley, Alan, T-30
Bromley, Sydney, F-18
Bronhill, June, P-174, D-125
Brook, Clive, F-8
Brook, Emily, P-20
Brook, Faith, P-174
Brook, Leslie, P-105
Brook-Jones, Elwyn, P-117
Brown, Arvin, P-176, P224
Brown, Hester Paton, P-156
Brown, Jeremy, P-160
Brown, Nancy, P-59
Brown, Pamela, T-25
Brown, Tim, P-201
Brown, W. Earl, T-27
Browne, Irene, P-67, P-75,
    P-78, P-87, P-135, P160, F-8
Browne, Laidman, P-84
Browne, Sam, D-81
Browne, W. Graham, P-28,
    P-49, P-79
Browning, Jacqueline, P-109
Bruce, Kate, F-1
Bruce, Mona, T-49
Bruce, Nigel, P-37, P-48
Brune, Adrienne, P-56
Brunel, Adrian, F-3

Bryan, Dora, P-111, P-121,
    P-128,T-60
Bryan, Robert, P-186
Bryant, Peggie, P-2
Bryden, Ronald, T-56
Bryne, Barbara, P-210
Brynner, Yul, F-21, F-23, T-68
Brytt, Kelly, P-160
Buchanan, Elsa, R-16
Buchanan, Jack, 7, P-33,
    P-138, B-119
Buchwald, Art, F-23
Buck, Dennis, P-213
Buckley, Donald, P-12
Bufman, Zev, P-203
Buka, Donald, R-41
Bull, Francis H., P-29
Bullock, H. Ridgely, Jr., P-141
Bunnage, Avis, T-81
Bunny Lake Is Missing, F-26
Burke, Patricia, P-174
Burnably, Davy, P-28
Burnell, Janet, P-69
Burns, Mark, P-215
Burns, Pamela, T-60
Burr, Anne, R-41
Burr, Marilyn, P-152
Burridge, Geoffrey, P-181
Burroughs, Jackie, P-194
Burrows, John, P-181
Burston, Reginald, P-58, P-75,
    D-16, D-54, D-55, D-56
Burton, David, P-52
Burton, Hal, T-40, T-56
Burton, Harry, P-225
Burton, Kate, P-202
Burton, Molly, P-17
Burton, Richard, P-203, F-28,
    T-68, T-69, D-96
Burton, Sarah, P-90, P-113,
    P-146
Bush, Vannevar, T-12
Butcher, Cyril, P-109
Butler, George, P-88
Butler, Janet, P-126
Buzard, Helen, T-85
Byng, Douglas, 10, P-37, P-56
Byron, Athur, P-52, F-7

Cadell, Simon, P-204, P-211,

    P-219
Caeser, Irvin, P-27
Caine, Michael, F-30
Calloway, Ann Hampton,
    D-181
Calthrop, Christopher, P-117
Calthrop, Donald, P-31, P-17,
    P-27
Calthrop, G.E. (Gladys), 7, 11,
    P-35, P-37, P-38, P-45, P-48,
    P-51, P-53, P-57, P-58, P-61, P-
    67,P-70,P-71, P-74, P-75, P-79,
    P-80, P-83, P-84, P-88, P-90, P-
    92, P-97, P-100, P-105, P-107,
    P-109, P-111, P-115, P-126, F-
    15, T-68
Calvert, Phyllis, P-164, P-175
Camarata, Tutti, T-10
Camera Three, T-70
Cameron, Charles, P-112
Cameron, Rita, P-163
Camiller, George P-177
Campbell, Alan, P-71
Campbell, J.M., P-22
Campbell, Jean, D-153
Campbell, Judy, P-99, P-100,
    P-101, P-124, P-174
Campbell, Naomi, R-21
Campbell, Patton, P-141
Campbell, Violet, P-48
Campbell, Virginia, T-1
Campbell, Winifred, P-75,
    P-78
Can-Can, R-55
Cantiflas, F-21
Cantor, P-175, P-179, P-189
Capell, Peter, R-39, R-47
Cardin, George, P-107
Cardinall, Roberto, D-121
Carew, Denis, P-88
Carey, Brian, P-111
Carey, David, P-109
Carey, Eileen, P-58
Carey, Joyce, P-43, P-99,
    P-100, P-101, P-129, P-143, P-
    144, P-145, P-147, P215, F-15,
    F-17, F-18, T-68
Cargrill, Patrick, P-175
Carino, Arthur, P-79
Carlisle, Marion, P-77

Carlisle, Tom, P-67
Carmichael, Ian, P-121, P-128, P-174, T-74
Carnegie, Hattie, P-113
Carney, Art, T-23
Carney, George, F-15
Carnival of the Animals, 23, P-142, T-23
Carnovsky, Morris, P-145
Carpenter, Peter, P-43, P-215
Carpenter, Sue, T-81
Carr, George, P-47
Carr, Jane, T-85
Carr, Jason, P-223
Carr, Mary Ann, P-90
Carricart, Robertson, P-208
Carrie, P-216
Carrol, Agatha, P-69
Carroll, Helene, P-203, P-208
Carroll, Leo G. P-39
Carroll, Madeleine, R-16
Carson, Jean, P-117
Carte, Eric, P-215
Carten, Audrey, P-84
Carten, Kenneth, P-70, P-83, P-88, P-90, P-15, D-59
Carten, Waveney, P-84
Carter, Jack, P-152
Carver, Cherry, P-24
Carver, Lynne, F-13
Case, Gerald, P-100, P-101, P-116, F-15
Casey, Brian, P-171
Casmore, Victor, P-171
Cason, Barbara, P-180
Casson, Lewis, P-29, P-153, B-28
Castillo, P-108
Castle, Anne, P-144, T-24
Castle, Charles, T-68
Castle, Gene, P-161
Caswell, Richard, P-218
Cathey, Dalton, P-200
Cavalcade, 13, 16, 17, 27, P-67, P-207, P-209 F-8, R-5, R-12, R-16, T-7, T-9, D-7, D-8, D-9, B-69, B-74, B-83
Cavanagh, Lilian, P-49
Cavanagh, William, P-56
Cavanaugh, Paul, F-7

Cavell, Butch, R-47
Cavendish, Norah, P-214
Cavett, Dick, T-63
Cecil, Jonathan, P-181
Cecil, Nora, F-10
Cecil, Sylvia, P-109, P-117, D-70, D-72, D-73
Ceeley, Leonard, P-77
Ceiffe, Alice Belmor, P-40
Cellier, Frank, P-49, P-76, R-17,
Cenedella, Robert, R-38
Cey, Jacques, F-20
Chagrin, Nicholas, P-156
Chamberlain, George, P-79
Chamberlain, Martin, P-193
Chamberlain, Richard, P-214
Chambers, Haddon, P-20
Champion, Gower, P-161
Chance, Michael, P-216
Chaney, Stewart, P-98
Channon, Dennis, T-59
Chaplin, Saul, F-29
Chapman, John, R-52
Chapman, Robert, T-13
Chapman, Stella, P-111
Chappell, E., R-21
Chappell, William, P-121, P-126, P-128, P-143
Charig, Philip, P-27
Charity Gala, P-158
Charles B. Cochran's, P-64
Charles, Maria, P-227
Charley's Aunt, 4, P-14
Charlot's Revue, P-33, P-34
Charlot's Revue of 1926, P-42, F-5
Charlot, André, 6, P-22, P-32
Chase, Ilka, P-190, T-8
Chase, Pauline, 3, P-12
Chater, Geoffrey, P-191
Chater, Gordon, T-20
Chautard, Emile, F-10
Chelsea Buns, 7, B-34
Checkpoint, P-178
Chelson, Peter, T-80
Chelton, Nick, P-216
Cherrell, Gwen, P-185, T-69
Cherry, Helen, T-35
Chester, Betty, P-24

Chester, Sybil, P-34
Cheston, Dorothy, P-24
Chevalier, Albert, P-15
Chevalier, Maurice, P-106, T-68
Chiarletti, Guido, P-4
Chicago, B-38
Childs, Gilbert, P-28
Chisholm, Robert, R-38
Choice of Coward, A, T-34-36
Christensen, Margaret, P-156
Christie, Dinah, T-66
Christmas, Paul, P-150
Christopher, Thomas, P-187
Church, John, P-167
Ciannelli, Edward, F-11
Circle, The, R-20
Claire, Imogen, P-217
Claire, Ina, P-76
Claire, Mary, P-46
Clancy, Deidre, P-216
Clare, Mary, P-67, P-153
Clare, Wyn, P-32
Clark, Alexander, T-3
Clark, E. Holman, P-11, P-25
Clark, Jacqueline, F-17
Clark, John Nesbet, P-180
Clark, Peggy, P-145, P-160
Clarke, Cecil, T-69
Clarke, Cuthbert, P-17
Clarke, Dorothy, P-32
Clarke, Philip, P-67
Clarke, Richard, P-190
Clarkson, David, P-25
Clarkson, Joan, P-56,
Clarkson, John, P-195
Clay, Cassius (Mohammed Ali), T-42
Clayburgh, Jill, P-208
Clayton, Jack, R-12
Clement, Clay, F-7
Clements, John, P-105
Clether, Brenda, P-78
Cliff, Laddie, P-28, P-34
Clift, Montgomery, T-1
Clifton, Eileen, P-78
Clinton-Baddely, Enid, P-67
Clinton, Mildred, P-139
Clive, Madeleine, P-139
Clubborn, Arnold, P-9

Clulow, John, P-11
Co-Optimists, The, P-28
Coates, Norman, P-195, P-204
Cochrans 1931 Revue, D-6,
   D-10
Cochran, Charles B. 7, 10, 11,
   14, 15, P-37, P-56, P-57, P-61,
   P-67, P-70, P-74, P-75, P-78
Cochran, Mabel, P-146
Coco, T-65
Codrighton, Ann, P-56, P-70
Codron, Michael, P-159, P-220
Coe, Fred, T-8
Coffey, Denise, P-163
Cohan, George M. B-184
Cohen, Alexander, T-65
Cohen, Jonathan, P-219
Colbert, Claudette, P-120,
   P-127, F-7, T-11
Cole and Coward, P-222
Cole, Julie Dawne, P-215
Coleman, Ronald, R-20, R-33
Coleridge, Sylvia, P-126, P-129
Collier, Constance, 14, P-68,
   P-74
Collier, Patience, P-144, T-24
Collingwood, Charles, T-86-94
Collins, Frank, P-56
Collins, Joan, P-220, P-224,
   T-86-94
Collins, Michael, D-121
Collins, Paul, P-190
Collinson, Frank, D-23, D-24
Collinson, Peter, F-30
Colman, Booth, P-113
Colson, Kevin, P-157
Colt, Alvin, P-167
Comden, Betty, F-11
*Come Into The Garden
   Maud*, P-165, P-187, B-107, R-
   76
Compton, Fay, P-97
Compton, Sidney, P-14
Comstock, Francis Marion
   P-77
Concerto, 11, F-3
Conery, Edward, P-202
Conklin, John, P-178
Conley, Jay, P-77
Connard, Phyllis, P-71, P-139

Connell, Howard, T-22
Connolly Mark, P-40
Connolly Patricia, P-214
Conroy, Fran, T-23
Conroy, Jean, P-153
Constable, William, P-152
Constant Nymph The, 9, P-46
   B-140, B-141
Conventry, Edward, P-56
Conversation Piece, 14, P-75,
   P-78, P-146, R-9, R-14, R-68,
   D-16, D-17, D-80, D-96,B-69,
   B-75, B-84, B-130,
   B-137, B-215, B-227
Converse, Frank, P-208
Conway, Tom, P-43
Cook, Donald, P-114, P-172
Cook, Mildred, P-146
Cook, Robert, T-58
Cook, Roderick, 27, P-160,
   P-170, P-180, P-188, P-194,
   P-213, T-66, T-75
Coolidge, Philip, T-8
Cooper, Edward, P-68, P-88
Cooper, Gary, 17, F-10, F-11,
   R-8,
Cooper, Gladys, 6, 21, P-124,
   B-119, B-203
Cooper, Rowena, P-191
Cooper, Roy, P-190
Cooper, Sally, P-209
Cooper, Stuart, T-43
Coote, Robert, P-174
Copeland, Joan, P-146
Corbett, Geoffrey, P-152,
   D-129
Corbett, Leonora, 19, P-98,
   R-38, T-3
Corbett, Hilary, P-194
Corcoran, Elizabeth, P-70,
   P-75, P-78
Corcoran, Robert, R-55
Cordell, Cathleen, P-91, R-38
Corey, Wendell, T-6
Corn Is Green, The, P-203
Cornish, Richard, P-177
Coslow, Sam, D-15
Cossart, Ernest, F-11
Cossart, Valerie, P-68, P-80,
   P-98, R-38, T-3

Cotton, Joseph, T-9
Coulouris, George, F-23
Councell, Elizabeth, T-73
Countess Maritza, D-123
Country, Girl, A, 2, P-1
Courlay, Jock, T-22
Courtenay, Tom, T-82
Courtneidge, Cicely, 4, P-15,
   P-163
Courtneidge, Robert, P-15,
   P-30
Coward, T-95
Coward NY Memorial, P-184
Coward, Eric, P-6
Coward, Violet, 1, 2
Cowardy Custard, 26, P-181,
   D-135
Cowl, Jane, 9, P-43, P-215
Cowley, Eric, P-68, P-74
Cox, Catherine, P-213
Cox, Michael Graham, P-168
Crabbe, Gary, P-154
Craig, Jerry, P-161
Craig, Michael, F-29
Craig, Russell, P-216
Crandall, Elizabeth, P-77
Crane, Harold, P-139
Craven, Gemma, T-74
Crawford, Broderick, P-80
Crawford, Dan, P-215
Crawford, J.R. P-14
Crawford, Mimi, P-17
Crawford, Neil, P-95
Craydon, Letty, P-157
Cree, Patricia, P-135
Crenna, Richard, F-29
Crews, Laura Hope, P-40
Cribbins, Bernard, T-86-94
Crime Without Passion, 17
Croft, Paddy, P-190
Cronin, Jackie, P-161
Cronyn, Hume, P-187
Cronyn, Tandy, T-49
Crouse, Lindsay, P-190
Crowe, Sara, P-220, P-227
Cruttenden, Abigail, P-227
Cullum, Charles, P-124
Cullum, John, P-203, T-47
Culver, Roland, P-168
Cummings, Constance, P-166,

F-17
Cummings, Ina, P-150
Cunningham, Neil, T-85
Cunningham, Philip, P-24
Cunningham, Zamah, T-23
Curra, Roland, P-205
Currah, Brian, P-165
Curran, Homer, P-113
Currie, Clive, P-30
Currie, Finlay, F-26
Curtis, Tony, F-25
Curzon, George, P-51
Cusack, Cyril, T-60
Cuthbertson, Allan, P-112
Cutler, Kate, P-25, P-30, P-35,
    P-69
Cutts, Graham, F-2
Cutts, Marilyn, P-205
Cutts, Patricia, T-13

d'Alba, Julia, D-125
d'Ambricourt, Adrien, F-10
d'Esterre, Lisa, P-88
Daisy Chain, The P-5
Daisy Mayme, B-38
Dale, Grover, P-154, P-156
Dalton, Doris, P-108
Damita, Lili, F-2
Dana, F. Mitchell, P-200
Dana, Mitchell, P-213
Dane, Clemence, D-30, D-88
Daniels, Danny, P-161
Danerman, Paul, T-85
Daniel, Jennifer, T-57
Daniels, Marc, T-23
Danner, Blythe, P-214
Danses Concertants, P-178
Darbyshire, Michael, P-117
Dare, Zena, 10, T-68
Darling, S. Grenville, P-11
Darling, William S., F-8
Darnborough, Anthony, F-19
Darwall, Barbara, P-200
Darwell, Jane, F-10
Daubeny, Peter, P-116, T-68
Davenport, Bromley, P-35
Davenport, Harry, P-40
Davey, Nuna, F-18
David Frost Show, The, T-51,
    T-64

David, Clifford, T-47
David, John, P-218
David, Worton, D-46
Davidson, Gordon, P-220
Davidson, Lawrence, P-151
Davies, Betty Ann, F-20, T-4
Davies, Gareth, P-156
Davies, Irving, T-74
Davies, Tudor, P-181
Davis, Betty, P-56
Davis, Brian, P-77
Davis, George, F-6
Davis, Joe, P-164, P-165,
    P-175, P-179, P-206
Davis, Ray, T-55
Davis, Winifred, P-75, P-78,
    P-88
Dawn, Julie, D-121
Dawson, Beatrice, P-179,
    P-189
Day, Edith, P-153, P-156
Day, Frances, P-103
De Banzie, Brenda, F-27
de Casalis, Jeanne, P-82
De Havilland, Olivia, R-50
de Legh, Kitty, P-95
De Lissa, Arthur, P-3
de Lungo, Ton, P-46
DeMille, Cecil B., R-14, R-16
De Souza, Edward, P-159,
    R-69
De Wit, Jacqueline, T-27
Dean, Basil, P-9, P-39, P-41,
    P-43, P-44, P-45, P-46, P-48, P-
    51
Dean, Leamond, P-146
Dean, Lee, P-218
Deane, Dacia, F-4
Debenham, Ciceley, P-15
Debenham, Dorothy, P-59
Deeley, Michael, F-30
DeKordova, Frederick, T-11
Delaney, Maureen, P-153
Dellaway, George, P-23
Delman, Elaine, P-181
Delve, David, P-206
Delysia, Alice, 8, P-37, D-46,
    D-119
Demeger, Robert, P-209
Dench, Judi, T-83

Dene, Zulema, P-201
Denham, Maurice, P-116,
    R-75
Denison, Michael, P-174
Dennis, Eileen, P-16
Dennis, Jon, P-157
Dennis, Jonathan, P-174
Dennis, Ray, P-90
Denny, Reginald, F-6
Dereeder, Pierre, P-77
Design For Living, 6, 14, 15,
    16, 19, 27, P-71, P-91, P-186,
    P-205, P-208, F-10, R-8, T-37,
    T-70, T-72, T-95, B-22, B-54,
    B-69, B-74, B-85, B-144
Desmond, Florence, P-37,
    P-57
Deutsch, Nicholas, P-180
Deval, Jacques, P-84
Devereau, Ed, T-84
Devine, George, P-151, T-25
Devine, Lauri, P-56
Devis, Pamela, P-117
Devlin, Cory, P-145
Devon, Patricia, P-148
Dewell, Michael, P-167
Dick Cavett, Show, The, T-63
Dickens, C. Stafford, P-154
Dickenson, Sandra, T-85
Dietrich, Marlene, 26, P-104,
    F-21, T-7, D-84, D-116, D-183
Diffen, Ray, P-187
Dillingham, Charles, P-39
Dillon, Mia, P-210
Dinah Shore Show, The, T-27
Disney-Roebuck, C., P-45
Diss, Eileen, P-191, T-59
Diversions, P-178
Dixon, Arthur, P-23
Doble, Frances, 10, F-3
Docker, Robert, P-206, R-68
Dods, Marcus, R-68
Dodsworth, T-8
Dolan, Lindsay, P-209, P-216,
    T-82
Dolan, Robert Emmett, R-20
Dolin, Anton, P-152
Dolman, Richard, P-31, P-37
Dolores Sisters, The, P-32
Dominic, Zo, P-219, P-223

Donald, James, P-100, P-101, F-15
Donald, Shirley, P-157
Dondlinger, Mary Jo, P-226
Donen, Stanley, 23, F-23, F-24
Donlin, James, F-10
Donohoe, Amanda, T-80
Don't Count The Candles, T-50
Dorow, Dorothy, D-121
Dossor, Alan, T-80
Dotrice, Roy, P-210
Dougherty, Francis A, P-167
Douglas, James B. P-194
Douglas, Johnny, D-125
Douglas, Kirk, T-17
Douglas, Melvyn, F-14
Douglas, Susan, R-41
Douglas, Wallace, P-79
Dowse, Mark, P-186
Drage, Maie, P-58
Dragon, Carmen, R-45, T-8
Drake, Alfred, R-35
Drake, Julie, P-160
Drayton, Noël, T-9
Drewes, Lorna, P-117
Drover, Dorothy, P-67, P-78
Drury, Peter, P-111
Dryden, Robert, R-39, R-47
du Maurier, George, B-119
DuSautoy, Carmen, P-227
Duchess of Kent, P-127
Dudley, Bronson, P-90
Dudley, Philip, T-57
Duff, Harry, P-4
Duggan, Charles H., P-224
Duke, Edward, P-220, P-224, T-86-94
Dukes, Ashley, P-41
Dullea, Keir, F-26
Duna, Steffi, P-70
Duncan, Laura, P-90
Duncan, Victoria, P-201
Dunham, Joanna, T-35
Dunkinson, Harry, F-10
Dunn, Geoffrey, P-131
Dunn, Michael, F-28
Dunne, Irene, R-11, R-43
Dunning, Jessica, P-153
Dunnock, Mildred, F-28

Dupree, Frank, P-10
Dupuis, Paul, P-116
Durante, Jimmy, 22
Dvorsky, Peter, P-194
Dwyer, Leslie, F-15
Dyall, Franklyn, F-4
Dyall, Valentine, F-18
Dyer, David, P-216
Dyke, John Hart, P-175

Eamonn Andrews Show, The, T-42
Earl Mountbatten, T-68
Earle, Edward, D-164
Eason, Myles, P-117
Easy Virtue, 9, 11, 27, P-43,P-44, P-215, F-3, F-4, B-67, B-75, B-87
Ebb, Fred, P-210
Eccles, Jane, T-34
Ed Sullivan Show, The, 23, T-14, T-17, T-32
Eddison, Robert, P-92
Eddleman, Jack, P-160
Eddy, Nelson, 16, F-13, D-75, D-76, D-124, D-157
Edlin, Tubby, P-32
Edmett, Nicky, P-144
Edmond, Terence, T-58
Ednay, Benjamin, T-69
Edney, Florence, T-1
Edro, J.K., P-4
Edwards, Ben, P-176
Edwards, Lumena, P-79
Elburn, Betty, P-75
Elder, Eldon, P-141
Elias, Rosalind, D-123
Elkin, Clifford, P-143
Elkins, Margreta, D-102
Elliot, Denholm, P-167, D-169
Elliot, Frank, F-4
Elliott, Don, P-169
Elliot, Madge, 20
Ellis, Carrie, T-86-94
Ellis, Mary, P-112, P-135, F-19
Elphinstone, Derek, F-15
Elsie, Lily, B-119
Elson, Charles, P-114, P-139
Elson, Isobel, T-1
Elwood, James, R-76

Emery, Polly, R-17
Emiston, Liz, P-171
ENSA Tour, P-103
Engel, Lehman, D-96, D-123, B-130
Ensor, Derek, P-185
Erickson, Mitchell, P-189
Erskine, Eileen, F-16
Erskine, Howard, P-169
Esler, Eileen, P-2
Esmond, Annie, P-76
Esmond, Jill, P-63
Essison, Robert, P-110
Estensen, Elizabeth, P-209
Ettori, Claudye, F-28
Eula, Joe, P-172
Evans, David, P-154
Evans, Edith, 25, P-27, P-162, T-25, T-54, T-60, T-68
Evans, Madge, P-52
Evans, Peter, P-109
Evans, Rex, D-96
Evans, Ronald, P-109
Evans, Tudor, P-109
Evelyn, John, P-59
Evensen, Marlon, P-43, P-215
Everett, Rupert, P-217, P-221
Everley, Greegg, P-75

F.E.S. Plays Ltd., P-153
Fahy, Tom, P-209
Fairbanks, Jr., Douglas, P-127, P-190, D-88
Fairbanks, Douglas, P-82
Fairchild, William, F-29
Fairfax, Diana, P-168
Fallen Angels, 8, 10, 13, 26, 27, P-36, P-69, P-116, P-141, P-166, P-195, T-30, B-67, B-72, B-75, B-86, B-229, B-242
Fallender, Deborah, R-73
Family Album, P-83, P-177, T-86-94, D-81
Fancy, Brett, P-209
Fane, Dorothy, F-3
Farago, Peter, P-211
Farebrother, Violet, F-4
Farey, Charles, P-56
Faris, Alexander, P-216
Farrah, Paul, P-201

Farrer, Ann, P-84
Farrow, Claude, P-75, P-78
Faulkner, David, P-150
Faull, Ellen, D-97
Fay, Anna Eva, 1
Fayne, Greta, P-37
Fearon, José, P-58
Feilding, Harold, P-157
Feist, Gene, P-195
Fellows, Julian, P-198, T-73
Felstead, Betty, P-135
Felton, John, P-160
Fenn, Jean, P-154
Fenn, Roger, T-86-94
Fenner, Jill, P-217
Fenwick, Lucy, P-216
Ferber, Edna, 15, P-79
Ferneau, Yvonne, F-20
Ferrer, José, P-160
Ferrier, Pat, P-154
Ferris, Pam, T-80
Feydeau, P-150, P-151
Fiander, Lewis, P-174, P-209,
    P-212
Fickett, Homer, R-38, R-39,
Field Figures, P-178
Field, Lila, 2, P-2
Fielding, Fenella, P-193
Fielding, Harold, P-156
Fig Leaves Are Falling, The,
    P-170
Fildes, Audrey, P-112
Fingerhut, Arden, P-210,
    P-221
Finkel, Bob, T-27
Finlay, Donald, P-124
Finlay, Frank, T-58
Firbank, Ann, T-69
Fisher, Jules, P-161
Fisher, Terence, F-19
Fitch, Robert, P-160
Fitchew, Michael, P-216
Fitzgerald, Walter, F-15
Fitzgibbon, Maggie, P-157,
    P-174
Fitzpatrick, Michael, T-84
Fitzwilliam, Neil, P-174
Flack, Leslie, P-67
Flacks, Niki, P-189
Flanders and Swann, D-166

Fledermaus, Die, 10
Fleetwood, Betty, F-16
Fleischmann Hour, The, R-4,
    R-5, R-6, R-7, R-8
Fleming, Ian, P-29
Fleming, Lucy, P-168
Fleming, Michael, P-198, T-73
Flemington, Sarah, P-163
Flemming, Lucy, T-54
Flemyng, Gordon, T-45
Fletcher, Robert, P-161
Flickett, Homer, R-38
Floyd, Gwen, P-100, P-101
Flynn, Errol, P-127
Foch, Nina, P-167
Folliot, Gladys, P-23
Fontana, George, P-57
Fontanne, Lynn, 6, 9, 14, 22,
    P-71, P-73, P-80, P-127, P-129,
    P-139, F-6, T-63, T-65, B-256
Foot, Freddie, T-60
Forbes, Brenda, P-139, T-10
Forbes, Bryan, P-174
Forbes, Meriel, P-151
Forbes, Sheila, P-156, P-160
Force, Joan, P-167
Ford, Aly, P-67
Ford Star Jubilee, 23, T-9
Ford, Laurel, P-181
Ford-Davies, Oliver, P-177
Forsyth, Bruce, F-29, T-60
Forsyth, John, T-7
Fortescue, Kenneth, P-185
Forwood, Anthony, P-126
Fosse, Bob, P-161
Foster, Basil, P-12
Foster, Herbert, P-167
Foster, Julia, R-75
Fowler, Harry, T-82
Fox, Claire, P-209
Fox, Richard, P-163
France, Alexis, P-131
France, C.V., P-17
Franchi, Sergio, T-63
Francis, Andrew, P-205
Francis, Clive, P-193
Francis, Dick, P-57
Francis, Raymond, T-83
Francis, Ronald, P-117
Frank, Carl, R-39, R-47

Frank, Dorothy, P-154
Frankel, Benjamin, D-57,
    D-58, D-59
Frankel, Cyril, P-185
Franklin, Gretchen, P-174
Franklin, Harold, P-78
Franklin, Sidney, F-6
Fraser, Ann, P-154
Fraser, Bill, F-20
Fraser, Moyra, T-86-94
Frasher, James, P-154
Freedman, Bill, P-219, P-223
Freeland, Brian, P-162
Fremantle, Peggy, P-47
French, Arthur, P-208
French, Harold, 3, P-9, P-13,
    P-91,
French, Hugh, P-88, P-90,
    P-92, D-59, D-62
French, Samuel, P-25
French, Valeri, P-195
Fresnay, Pierre, 14, P-78
Fried, Michael, P-195
Friedman, Maria, T-82
Friend, Mark, P-225
Friend, Philip, F-15
Friendly, Fred W., T-18
Froeschel, George, F-14
Front Page, The, 17, T-18
Frost, David, T-51
Frow, Gerald, P-181
Fry, Bill, P-32
Fry, Billy, P-67
Fumed Oak, 17, P-83, P-116,
    P-167, P-171, F-20, T-86-94
Funny Girl, 25
Furse, Robert K., P-91
Future Indefinite, 22, B-53
Fyson, Leslie, R-68, D-125

Gabain, Marjorie, P-46, P-53
Gabor, Eva, P-147
Gabor, Zsa Zsa, 22
Gaige, Truman, P-77
Gale, John, P-164, P-198, T-73
Gale, Matthew, P-209
Gale, Peter, P-181
Gallery First Nighters', P-155
Galloway, Pat, T-75
Gallup, Frank, R-35

Gamble, Warburton, F-7
Gamley, Ailsa, P-135
Gamley, Douglas, T-59, D-102
Gampel, Chris, P-160
Gardner, Ian, P-198, T-73
Gardner, Rick, T-73
Garland, Geoff, P-167
Garland, Judy, 11
Garland, Patrick, P-193, T-56
Garnett, Richard, P-227
Garrick, Beulah, P-195, T-13
Garroway, Dave, R-57
Garry, Charles, P-46
Garson, Greer, P-84, R-44
Gatrell, John, P-88. D-59
Gatson, Marjorie, R-14
Gatteys, Bennye, T-27
Gautier, Jacques, P-117
Gavin, Gene, P-154, P-32,
    P-34, P-50, P-56, D-43
Gaynes, Gay, T-84
Gaynor, Grace, P-150
Gaynor, Mitzi, F-23
Genister, John, T-86-94
Gentle, Jackie, P-163
Gentlemen Prefer Blondes, 9
Gentles, Avril, P-147
George and Margaret, P-87
George, A.E., P-20
George, Bruce, P-174
George, George W. P-171,
    F-27
George, Marie, P-11
Gershwin, George, F-29
Gershwin, Ira, F-29
Getze, Tilda, P-90
Gibbons, Carroll, D-1, D-2,
    D-3, D-28, D-29
Gibson, Alan, T-59
Gibson, Felicity, T-57
Gibson, Leonard, P-90
Gibson, Madeleine, P-57
Gibson, Margaret, P-135,
    P-185
Gideon, Melville, P-28
Gielgud, John, 7, 9, 23, 26, 27,P-
    35, P-144, P-174, P-179, P-183,
    P-189, P-207, F-21, T-68, T-95,
    B-140, B-141
Gielgud, Val, R-12

Gilbert, Howard, P-109
Gilbert, Ruth, T-6
Gilchrist, Connie, F-14
Gilford, Jack, P-150
Gill, John, P-129
Gill, Richard, P-117
Gill, Tom, P-135
Gillian, David, T-85
Gillmore, Margalo, 27, P-154,
    P-184
Gilmore, David, P-209
Gilmore, Lowell, T-1
Gilpin, John, P-152
Gingold, Hermione, P-116,
    P-196, T-68, D-164
Ginner, Ruby, P-6
*Girl Who Came To Supper,
    The* 25, P-160, P-178, R-73, T-
    31, T-32, D-109, D-131, D-179,
    B-176, B-249
Gish, Dorothy, F-1
Gish, Lillian, F-1, B-119
Glade, Carol, P-160
Glass Menagerie, The, 6, 17
Glassford, David, P-39
Gleason, John, P-190
Glenister, Robert, T-82
Glenn, Don, P-120
Glenville, Peter, P-112
Glenville, Shaun, P-14
Globe Revue, The, P-138,
    D-40
Glossop, Roger, P-209
Glover, David, P-172
Glover, John, P-208
Glyn, Patricia, F-19
Glyn, Trevor, P-59
Glynn, Victor, T-80
Glynne, Mary, P-12
Go-Forth (Boom), F-28
Goddard, Daphne, T-83
Godfrey, Fred, P-45
Godwin, Christopher, P-227
Gold, Jack, T-82
Gold, Max, P-225
Golden Hour of Drama, T-39
Golden, Richard, P-151
Goldenberg, William, P-161
Goldfish, The, 2, P-2, P-17
Good, Gladys, T-68

Goodall, Edith, P-18
Goodchild, Tim, P-181
Goodman, Leonard, P-78
Goodner, Carol, T-3
Goodrich, Louis, P-11
Gordon, Arne, T-49
Gordon, Barbara, P-194
Gordon, Donald, P-59
Gordon, Dorothy, F-20
Gordon, Josephine, P-174
Gordon, Max, P-71
Gordon, Ruth, T-44
Gordon, Zoe, P-4, P-59
Gore, Altovise, P-161
Gorha, Cas, T-95
Gorie, John, T-54
Gottlieb, Jon, P-221
Gough, Michael, P-126
Gower, John, P-174
Graavey, Ferdinand, 16, F-9
Grace, Nicholas, T-86-94
Gradwell, Charmain, P-209
Graeme-Brooke, Douglas,
    P-59
Graham, Morland, P-87
Graham, Sheilah, P-56
Graham, Violet, P-3
Grammer, Sydney, P-75, P-78,
    D-56
Granat, Frank, P-171, F-27
Grand Tour, The, P-178
Grandage, Michael, P-209
Grant, Cary, F-24, R-20, T-65,
    B-157
Grant, Deborah, P-218
Grant, Eddie, P-56
Grant, Joyce, P-177
Grant, Kim, P-156, P-174,
    P-206,
Grant, Pamela, P-129, P-163
Granville, Bonita, F-8,
Grass is Greener, The, F-24
Graveney, Henry, T-45
Graves, Peter, P-135, P-174
Gray, Charles, T-54
Gray, Dulcie, P-174
Gray, Jennifer, P-100, P-101
Gray, Linda, P-88
Gray, Peter, P-110, P-124,
    T-20

Gray, Timothy, 25, P-161, P-163
Graye, Carol, P-109
Great God Brown, The, B-36
Great Name, The, 2, P-3
Green, Adolph, F-11
Green, Babbie, P-221
Green, Guy, F-27
Green, Keith, P-144
Green, Lois, P-135
Green, Martyn, T-8
Green, Philip, P-135
Green, Ruby, P-90
Green, Simon, 209
Greenbaum, Hyam, P-70
Greene, Graham, F-22
Greenwald, Raymaond J., P-213
Greenwell, Peter, P-155, T-74
Greenwood, Clifford, P-83, D-19, D-81
Greenwood, Jane, P-176
Greenwood, Joan, P-166
Greet, Claire, P-47, P-23
Gregg, Everley, P-61, P-80, P-83, P-91, F-11, F-1 , F-19
Gregg, Hubert, P-174, F-15, R-68
Gregg, Paul, P-205
Gregory, Dora, F-15
Gregory, John, D-163
Grenfell, Joyce, 20, P-174, T-68, D-64, D-65, D-82, D-92
Griffies, Ethel, F-7, D-96
Griffin, Tom, P-216, D-120
Griffis, William, P-150
Griffith, D.W., F-1
Griffiths, Jaye, P-209
Grimaldi, Marion, P-135, P-174
Grimes, Tammy, 25, P-150, P-161, P-172, P-189
Grimshaw, Nicholas, P-143
Grimston, Harold Robert, P-2
Grizzard, George, P-170
Grose, Lionel, F-15
Grose, Molly Pickering, P-226
Gross, Paul, P-154
Grossmann, Suzanne, P-172
Groves, Fred, P-56, P-67

Guard, Philip, P-111
Guardsman, The, 16, F-6
Gueroult, Denys, R-67
Guinan, Patricia, P-167
Guiness, Alec, F-22
Gullan, Campbell, P-71
Gurney, Rachel, T-83
Gutierrez, José, P-160
Guys and Dolls, 21

H.M. Tennent Ltd., 19, 23, P-124, P-129, P-139, P-143, P-144, P-151, P-164, P-165, P-175, P-179, P-189,
Hackforth, Norman, P-164, D-37, D-39, D-40
Haden, John, P-193
Hagan, Molly, P-221
Haggard, Piers, T-55
Hale, Binnie, P-96
Hale, Sandra, T-81
Hale, Sonnie, 10, 11, P-56
Halinka, Anna P-135
Hall, Geogine, P-202
Hall, Irlin, P-109
Hall, Margaret, P-161
Hall, Walter, P-225
Hall, Willis, F-27
Hallard, C.M., P-45
Halle, John, P-177
Halsey, Janice, P-193
Hamilton, Anna, P-163
Hamilton, Cosmo, P-23
Hamilton, Dorothy, P-91
Hamilton, Guy, P-174
Hamilton, Hazel, P-23
Hamilton, Lance, P-116, P-145, P-146, T-12
Hamlisch, Marvin, P-214
Hammerstein, Oscar, D-18, D-27
Hammond, Kay, P-97, P-105, F-9, F-17
Hampden, Burford, P-2
Hampshire, Susan, P-174, P-223, D-122
Hampton, Grayce, P-43, P-80
Hancock, Christopher, T-58
Hancock, Lucy, T-80
Handle, Irene, F-18

Handley, Broian, P-163
Hands Across The Sea, 17, P-83, P-84, P-201, T-86-94
Haney, Sheila, P-194
Hanley, Dell, P-160
Hannah, Chris, T-86-94
Hannele, 3, P-9
Hannen, Nicholas, P-126
Happy Family, The, Pf-17
Haraldson, Marian, P-160
Harbord, Carl, P-78, T-1
Harcourt, George, P-39
Harding, Jeff, P-205
Harding, John, T-83
Harding, Lyn, P-18
Harding, Phyllis, P-18, P-57, P-70, P-78, P-80
Hardman, Lwrence, R-17
Hardwick, Paul, P-193
Hardwicke, Sir Cedric, R-30
Hardwicke, Edward, R-73
Hardy, Cherry, P-120, P-146
Hardy, Robert, T-49
Hare, Betty, P-67, P-70, P-83, P-109, P-129, P-153, P-156, P-174
Hare, Doris, P-70, R-73, D-53
Hargreaves, Janet, P-215
Harker, Joseph & Philip, P-26
Harkin, Dennis, F-18
Harman, Victor, P-117
Harmon, April, P-32
Harn, Bill, P-70
Harris, Doris, P-2
Harris, George W., P-43, P-44, P-45, P-48
Harris, Judieth, T-68
Harris, Leonore, P-108
Harris, Lionel, T-20
Harris, Radie, 27, P-184,
Harris, Robert, P-43, P-47, P-49, P-215
Harris, Rosemary, P-210, T-44
Harris, Sam, P-39
Harrison, Kathleen, F-15
Harrison, Mona, P-3, P-36, P-79
Harrison, Rex, P-91, P-160, F-17, T-5
Harrison, W.A.H., P-67

Harrity, Rory, P-150
Harron, Robert, F-1
Hart, Cecilia, P-190, P-208
Hart, Josephine, P-217, P-221
Harte, Jerry, T-84
Harter, Sarah, P-159
Hartnell, Norman, P-57
Hartung, Robert, T-44
Harty, Patricia, P-154
Harvey, Alton, P-157
Harvey, Elwyn, P-146
Harvey, James, P-3
Harvey, Laurence, T-55,
    D-101, D-164
Harvey, Morris, P-34
Harvey, Patrick, T-58
Harwood, Marjorie, P-69
Haskell, Judith, P-161
Hastings, J.B., P-37, D-46
Hatch, Wilbur, R-40
Hatherton, Arthur, P-27
Hauptmann, Gerhardt, P-9
Hauxvell, John, D-121, D-123
Havers, Nigel, T-84
Hawthorne, David, P-46
Hawtrey, Charles, 2, 3, P-3,
    P-4, P-7, P-11, P-20, P-25,
Hay Fever, 6, 8, 13, 14, 25, 26
    27, P-38, P-40, P-68, P-69, P-74,
    P-95, P-124, P-162, P-168, P-
    176, P-206, P-210, P-227, F-30,
    R-17, R-41, R-75, T-1, T-2, T-
    25, T-54, , T-56, T-95, B-30, B-
    67, B-74, B-88, B-147, B-229
Haydn, Richard, P-88, P-90
Haydon, Julie, 17, F-11
Haye, Helen, 5, P-18, P-27
Hayes, Carlton, P-140
Hayes, Claire, P-216
Hayes, Helen, 17, 27, P-81,
    P-184, F-11, R-35, R-46, B-117
Hayes, Margaret, T-8
Hayes, Patricia, T-81
Hayes, Tommy, P-56, P-57,
    P-70, P-75, P-79, P-88
Hayward, Louis, P-74, P-75,
    P-80, D-55
Hazell, Hy, P-174
Heal, Joan, P-128, P-174
Hearn, James, P-3

Heart of a Woman, T-9
Hearts of The World
    (Cavalcade), F-1
Heatherley, Clifford, P-58, F-9
Heawood, John, P-146, T-60
Hecht, Ben, 17, P-181, F-10,
    F-11
Hector, Louis, T-8
Hedderwick, Cari, P-179
Hedley, Jack, T-69
Heflin, Van, R-44
Heilbron, Vivien, T-58
Highley, Bruce, P-190
Helbig, Herbert, P-180
Hellier, Marjorie, P-112
Hello, Dolly!, 25
Helms, Alan, P-154
Helpmann, Robert, P-135
Hembrow, Victor, P-24
Henderson, Dick, F-8
Henderson, Florence, P-160
Henderson, Jo, P-195
Henderson, Marcia, T-9
Henderson, Skitch, T-29
Henderson-Tate, David,
    P-156
Henley, Drewe, P-164, P-185
Henley, Joan, R-17
Henri, Marc, P-57
Henriques, Pauline, P-112
Henritze, Bette, P-202
Henry, Leonard, P-34
Henry, Mark, P-34
Henry, Richard, T-54
Henson, Gladys, P-71, P-74,
    P-80, P-87, P-88, P-90, P-92
Henson, Nicky, P-174
Hepburn, Audrey, F-25
Hepple, Jeanne, P-167
Herbert, A.J., P-120
Herbert, Diana, T-8
Herbert, F. Hugh, T-8
Herbert, Evelyn, P-77
Herbert, Rachel, P-211
Herrmann, Bernard, R-21
Hersholt, Jean, F-6
Heslewood, Tom, P-4
Hesterberg, Trude, F-2
Hewer, John, P-156, P-157
Heyman, John, F-28

Heywood, Tim, P-215, P-225
Hibbert, Geoffrey, F-15
Hick, C. Bailey, P-43, P-215
Hickey, Bill, T-47
Hickey, William, T-23
Hickman, Charles, P-95, P-185
Hicks, Barbara, P-151, P-162
Hicks, Sir Seymour, 17
Hickson, Joan, P-191
High Spirits, 25, P-146, P-161,
    P-163, D-110, D-133, D-134, D-
    177, D-178, B-165, B-249
Hignell, Rose, P-58, P-109
Hill, Benny, F-30
Hill, Noël, P-215
Hill, Renee, P-117, P-124
Hill, Rosemary, T-59
Hiller, Wendy, R-61
Hinchco, Tamara, T-58
Hindle, Madge, T-83
Hinton, Tyrell, P-2
Hitchcock, Alfred, 11, F-4
Hoare, Philip, T-95
Hobbes, Haliwell, P-24, P-43,
    P-215
Hobson, Valerie, F-20
Hodge, Edward, F-18
Hodge, Patricia, P-212, P-219
Hoey, Dennis, T-1
Hogan, Bob, P-163
Hogarth, Lionel, P-43, P-215
Holden, Fay, F-13
Holden, William, F-25
Holder, Geoffrey, T-47
Holland, Anthony, P-116,
    P-185
Holland, Jack, P-56
Holland, Robert, R-12
Holliday, David, P-156
Holliday, Judy, 24, P-154
Hollis, Alan, P-35, P-39, F-3
Hollis, Stephen, P-195
Holloway, Baliol, P-9
Holloway, Jean, R-45
Holloway, Julian, P-174
Holloway, Stanley, P-28,
    P-174, F-16, F-18, F-20
Holm, Celeste, P-161,
Holm, Ian, T-83
Holmes, Jill, P-163

Holmes, Peter, P-160
Holmes, Tracey, P-59
Holt, Carol, P-225
Holtzman, Fanny, 16, B-14
Home and Colonial (South Sea Bubble), P-143, B-255
Home Chat, 9, 13, P-51, P-69, B-73, B-76, B-89
Home, Sally, P-177
Hood, Curtis, P-154
Hope, Bob, P-138, P-184
Hopkins, Miriam, 17, F-10
Hopper, Hedda, R-22
Horden, Michael, P-19
Horlock, David, P-212
Horne, David, P-144
Horner, Richard, P-161
Horsey, Helen, P-109, P-111
Horsley, Bill, P-135
Horsley, John, T-83
Horspool, Maurice, R-61
Horton, Edward Everett, F-10
Horton, Helen, P-205, T-84, T-85
Hossack, Grant, P-174
Houseman, John, R-21
Houston, Donald, T-43
Howard, Cuthbert, P-2
Howard, Lance, T-10
Howard, Norah, P-14, P-58, P-70, T-13, D-96
Howard, Thomas, F-17
Howard, Trevor, F-18, F-27, T-8
Howe, George, P-193
Howell, Jonathan, P-212
Howell, Ursula, T-34, T-84
Howes, Bobby, P-92, P-103
Howes, Sally Ann, T-29
Howland, Beth, P-161
Howlett, Stanley, P-117
Hoyt, Julia, P-68
Hubbard, Elizabeth, P-202
Huby, Robert, P-121
Huebling, Craig, P-150
Hughes, Hazel, P-186, T-54
Hughes, Ian, P-201
Hughes, Michael, P-193
Hughes, Mick, P-193, P-227
Hughes, Raymond, T-60

Hughes, Spike, P-70
Hulbert, Jack, 4, P-15, B-160
Hully, Tony, P-92
Hume, Doreen, D-163
Hume, Roger, P-211
Humphirse, Alison, T-95
Humphry, John, P-131
Hunt, Chris, T-95
Hunt, James, P-163
Hunt, Martita, F-20, F-26
Hunt, Peter, P-170
Hunt, Wish Mary, P-154
Hunter, Ian, P-143, F-4, F-13
Hunter, Peter, P-212
Huntley, G.P., P-57
Huntley, Raymond, P-105
Huntley-Wright, Betty, P-58
Hurst, David, P-150
Hurst, James, P-154
Hutchinson, Leslie, P-56
Hutchinson, Stuart, P-216
Hutt, William, P-153, P-154
Huxley, Carol, D-97
Hylton, Jack, D-78
Hylton, Millie, P-23
Hyman, Prudence, P-112
Hymes, Phil, T-47
Hyton, Anne, P-44

I'll Leave It To You, 6, 13, P-25, P-69, B-76, B-90
Iagnocco, Ray, P-187
Ibetson, Arthur, T-69
Ida Collaborates, 5, P-19
Idear, P-57
In Which We Serve, 19, F-14, R-29, R-30, R-31, T-95, B-30
Inescort, Elaine, P-58
Ingham, Winefride, P-109, D-71
Inglis, Jean, P-117
Ingram, Pamela, P-175
Innes, George, P-221
Ireland, Anthony, P-112
Irvine, Robert, F-4
Irving, Ernest, P-56, D-142
Irving, John, T-9
Irwin, Carol, R-39
Island Fling, P-143, B-255
Italian Job, The, F-30

Ives, Burl, F-22
Ivey, Dana, P-202, P-214
Izen, Rachel, P-216
Izzard, Bryan, T-86-94

Jackson, Anna, P-90
Jackson, Felix, T-6
Jackson, Gordon, P-174
Jackson, Nancie, T-57
Jacob, Fordon, D-129
Jacob, Naomi, P-30
Jacobi, Derek, 25, P-162, P-207
Jacques, Hattie, T-35
Jaffe, Carl, P-109
Jaffe, Henry, T-27
Jakob, Vera, T-86-94
James, Finlay, P-205, P-214
James, Graham, P-174
Janney, Leon, P-120
Jason, Neville, D-125
Jayston, Michael, P-197, T-95
Jean, Desmond, P-59
Jean, Isabel, P-84, P-126, F-3
Jeans, Ronald, P-32
Jeans, Ursula, 10, F-8
Jefferies, Douglas, P-25
Jeffries, Ellis, P-20
Jellinek, Tristram, P-217
Jenkins, George, P-113
Jenkinson, Jerry, P-217
Jenn, Myvanyn, D-181
Jennings, Alex, P-209, T-95
Jensen, John, P-194
Jephcott, Dominic, T-86-94
Jerrold, Mary, P-20, F-20
Jesse, Stella, P-25
Jewell, Isabel, F-10
Jewesbury, Edward, T-86-94
Joel, Doris, 5, P-22
Johns, Glynis, 27, P-174, P-184, T-49
Johnson, Arte, T-27
Johnson, Celia, P-168, P-174, F-15, F-16, F-18, F-19, R-70, T-54, T-59, T-68
Johnson, Dorothy, D-97
Johnson, Geoffrey, 26, 27, P-184
Johnson, Gloria, P-163

Johnson, Jill, P-198, T-73
Johnson, Molly, P-101
Johnson, Richard, P-191
Johnson, Roy, P-120
Johnston, Alick, P-46, P-76
Johnston, Barney, P-160
Johnston, Colin, P-49
Jon, Robert, P-213
Jonah, Willie, P-186
Jones, Alan, P-77
Jones, Arthur, P-59
Jones, Caroline, T-9
Jones, Griffith, P-88, P-129,
    T-35
Jones, Henry, T-6
Jones, Peter, P-126
Jones, Simon, P-224
Joseph, Philip, T-85
Jourdan, Louis, B-209
Journey's End, P-60, P-225
Joy, Robert, P-210
Joyce, Phyllis, P-40
*Joyeux Chagrins (Present
    Laughter)*, 21, P-115
Judels, Charles, F-13
Judge, Ian, P-216, D-120
Julia, Raul, P-208
Julian Kane, 5
Justice, Barry, T-49, T-57

Kaler, Berwick, P-209
Kaliz, Armand, F-10
Kander, John, P-146, P-210
Kane, Richard, T-86-94
Kapoor, Shashi, F-27
Karaviotis, Joseph, P-216
Karol, Tom, P-193
Kaszner, Kurt, P-150, T-47
Katselas, Milton, P-203
Kauflin, Jack, P-161
Kaufman, George S., 14, P-79
Kaufman, Martin, P-222
Kawahara, Takashi, T-84
Kay, Anthony, P-109
Kay, Hershy, P-178
Kaye, Danny, P-127
Kaye, Gloria, P-146
Kean, Edmund, 18
Kean, Marie, P-194
Kearns, Vivien, P-117

Kedrova, Lila, P-211
Keffe, Dorothy, P-67
Keep, Claire, P-35
Keith, Lawrence, P-161
Keith, Penelope, P-206, P-207,
    T-71
Keith, Sheila, P-164
Kellogg, Marjorie Bradley,
    P-202
Kelly, Clyde, P-77
Kelly, George, B-38
Kelly, Sean, P-151
Kelso, Vernon, P-43, P-215
Kemball, Colin, P-117
Kemble, Cooper, Anthony,
    P-68
Kemble, Colin, D-74
Kemp-Welch, Joan, T-34
Kendall, Chrissie, T-82
Kendall, Gail, P-117
Kendall, Henry, P-27
Kendall, Jo, T-80
Kendall, Kay, B-209
Kendall, Madge, 12
Kendall, Pat & Terry, P-37
Kennedy, Bill, P-161
Kennedy, Cheryl, P-174
Kennedy, Madge, 13, R-4
Kennedy, Margaret, 9, P-46
Kennedy, Robert, P-218
Kenny, Joyce, P-47
Kent, Kenneth, P-46
Kent, Michael, P-111
Kenyon, Nancye, P-27
Kern, Jerome, D-18, D-26,
    D-27
Kernan, David, P-174, T-74
Kerr, Deborah, F-24
Kerr, G., R-5
Kerr, Molly, P-35, P-39
Kershaw, Willette, F-3
Kibrig, Joan, P-146
Kidd, Michael, F-29
Kilgren, Cheryl, P-154
Kilty, Jerome, P-139
Kimbrough, Charles, P-210
Kinder, David, P-216
King and I, The, 21, B-249
King's Singer, The, D-166
King, Ada, P-45, P-53

Kirby, Max, P-59
Kirk, Lisa, P-208
Kirk, Mark-Lee, T-9
Kirkwood, Pat, P-117, P-174,
    D-72, D-73
Kirsten, Dorothy, R-47
Kiss Me, Kate, 9
Klausner, Terri, P-200
Knapp, Bridget, P-154
Knapp, Terence, P-174
Kneebone, Tom, P-170, T-66
Knight of the Burning Pestle,
    5, P-24, P-26
Knight, David, P-174
Knight, Peter, T-74
Knight, Ray, T-84
Knightley, Will, P-225
Knode, Charles, T-59
Knowles, Michael, P-218
Kock, Howard, R-21
Kohler, Estelle, P-201
Kostelanetz, André, 23, P-142,
    D-85
Koushouris, John, T-10
Kovac, Ernie, F-21
Kraly, Hans, F-6
Kroeger, Berry, P-120
Kronman, harry, R-40
Kruger, Otto, 13, P-63, R-4
Kruschen, Jack, P-174
Kulukundis, Eddie, P-201,
    P-223
Kunkerly, Kathy, P-163
Kurnitz, Harry, 25, P-160, F-23
Kurvenal, Christian, P-159

L.O.P. Ltd., P-151
Labour, Elain, P-160
Lacey, Joantha, T-80
Lack, Simon, P-124
Ladbrook Sara-Jane, T-58
Lady Windermere's Fan, 22,
    P-135
LaGuardia, Fiorello, R-32
Lahr, John, T-95
Lahti, Christine, P-202
Laine, Cleo, P-174, T-55, T-74
Lamb, Celia, P-109
Lamb, Reginald, P., P-4
Lamb, Rosemary, R-76

Lambelet, Kathleen, P-59
Lambert, Jack, P-117
Lambert, Muriel, P-46
Lambton, Anne, P-217
Lamont, Fiona, P-216
Lamour, Dorothy, 8
Lancaster, Lucie, P-160, T-8
Lancaster, Osbert, T-68
Landers, Dana, P-221
Landi, Elissa, P-46
Landi, Jami, P-160
Landis, Jessie Royce, F-20
Landon, Avice, P-164
Landon, Ross, P-88, P-91,
    D-59
Landor, Rosalyn, P-206
Landwehr, Hugh, P-221
Lane, Dorothy, P-84
Lane, George, P-111
Lane, Maurice, P-163
Lane, Nathan, P-202
Lang, Belinda, P-198, T-73
Lang, Doreen, P-98, T-3
Lang, Joan, P-95
Lang, Otto, T-9
Lang, Robert, P-162
Langella, Frank, P-208
Langford, Bonnie, T-86-94
Langford, William, P-114
Langton, Diane, T-86-94
Lanti, Al, P-161
Larchet, George, P-95
Larkin, Mary, T-58
Larrimore, Francine, P-48
Larry, Sheldon, T-70
LaRue, Danny, P-174, T-68
Lascelles, Eric, P-2
Last Resource, The, R-3
Latham, Philip, T-59
Lathbury, Stanley, P-23
Laurent, Henri, P-3
Laurie, Hugh, T-81
Laurie, John, P-88
Laurie, St. John, P-75, P-78
Lavelle, Bradley, T-85
Lavers, Colin, T-86-94
Lawrence, Bill, R-40
Lawrence, Gertrude, 3, 7, 11,
    12, 13, 16, 17, 21, 25, P-9, P-32,
    P-33, P-34, P-42, P-58, P-61, P-

62, P-63, P-83, P-113, P-204,
    P212, P219, F-6, F-29, R-15, R-
    19, R-21, R-32, R-51, T-80, D-5,
    D-20, D-21, D-22, D-44, D-45,
    D-47, D-51, D-52, D-86, D-87,
    D-88, D-92, D-152, D-153, B-
    119, B-168, B-184, B-193, B-256
Lawrence, Henry, P-154
Lawrence, Miriam, P-161
Lawrence, Vernon, T-74
Lawton, Fran, F-8
Laye, Evelyn, 11, 12, P-59, R-
    36,R-70, D-50, D-159
Laye, Gilbert, P-23
Layton, Joe, 25, P-156, P-157,
    P-160, P-178, T-47, D-115
Lea, Barbara, D-181
Leach, John, D-102
Leach, Rosemary, T-69
Lean, David, F-15, F-16, F-17,
    T-95
Leavins, Arthur, R-68
Lee, Auriol, P-29, P-39, P-41
Lee, Bernard, P-111
Lee, John, P-164
Lee, Renee, P-161
Lee, Vanessa, P-135, P-174,
    R-58, D-121, D-163
Leech, Richard, P-124
Leeds, Barbara, T-1
Leeds, Sandy, P-160
Leggatt, Alison, P-67, P-83,
    P-174, F-16
Leggatt, Norman, P-163
Legrand Michel, F-27
Leichke, Harry, F-2
Leigh, Adele, D-122
Leigh, Janet, T-17
Leigh, Louise, P-22
Leigh, Vivien, 23, P-82, P-127,
    P-143, P-151, T-12, T-15
Leighton, Margaret, P-131,
    F-19, T-57, D-106, D-107
LeMessena, William, P-141,
    P-214
LeMessurier, Jon, T-69
Lenn, Robert, P-161
Lenska, Rula, P-218, T-72
Leon, Sydney, P-24
Leonard, Queenie, P-57, P-64

Leonard, Robert Z. F-14
Lerner, Alan Jay, B-169
Les Amants Terrible (Private
    Lives), 16, F-12
Lesley-Green, Carol, P-16
Leslie, Cole, 23, 26, P-184,
    T-68, B-170
Leslie, Enid, P-3
Leslie, Fred, P-80
Leslie, Lew, P-50
Leslie, Sylvia, P-59, P-78
Lester, John, P-201
Lester, Margot, P-40
Levey, Harold, R-38, R-39
Levin, Herman, 25, P-160
Levine, Maurice, P-196, T-75
Levy, José G., P-29
Lewis, Dianna, F-13
Leis, Fred, P-15, P-23
Lewine, Richard, T-10, T-11,
    T-13
Lewis, J.J., P172
Lewis, Martin, P-97, R-12
Lewis, Michael, P-139
Lewis Ronald, P-143
Lewis, Russell, P-113
Liberace, 22, B-205
Libin, Paul, P-202, P-208
Lieberson, Goddard, D-96
Light Blues, The, 4, P-15
Lillie, Beatrice, 10, 14, 17, 25
    P-33, P-42, P-65, P-57, P-73, P-
    90, P-92, P-161, F-5, F-21, T-5,
    T-29, D-47, D-60, D-61, D-62,
    D-63, D-86, D-92, D-101, D-
    145, D-146, D-147, D-148, D-
    149, D-150, D-151, B-182,
    B-165, B-173, B-226
Lilo, R-55
Limpus, Alan B., P-49
Limpus, Alban P., P-38
Lincoln, Diana, P-116
Lind, Cherry, R-68
Linden, Jennie, T-34
Linden, Leon, T-43
Linden, Marta, P-108
Linden, Robert, P-170
Lindsay, Margaret, F-8
Linley, Betty, P-68
Linnit & Dunfree Ltd., P-163

Lister, Francis, P-45
Lister, Lance, P-37, P-56
Lister, Moira, P-110, P-174, R-69
Lister, Rupert, P-49
Little Fowl Play, A P-7
Little, Caryl, P-174, T-55
Littler, Prince, P-109
Livesay, Sam, P-76
Livesay, Roger, P-24
Livingston, Sidney, T-80
Lloyd, Doris, T-9
Lloyd, Frank, F-8
Lloyd, Hugh, P-201
Loan, Leonard, P-48
Locke, Shamus, P-135
Lockwood, Margaret, P-185
Loden, Barbara, P-150
Loder, John, R-52
Loesser, Frank, P-14
Lohr, Marie, P-153
Lomax, Rosemary, P-88, P-90
Lombard, Carole, R-20
London Calling!, 7, P-32, D-10, D-19, D-44, D-45, D-46, D-152, D-156
London Morning, 23, P-152, D-129
London Topical Talk, R-34
London, Jack, P-67
Long Island Sound, T-85
Long, William Ivey, P-224
Look After Lulu, 23, 27, P-150, P-151, P-193, T-19, T-48, B-17, B-71, B-91
Lordan, Elaine, T-81
Loren, Sophia, T-69
Losch, Tilly, 10, P-56, P-57
Losey, Joe, F-28
Lotinga, Doreen, R-12
Lotterby, Sidney, T-86-94
Loudon, Dorothy, P-170, D-164
Lovat, Nancie, P-15
Lowenfeld, Henry, P-11
Lowrrie, Arthur, P-32
Lubitsch, Ernst, 16, F-10
Luboff, Norman, R-45
Lucas, Philip, F-19
Ludlow, Patrick, P-59, F-9

Luguet, André, F-12
Lui, Kalen, F-27
Luke, Peter, T-30
Lumb, Geoffrey, T-44
Lumley, Joanna, P-204, P-211
Lumley, Molly, P-75, P-88, P-153
Lunt, Alfred, 6, 9, 13, 14, 15, 22, P-71, P-73, P-80, P-127, P-129, P-139, F-6, T-63, T-65, B-22, B-256
Lupino, Richard, T-9
LuPone, Robert, P-170
Luscombe, Tim, P-21, P-220
Lustgarten, Edgar, R-71
Lyell, Kathleen Ross, P-2
Lyle, Rita, P-70
Lynch, Nancy, P-154, P-160
Lynch, Thomas, P-208
Lynley, Carol, F-26
Lynn, Iola, P-145
Lynn, Jonathan, P-201
Lynn, Mary, P-92
Lynne, Gillian, P-177, T-55
Lyric Revue, The, P-121, D-37
Lytton, Doris, P-11

MacArthur, Charles, 17, P-81, F-11
MacCormack, Edward, P-84
Macdermott, Norman, P-35
MacDonald, Jeanette, 16, F-13, R-45, D-77, D-124, D-158, D-160, D-161, B-211
MacDonald, Murray, P-168
MacDonald, Stephen, P-217
Macfarlane, Peter, P-43, P-215
MacGill, Sheila, F-8
MacGowan, Kenneth, P-52
MacKay, Alex, P-161
MacKay, Ann, P-216
Makay, Percival, D-18
MacKenzie, John, T-51
Mackie, J. Marr, P-135
MacLaine, Shirley, F-21
MacLiammoir, Michael, T-68
MacNaughton, Alan, P-177, T-59
MacOwan, Michael, P-126, P-131, T-40

MacOwan, Norman, P-4
Macrae, Arthur, P-67, P-87, P-143
MacRae, Gordon, R-45, R-48, R-53
Mad About The Boy, T-70
Madden, Clara, T-59
Maddox, Daphne, P-111
Madeira, Jean, T-17
Mademoiselle, P-84
Main, Marjorie, F-14
Mainbocher, P-114, T-10
Maitland, Mollie, P-30
Makeham, Eliot, R-12
Malcolm, Christopher, P-186
Malet, Arthur, P-150
Malina, Luba, P-145
Mandell, Pamela, T-85
Mander, Miles, F-9
Manetto, Corina, P-146
Manie, Ambrose, P-30
Mann, Jack, P-203
Mann, Theodore, P-202, P-208
Mannheim, Lucie, F-26
Manning, Hugh, P-131
Mantel, Doreen, T-84
Mantovani, P-107, P-109, P-117, D-36, D-64, D-66, D-67, D-68, D-69, D-70, D-70, D-72, D-73, D-74
Manulis, Martin, P-114
Mapp, Neville, P-112
Maranne, André, T-82
March, Elspeth, P-11
March, Fredric, 17, F-7, F-10
Marchant, William, T-43, T-48, T-49, B-178
Margetson, Arthur, P-51
Margolies, Miriam, T-74, T-86-84
Maria, Jaqueline, P-161
Mariano, Patti, P-154
Markle, Fletcher, R-41
Markson, Hadassah, B., P-196
Marlay, Andrew B., P-195
Marmount, Pam, P-135
Marquand, John, P-95
Marquise, The, 9, P-49, P-52, T-59, B-58, B-76, B-92
Mars, Marjorie, F-18

Marsh, Jean, T-70
Marshall, David, T-49
Marshall, Herbert, P-30, P45,
    R-16, R-40, R-43
Marshall, Very, T-13
Marsland, Nancy B., P-43,
    P-215
Martel, Gillian, T-58
Martell, Philip, P-135
Martin, Ann, P-109
Martin, Charles, R-26, R-29
Martin, Denis, P-109
Martin, Edie, P-67
Martin, Hugh, 25, P-161
Martin, Jessica, T-86-94
Martin, Mary, 20, 22, P109,
    P-125, P-130, T-10, D-67, D-68,
    D-71, D-105, B-179, B-198
Martin, Millicent, P-177,
    P-181, R-75
Martin, Rosemary, P-159
Martin, Troy Kennedy, F-30
Martindale, Gilian, P-156
Marvelous Party!, T555
Marx, Chico, R-20
Marx, Groucho, R-20
Mason, Herbert, P-32
Mason, James, P-69
Mason, Reginald, P-120
Mason, Virginia, T-55
Massary, Fritzi, P-88, D-57
Massey, Anna, F-26, T-54
Massey, Daniel, 5, P-31, F-15,
    F-29, R-70, T-95
Massey, Raymond, 10, P-47,
    P-5, B-180
Massine, Leonide, P-37
Masterson, Valeri, P-216,
    T-55, D-120
Matalon, Vivian, P-165, P-187
Matera, Barbara, P-172
Mather, Aubrey, P-46
Mathews, George, T-47
Mathias, Sean, P-223
Matter Of Innocence, A, F-27,
    T-43
Mattews, A.E., P-48
Matthews, Art, P-160
Matthews, Jessie, 10, 11, P-56,
    P-174

Matz, Peter, P-140, 146, T-10,
    D-97, D-98
Maud, P-165
Maude, Jacqueline, P-164
Maugham, W. Somerset, F-20,
    B-27, B-181
Maxwell, Edwin, F-7
Maxwell, Elsa, 6
Maxwell, Roberta, P-176
May, Ada, P-64
May, Bunny, P-174
May, Jack, F-18
Mayer, Edwin Justus, F-7
Maynard, Ted, T-85
Mazin, Stan, P-161
McAlister, David, P-204
McAuliffe, Nichola, T-82
McCallum, Charley, P-157
McCallum, David, T-24
McCallum, Joanna, P-209
McCambridge, Mercedes,
    R-33
McCarthy, Daniel, P-11
McCarthy, John, P-11, P-207
McCarthy, Julia, P-205
McCormick, Myron, T-23
McCowen, Alec, T-71
McDermott, Hugh, P-124
McDonald, Graeme, T-57
McDowall, Roddy, P-150
McDowell, Norman, P-152
McEwan, Geraldine, P-188,
    P193
McGee, Henry, T-86-94
McGrath, Joe, P-161
McGrath, Katherine, P-190
McGrath, Pat, P-109, D-66
McGroder, Jack, P-200
McGuigan, William, P-67
McIntire, Paddy, T-55
McIntyre, James, P-91
McKail, David, T-57
McKechnie, James, R-61
McKellen, Ian, T-54
McKenna, Siobhan, T-18
McKenzie, Julia, D-170
McLaughlin, Gibb, F-9
McLennan, Rod, P-174
McManus, John, P-85, P-90
McMichael, Peter, T-81

McMorrough, Lynett, P-218
McNamara, Dermot, T-8
McNutt, Paterson, P-68
McRae, Carmen, D-165
McRae, Maureen, P-194
McWhinnie, Donald, T-58
Meadows, Julie, P-163
Me and The Girls, T-82
Mead, Margaret, T-64
Meadmore, Michael, T-86-94
Meadows, Leslie, P-171
Measor, Beryl, P-99, P-110,
    P-101, T-4
Meet Me Tonight, F-20
Mehuhin, Yehudi, 26
Meiser, Edith, P-120
Melville, Alan, R-73, T-57,
    T-67
Menjou, Adolph, R-14, R-22
Menuhin, Yehudi, 27, P-183
Menzies, Angus, P-90, P-109
Menzies, Rod, P-194
Mercer, Beryl, F-8
Mercer, Marian, P-176
Merival, John, P-174
Merkel, Una, F-6
Merman, Ethel, 22, P-73,
    P-154
Marrall, Mary, P-79, F-20
Merrick, David, P-172
Merry Widow, The, 2
Messel, Oliver, P-57
Messina, Cedric, T-54, T-59,
    T-71
Metaxa, George, P-58, D-49
Meyer, Greta, F-14
Michael, Ralph, P-111, P-124
Michaels, Louis I., P-193
Michel, Leonard, P-75, P-78
Michell, Keith, P-160, P-161,
    R-73
Michelmore, Jenny, P-209
Michie, Ian, P-225
Middle East Diary, B-48
Middleton, George, P-27
Middleton, Sally-Ann, P-16
Mielziner, Jo, P-52, P-54
Mike Sammes Singers, P-174
Miles, Bernard, F-15
Miles, Margaret, P-117

Millar, Gertie, 2
Miller, Gilbert, P-20, P-25, P-27
Miller, Louis, P-59
Mills, Clifford, P-4
Mills, Gordon, P-108, P-120
Mills, Grace, P-108
Mills, Hayley, F-27
Mills, John, P-60, P-67, P70, F-15, F-16, T-68, T-95
Mills, Juliet, F-15
Mills, Michael, T-60
Milman, Martin, P-193
Milman, Yvette, P-193
Milne, Alexis, P-112
Milton, Billy, P-57, P-58
Minskoff, Jerome, P-214
Minty, Jeanette, P-152
Miracle in 49th Street (The Scoundrel), 17, F-11, B-162
Mireille, P-59
Mirvsch, Ed, P-194
Mitchell, Arthur, P-170
Mitchell, Byron, P-139
Mitchell, David, P-203
Mitchell, Esther, P-120
Mitchell, Sheila, P-198, T-73
Mitchell, Terry, P-174
Mitchum, Robert, F-24
Moffat, Alice, P-27
Moffatt, John, P-174, P-131, P-181
Mohyeddin, Zia, T-43
Moiseiwitsch, Tanya, P-112
Molecey, John, P-111
Molyneux, 6, P-76, P-84, P-165
Molyneux, Eileen, P-32
Molyneux, William, T-8
Monast, Fernand, P-163
Monkman, Dorothy, P-67
Monkman, Phyllis P-8, P-34
Monroe, Donna, P-160
Montagnese, John, P-200
Montgomery, Earl, P-150
Montgomery, Robert, 16, F-6, R-7, R-22
Moody, Dorothy, 3, P-9
Moody, Ivy, P-9
Moonlight Is Silver, D-88
Mooney, Roger, P-195

Moore, Dudley, T-42
Moore, Grace, T-85
Moore, Hilda, P-3, P-38
Moore, John, P-143
Moore, Mary, P-25, P-46
Moore, Roger, T-13
Moore, Ruswsell, T-75
Morales, Carmen, P-160
Moray, Stella, P-156, P-174
More, Kenneth, P-111
Moreno, Rosit, F-11
Morgan, Al, T-29
Morgan, Eric, P-24
Morgan, Fidelis, P-217
Morgan, Helen, P-66
Morgan, James, P-113, P226
Morgenthau, Henry, R-28
Morlay, Gaby, F-12
Morley, John, P-135
Morley, Robert, P-174, P-199
Morley, Sheridan, P-199, P-204, P-212, P-219, P-223, P-226, T-61, B-192, B-193, B-194
Morley, Susannah, P-225
Morell, Henry, P-4
Morrill, Priscilla, P-167
Morris, Jonathan, P-146
Morris, Leonard, P-88
Morris, Richard, T-84
Morrish, Ann, T-30
Morrow, Alex, P-163
Mort, Patricia, T-57
Morthen, Michael, P-174
Mortimer, Charles, P-59
Mortimer, John, P-26, T-67
Mortimer, Penelope, P-26
Morton, Hmphrey, P-44
Mosley, Peter, P-109
Moss, Farries, P-69
Moss, Marjorie, P-57
Moss, Sandra, P-214
Motley, P-153, P-162, P-168
Mount, Peggy, P-218
Mousetrap, The, 19
Mowbray, Alan, F-14
Mower, Margaret, P-154
Moxon, Henry, T-83
Mr. & Mrs. Edgehill, T-83
Mr. & Mrs., P-171
Mrs. Capper's Birthday, T-48,

T-81, D-171
Mundie, Malcolm, P-201
Muir, Gavin, P-40
Mundin, Herbert, F-8
Muntz, Betty, P-37
Marai, Ilona, P-160
Murray, Barbara, T-34
Murray, Brian, P-210, P-214, P-226
Murray, William, P-111
Murrow, Edward, R., 23, T-12, T-18, B-203
Musical Jubilee, A, P-189
Musser, Tharon, P-167, P-203
My Fair Lady, 25, B-249

Nadell, Rosalind, D-97
Naires, Carey, P-160
Naismith, Laurence, P-131
Napier, Alan, P-58, P-74
Nare Geoffrey, P-87
Nash, Ogden, P-142, D-85
Natwick, Mildred, 19, P-98, R-38, R-52, T-11, B-204
Neagle, Anna, P-174, P-185, F-9, T-68, D-79
Neame, Ronald, F-15
Neil, Rebecca, P-209
Neill, Terence, P-48, P-68
Neilson, Richard, P-190
Nelson, Ralph, T-13
Nelson, Richard, P-202, P-214, P-224
Nervo and Knox, P-103
Nesbitt, Cathleen, 27, P-46, P-184, D-96
Nesbitt, Robert, P-174
Nettles, John, T-86-94
Never Say Die, 3, P-11
Neville, Anthony, P-59
Neville, John, P-171
Nevinson, Nancy, T-82
New, Barbara, T-59
New, Derek, P-171
Newley, Anthony, T-86-94
Newman, Stanley, P-24
Newton, Daphne, P-110, P-143, P-175
Newton, Pauline, P-51
Newton, Robert, P-58, F-16,

F-21
Ney, Mariey, P-46
Nicholas, Betty, P-32
Nichole, Allegra, P-129
Nicholls, Anthony, P-162
Nichols, Dandy, P-111, P-174,
    T-43, T-58, T-72
Nicholson, Nora, P-153
Nicholson, Sheila, P-107
Nicholson, Steve, T-86-94
Nicholson, William, P-37, P-49
Night of 100 Stars, P-136,
    P-149
Ninety Years On, T-38
Niven, David, F-21, R-16,
    R-47, T-68
Noble, Ray, D-6, D-9, D-11,
    D-53
Nodin, Gerald, P-58, P-59,
    P-70, P-88
Noël, P-181
Noël and Gertie, P-199, P-204,
    P-212, P-219, P-223, P-226, D-
    137, B-149
Noël Coward In Two Keys,
    P-187, R-76
Noël Coward Company, The,
    13, P-62, P-69
Noël Coward's Sweet Potato,
    26, P-170
Northen, Michael, P-156,
    P-163
Norton, Jim, T-49
Not Yet The Dodo, B-60
Novello, Ivor, 9, 11, 20, P-53,
    F-3, D-163, B-119, B-250
Nude With Violin, 23, P-144,
    P-145, P-147, T-16, T-21, B-79,
    B-93, B-204, B-234
Nugent, Moya, P-12, P-25,
    P-56, P-67, P-70, P-75, P-83, P-
    87, P-90, P-92, P-97, P-109, P-
    129, D-54, D-56
Nurock, Ken, T-70
Nype, Russell, P-169

O'Brian, Gipsy, P-43, P-215
O'Casey, Sean, T-23
O'Connor, Una, P-67, F-8,
    F-16

O'Farrell, Mary, R-12
O'Hara, John, B-210
O'Hara, Maureen, F-22
O'Hara, Patricia Quinn, P-139
O'Keefe, Lester, R-35
O'Keefe, Mary Elen, P-154
O'Keefe, Paul, P-154
O'Mahoney, Nora, T-9
O'Naut, Ayre, 2, P-2
O'Neil, Paddy, T-81
O'Neill, Anne, P-216
O'Neill, Eugene, T-23, B-36,
    B-38, B-136
O'Neill, Joy, P-109
O'Shea, Tessie, P-160, P-174,
    T-32
O'Sullivan, Kate, T-86-94
O'Toole, Peter, P-194
Oberon, Merle, T-9
Oenslager, Donald, P-108
Oglivy, Ian, P-205
Oh Coward!, 26, 27, P-180,
    P-188, P-200, P-213, T-66, T-75,
    D-136
    Gala Performance, P-182
Ohmead, Isobel, P-59, P-112
Okrent, Mike, T-81
Oldak, Violet, P-88
Oldaker, Max, P-88
Oldfield, Kenn, P-204
Oliver, Nora, P-56
Oliver, Prudence, T-86-94
Oliver, Tim, P-209
Olivier, Laurence, 12, 15, 25,
    27, P-61, P-62, P-63, P-76, P-79,
    P-127, P-183, F-26, R-70, T-61,
    T-67, T-95, B-116
Ollerenshaw, Maggie, T-80
Omnibus: Noël Coward, T-56
On With The Dance, 7, 8,
    P-37, D-26, D-42, D-47
Operette, 18, P-88, R-68, D-23,
    D-24, D-25, B-75, B-94, B-237
Orellano, P-58
Orndel, Cyril, T-69
Ortega, Eva, P-90
Orton, Joe, P-214
Osborne, John, T-95
Osterman, Lester, P-161
Osterwald, Bibi, T-6

Osyter, Jim, P-195
Our Man In Havana, 23, F-22
Our Town, T-8
Ovie, Fannie, P-9
Owen, Alan, R-68
Owen, Howard, P-7
Owen, Reginald, P-4, P-14
Oxman, Ken, R-76

Paar, Jack, T-26, T-63
Pacey, Steven, P-225
Pacific 1860, 20, P-109,
    P-138, D-34, D-35, D-42, D-
    126, D-127, D-127, D-164, B-78,
    B-95, B-179, B-197, B-237
Packer, Peter, T-9
Pagan, Peter, P-160
Page, Geraldine, P-214
Page, James, P-14
Painter, Abigail, P-209
Palcine, Anita, P-169
Paley, Natasha, 9
Palham, Peta, P-163
Palk, Anna, P-164
Palmer, Hilde, P-92
Palmer, Lilli, P-165, R-40,
    T-68
Palotta, Irene, P-2
Pangborn, Franklin, F-10
Parfitt, Judy, T-84
Parker, Cecil, 19, P-46,
    P-84, P-97
Parsons, Terry, P-218
Pascal, Francoise, T-71
Passing Fancy (The Girl Who
    Came To Supper), 25
Past Perfect (unfinished
    autobiography), B-138
Patch, Wally, F-15
Paterson, Pat, F-9
Patrick, Gail, F-14
Patrick, Nigel, P-84, P-164,
    P-174, P-175, F-20
Patterson, Dick, F-27
Patterson, Sean, P-215
Pattrick, Sheila, P-75, P-78
Paul, Andrew, T-81
Paul, Ren, P-146
Paull, Guy S., T-13
Pavlow, Murial, R-12

Pawson, Hargrave, P-74
Paye, Robin Fraser, P-191,
    T-71
Payn, Graham, 12, 14, 20, 21,
    23, 25, 26, P-70, P-109, P-113,
    P-117, P121, P-128, P-135, P-
    153, P-163, P-164, P-174, P-184,
    F-19, T-68, T-95, D-65, D-66,
    D-67, D-71, D-72, D-82, B-171
Payne, Edgar, P-3
Pays, Amanda, T-83
Payton, Mark, AP-206
Peace In Our Time, 21, P-111,
    B-2, B-78, B-96, B-150
Peacock, Kim, P-75
Peacock, William, P-143
Pearce, Alice, P-141, P154
Pearson, Leslie, P-135
Pease, Jacqueline, T-85
Peek, Anthony, P-111
Peel, Eileen, F-15
Pedrick, Gale, D-167
Pegler, Mary, P-220
Peile, F. Kinsey, P-35, F-3
Pelissier, Anthony, P-67, P-79,
    P-83, P-90F-20
Pentecost, George P-190
Percassi, Don, P-161
Perceval, Robert, P-193
Percival, Kate, P-193
Percy, Esme, F-9
Peretz, Daphen, P-109
Perilli, Maria, P-109, D-71
Perkins, Osgood, P-80
Perkins, Alberta, P-80
Perkins, Don, P-195
Perleman, S.J., F-21
Person To Person, 23, T-12
Peter Pan, 3, 22, P-12, T-8
Peters, Charles, P-83
Peters, Lucy, P-109
Peters, Roger, P-210
Petrified Forest, The, T-8
Peterson, Alan, P-154
Petherbridge, Edward, P-223
Pettingel, Fran, F-20
Peyton, Bruce, P-160
Philippe, Lorna, R-69
Phillips, Eric, P-143
Phillips, Helean, F-10

Phillips, Margaret, P-141
Phillips, Sian, T-86-94, R-76
Phillot, Gordon, P-129
Phillpotts, Ambrosine, P-112
Piazza, Fernado, F-28
Pickering, Donald, P-206,
    T-71
Pierce, Norman, F-15
Pierce, Sally, T-13
Pierre, Oliver, T-82
Pigeon, Norman, F-28
Piggot, Tempe, F-8
Pilbrow, Richard, P-191
Pinter, Harold, P-191, P-214,
    P-227
Piper, Evelyn, F-26
Piper, Frederieck, F-15
Pithey, Wensley, T-59
Pitot, Genevieve, P-160
Platt, Ian, P-216
Platters, The, T-17
Playfair, Arthur, P-3
Playfair, Nigel, P-24, P-26
Pleis, Jack, D-165
Plummer, Christopher, P-160
Pocher, Ruth, T-34
Podmore, William, P-43,
    P-215
Pogson, Kathryn, T-81
Pohlmann, Eric, F-23
Poindexter, H.R. P-189
Point Valaine, 15, 17, 21, P-79,
    P-112, P-139, B-22, B-54, B-79,
    B-97, B-97, B-197
Pointing, Audre, P-59
Poleri, David, T-8
Pollack, Horace, P-48
Pollock, Elizabeth, P-47
Polly With A Past, 6, P-27
Pond, Helen, P-169, P-170,
    P-180
Pons, Helene, P-154
Pons, Lily, R-14, D-96, B-130
Ponti, Carol, T-69
Pooley, Olaf, P-111
Pope, Muriel, P-20, P-25
Porter, Cole, 22, P-222, F-29,
    D-167, B-136, B-145
Porter, Michael, T-56
Porter, Stephen, P-172, P-190

Porterfield, Christopher, T-63
Possell, Janene, T-84
Post Depression Gaieties,
    P-81
Post, W.H., P-11
Post-Mortem, 27, P-60, P-225,
    T-52, B-68, B-74, B-98, B175
Potts, Nancy, P-190
Pound On Demand, T-23
Pounds, Mary, P-58
Powell, Anthony, P-179,
    P-189
Preminger, Otto, F-26, T-8
Prentice, Charles, P-75
Prentice, Keith, P-154
Prescott, Neville, P-126
Prescourt, Frieda, P-40
Present Indicative, 5, 18, B-42
Present Laughter, 18, 19, 20,
    21, 23, 26, 27, P-100, P-108,
    P110, P-120, P-147, P-?, P-164,
    P-190, P-194, P-198, P-202, T-
    34, T-45, T-73, T-95, D-106, D-
    169, B-2, B-23, B-70, B-77, 99,
    B147, B-238
Preston, Kathy, P-161
Pretty Polly Barlow, F-27,
    T-43, B-57
Price, Dennis, P-100, P-101,
    T-54
Price, Stanley, T-80, T-84,
    T-85
Priestly, Manfred, P-111,
    P-117
Prinsep, Anthony, P-36
Printemps, Yvonne, 14, P-75,
    P-78, D-16, D-54, D-55
Pritchard, Mark, P-201
Pritchard, Nicholas, T-85
Pritchard, Tessa, P-201
Pritchett, James, P-154
Private Life, A, T-79
Private Lives, 7, 12, 13, 16, 19,
    24, 26, 27, P-38, P61, P-63, P-69,
    P-105, P-114, P-124, P-129, P-
    159, P-169, P-172, P-179, P-189,
    P-197, P-198, P-203, P-214, P-
    220, P-224, F-6, F-12, F-29, F-
    30, R-4, R-7, R-13, R-21, R-26,
    r-60, R-68, R-69, R-75, D-5, D-

153, T-20, T-71, D-169, B-30, B-68, B-74, B-100, B-116, B-147, B-175, B-189
Producer's Showcase, T-8
Prosser, David, F-27
Protzman, Albert, T-3
Prouse, Derek, P-129
Prowse, Philip, P-191, P-217, P-221
Prud'homme, Cameron, R-39
Pryor, Maureen, P-111
Pryor, Roger, R-22, R-38, R-39, R-47
Pughe, Cyntha, R-69
Purnell, Lousie, P-162
Purveur, Eric, P-67

Quadri, Therese, P-63, P-114, P-145, P-147
Quadrille, 22, P-129, P-139, B-22, B-54, B-78, B-101
Quaker Girl, The, 2
Quartet, F-20
Quayle, Anthony, P-151, T-60
Queen Was In The Parlour, The, 9, 10, 11, 13, 16, P-45, P-69, F-2, F-7, B-76, B-102
Quilley, Denis, P-174, P-163, T-86-94
Quilter, Roger, P-4
Quine, Richard, F-25
Quinn, Patrick, P-213
Quinney, Maureen, P-135

Rabett, Catherine, T-82
Rabb, Ellis, P-150
Rabke, Henry, P-77
Raglan, James, P-44
Rain Before Seven, P-69
Raine, Gillian, P-129, T-58
Raine, Patricia, P-144
Rainger, Ralph, D-15
Rains, Claude, 17, P-27
Rains, Jack, P-160
Rameau, Hans, F-14
Ramsay, Ramak, P-189
Randell, Pamela, P-88
Randolph, Elsie, P-174
Rangel, Germinal, P-189
Rank, J. Arthur, F-19, F-20

Raskin, Carolyn, T-27
Rat Trap, The, 9, P-47, B-72, B-76, B-103
Rathbone, Basil, R-55
Rathbone, Irene, P-30
Rattigan, Terrence, 25, P-160, T-38
Rawlings, Margaret, P-131
Rawnsley, David, F-15
Rawson, Tristan, P-79
Ray, Andrew, T-58
Ray, Phil, P-10
Ray, Scott, P-160
Ray, Ted, F-20
Rayel, Jack, T-8
Rayland, Walter, P-67
Raymond, Cyril, F-18
Raymond, Gary, P-193
Rayner, Minnie, P-38
Raynor, Arnold, P-14
Read, John B. P-178
Reader, Nina, P-139
Reader, Ralph, P-83
Red Peppers, 17, 23, P-83, P-177, P-201, F-20, R-15, R-20, R-60, R-68, T-5, T-8, T-23, T-60, T-86-94, D-20
Redfield, William, T-47
Redgrave, Lynn, 25, P-162, T-43
Redgrave, Michael, 24
Redgrave, Vanessa, P-186
Redmond, Moira, T-30
Reed, Alan, P-26
Reed, Carol, F-22
Reed, Michael, P-216, D-120
Reed, Robert, F-29
Reed, Stella, P-2
Reeder, George, T-47
Reeke, Rita, T-81
Reeves, Ruth, P-97
Regester, Robert, P-186
Reid, Beryl, P-175, F-29
Reinhardt, Stephen, P-170
Reisman, Leo, D-13
Reiss, Amanda, P-175
Relative Values, 21, P-124, P-185, B-71, B-789, B-104, B-204
Relph, George, P-51

Relph, Irene, P-111
Relph, Michael, P-124
Rennison, Charles, P-129
Revill, Clive, F-26
Reynolds, Dorothy, P-156, P-174
Reynold, Owen, P-95
Rhodes, Burt, T-86-94
Rice, Elmer, R-32
Rice, Peter, T-73
Richard, Cliff, P-174
Richards, Jack, P-77
Richard, Jim, T-58
Richards, Jon, P-154
Richards, Rosa, F-2
Richardson, Ian, T-80
Richardson, Ralph, F-22
Richardson, Tony, P-151
Richter, Paul, F-2
Rider, Duncan, P-88
Ridges, Stanley, F-11
Rimmer, Shane, T-83
Ringwood, Bob, P-201
Riskin, Susan, R-76
Ritch, David, T-30
Ritchard, Cyril, 20, 27, P-150, P-174, P-184
Ritchie, Bill, T-80
Ritman, William, P-187
Riva, Maria, T-7
Rivers, Max, P-37, P-56, P-57, P-174
Roberts, Anthony, P-174
Roberts, John, P-171
Roberts, Neil, P-225
Roberts, Rachel, T-44
Roberston, Adam, T-82
Robertson, Alex, P-75, P-78
Robertson, Nancy, T-75
Robertson, Stuart, F-9
Robey, George, 3
Robin, Leo, D-15
Robings, Douglas, P-144
Robinson, Elizabeth, D-102
Robson, E.M., P-24
Robson, Mary, P-23, P-35, P-47
Roden, Peter, T-69
Rodgers, Enid, P-190
Rodgers, Richard, T-47, D-111, B-215

Rodomsky, Saul, P-201
Roerick, William, P-113
Rogers, Bubbly, P-117
Rogers, Doris, P-112
Rogers, Erica, P-221
Rogers, Ginger, T-8, B-216
Rogers, Marjorie, P-58
Rogers, Paul, F-22
Rogges, Klein, F-2
Roland, Kathleen, P-190
Roman, Paul Reid, P-160
Roose-Evans, James, 24,
    P-159
Roper, David, T-85
Rorke, Mary, P-3
Rose, George, P-131, T-70
Rose, Philip, P-117
Rose, Reva, P-150
Rosenthal, Jack, T-81
Ross, Adrian, P-17
Ross, Jamie, P-180, P-188,
    T-75
Ross, Marion, T-11
Ross, Sidney, P-52
Ross, Winston, P-147
Rossington, Norman, T-86-94
Roth, Ann, P-202, P-208
Routledge, Patricia, P-174,
    P-181, F-27, R-74, T-47, D-169
Roven, Glen, P-181
Rowles, Polly, P-150
Roy, William, P-222, D-167
Royal Ballet, The, P-178
Royal Family, The, 15, P-79
Royal Gelatin Hour, The,
    R-13, R-15, R-19
Royston, Roy, P-9
Rudy Vallee Show, The, P-9
Rumann, Sig, F-13
Ruparell, Jay, T-83
Rush, Deborah, P-210
Russel, Christabel, P-57
Russel, Hopper, P-59
Russell, Charles, P-111, P-116,
    P-145, P-146, T-12, B-204
Russell, Evelyn, P-154
Russell, Geoffrey, P-163
Russell, Rosalind, 24, P-154,
    R-55
Rutherford, Margaret, P-97,

F-17
Ryan, Joan, P-163
Ryder, David, P-151
Rye, John, D-167
Rynn, Margie, P-224

Saal, Sylvia, P-108
Sacher, Gustav, P109
Sadovy, Liza, T-86-94
Sail Away, 24, P-154, P-156,
    P-157, P-178, T-84, D-37, D-
    108, D-130, D-131, D-180, B-
    138, B-139, B-176, B-178, B-226

Saint-Saens, D-85
Sainthill, Loudon, P-157,
    P-121, P-127, P-131, P-156
Salew, John, P-19
Sallis, Peter, P-151
Salter, Jane, P-209
Sampson, Roy, P-225
Sampson, Paddy, T-66
Samuels, Lesser, F-13
Sanders, George, P-75, P-78,
    P-160, F-13, R-14, D-56
Sanderson, Louise, P-215
Sandison, Gordon, B-216
Sands, Dorothy, P-139
Sanson, Robert, F-14
Sarner, Alexander, P-76
Sass, Enid, P-95
Satchell, Winifred, P-32
Saunders, Greg, P-209
Savigear, Raymond, P-135
Saville, Victor, F-13
Saving Grace, The, 5, P-20
Savory, Gerald, P-87
Scaasi, P-147
Scales, Prunella, P-168
Scandal, 5, P-23
Scanlon, Edward J. P-77
Schayer, Richard, F-6
Schlesinger, John, P-174
*Schlitz Playhouse of the
    Stars*, T-6
Schneider, Charles, P-170
Schnetzner, Stephen, P-195
Schofield, Charles, P-79
Schofield, Johnnie, F-15
Schon, Bonnie, P-170

Schrank, Joseph, T-27
Schraps, Ernest, P-77
Schwartz, Arthur, R-55
Scofield, Paul, T-74, T-78,
    D-101, D-169
Scotford, Sybil, P-161
Scott, Avis, P-110, F-18
Scott, Campbell, P-210
Scott, Dennis, P-154
Scott, Derek, T-45
Scott, Donald, P-135
Scott, Douglas, F-8, R-16
Scott, Geoffrey, P-185
Scott, George, C., P-202, P-208
Scott, Harold, P-46
Scott, Hutchinson, P-163,
    P-164, P-174
Scott, Joan Clement, P-43,
    P-215
Scott, Maidie, P-10
Scott, Richard, P-111, P-129
Scott-Gatty, Alex, P-23
Scoundrel, The, 17, F-11,
    B-142, B-162
Scovotti, Jeanette, D-123
Scully, Sean, P-160
Seabury, William, P-27
Seader, Richard, P-213, T-75
Second Man, The, 10, P-55
Segal, David F., P-169
Selfe, George, P-117
Selinsky, W., R-35
Sell, Colin, P-209
Selwyn, Arch, P-59, P-78, P-57
Semi-Monde, 27, P-191
Semmler, Alexander, R-41
Senn, Herbert, P-169, P-170,
    P-180
Seppings, Grace, P-4, P-9
Set To Music, 18, P-70, P-90,
    R-20, D-164, B-165
Sevening, Nina, P-12
Seymour, Carolyn, P-210
Shaber, David, P-146
Shackleton, Robert, P-90
Shadow Play, 17, 18, P-83,
    P-85, P-201, R-19, R-35, R-60,
    T-8, T-86-94, D-164, B-165
Shadows of The Evening,
    P-165, B-107

Shaefer, George, T-44

Shale, Betty, P-56, P-67, P-75, P-78

Shallcross, Alan, T-80

Shanahan, Alice, P-154

Shand, Neil, T-74

Shand, Ron, P-157

Sharaff, Irene, P-160

Sharkey, Anna, P-181

Sharp, Eileen, P-49

Sharpe, Jenny, T-95

Shaw, Billy, P-56

Shaw, Colin, T-81

Shaw, Francis, T-82, T-84

Shaw, George Bernard, P-30, P-131, P-132, T-47, B-245

Shaw, Glen Byam, R-17

Shaw, Jerome, T-10

Shawley, Robert, T-8

Shearer, Norma, 16, F-6, F-14

Sheffield, Reginald, 3, P-11, P-40

Sheldon, George V., F-18

Shelley, Carole, P-170, P-176, T-70

Shelley, Norman, R-17

Shelton, Mari, P-160

Shelton, Sloan, P-167

Shepard, Ruth, P-160

Shephard, Keith, P-69

Sheridan, Dinah, P-174, P-198, T-73

Sheridan, Nancy, T-1

Sheridan, Richard, D-167

Sherman, Loren, P-224

Sherriff, R.C., P-60

Sherrin, Ned, T-74, T-95

Sherry, Craighall, P-46

Sherwin, Jeanette, P-39

Sherwood, Henry, P-185

Sherwood, Sidney, P-4

Sherwood, Sydney, P-3

Shields, Syd, P-56

Shillying, David, P-204

Shimkus, Joanna, F-28

Shine, Wilfred E., P-9

Shore, Dinah, T-73

Short, Andrew, P-215

Short, Bobby, D-187

Show of Shows, F-5

Siddons, Alathea, P-157

Siegel, Arthur, D-181

Sieveking, Margot, P-46

Sigh No More, 20, P-107, R-68, D-31, D-32, D-33, D-164

Sillman, Leonard, P-176

Sillward, Edward, P-12

Siverman, Stanley, P-203

Sim, Millie, P-35, P-58, P-70

Simkins, Michael, P-209

Simmons, Jean, F-24

Simmons, Kay, P-77

Simms, Stephen, D-86-94

Simone, Sidney, D-39, D-40

Simpson, Peggy, P-105

Sims, Joan, T-86-94

Sinatra, Frank, 22, F-21

Sinclair, Edward, P-67

Sinclair, Hugh, 21, P-34, P-105

Sinclair, Malcolm, T-82

Sinden, Donald, P-198, T-73

Siretta, Dan, P-154, P-160

Sirocco, 9, 10, P-53, B-73, B-76, B-105, B-250

Sissle, Nobel, P-32

Sitwell, Edith, 7

Skipworth, Alison, F-7

Slattery, Tony, T-86-94

Sleeper, Martha, F-11

Sleeping Prince, The, 25, P-160

Sloan, Everett, R-41

Sloman, Roger, T-81

Small World, T-18

Smee, Derek, T-43

Smith, Alice, F-19

Smith, Beatrice, P-9

Smith, C. Aubrey, P-27

Smith, Geddeth, P-167

Smith, Gloria, P-160

Smith, Maggie, 25, P-179, P-189, T-25

Smith, Martin, P-216

Smith, Oliver, P-145, P-160, P-190

Smith, Paul, P-150

Smith, Tony, T-85

Smith, Ursula, P-171

Smith, Valerie, P-163

Smithson, Laura, P-67

Smylie, Pat, P-112

Snow, Peter, P-143

Snowdon, Eric, R-40

Snyder, Bruce, P-215

Snyder, William, P-146

Some Other Private Lives, P-62, P-69

Somers, Jimsey, R-39, R-47

Somerset, C.W., P-4

Sondheim, Stephen, P-212

Song At Twilight, A, 25, P-165, P-187, T-70, T-95, B-107, R-76

Soper, Gay, P-174

Song By Song By Coward, T-74

Songs of Coward, T-62

South Bank Show, The, T-95, T-77

South Pacific, 21, P-125, P-130,

South Sea Bubble, 23, P-143, T-12, T-15, T-70, B-79, B-106, B-209, B-255

Sovey, Raymond, P-150

Spangled Unicorn, A, 7, B-41

Spaull, Colin, P-198, T-73

Speaight, Robert, R-21

Spence, Johnnie, P-171

Spencer, Helen, P-38, P-51, P-74

Spencer, Marian, P-129, T-4

Spialek, Hans, P-90

Spriggs, Elizabeth, P-191

Spring, Joy, P-70

Spurgeon, Jack, P-70

Squire, Ronald, P-3, T-4

Squires, Douglas, P-174

Squires, Tod, P-67

St. Helier, Ivy, 11, 16, P-58, P-70, F-9, D-48

Stack, William, P-23

Stacy, Neil, P-218

Stafford, Cecil, P-56

Stamp-Taylor, Enid, F-4

Stanbridge, Martyn, P-217

Stander, Lionel, F-11

Standing, John, P-174, P-179, P-189, P-201, P-227, T-86-94

Standing, Wyndham, F-10

Stanford, Don Fitz, P-117
Stanion, Bryan, P-185
Stanley, Zane, T-84
Stannard, Eliot, F-3, F-4
Star!, 5, P-31, P-29, T-56, D-168
Star Chamber, P-83
Star Danced, A, R-51
Star Quality, T-49, T-80, D-170, D-171, B-49, B-65
Star, Bill, T-47
Star, Pat, T-83
Starace, Dinka, P-56
Steel, Edward, P-156
Steele, Vernon, F-10
Stelfox, Shirley, P-209
Stennet, Macleary, P-71
Stephens, Ann, F-15
Stephens, Jill, F-15
Stephens, Robert, 25, P-179
Stephenson, Sir William, 19
Sterland, John, P-144
Sterling, Jan, P-108
Stern, Ernst, 11, P-58
Sterroll, Gertrude, P-44
Stevens, Gloria, P-154
Stevens, John, P-92
Stevens, Marti, P-163
Stevens, Ronnie, T-55
Stevenson, Colette, T-82
Steward, Athole, P-38, P-75, P-78
Steward, Marney, T-75
Stewart, Paul, R-21
Stewart, Robb, P-117, D-30
Steward, Robert, P-216
Still Life, 18, 20, P-83, P-167, P-171, F-18, R-37, R-39, R-61, T-5, T-8, T-69, T-86-94
Stirling, Richard, P-215, P-225
Stock, Nigel, P-193
Stoddard, Haila, P-169
Stoker, Willard, P-116
Stokes, Alan, T-86-94
Stone, John, P-185
Stone, Peter, T-47
Stoney, Franc, P-3
Storri, Terri, P-37
Stothart, Herbert, P-27
Stott, Wally, D-41, D-83

Strachan, Alan, P-181, P-197, P-198, P-204, P-205, P-219, P-227, T-73
Strathallan, David, 19
Stratton, Chester, P-120
Straub, John, P-167
Streatfield, Philip, 3, 4
Strickland, Helan, F-11
Stride, John, P-186
Stritch, Elaine, 24, P-154, P-155, P-156, P-169, T-23
Stuart, Lois, P-25
Stuart, Sir Campbell, 18
Stuart, Sir Simeon, F-3
Stubbs, Una, P-174, P-181
Sturgeon, Jaime, P-205
Suedo, Julie, F-3
Suite In Three Keys, 25, P-165, P-187, R-76, T-78, B-71, B-107, B-161
Sullavan, Margaret, T-6
Sullivan, Ann, P-109
Sullivan, Ed, 22, P-160, B-203
Summerfield, Eleanor, P-174
Summerhayes, Jane, P-226
Sumpson, Tony, P-155
Surprise Package, 24, F-23
Susan and God, R-32
Susands, Patrick, P-38, P-79
Susskind, T-23
Sutherland, Joan, T-68, D-102
Swenson, Inga, T-47
Swift, Anne, P-208
Swift, Clive, T-85
Swift, David, T-80
Swinburne, Norah, P-23
Swinstead, Joan, P-110
Swiss Family Wittlebot, 1, R-1
Sydow, Jack, P-167
Sylva, Vesta, P-59
Syms, Sylvia, P-131, P-225

Talent To Amuse, A, P-22
Tabori, Kristopher, T-70
Talbot, Winifred, P-59
Tamavoh, Louis, P-112
Tandy, Jessica, P-187
Tannen, Julius, P-73
Tanner, Gordon, P-124
Tarras, Mildred, T-44

Tarver, E.W., P-11
Tasker, Jill, P-224
Tate, Reginald, P-76
Tatler, Eileen, P-117
Tawde, George, P-17
Taylor, Bill, T-86-94
Taylor, Elizabeth, P-203, F-28
Taylor, Howard, F-28
Taylor, Ken, T-92
Taylor, Laurette, 6, 8, P-38
Taylor, Marjorie, P-69
Taylor, Mitchell, P-160
Taylor, Noël, T-44
Taylor, Ross, P-171
Taylor, Valeri, R-17
Tearle, Godfrey, P-12
Teeters, Clarence, P-200
Teitel, Carol, P-195
Telford, Frank, T-6
Tempest, Dame Marie, 8, P-38, P-49, P-79, R-17
Temple, Dot, 3, P-79
Templeman, Simon, P-221
Tennent Productions, P-131
Tennent, H.M., P-97, P-100, P-105, P-111
Ternents, Billy, R-31
Terry, Hazel, P-111
Terry-Lewis, Mabel, P-43, P-215
Terribly Intimate Portraits, 7
Thacker, Russ, P-200
Thatcher, Billy, P-101
Thatcher, Heather, P-75, F-14, D-54, D-56
Theatre Royal, P-79, B-116
Theodore, Lee, P-170
Thesiger, Ernest, P-37
Third Little Show, The, 14, P-65, P-70
This Happy Breed, 1, 18, 20, 23, P-101, F-16, T-12, T-13, T-28, T-56, T-58, B-3, B-70, B-77, B-108, B-132, B-150, B-203, B-221
This Is Noël Coward, T-68
This Was A Man, 9, P-48, B-73, B-76, B-109
This Year of Grace, 10, 11, 14 P-56, P-57, D-1, D-2, D-3, D-4,

D-41, D-142, B-75, B-110, B-165, B-173
Thomas, Clive, T-80, T-86-94
Thomas, Dorothy, P-3
Thomas, Jeannie, P-4
Thomas, Mary, D-121
Thomas, Richard, F-18
Thomas, Samuel, P-77
Thompson, Frank, P-145
Thompson, Kay, 24, P-154, P-161
Thompson, Leslie, P-67
Thompson, Peggy, P-109
Thompson, Walter, P-30
Thorn, Bert, T-8
Thorndike, Sybil, 24, P-153, T-68, B-28
Thornton, Angela, P-145, P-147, P-190
Thornton, Tom, P-161
Thorpe, George, P-40
Thorpe, Richard, P-59, T-30
Those Were The Happy Days, F-29
Thurber, James, T-19
Thurman, David, P-150
Thurston, David, P-150
Thurston, Robert, P-145, P-147
Tickner, Martin, P-175, P-211
Tillinger, John, P-176
Tilton, James, P-172
Titheradge, Dion, P-34
Titheradge, Madge, 15, P-45, P-51, P-79, P-84
Titheradge, Meg, P-101
Titmuss, Phyllis, P-22
To Step Aside, B-43
Toast of the Town, T-7
Toback, Hannah, P-77
Today Show, The, T-29
Todd, Ann, T-24
Todd, Elizabeth, P-109
Todd, Michael, F-21
Together With Music, 23, T-10, T-11, T-95, D-103, D-104, D-105, B-179, B-205, B-221
Toguri, David, P-201, P-219
Toles, Mike, P-160
Tommon, Marie, P-189

Toms, Carl, P-93, P-206, P-211, P-212, P-219, P-220, P-223
Tonge, Lilian, P-80
Tonge, Philip, P-4, P-71, P-80, P-98, P-113, T-3, T-11
Tonight At 8, P-177
Tonight At 8:30, 7, 17, 21, 26, P-83, P-85, P-113, P-167, P-171, P-201, F-14, F-18, R-15, R-16, R-19, R-22, R-35, R-37, R-39, R-40, R-44, R-46, R-47, R-54, R-61, R-68, T-5, T-6, T-8, T-23, T-27, T-60, T-70, T-86-94, D-19, D-180, B-69, B-70, B-77, B-111, B-184, B-216
Tonight Is Ours, 16, F-7
Tonight Show, The, T-26
Tony Awards, The, T-65
Toser, David, P-170, P-213
Tosh, Maurice, P-4
Tottenham, Merle, P-67, F-8, F-16
Tours, Frank, P-57, P-113
Townley, Toke, F-20
Toye, Wendy, P-107, P-174, P-181
Tozer, J.R., P-11
Transatlantic Productions, 9, 15, P-139, B-22
Traveler's Joy, D-170, D-171
Travers, Ronald, T-58
Travilla, T-8
Traylor, William, P-145, P-147
Tree, Lady, P-45
Tregidden, Brian, T-60
Trent, Bruce, D-163
Trevor, Ann, P-30, P-38, P-74, P-17
Trevor, Austin, P-36, P-58
Trio, F-20
Tripp, June, P-2
Trotter, Alan, P-6
Trouncer, Cecil, P-131
Troy, Louise, P-146, P-161, P-208
Trubshaw, Michael, F-20
Truex, Ernext, P-65
Truex, Lillie, P-65
Tu, Poulet, T-43
Tucker, Ian, P-170

Tucker, Leonard, P-211, P-215, P-219, P-220, P-223
Tucker, Robert, P-170
Tuddenham, Peter, P-117, R-69, D-74
Tudor, Nicholas, P-205
Turner, Aidan, P-108
Turner, Eileen, D-97
Turner, John Hasting, P-31
Turner, Marcell, P-67, P-88
Turner, Yolanda, P-88, T-20
Twentieth Century, 17
Tyler, Grant, P-109
Tyson, Cicely, P-203

Underdown, Edward, P-70, P-83
Up And Doing, P-96
Urbanski, Douglas, P-214
Ure, Gudrun, R-69
Ustinov, Peter, D-101

Valentina, P-161
Valentine, James, P-146
Valli, Romolo, F-28
Vallone, Raf, F-30
Van Der Vlis, Diana, P-190
Van Dyke II, W.S., F-13
Van Thal, Dennis, P-92
Van-Tempest, A., P-11
Vanburgh, Irene, P-88
Vance, Dennis, T-22
Vanderbilt, Gloria, T-8
Vanderlyn, Veronica, P-67
Vanne, Marda, P-43, P-51, P-215
Vansittart, Rupert, P-216
Varden, Evelyn, P-108, R-41
Varden, Norma, F-14
Vardy, Mike, T-83
Vardey, Beatrice, P-111
Varela, Santiago, T-84
Varney, Guy, T-49
Varney, Reg, T-86-94
Vaughan, Lorrain, P-216
Vaughan, Terry, P-157
Vaughn, Carles, B. P-3
Vazquez, Yolanda, P-217
Veerney, Sylvia, P-117
Veness, Amy, F-16

Venning, Una, P-153
Verdon, Gwen, P-161, R-55
Verne, Jules, F-21
Verney, Guy, F-16
Verno, Peter, P-163
Vernon, Charles, B. P-3
Vernon, John, T-61
Vernon, Richard, P-168, T-59
Vicary, Helen, P-4
Villiers, James, P-179, T-30
Villiers, Mavis, P-156
Vincent, Henrietta, F-18
Vine, Douglas, P-111
Vines, Margaret, P-79
Vokes, Pete, P-67, P-8
Von Furstenberg, Betsy,
   P-169
Von Mayrhouser, Jennifer,
   P-210
VonScherler, Sasha, P-146,
   P-150
Vortex, The, 5, 7, 8, 9, 11, 27,
   P-35, P-39, P-69, P-126, P-217,
   P-221 F-3, T-24, T-36, T-56, T-
   57, T-70, T-70, T-95, B-67, B-72,
   B-74, B-112, B-140, B-141, B-
   200, B-215, B-242, B-250
Voss, Philip, T-82
Votos, Christopher, P-154

Wade, Philip, P-44
Wade, Robert, T-3
Wade, Uel, P-196
Wadsworth, Chris, T-86-94
Waiting In The Wings, 24,
   P-153, B-28, B-71, B-79, B-113,
   B-243
Wakefield, Hugh, F-17
Wakefield, John, D-102
Walbrook, Anton, P-91
Walbye, Kay, P-200
Walden, Russell, P-200
Waldhorn, Gary, T-81
Walken, Ronnie, P-161
Walker, Britt, T-85
Walker, Carol, P-157
Walker, Chris, T-81
Walker, Danvers, T-34
Walker, Janet Hayes, P-226
Walker, Kathryn, P-203

Walker, Lillias, T-43
Walker, Nancy, P-141
Walker, Nella, F-14
Walker, Rhoderick, P-113,
   P-129, P-139, T-13
Walker, Stuart, T-71
Wall, Max, T-81
Wallace, Anne, P-161
Wallace, Brian, P-221
Wallace, Nellie, P-10
Wallace, Mike, R-55
Wallbank, John, P-201
Walley, Norma, F-9
Walsh, Kay, F-15, F-16, F-2?
Walton, Clive, P-216
Walton, Tony, P-146
Wannamaker, Sam, R-39
War In The Air, 3, P-10
Warburton, John, F-8
Ward, Leon, P-163
Ward, Mackenzie, P-48
Ward, Penelope Dudley, P-90,
   F-15
Ward, Ronald, P-30
Ward, Tara, T-9
Ward, Trevor, P-111
Warde, Victoria, T-9
Ware, Kenneth, P-70
Wareing, Lesley, R-12
Warenskjold, Dorothy, R-53
Waring, Barbara, F-12
Waring, Derek, P-181
Wark, Robert, P-145
Warneford, Fred, P-2
Warner, Jack, F-20
Warner, Richard, P-87
Warren, Arthur, P-56
Warren, John, F-19
Warren, Marcia, P-211
Warwick, Cecil, P-17
Warwick, John, P-109
Warwick, Norman, P-117,
   P-174, D-74
Warwick, Richard, T-57
Warwick, Stephen, P-174
Washbourne, Mona, P-124,
   P-145, P-147
Waterhouse, Keith, F-27
Waters, Jan, P-163
Waters, Moray, F-24

Waters, Naomi, P-70
Waterson, Juanita, T-85
Waterston, Sam, P-176
Watford, Gwen, P-198, T-73
Watkins, Maurine, B-38
Watson, Betty Jane, P-154
Watson, Caven, F-15
Watson, Derwent, P-217
Watson, Henrietta, P-51
Watson, Janet, P-226
Watson, Moray, P-206
Wattis, Richard, T-25
Wayne, Fred, T-6
Ways and Means, 18, P-83,
   P-167, F-20, T-86-94
We Were Dancing, 18, P-177,
   F-14, R-22, D-88
Weatherly, Peter, T-69
Weatherwise, P-69
Webb, Alan, P-83, P-87, P-91,
   P-143, F-19
Webb, Clifton, 6, 19, P-98,
   P-108, R-38, T-85
Webb, Gillian, P-144
Webber, Andrew Lloyd, 21
Webster, Bruce, P-139
Webster, Margaret, P-153,
   B-243
Weeks, Barbara, R-39, R-47
Weeks, Emlyn, P-109
Weguelin, Thomas, P-24
Weiss, Marc, B. P-208
Welch, Clare, P-168, P-216
Welch, Elisabeth, P-174
Weldon, Duncan C. P-193,
   P-205, P-214
Welles, Orson, R-21
Wellesley, Arthur, P-36
Wells, Deering, P-44
Wells, Veronica, F-28
Welsh, Jane, P-64
Wensak, Annie, T-82
Werner, Fred, P-161
Werth, Anna, P-77
West, Claudine, F-6, F-14
Weste, Harry, P-109
Westwood, Patric, P-117
Weymouth, Sara, P-216
What Mad Pursuit?, T-85,
   T-178

What's My Line?, T-19, T-33
Wheeler, Cyril, P-91
Whelan, Gordon, D-50
Where The Rainbow Ends, 2, 3, 4, P-4, P-5, P-8, P-13, T-3
Where's Charley?, P-14
Whilton, Irene, T-80, T-82
White Ensign (In Which We Serve), F-15
White, Joan, T-44
White, Leonard, T-43, T-48, T-49
White, Sheila, P-117, P-174
Whitebirds, P-50
Whitfield, June, P-117, P-174
Whitmore, Dean, T-27
Weigert, René, P-180
Wilcox, Herbert, F-9, T-68
Wilcox, Paula, T-81
Wild Heather, 5, P-18
Wilde, Oscar, 11, 22, P-135, T-25, B-225
Wildeblood, Peter, T-34
Wilder, Duan, P-169
Wilding, Michael, F-15
Wilkingson, Norman, P-24
Williams, Hope, F-11
Williams, Hugh, F-9, F-24
Williams, Iva, P-4
Williams, Ivy, P-29
Williams, Jill, P-32
Williams, John, P-176, B-204
Williams, John A., P-198
Williams, Keith, T-73
Williams, Lionel, P-3
Williams, Margaret, F-24
Williams, Rita, D-121
Williams, Simon, P-168, T-86 T-94
Williams, Tennessee, 6, F-28
Williams, Tony, P-32
Williamson, Susan, P-191
Willmore, Alfred, P-2, P-12
Wilmot, Richard, T-59
Wilson, Dennis, T-60
Wilson, Ian, F-20
Wilson, John C., 9, 15, 19, P-76, P-79, P-80, P-83, P-84, P-87, P-88, P-97, P-98, P-100, P-105, P-108, P-111, P-114,

P-124, P-129, P-139
Wilson, Julie, P-222
Wilson, Neil, P-186
Wilson, Sandy, B-250
Wilson, Stella, P-67
Wilson, Willeen, P-84
Wimbush, Martin, T-83
Windom, William, P-141
Wingrove, Charles, P-67
Winn, Godfrey, P-49
Winter, Sophia, P-209
Winwood, Estelle, T-3, T-8
Wisdom, Norman, P-138
Wise, Robert, F-29
Wise, Sybil, P-111, P-129
Wiseman, Philip, P-146, P-166
Wither, Googie, P-105
Wittstein, Ed, T-44
Wodehouse, P.G., P-27
Wodeman, Joyce, P-69
Wojewodski, Robert, P-221
Woman and Whiskey, P-21
Wonderful Town, R-55
Wood, G., P-167
Wood, Peggy, 11, 18, 19, P-58, P-88, P-98, R-6, R-39, D-48, D-49, D-58, B-251, B-252
Wood, Wallace, P-43
Woodland, Rae, R-68
Woods, Aubrey, T-80
Woods, Richard, P-154, P-202, P-208
Woods, Tom, P-51
Woodson, William, P-146, R-41
Woodward, Charles, P-187
Woodward, Edward, 25, P-161
Woolfe, Betty, P-111, P-143
Woollcott, Alexander, 2, P-81, F-11, B-1, B-232, B-254
Words and Music, 14, P-70, D-11, D-12, D-41, B-75, B-114
Worsley, Pat, P-75, P-78, D-56
Worth, Irene, P-165, P-174
Worth, Maggie, P-160
Wrede, Casper, T-25
Wrick, Mary, P-77
Wright, Cobina, T-85
Wright, Mark, P-169
Wright, Norman, R-69

Wyatt, Peter, P-151
Wyndham, Joan, P-76
Wyngarder, Peter, T-34
Wynne, Arthur, P-2
Wynne, Esmé, 4, P-4, P-14, P-19, P-21, P-25
Wynne, Eve, P-42
Wynter, Mark, P-174
Wynyard, Diana, P-91, F-8

Yarde, Margaret, P-46
Yarrow, Arnold, P-151
Yeargan, Michael H., P-210
Yellend, David, T-80
Yoicks!, P-31
York Theatre Company, P-226
York, Cameron, P-77
York, Susannah, P-174, T-80
Yorke, Erica, P-117
Yorke, Mavis, P-4
Young Idea, The, 5, P-30, B-76, B-115
Young, Gig, T-8
Young, Howard, P-113
Young, Kay, F-15
Young, Loretta, R-33
Young, Raymond, P-117
Young, Victor, F-21
Your Hit Parade, R-18
Yuki, P-205

Zahn, Mary, P-160
Zanack, Darryl, T-22
Zaslow, Michael, P-226
Ziegfeld Follies of 1931, P-66
Ziegfeld, Florenz, 12, P-59
Ziegler, Anne, D-82
Zimbalist, Efrem, Jr., P-141
Zimmerman, Harry, P-161, T-27
Zimmerman, Matt, P-163
Zinkeisen, Doris, P-31, P-37, P-135
Zinser, William, T-31
Zirato, Bruno, R-55
Zoya, Deric, P-24
Zousmer, Jesse, T-12
Zucco, George, P-79

About the Author

STEPHEN COLE is a former actor with many regional and film credits. He has written the lyrics for several musicals, and has worked as a press agent and production assistant for several Broadway shows. He is currently affiliated with the Rodgers and Hammerstein Organization.

Titles in
Bio-Bibliographies in the Performing Arts

Milos Forman: A Bio-Bibliography
Thomas J. Slater

Kate Smith: A Bio-Bibliography
Michael R. Pitts

Patty Duke: A Bio-Bibliography
Stephen L. Eberly

Carole Lombard: A Bio-Bibliography
Robert D. Matzen

Eva Le Gallienne: A Bio-Bibliography
Robert A. Schanke

Julie Andrews: A Bio-Bibliography
Les Spindle

Richard Widmark: A Bio-Bibliography
Kim Holston

Orson Welles: A Bio-Bibliography
Bret Wood

Ann Sothern: A Bio-Bibliography
Margie Schultz

Alice Faye: A Bio-Bibliography
Barry Rivadue

Jennifer Jones: A Bio-Bibliography
Jeffrey L. Carrier

Cary Grant: A Bio-Bibliography
Beverley Bare Buehrer

Maureen O'Sullivan: A Bio-Bibliography
Connie J. Billips

Ava Gardner: A Bio-Bibliography
Karin J. Fowler

Jean Arthur: A Bio-Bibliography
Arthur Pierce and Douglas Swarthout

Donna Reed: A Bio-Bibliography
Brenda Scott Royce

Gordon MacRae: A Bio-Bibliography
Bruce R. Leiby

Mary Martin: A Bio-Bibliography
Barry Rivadue

Irene Dunne: A Bio-Bibliography
Margie Schultz

Anne Baxter: A Bio-Bibliography
Karin J. Fowler

Tallulah Bankhead: A Bio-Bibliography
Jeffrey L. Carrier

Jessica Tandy: A Bio-Bibliography
Milly S. Barranger

Janet Gaynor: A Bio-Bibliography
Connie Billips

James Stewart: A Bio-Bibliography
Gerard Molyneaux

Joseph Papp: A Bio-Bibliography
Barbara Lee Horn

Henry Fonda: A Bio-Bibliography
Kevin Sweeney

Edwin Booth: A Bio-Bibliography
L. Terry Oggel

Ethel Merman: A Bio-Bibliography
George B. Bryan

Lauren Bacall: A Bio-Bibliography
Brenda Scott Royce

Joseph Chaikin: A Bio-Bibliography
Alex Gildzen and Dimitris Karageorgiou

Richard Burton: A Bio-Bibliography
Tyrone Steverson

Maureen Stapleton: A Bio-Bibliography
Jeannie M. Woods

David Merrick: A Bio-Bibliography
Barbara Lee Horn

Vivien Leigh: A Bio-Bibliography
Cynthia Marylee Molt

Robert Mitchum: A Bio-Bibliography
Jerry Roberts

Agnes Moorehead: A Bio-Bibliography
Lynn Kear

Colleen Dewhurst: A Bio-Bibliography
Barbara Lee Horn

Helen Hayes: A Bio-Bibliography
Donn B. Murphy and Stephen Moore

Boris Karloff: A Bio-Bibliography
Beverley Bare Buehrer

Betty Grable: A Bio-Bibliography
Larry Billman

Ellen Stewart and La Mama: A Bio-Bibliography
Barbara Lee Horn

Lucille Lortel: A Bio-Bibliography
Sam McCready